The Undergraduate Woman: Issues in Educational Equity

The Undergraduate Woman: Issues in Educational Equity

Edited by
Pamela J. Perun
Wellesley College

LexingtonBooks
D.C. Heath and Company
Lexington, Massachusetts
Toronto

*This book is dedicated to Miriam Chamberlain
because the fruits of her work at the
Ford Foundation in support of
innovative programs and research
on women in higher education should soon
make the findings of this book obsolete.*

Library of Congress Cataloging in Publication Data

Main entry under title:

The Undergraduate woman.

Papers from a conference, jointly sponsored by the Higher Education
Resource Services and Wellesley College Center for Research on Women, held
at Wellesley College, Sept. 1979.
Includes index.
1. Women college students—United States—Congresses. I. Perun,
Pamela J. II. Higher Education Resource Services (U.S.) III. Wellesley
College. Center for Research on Women.

LA227.3.U44	378'.0088042	80-8596
ISBN 0-669-04304-4		AACR2

Copyright © 1982 by D.C. Heath and Company

Published simultaneously in Canada

Printed in the United States of America

International Standard Book Number: 0-669-04304-4

Library of Congress Catalog Card Number: 80-8596

Contents

Contents

Foreword

The complex issues surrounding questions of sex equity in higher education have been addressed from a variety of perspectives in the last decade. Yet amid much controversy over affirmative-action guidelines, goals, and time-tables, some central equity concerns regarding the process of college education itself have received little concerted attention, although many aspects of these questions have been the subject of research by scattered scholars in various disciplines. The need to define sex-equity issues in higher education as a discrete research field, addressable through the differing perspectives of several disciplines, seemed clear and urgent. In recognition of this need, Higher Education Resource Services and the Wellesley College Center for Research on Women jointly sponsored the research conference that forms the basis of this book. The conference was held at Wellesley College in September 1979 and brought together a group of some fifty scholars from the social and biological sciences and the humanities, as well as college presidents and educational policymakers.

After much thought, the planning committee decided to limit the focus of the conference, and hence of this book, to the traditional-age undergraduate, for two reasons. First, we believe that despite the rapidly growing number of older students in higher education, the late-adolescent/young-adult group will continue to be the core of undergraduate students, those for whom the policies and practices of academic institutions are primarily designed. Second, the inclusion of older female students would have diluted one of the central issues of interest to us—that is, the conflict, unique to young women, about the primacy of career preparation as opposed to marriage and family. For a young man this issue presents little difficulty; he can do both and have the full support of society in the process. Indeed, the system of higher education is geared to *his* timetable. A young woman, on the other hand, finds few or no social and institutional supports in her efforts to combine family and career. Further, she knows that time is against her if she postpones marriage and children; postponing a career commitment may seem the lesser of two evils.

The purposes of higher education, therefore, have historically been conceived of as different for women and men—a difference conditioned by the traditional expectation that a college education should prepare men for professional and public leadership roles and women for family and perhaps community roles. Predictably, then, the outcomes of that education have differed significantly for the two sexes; whereas college-educated men trained for the learned professions and went on to shape those professions, including higher education itself, in their own image, college prepared women for, at most, only the traditional "female" occupations—school teaching, nursing, librarianship, secretarial work. More commonly, higher education for women has been seen as a form of finishing school or perhaps even an opportunity to learn for the sake of learning, rather than as preparation for rewarding careers.

It should have come as no surprise, therefore, to find that institutions of higher education dealt differently with men and women. That, indeed, was thought to be part of their mission. But in the last two decades the automatic assumption that men and women will lead different lives, and therefore need different kinds of education, has given way to concerns for greater equality—under the law, in education and employment, and in personal relationships. It has also been called into question by young women themselves. Increasingly, as divorce statistics mount and inflation drives millions of married women into the labor market, women have become aware that they will have to work outside the home for most of their adult lives. Preparation for a career thus assumes an urgency for young women that it did not have in the past. They are beginning to make the same cost-benefit calculations that are traditional for men—what are the trade-offs going to be among opportunity costs, human-capital formation, and expected returns to educational investment? But models of these processes are still scarce for women; too many of the factors in the equation are unpredictable, and the choices exceedingly difficult. Our purpose, then, was to begin a systematic assessment of how young women, on the one hand, and institutions of higher education, on the other, have responded to these pressures for sex equality.

The dual emphasis—on the individual and the institution—is crucial to our understanding of equity issues. Too much of the writing and scholarship on women students in higher education has focused on women's defects or shortcomings with respect to an institutional structure designed by men for men. We wanted to examine to what extent colleges and universities were attempting to meet equity problems at least part way. In a period when more than half of undergraduate students are female, one might rationally expect the educational system to adapt to this changed circumstance. Enlightened self-interest alone would suggest a new emphasis on structures, curricula, and services to meet the needs of this new majority, particularly as we enter into the inexorable demographic decline.

Among the most pervasive and far-reaching of equity concerns is the issue of equal access to higher education. Which college a student attends is important—not only as a matter of reputation or social status, but also as a question of quality. Too many of the best institutions, those that offer a comprehensive range of curricular choices and high-quality faculties, are still maintaining biased sex ratios in admissions. Could new approaches to student recruitment—perhaps with lessened emphasis on football—attract more of the ablest women to such institutions? Are there more efforts to be made in the area of financial aid for women? Are there steps the institutions might take to facilitate equal employment and pay, so that women students, like men, could pay a greater share of educational costs from their own earnings?

The area of most pressing concern to us was what happens to female students during the traditional four years of college. Numerous studies have concluded that women's growth in general competence and knowledge during college does not match that of men. Is this effect traceable to institutional failures to put the same high demands on women as on men, to challenge them to explore nontraditional fields and more venturesome career choices? What are the silent messages conveyed by institutions whose power structure and reward systems overwhelmingly demonstrate male leadership and female supporting roles? To what extent does a curriculum that almost universally neglects women as creators of art or science, history or literature dampen the aspirations women students bring with them?

Such questions reach to the heart of the academic enterprise, challenging deeply held assumptions not simply about appropriate sex roles but also about objectivity in the pursuit of truth and justice in the distribution of rewards. More immediately, in an academic context, they demand clarification of institutional goals—always a difficult issue. In the decades ahead, when no major college or university can survive without women students, none can afford a dual philosophy that provides, at best, only a broad liberal education for women but purposeful professional training for men.

The time scale for real change in higher education is a long and uncertain one; as in any evolutionary process, some promising avenues turn into dead ends. For an individual that is not a consoling thought. Young women just entering college are gambling with their prime childbearing years if they lay plans to pursue professional training for the next ten years or more. It is therefore not surprising that a close examination of educational statistics does not yet demonstrate a mass movement of women into the professions. But a strong trend in that direction began about a decade ago, and the educational patterns of men and women with respect to purpose, timing, and curricular choices have converged rapidly since the virtual abolition of enrollment quotas in graduate and professional schools in the early 1970s.

Yet among the pressures of financial stringency, expectations of declining enrollments, curtailment of graduate programs, unemployment for Ph.D.'s and threats to the continued vitality of the scholarly enterprise, sex-equity issues are still often neglected. Attention to these concerns, far from depleting already scarce resources, can serve to renew academic institutions and rededicate them to the quest for a system of higher education that will serve the needs of women and men equally. We hope that this book will open a dialogue toward that end.

Lilli S. Hornig

Acknowledgments

Many of the chapters in this book were first presented at our Research Conference on Educational Environments and the Undergraduate Woman, Wellesley College, September 1979. The conference was jointly supported by the Fund for the Improvement of Postsecondary Education; the Wellesley College Center for Research on Women; and Higher Education Resource Services, the latter through a grant from the Ford Foundation. Special thanks are due to those who served on the planning committee—Carolyn Elliott, Lilli Hornig, Jeanne Speizer, Blythe Clinchy, and Carol Gilligan—for their assistance in organizing and orchestrating the conference. Carol Stoel and Alison Bernstein also donated their time as advisors to the conference, and we thank them for their many helpful suggestions and comments.

We are greatly indebted to the Spencer Foundation for a generous grant in support of the editing of the conference papers into their present form. This grant also permitted us to commission additional papers for this book, thus providing us with the opportunity to generate original research on special, previously neglected topics in the literature. But beyond its financial support, the Spencer Foundation, through President H. Thomas James, made some very helpful comments on the format of this book that substantially increased its scope and therefore its contribution to the field. We thank the Spencer Foundation for both its financial and substantive contributions to this project.

Throughout this year of preparing, editing, and processing the chapters for publication, Jacqueline Fields, Patricia Bell Scott, Jeanne Speizer, Florence Ladd, and Lilli Hornig donated their services as consultants and advisors to the project. Their contributions are gratefully acknowledged here. The unsung but true heroine of this book, however, is Margaret May, whose excellent secretarial skills were exceeded in importance to this project only by her patience, tact, and care.

Part I
Historical and Recent Trends in College Attendance by Women

The Undergraduate Woman: Theme and Variations

Pamela J. Perun

*Now we are here to consider facts; now we must fix our eyes upon the pro-
cession—the procession of the sons of educated men. There they go, our
brothers who have been educated at public school and universities, mounting those steps, passing in and out of those doors, ascending those pulpits,
preaching, teaching, administering justice, practising medicine, transacting
business, making money. It is a solemn sight always—a procession like a
caravanserai crossing a desert . . . a sight that has often caused us, you may
remember, looking at it sidelong from an upper window, to ask ourselves
certain questions. But now, for the past twenty years or so, it is no longer a
sight merely, a photograph, or fresco scrawled upon the walls of time, at
which we can look with merely an esthetic appreciation. For there, traipsing
along at the tail end of the procession, we go ourselves. And that makes a
difference. . . . The questions we have to ask and to answer about that procession during this moment of transition are so important that they may
well change the lives of all men and women for ever. For we have to ask
ourselves, here and now, do we wish to join that procession? Above all,
where is it leading us, the procession of educated men?*

—Virginia Woolf, *Three Guineas* (1938)

The Theme

It is a commonplace observation these days that higher education faces an
uncertain future. An undersupply of undergraduates, an oversupply of
Ph.D.s, phenomenally high tuition fees at private institutions, ever higher
operating costs, and now the prospect of a severely restricted federal role at
all levels of higher education are among the major issues confronting U.S.
colleges and universities in the 1980s. These problems are serious indeed,
having been caused by long-term demographic, economic, and social trends
to which higher education has been both a contributor and beneficiary. As
such, these problems have long been visible on the horizon to educators,
administrators, and policy analysts and much effort has been devoted to

3

anticipating their impact on the structure and functions of higher education. The many studies and reports issued between 1967 and 1980 by the Carnegie Commission on Higher Education and its successor, the Carnegie Council on Policy Studies in Higher Education, alone attest to the thoroughness by which the future of higher education has been projected, analyzed, debated, and interpreted. Although it is a truism that "for American higher education these are troubled times. (They always were.)" (Gradd [pseud.] 1974, p. 342), the 1980s promise to be a decade of more bad news than good. Higher education, however, should be adequately prepared for this decade, given the prior investment in forecasting every possible trend and its consequences.

Every possible trend except one, that is. There *was* some good news for higher education in the 1970s that should positively affect its future in the 1980s but from a totally unexpected source. In unprecedented numbers women entered, reentered, and remained in postsecondary education. Women of both the traditional age and the growing reentry student populations are now an important constituency in higher education. Before too long, they may well become its *majority* constituency at the undergraduate level. The Census Bureau (1980) recently announced that for the first time since World War II female students outnumber male students and that women are continuing to enroll at higher rates than men. Projections of future levels of enrollment by women are that this trend will persist and possibly accelerate (Carnegie Council on Policy Studies in Higher Education, 1980).

To the surprise of almost everyone, then, the 1970s witnessed a remarkable demand by women for postsecondary education. Yet the significance of this trend for higher education in the 1980s remains largely unexamined. Whether due to a failure to anticipate its appearance or to a lack of interest in its implications, or even to a simple ignorance of its occurrence, this trend has been given little attention by educators, policy analysts, or scholars to date. The increased presence of women in undergraduate education has been overlooked even by those most concerned with the status of women in higher education. Throughout the 1970s, many studies by the various disciplines, by individual institutions, by government agencies, and by feminist action groups focused attention on the role and status of women in academic administration (Astin 1977a; Berry 1979; Biklen and Brannigan 1980) and in the faculty and graduate-student ranks (Carnegie Commission on Higher Education 1973; Rossi and Calderwood 1973; Feldman 1974; Furniss and Graham 1974; Centra, 1974; Howe 1975; Wasserman, Lewin, and Bleiweis 1975; Harmon 1978; Astin and Hirsch 1978; Cole 1979; Commission on Human Resources 1979). Concern for assuring equal educational and occupational opportunities for highly educated women has therefore been well documented. Similar concern for women in those critical undergraduate years of preparation and decision has yet to be demonstrated. To date, researchers and policy analysts have failed to put forth the needs of women as a legitimate and necessary priority for the future. A survey of recent books (Astin 1977b; Bowen 1977; Smith and Bernstein 1979) analyzing the contemporary status of higher education reveals that women undergraduates do not receive the attention they merit in terms of their numbers alone.

Attempts to explain the apparent lack of interest in the undergraduate experiences of women can only be an exercise in speculation at the present time. Perhaps the admission of women to previously all-male elite institutions in the 1970s has created the impression that the equal treatment of male and female undergraduates is now an accomplished fact. Perhaps the assumption has been that the increasing numbers of women could be assimilated and their diverse needs could be accommodated without significant institutional change by colleges and universities. Certainly a corollary to that assumption has been that any difficulties encountered by women undergraduates are rooted in their experiences prior to college, that is, in their socialization, in their aspirations, or in their academic preparation. Frequently, the responsibility for the success or failure of undergraduate education of women is attributed solely to the individual student without consideration of the institutional context and its relationship to the achievements, or lack thereof, of female students. Verification of the rationale underlying this lack of critical inquiry into the settings and processes of undergraduate education for women must await future research. But, whatever the ultimate assignment of responsibility, it is very clear that undergraduate education of women merits some long overdue attention in light of the increased propensity of women to obtain baccalaureate degrees and their increased presence on college compuses.

Hence, from the perspective of the institution of higher education, this is now an appropriate time to examine the undergraduate education of women. From the perspective of individual women as well, there are equally compelling reasons for doing so. Primary among them is that, many years after Virginia Woolf originally described the procession of educated men, educated women still find themselves at its tail end. Although the linkages between education and occupation, education and income, and education and inter-generational mobility (Hauser and Featherman 1977; Sewell, Hauser, and Wolf 1977) are well documented for men, the effect of education in women's lives is much less clear. Research into the process of occupational achievement for women is still in its infancy (Sweet 1973; Tyree and Treas 1974; Treiman and Terrell 1975; Taeuber and Sweet 1976; Wolf and Rosenfeld 1978); the evidence to date suggests that the educational outcomes of men and women have historically been very different and that those differences persist among contemporary generations.

The picture that is beginning to emerge from this research into the linkages between educational attainment and outcomes for women presents a paradox. It is clear that educational attainment by women is strongly related to labor-force participation.

> Whether a women is in the labor force or not is affected greatly by the amount of schooling she has had . . . the more education a women has received, the greater the likelihood that she will be engaged in paid employment . . . women with college degrees are more likely than other women to be in the labor force . . . the highest labor force participation rates were for women with 4 years of college or more . . . even when the data on women were distributed by marital status and age, the pattern of greater labor force participation among women with higher educational attainment generally held true. [Women's Bureau 1975, pp. 187–188]

But in the labor force, women and men of equivalent educational attainment are differentially distributed among occupation groups. In 1978, for example, men and women with at least a B.A. "were likely to be in professional and technical occupations . . . (66 percent of the employed women, 53 percent of the men) and . . . in managerial occupations (9 percent of women, 25 percent of the men). Most college-educated women did not enter professional and managerial occupations were employed in clerical occupations (15 percent)" (Bureau of the Census 1980, p. 60). Educational attainment, however, appears *not* to be significantly related to income. At every educational level, women's median income is far below that of similarly educated men. Among college graduates, the median income of women is only 59 percent of that earned by men (Women's Bureau 1975). This income differential is maintained throughout the life course and "is not simply the result of a skill differential, as defined by differing occupational levels or educational attainment, for it exists within all major occupations and education groups. What is striking is that women's earnings constitute a similar fraction of men's earnings with all these groups, and that this relative earnings position of women has shown little if any change over time" (Lloyd and Niemi 1979, p. 174).

It appears, then, that although educational attainment is an important determinant of women's attachment to the labor force, it does not significantly affect the types of jobs they hold or the incomes they receive from those jobs. In other words, women do not receive the same return on their educational investment that men do. In fact, any return on women's educational attainment apparently accrues to their husbands. According to one estimate "husband's earnings increase about 6.5 percent for each year of his schooling and 3.5 percent for each year of his wife's schooling (Lloyd and Niemi 1979, p. 121). Explanations of this paradoxical situation are as yet incomplete. The sex segregation of occupations (Oppenheimer 1970), the differences between men's and women's adult lives (Perun and Bielby 1981), and the conditions and contingencies of women's work and family roles (Featherman 1980) have been identified as some of the major contributors to the persistent gap between women's educational attainments and occupational achievements. The role that education itself plays in maintaining this gap has received little attention, however. Recognition of the postcollege factors influencing this process is based on substantial research in the last ten years by sociologists, demographers, and economists. Parallel research into the contribution of the educational experience itself does not yet exist.

In light of women's increased attachment to the labor force (Bureau of the Census 1980), increased investment in graduate and professional training (Feldman 1974; Bureau of the Census 1980), and increased presence in undergraduate education through the 1970s, education may well be a major explanatory variable in the analysis of the contemporary status and roles of American women. A constant theme in the research on women's labor-force participation has been the importance of educational credentials for women's occupational advancement (Lloyd and Niemi 1979). As Featherman notes, "women apparently must rely more heavily on formal credentials for access to jobs . . . it is probable that educational credentials retain their importance across the working lives of women; men use credentials for initial entry and then their experience becomes more prominent" (Featherman 1980, p. 710). Perhaps, then, it is now necessary to examine by what means and toward what ends that credential is acquired before we can understand why it brings so many fewer rewards to women than to men.

The intent of this book is to initiate a comprehensive examination into the processes and settings of undergraduate education for women. As such, it reflects an important shift in the history of educated women in terms of ultimate goals. For the past one hundred years or so, which represents the only history educated women have had, the central goal has been coeducation. Gaining access to institutions and programs has in itself been a long hard-fought struggle by women, one successfully concluded only in the last decade when many previously male-only elite institutions opened their doors to women at last (Conway 1974). Now that the goal of coeducation in terms of access to educational institutions has been reached, the process of education itself becomes the focus of attention. Assuring that coeducation is equal education for men and women is the task for the future. Any assumption that equal access will inevitably result in equal educational experiences and outcomes by women and men is unrealistic and naive. As the Carnegie Council notes, "it is tautological, or nearly so, that educational opportunities will tend to equalize the earnings of men and women only if they use similar opportunities in similar proportions, and if they can and do use their educational qualifications similarly at each stage of job choice and job progression'' (Carnegie Council on Policy Studies in Higher Education 1980, p. 268). Therefore, there is no reason for optimism that the struggle by women to join the procession of educated men has been won. A more realistic assessment of our progress is that the struggle has merely moved to another stage, one more complex and difficult but one perhaps with more promise for the ultimate equality of women and men.

In contrast to the previous stage of the struggle, which was largely conducted from the outside, the present stage will take place inside the institution of higher education. Its focus of inquiry is a broad one, encompassing all aspects of the process of education that may hinder the equality of opportunity or the achievement of equal educational outcomes for both women and men. Because this stage of the struggle is so new, no single theoretical perspective or sound empirical basis as yet exists to guide this inquiry into the processes and settings of undergraduate education. Perhaps no single conceptual perspective will ever be adequate in light of the complexity and diversity of the issues, but no such limitation need apply to constructing a body of research findings to illuminate those very issues. Given that efforts to identify the critical tasks of this stage are currently underway, building that research base becomes an urgent contemporary priority.

These chapters in this book are therefore intended as the first step toward constructing that empirical base. Drawn from a variety of disciplines with different methodological approaches and theoretical perspectives, this book represents the state of the art in research into undergraduate education for women as of 1980. The unifying theme of the book is the undergraduate woman, and each chapter reflects a different facet of the undergraduate experience of women. No claim is made that this collection is all-inclusive or definitive. In many important areas no research tradition yet exists; in others the data are of poor quality or the earlier research is obsolete. The primary purpose of the book, then, is to stimulate research into ignored areas and to revive research traditions into topics neglected of late. Both women's lives and higher education have been transformed in recent years, and new research initiatives are needed in all relevant disciplines if we are to understand the profound applications and implications of these social changes. The secondary purpose is to bring the concerns of women undergraduates, the overlooked majority in contemporary education, into prominence. This survey of research issues and findings is intended to be a resource for scholars, educators, and policy analysts. Previously, such empirical evidence has been scattered throughout the social sciences and the humanities. By providing a comprehensive, multidisciplinary approach to the topic of undergraduate education for women, we hope to stir their interest and to direct their attention to this important area of concern. The ultimate purpose of this book, however, is to improve the science and practice of undergraduate education for men and women alike. No longer is it acceptable to have a system of higher education which provides an education for women separate and distinct from that provided for men. Our goal now is to fashion a system of higher education in which gender is an irrelevant concern so that all individuals can be educated according to their needs and abilities. This book is offered in the confident expectation that it can and will provide answers to those questions posed by Virginia Woolf about an experience she herself was denied: "What, then, is this 'university education' of which . . . [our] sisterhood has heard so much and to which they have contributed so painfully? What is this mysterious process that takes about three years to accomplish, costs a round sum in hard cash, and turns the crude and raw human being into the finished product—an educated man or woman?" (Woolf 1938, p. 24).

Variations on the Theme

The organizational plan of the book is a temporal one in which the social-psychological and social-structural factors affecting undergraduate education for women, *before, during,* and *after* the college years are examined. In part I, the experiences of contemporary undergraduate women are set within a historical context. Joyce Antler's chapter, "Culture, Service, and Work: Changing Ideals of Higher Education for Women," documents trends in college attendance by women as well as the varieties of college experience available to them in different eras. In addition, she traces the evolving meaning of undergraduate education for women by analyzing the ways in which the curriculum deemed appropriate for women has changed as a function of historical time and social change. The chapter by Barbara Heyns and Joyce Bird, "Recent Trends in the Higher Education of Women," concentrates on the more recent history of college attendance by women. Profound changes occurred during the 1960s and 1970s, not only in terms of the absolute numbers of women pursuing baccalaureate degrees but also in the racial, socioeconomic, and age composition of the undergraduate population. This chapter discusses those changes and their implications for higher education in the future.

In part II the focus shifts to the precollege years when critical decisions about college attendance are made and important hurdles must be passed before admission to higher education. In "Mapping the Road to Academe: A Review of Research on Women, Men, and the College-Selection Process" by Katharine Hanson and Larry Litten, a model of the college attendance process is presented. Literature pertinent to the model is critically evaluated to determine what differences, if any, exist in the ways in which men and women decide and plan to go to college and whether those differences are related to individual differences or to institutional practices. Marlaine Lockheed, in "Sex Bias in Aptitude and Achievement Tests Used in Higher Education," discusses methods of test construction and the presence or absence of test bias therein. In addition, she evaluates the literature on sex bias in test scores and suggests probable factors associated with test score differences related to gender. In "Sex Differences in the Significance of Economic Resources for Choosing and Attending a College," Rachel Rosenfeld and James Hearn analyze a national, longitudinal data set to determine whether economic resources have a differential impact on the ability of women to attend college. One of the most important changes in higher education to occur during the 1970s was the marked increase in the federal role in financing college educations; during those years, the costs of attending college also increased dramatically. This chapter looks at the role that economic resources play in college attendance by women as a function of such changes.

In part III, the college years themselves are under scrutiny. From such a vast and significant area of research several topics have been selected for special examination. The chapter by Blythe Clinchy and Claire Zimmerman, "Epistemology and Agency in the Development of Undergraduate Women," comes from the domain of developmental psychology and charts the process and progress of cognitive development among women during their undergraduate years. In "Social Psychology Looks at But Does Not See the Undergraduate Woman," the discipline of social psychology itself is the focus of attention. Sumru Erkut discusses how an earlier promising tradition of research on undergraduate women diminished in importance within the discipline and suggests what might and should be done to revive it in future research. Helen Astin and Patricia McNamara in "Educational and Career Progress of Chicana and American Indian College Women" describe the educational experiences and outcomes of two populations, Chicana and American Indian college women, very new to higher education. The history of these minorities in higher education is just beginning to be written, and this chapter both documents their initial experiences in college and begins to account for the role that college plays in their later life achievements. In Jacqueline Fleming's chapter, "Sex Differences in the Impact of College Environments on Black Students," the experiences of black students in black schools and white schools are contrasted. The increased presence of black students in white schools is similarly a phenomenon of the 1960s and 1970s, whereas black schools themselves have a long and important history of service to the black community. The question of which educational environment best facilitates the individual development and occupational achievement of black men and women is still open, and Jacqueline Fleming's research is an important contribution to that debate. Sheila Bennett's research presented in "Undergraduates and Their Teachers:

An Analysis of Student Evaluations of Male and Female Instructors" examines the reciprocal relationships between two phenomena which grew in significance during the 1970s: student evaluations of teachers and an increased proportion of female faculty. As faculty positions have diminished in number due to decreased enrollments and high tenure ratios, student evaluations of their teachers have assumed greater importance in tenure and promotion decisions. Because women faculty cluster at the lower ranks where such decisions are critical turning points in their careers, student evaluations have become important determinants of those decisions. This chapter discusses the ways in which students, both male and female, may differentially perceive their instructors and consequently may demand and expect different faculty styles as a function of gender, both their own and their instructors'. Finally, in "Sex Differences in the Implications of the Links Between Major Departments and the Occupational Structure," James Hearn and Susan Olzak analyze the ways in which social-psychological characteristics of students and social-structural aspects of occupations differentially affect male and female students. By conceptually linking choice of major, department climates, and occupational aspirations, they present an innovative discussion of the means by which postcollege plans may subtly but profoundly shape the college experiences of women.

In part IV the issue of educational outcomes is addressed. Marsha Brown, in "Career Plans of College Women: Patterns and Influences," analyzes changes in the career plans of undergraduate women over time and in relation to the type of college they chose to attend. Her chapter documents the volatility of those plans and suggests factors associated with both the maintenance and the abandonment of high career aspirations by women. In "Career Commitment of Female College Graduates: Conceptualization and Measurement Issues," Denise Bielby takes the analysis of women's career plans one step further. Her chapter examines a decade of research on career commitment and its relationship to education among women and presents a critical analysis of the concept itself that should serve as a model for future research. Karl Alexander, Thomas Reilly, and Bruce Eckland in "Family Formation and Educational Attainment" then discuss the implications of marital plans for educational attainment among men and women. By focusing on the age of marriage as a critical determinant of women's adult life histories, their analysis documents the relationship between marriage and educational attainment among women using a life-course perspective. In "Life After College: Historical Links Between Women's Education and Women's Work," Pamela Perun and Janet Giele also use a life-course perspective. By analyzing the life histories of the graduates of a single-sex college since the turn of the century, they discuss the ways in which women's lives after college are structured as a function of individual decisions, historical eras, and social conditions, and they examine the changing function of a college education in women's lives in light of changing definitions of women's work. In the concluding chapter, 'Issues of Educational Equity in the 1980s: Multiple Perspectives," women from a variety of constituencies in higher education present the equity issues they would like to see brought to the forefront in this decade. Jeanne J. Speizer, an educator, discusses an issue of equity in the classroom, and Mary Ann Gawelek, Lourdes Rodríguez-Nogués, and Oliva M. Espín, all counseling psychologists, illustrate issues of equity in the counseling center. Carmen R. Besterman, a community-relations analyst, presents some equity issues in higher education for Hispanic women. Pamela J. Perun, a human developmentalist, and Florence C. Ladd, a psychologist, raise issues of equity that affect the faculty and administrative ranks in higher education. Finally, Sumru Erkut, a social psychologist, and Lilli S. Hornig, a chemist and a human-resource analyst, discuss equity issues that link the institution of higher education to the family and to the world of work.

Bibliography

Astin, Alexander W. "Academic Administration: The Hard Core of Sexism in Academe." *UCLA Educator* 19(1977a):60–66.
————. *Four Critical Years*. San Francisco: Jossey-Bass, 1977b.
Astin, Helen, and Hirsch, Werner, eds. *The Higher Education of Women*. New York: Praeger, 1978.
Berry, Margaret C., ed. *Women in Higher Education Administration: A Book of Readings*. Washington, D.C.: National Association of Women Deans, Administrators and Counselors, 1979.
Biklen, S.K., and Brannigan, M.B., eds. *Women and Educational Leadership*. Lexington, Mass.: Lexington Books, D.C. Heath and Company, 1980.
Bowen, Howard. *Investment in Learning*. San Francisco: Jossey-Bass, 1977.
Bureau of the Census. *A Statistical Portrait of Women in the United States: 1978*. Washington, D.C.: U.S. Department of Commerce. 1980.
Carnegie Commission on Higher Education. *Opportunities for Women in Higher Education*. New York: McGraw-Hill, 1973.
Carnegie Council on Policy Studies in Higher Education. *Three Thousand Futures: The Next Twenty Years for Higher Education*. San Francisco: Jossey-Bass, 1980.
Centra, John. *Women, Men and the Doctorate*. Princeton, N.J.: Education Testing Service, 1974.
Cole, Jonathan. *Fair Science: Women in the Scientific Community*. New York: Free Press, 1979.

Commission on Human Resources. *Climbing the Academic Ladder: Doctoral Women Scientists in Academe.* Washington, D.C.: National Academy of Sciences, National Research Council, 1979.

Conway, Jill. "Coeducation and Women's Studies: Two Approaches to the Question of Women's Place in the Contemporary University." *Daedalus* 103 (1974):239–249.

Featherman, David. "School and Occupational Careers: Constancy and Change in Worldly Success." In O.G. Brim, Jr, and J. Kagan, eds., *Constancy and Change in Human Development.* Cambridge, Mass.: Harvard University Press, 1980.

Feldman, Saul. *Escape from the Doll's House.* New York: McGraw-Hill, 1974.

Furniss, W. Todd, and Graham, Patricia Albjerg, eds. *Women in Higher Education.* Washington, D.C.: American Council on Education, 1974.

Gradd, Edward [pseud.] "The American Credo . . . of Higher Education." *Daedalus* 103 (1974):341–345.

Harmon, Lindsey. *A Century of Doctorates.* Washington, D.C.: National Academy of Sciences, 1978.

Hauser, Robert, and Featherman, David. *The Process of Stratification: Trends and Analyses:* New York: Academic Press, 1977.

Howe, Florence, ed. *Women and the Power to Change.* New York: McGraw-Hill, 1975.

Lloyd, C., and Niemi, B. *The Economics of Sex Differentials.* New York: Columbia University Press, 1979.

Oppenheimer, V. *The Female Labor Force in the United States.* Westport, Conn.: Greenwood Press, 1970.

Perun, P., and Bielby, D. "Toward a Model of Female Occupational Behavior: A Human Development Approach." *Psychology of Women Quarterly* (in press).

Rossi, Alice, and Calderwood, Ann, eds. *Academic Women on the Move.* New York: Russell Sage Foundation, 1973.

Sewell, W.; Hauser, R.; and Wolf, W. "Sex, Schooling and Occupational Careers." Working Paper no. 77–31, Center for Demography and Ecology, University of Wisconsin, Madison, 1977.

Smith, Virginia, and Bernstein, Allison R. *The Impersonal Campus.* San Francisco: Jossey-Bass, 1979.

Sweet, J. *Women in the Labor Force.* New York: Seminar Press, 1973.

Taeuber, K., and Sweet, J. "Family and Work: The Social Life Cycle of Women." In J.M. Kreps, ed., *Women and the American Economy: A Look to the 1980s.* New York: Columbia University Press, 1976.

Treiman, D., and Terrell, K. "Sex and the Process of Status Attainment: A Comparison of Working Men and Women." *American Sociological Review* 40 (1975):174–200.

Tyree, A., and Treas, J. "The Occupational and Marital Mobility of Women." *American Sociological Review* 39 (1974):293–302.

Wasserman, Elga; Lewin, Arie Y.; and Bleiweis, Linda H., eds. *Women in Academia: Evolving Policies Toward Equal Opportunities*. New York: Praeger, 1975.

Wolf, W., and Rosenfeld, R. "Sex Structure of Occupations and Job Mobility." *Social Forces* 56 (1978):823–844.

Woolf, Virginia. *Three Guineas*. New York: Harcourt, Brace and World, 1938. Reprinted with permission.

Women's Bureau. *1975 Handbook of Women Workers*. Washington, D.C.: U.S. Department of Labor, 1975.

Culture, Service, and Work: Changing Ideals of Higher Education for Women

Joyce Antler

The higher education of women is a feministic movement, the natural expression of a fundamental principle that is that women being first of all human beings, even before they are feminine, have a share in the inalienable right of human beings to self-development.
—Mary Emma Wooley, *Life and Letters of Mary Emma Wooley* (1955)

The field of education was the first to feel the force of the American woman's growing concern for self-development. Though opportunities for women in higher education gradually increased throughout the nineteenth century, the struggle to win for women the right to a college education was not achieved until the twentieth.[1] For many girls growing up in the United States after the Civil War, the attainment of a college education became a burning desire, crucial to the widening of opportunities in other areas. Higher education was the one reform that included all the rest, commented M. Carey Thomas, president of Bryn Mawr College. An inevitable result of the agitation of the early women suffragists, it would itself inevitably lead to equal suffrage, she believed, as well as other political, legal, and economic reforms for the benefit of women (Thomas 1906).

Thomas expressed the desperate longing for a college education common to many women of her generation in a speech to the General Federation of Women's Clubs at the turn of the century.

> I was born with a desire to go to college and afterwards to a German university. It seems to me, in looking backwards, as if the world had been born of persons born to prevent me. As a child in Baltimore, during the war, I of course had never seen a woman who had been to college . . . but my desire to go was inborn, like the color of my eyes; and so overwhelming that everything had to give way before it. Grandparents, great-aunts and uncles, Pennsylvania and Virginia cousins, and even comparative strangers, entered into the controversy with a passion that would today be unimaginable. My own experience was the experience of hundreds of other women. In the sixties and seventies and earlier, women were born into the world over with this same passionate longing for college, and before it parents,

I would like to thank Patricia Albjerg Graham and Lynn Gordon for their comments on an earlier version of this chapter.

15

lovers and even husbands have yielded; and colleges and universities opened as if by magic. . . . [Thomas 1903]

The "passionate desire" for college education that emerged in the decades after the Civil War reflected in large part widening opportunities for female education in the United States as well as growing aspirations among women for knowledge and professional training. Although education at seminaries and normal schools had been available to women since the late eighteenth and early nineteenth centuries, the idea of advanced education for women, expressly modeled after the higher academic standards of college education for men, was not realized until the 1870s and 1880s. About fifty prewar female colleges, most of them church or community sponsored, had been established during the period 1825–1875, but lacking financial and organizational resources comparable to those of male institutions they were unable to develop academic programs of high quality on a continuing basis. Generally, these colleges offered courses of study above the standard of those given at female seminaries but below those of colleges for men (Woody 1929).

The opening of Vassar College in 1865 heralded a new era in the evolution of higher education for women. Vassar's endowment was considerably higher than those of existing female colleges, and its standards for admission and academic program compared favorably with men's colleges. Smith College, founded in 1875, offered a course of study even more closely paralleling that of men's colleges; Wellesley, also established in 1875, as well as the later colleges for women, including Bryn Mawr in 1885 and Mt. Holyoke in 1888 also met standards of male colleges.

Opportunities for women increased at coeducational institutions following the Civil War. Before the war only three private colleges in Ohio—Oberlin, Hillsdale, and Antioch—and two state universities—Utah and Iowa—admitted women.[2] The decline in student enrollments that accompanied the war, however, weakened opposition to the presence of women in educational institutions and led to their admission at several universities. By 1870 eight state universities accepted women (Newcomer 1959).

The growing interest in higher education for women during the middle and later decades of the nineteenth century has been attributed to several factors. The development of the public-school system prepared women who might not have had the opportunity to attend more expensive private academies for college-level work and instilled in many of them a desire for learning. At the same time, the growth of public schools sparked a demand for teachers, which men, more interested in new industrial and professional opportunities, failed to meet. Female teachers, furthermore, were cheaper than male ones who commanded salaries from two to four times those paid to women. The expansion of employment opportunities for women in public elementary and secondary schools encouraged the acceptability of higher education for women since it led to public acknowledgment of the need to educate females. Other factors that might have created increased interest in a college education for women include the vast increase of ladies' magazines and fiction primarily written for women in the second quarter of the nineteenth century, developments which promoted women's interest in reading, and thus, in learning; the increase of leisure time available to women, a product of industrial progress and the invention of labor-saving devices; the growth of employment opportunities for women outside the home, a result not only of industrialization but of women's experience as philanthropic volunteers during the Civil War; and finally, and perhaps most important, the spread of the women's rights movement, a consequence of role conflict experienced in the antislavery movement, which helped awaken women to their second-class status as citizens and impressed upon many of them the need for education to help attain desired political and legal ends. Reform of the old-time male colleges and the sudden development of secular, research-oriented universities in the post-Civil War era added new prestige to higher education generally and ensured that admission to college, for men as well as for women, was seen as desirable. The relative numerical decline of college students before the year 1869 ended; and in the period 1870–1910 the number of enrolled students nearly quintupled at a time when the nation's population doubled.[3]

Women's intense desire for a college education in the late nineteenth century sparked a correspondingly passionate controversy. According to many observers, college training form women was a radical departure that would have lasting, deleterious effects on the mental and physical health of women, their reproductive capacities, and their spiritual and emotional natures.

The opening salvo in the attack against higher education for women came from Dr. Edward Clarke, professor of medicine at the Harvard School of Medicine. In his influential *Sex in Education,* reprinted twelve times within a year of publication, Clarke (1873) argued on the basis of allegedly scientific evidence that intellectual activity violated the fundamental principles of feminine nature and was the major factor responsible for the ill health that seemed prevalent among American women. His assertion sprang from his belief that violation of women's "rhythmical periodicity" by excessive study led to the degeneration of their sex organs and eventually to uterine disease, hysteria, and insanity. His assertions were disputed by other physicians, including Mary Putnam Jacobi who won Harvard Medical School's coveted Boylston Prize in 1876 for her essay, *The Question of Rest During Menstruation,* which showed that "college-bred women were in no-wise incapacitated for their habitual mental exertion" (Jacobi 1890, p. 76). To dispel further the notion that the higher education of women led to physical incapacity, the Association of Collegiate Alumnae conducted a statistical review that found that the large majority of women graduates considered themselves to be in excellent health and felt that college training had added to their physical strength.[4]

Despite these findings, the medical profession by and large continued to claim that higher education had deleterious effects on the health of women. The question was entangled with the issue of alumnae's proclivity to marriage and reproduction. After 1890, when statistics about the marriage rate of the first generation of college women could be collected, a steady stream of literature appeared that purported to present evidence on either side of the question. Generally, the results showed a definite differential between the rate of marriage and childbearing of women college graduates and those of the female population at large. In his influential work *Adolescence,* G. Stanley Hall (1904) cited statistics, for example, from Vassar, Wellesley, and Smith that purported to show that less than 50 percent of alumnae married, a large number of whom were childless, and that for those who were mothers the average number of children was less than two. Since many experts believed that three children per marriage were necessary to perpetuate the race, the obvious conclusion was that college women had failed to reproduce themselves. "From the viewpoint of the eugenicist," one critic concluded, "colleges for women were 'an historic blunder'" (Goodsell 1924, p. 46).

Still other objections to college education for women were raised, among them that female students would distract males and lower standards in coeducational institutions, or that the "public life of colleges would deprive women of their natural delicacy, refinement and tenderness" (Eliot 1908, p. 103). Several educators feared that the respectability of college education for women would remain suspect until upper-class families sent their daughters to college, for amongst the leisure class college remained unfashionable.

Liberal Arts as a Goal of Higher Education: The Ideal of "Culture"

By the late 1890s, however, the increasing enrollment of women in institutions of higher learning offered evidence that as college doors, once firmly barred to women, were opening with rapidity, a growing number of families were willing to send their daughters to college, however dubious they remained about its effects on the health, morality, womanly charms, and future marriage and childbearing prospects of young girls. By the turn of the century, women constituted almost one-third of the student body at the nation's colleges, and their numbers were gaining steadily. During the period 1890–1910, for example, students at women's colleges increased by 348.4 percent, while at coeducational colleges the gain in numbers of enrolled women students—438 percent—was even greater. Over a similar period, male students' attendance at college increased by only 214.2 percent (Goodsell 1924).

One of the most significant developments in the progress of higher education for women was the growing number of institutions to become coeducational in the last third of the nineteenth century. In 1870 only 30.7 percent of colleges for men were coeducational. By 1898 fully 70.0 percent admitted both men and women, while 30 percent took men only (Thomas 1900). After 1900, the increase in number of women attending coeducational schools, though less marked, was still impressive. From 1910–1916, for example, the increase of women was 70 percent compared with 43 percent for men. "Women who have been to college are as plentiful as blackberries on summer hedges," Thomas stated in 1908, remarking upon the contrast with the situation twenty-five years earlier when, having gone on to do graduate work in Europe after college, she was thought "to be as much of a disgrace to my family as if I had eloped with the coachman" (Thomas 1908, p. 1).

Yet in spite of substantial progress made in overcoming opposition to the higher education of women, as evidenced by the increasing number of female students attending college, the struggle of women to achieve the right to an advanced education on equal terms with men remained far from complete. Most observers, however, agreed that the first battle had been successfully waged. By the turn of the century, the notion that women were capable of acquiring the education given to men no longer seemed in contention. The record of merit established by women at women's schools as well as at coeducational institutions (where women's high scholastic achievements often threatened male students, producing a backlash against equal opportunity) offered conclusive proof that there were few, if any, differences in abilities between the sexes. Women now began to focus on new educational issues that were to occupy their attention during the next twenty years. Having proven their intellectual equality with men, they turned to perhaps more troublesome questions about the ideals, values, and purposes of college education for women.

Because the debate about the higher education of women in the decades after the Civil War had focused to a great extent on the comparative abilities of men and women, women's colleges had attempted to establish the proof of their students' fitness for advanced study by adopting the program of men's colleges almost in their entirety. The curricula in women's colleges during the post-Civil War years were thus patterned after those in force at men's colleges during the early nineteenth century, with study of Greek, Latin, and mathematics generally prescribed. Women's colleges similarly adopted the "disciplinary" goals that lay behind this orthodox curriculum. According to these aims, first outlined in the influential Yale Report of 1828 (Brubacher and Rudy 1958), the production of mental culture and discipline, to be achieved through a prescribed curriculum consisting of "the thorough study of the ancient languages," was seen as the primary purpose of college education. Such a college curriculum (and particularly, the study of Greek) would discipline all the mental faculties, so the theory went, and serve as the basis of any later intellectual or vocational achievement. Even more significant than the intellectual benefits of such a course of cultural study, however, was the high moral character it would instill. The cultivated Christian gentleman, the manly educated man, was commonly recognized as the desired product of college training in the first half of the nineteeth century.[5]

At many women's colleges, culture as the ideal of higher education afforded a flawless justification for the new experiment of female education. College courses devoted to culture would prepare women to teach, the one occupation recognized by college founders as appropriate to unmarried females, and, above all, such a curriculum would promote the development of womanly women, not the de-feminized creatures so feared in the popular imagination. In this way, culture as an educational ideal upheld social norms about women's proper roles, even while challenging fundamental assumptions about the intellectual inferiority of women to men. But attainment of knowledge as the goal of education was thus subtly transformed as educators, rejecting certain traditional notions about the limitations of women's place, in part accepted the society's image of feminine nature. Because of this ambivalence, the development of character and the pursuit of culture, rather than learning for its own sake, often became the goals of higher education for women.

At men's colleges, however, widespread curricular innovations after 1870 transformed the ideal of culture and mental discipline as the linchpin of higher education (Brubacher and Rudy 1958). In 1869 President Charles Eliot of Harvard instituted an elective system at that college, charging that the traditional curriculum produced unmotivated students and routine teaching. Eliot wanted to make motivation internal, leaving it to students to follow their own interests and aptitudes and choose the courses in which they wanted to specialize. Implicit in the new system was the expectation that in their freedom students would become experts in the chosen fields. Such a concept diverged directly from the standard set by the old Yale report, which asserted that all students, too immature to know their own interests and future life courses, must follow an identical, prescribed curriculum. Not all colleges went as far as Harvard and Cornell, which by 1890 offered almost their whole curriculum as elective, but the movement toward election, diversification, and specialization was irresistible.[6]

One consequence of this change was the effect it had upon the perception of professional development. Whereas the old-time college produced high-minded Christian gentlemen of character fine enough to enter the law and ministry, now college was seen as a gateway to all professions, new vocations—like engineering, teaching, and architecture—as well as old. In the larger universities college students often took preprofessional courses in their anticipated area of specialty. Frequently, graduate courses in the arts and sciences as well as in professional fields were open to undergraduates. Students could also specialize in a field by grouping elective courses or following a major-minor concentration. All these measures further delineated the objectives of higher education at the turn of the century from earlier goals.

How did the ideal of culture articulated as the goal of higher education at women's colleges align with these developments? Historians usually suggest that women's colleges slavishly followed programs established at male institutions, or offered carbon copies of them. Only to a certain extent, however, is this true, for the disciplinary ideals of liberal culture that continued to dominate curricula at a good many of the women's colleges in the opening decades of the twentieth century had declined in importance at many private and public universities and even at some of the smaller elite male schools. Indeed, remarked one faculty member in 1930, the woman's college remained the only institution of higher learning in the United States where one might obtain "a gentleman's education" (McHale 1934, p. 3).

In 1915, for example, Latin or Greek, French or German, English composition, mathematics, and philosophy were still prescribed courses at most of the women's schools. Wrote one curriculum analyst, the woman's college was "never more on the defensive for its aim of 'culture' only. . . . Guided conservatively by the old guard which admits no aim except in terms of culture," she concluded, [the woman's college] "adjusts itself slowly to the socialization of education" (Robinson 1918, p. 108).

Although the old disciplinary goals remained in force at women's schools, many curriculum changes in the direction of greater elective choice were instituted after 1890. Wellesley adopted a new curriculum in 1893, significantly reducing the required number of courses; Vassar, in 1900-1901; Mt. Holyoke, in 1907-1908; at each of these schools a large number of new courses was steadily added. Nevertheless, with the exception of Radcliffe, which followed Harvard's free-elective standard, most women's colleges maintained a good number of required courses in the freshman and sophomore years (and some in the upper classes as well), putting them in the conservative group of institutions with regard to election. Most of the women's schools prescribed nearly half or more, in fact, of total courses. Nevertheless, the variety of new courses offered and the possibility of grouping elective courses allowed students considerable choice in determining their own programs. The movement toward election and specialization thus placed women's colleges squarely in the camp of modern educational reform, yet the extent of curriculum change at these institutions did not signify the abandonment of traditional culture and disciplinary ends. The new Wellesley curriculum of 1893-1894 (which endured for the next forty years) was adopted, for example, according to President Helen Shafer, because it offered "the widest election consistent (1) with the completion of certain subjects which we deem essential to all *culture,* and (2) with the continuous study of one or two subjects for the sake of *mental discipline* and *breadth of view* which belong to advanced attainment" (emphasis added) (Glasscock 1975, p. 138).

Social Activism in the Progressive Era: A New Ideal of Service

Despite the fact that in general women's colleges remained devoted to the old disciplinary studies, the changing interests of college women themselves, reflecting a new activism in society at large, came to modify the emphasis on general culture as the principal object of higher education for women. A new educational ideal, sometimes described as fitness for an active and useful life, began to be expressed—although haltingly—during the years after 1890. Although required course work at women's colleges was still geared to the creation of cultivated women, new, more practical courses as well as extracurricular lectures and activities suggested that the goals of college women were changing in a manner that corresponded to the main currents of modern education generally, as well as with new ideals of progressive social reform. The new ideal of service, although rooted in the ethic of selflessness traditionally promoted by women's colleges, reflected a conscious motivation to become effectively involved in worldly concerns outside as well as within the domestic arena.

The transition from pure culture to service as an ideal of higher education for women was marked by a new emphasis on action, direct and deliberate, which began to appear at women's college campuses after 1890, replacing previous interpretations of liberal education as passive. A preference for living life at first hand was one general evidence of this shift. Such a focus was compatible with the derogation of isolated mental activity and the aversion to the excessive refinement and cultivation of intellect that Christopher Lasch suggests similarly characterized many middle-class reformers of the period (Lasch 1965). Describing the difference "between the healthy life of action, and the morbid selfish life of thought," for example, the Vassar student magazine proclaimed in an 1891 editorial that "the college girl can do almost anything, but she cannot contentedly do nothing" (Marbury 1915, pp. 28–29).

At Vassar women began flocking into the rapidly expanding departments that dealt with economics, once considered a man's field, and social problems. Courses that seemed related to the vital problems of the age—socialism, labor problems, and charities and corrections—became popular almost overnight. Women's work, rather than women's rights, was frequently discussed and the idea expressed that it can be as great as men's and must be "judged and accepted or rejected on an equal basis with men's work" (Marbury 1915, p. 30). Charlotte Perkins Gilman's *Women and Economics* (1898), which argued that only through gainful employment could women win independence, became the bible of the Vassar student body (Blatch and Lutz 1940, p. 108). Lectures at the various colleges, with guest speakers who had pioneered in the solution to social problems, included topics such as socialism, urban slums, settlements, labor strife, and the educated woman in society. This remarkable new interest in outside affairs was noticeable on campus in a number of other ways. For the first time, newspapers began to play an important role on campus. Bulletin boards, detailing matters of social concern, were started. Graduating classes were urged to utilize their education, and approaches other than teaching, the standard vocation for unmarried women, were set before them, including opportunities in law, medicine, journalism, business, settlement work, and home economics. As one professor of economics at Vassar related, seniors asked only, "What can I do? Where can I be useful after leaving college?" (Mills 1929, p. 80). At many colleges student interest in social questions organized around a variety of campus societies that defined their function to include practical service in the community as well as the development of interest in social theories and problems. Among the most active of these clubs were socialist societies, college suffrage leagues, Christian associations, and especially, college branches of the college settlement associations (Folks 1916, pp. 51–53). In 1889–1890, a College Settlement Association (CSA), with Smith, Vassar, Wellesley, Bryn Mawr, and Harvard Annex (Radcliffe) as members, was formed for the purpose of extending the educating power of the settlement idea. Included in the association were the New York settlement on Rivington Street on the Lower East Side, and the Philadelphia and Boston (Denison House) college settlements. Within a few years, fourteen eastern women's colleges were represented in the association. Until the demise of the CSA in 1917, college girls frequently spent vacations at the settlements and undertook other forms of practical cooperation during the year with the poor immigrant families who lived in the neighborhoods of the settlements. Women students at coeducational institutions in the Midwest and the West also undertook settlement activities; for example, women at the University of California at Berkeley participated in the West Berkeley Settlement League, while University of Chicago students were active in the University of Chicago Settlement (Gordon 1980).

A widespread belief in the importance and revolutionary nature of the work of college settlement women typified the strong crusading zest common to educated women in the last decade of the nineteenth century as many of them set out in new, pathbreaking occupations.[7] The ideals of altruism and devotion to others as goals of college education carried over from earlier generations, but no longer were these qualities considered mere by-products of character-building or the development of a cultured intellect. By 1890 students at women's colleges agreed upon the aim of their training: "We want to be, that we may *do*" (Marbury 1915, pp. 37–39). Even as the goal of service gained prominence at women's colleges, the older ideal of service was never abrogated. What is significant is that the word *culture* was no longer used to describe only those graces that characterized civilized living. In these transition years, a new activism was implied in the definition of culture, one that involved a sympathetic and mature understanding of social problems outside the college campus and the motivation to become a part of their solution.

Specialized Training versus the Liberal Arts: Refocusing Educational Ideals on Women's Work

The reluctance of women's colleges to renounce the ideal of culture while adopting new goals of service and utility nevertheless created fundamental ambiguities about educational means and ends that began to surface in the first decade of the twentieth century. Concern about the relationship of goals of college education to the practical components of a woman's life after graduation slowly began to emerge as the paramount issue in women's education. After the first decade of the twentieth century the idea of education as "preparation for life" came to occupy the attention of college educators and administrators. At both women's colleges and coeducational institutions discussion of educational purpose now turned largely toward consideration of the vocational relevance of college curricula for women.

"The problem today is not how to gain admittance to a college but how to make effective use of ourselves after graduation" wrote Mary Van Kleeck in the *Smith Alumnae Quarterly* of January 1911 (Van Kleeck 1911, p. 75). Many colleges organized employment (or appointment) bureaus. In addition an appointment bureau organized by the Women's Educational and Industrial Union of Boston opened in 1910, followed in 1911, by the Inter-collegiate Bureau of Occupations in New York, established by the alumnae organizations of eight women's colleges (Adams 1912).

The work of the Associates of Collegiate Alumnae (ACA) added momentum to the vocational movement at women's and coeducational colleges. Beginning with two ACA-sponsored appointment-bureau conferences in 1911, one at Smith College and the other in New York City, which attempted to raise common issues and problems, studies, lectures, and meetings concerned with vocational opportunities for college women were organized. These meetings greatly increased accessibility of information about vocational matters and influenced the way in which colleges treated the question of vocational guidance. In the 1920s, however, the

American Association for University Women, successor to the ACA, concluding that colleges by themselves could not successfully undertake the task of collecting and disseminating national information on employment opportunities for women, proposed the creation of a new organization, the Institute of Women's Professional Relations. Established in 1929, the institute acted as a national clearinghouse for information and planning about the work experience of women, with the intention of using the data collected to organize college curricula and develop programs for "functional education" (Adams 1912; Palmer 1918; Talbot and Rosenbery 1931).

In addition to stimulating interest in how colleges could provide students with pertinent information about employment possibilities, educators turned their attention to the more problematic issue of whether college curricula should be modified to prepare women for future careers. The assumption of a fundamental dichotomy in the life experience of male and female college graduates based on women's "normal occupation" of motherhood determined the outlines of the debate about vocational versus liberal-arts training at women's colleges. Women educators often shared the assumptions of their male colleagues that marriage and motherhood, rather than any professional career, was the appropriate destiny for educated women. Others recognized that many college graduates would prefer self-supporting work to marriage, but always there was the acknowledgment, as one alumna put it, of that "persistent vicious alternative-marriage or career" (Howes 1922, p. 445). As they examined the consequences of the premise that marriage and career were irreconcilable options, some women educators began to suspect that imitation of men's college curricula, which they acknowledged had hitherto guided the paths of women's education, might be erroneous. One faculty member wrote:

> In the higher education what seemed good for men seemed double good for women but it has become evident that this college curriculum does not bear so definite and satisfactory a relation to the after lives of women as it does to those of men. It is constantly impressed upon a boy during these four years that he must find out what he is good for; he must either be fit or ready to be fitted to do something which will have a definite market value. But the destiny of the girl who goes to college is carefully concealed from her. She does not know whether she is to marry, to teach, or to live the life of leisure . . . [Smith 1898, p. 2]

This dilemma of choice made it difficult to design a vocationally relevant course for college women since, as observers pointed out, students never knew with certainty which option they would select. Should colleges equip women with only the standard cultural training, or should they prepare women specifically for self-support in a selected vocation or, alternatively, for wifehood and motherhood? Proponents of women's education were sharply divided over these possibilities.

The relationship of specialized training, particularly domestic science, to the curriculum at general arts colleges was not a new issue. The first Vassar prospectus of 1865 noted that while the household was "woman's peculiar province," it was the home, and not the college, that was "the proper school for this art." Concluding that "a full course in the arts of domestic economy cannot be successfully incorporated in a system of liberal or college education," a compromise had been offered at Vassar in which domestic economy was to be taught theoretically by lecture and textbook, with practical illustrations drawn from examples of college living (Journal of Home Economics 1911, p. 331; Marbury 1915, pp. 3–4). In the Midwest and Far West the Morrill Act of 1862, providing for the establishment of the land-grant colleges, gave impetus to learning related to "agriculture and the mechanical arts" as necessary to promote the "liberal and practical education of the industrial classes."

A four-year course in domestic science was introduced at the University of Illinois in 1875–1876. But not until 1890 when Marion Talbot gave lectures and conducted laboratory work in sanitation and dietetics at Wellesley College was the first real attempt initiated to introduce college courses in home economics on a scientific and systematic basis. The work continued at Wellesley only for two years, until Miss Talbot became dean of women at the University of Chicago, where she offered similar instruction.

In the next few years courses in domestic science were introduced at several state schools in the Midwest, among them the Universities of Chicago (in 1893), Wisconsin, Tennessee (in 1897), and Idaho. The first Lake Placid Conference in 1899 and its successive annual meeting that gave rise to the American Home Economics Association in 1909 provided further impetus to the development of educational efforts to foster courses of study in home economics at the college level. By 1910 over one-hundred colleges and universities were offering instruction in home economics, courses that were taken primarily by women. The largest group offering a five-year course leading to a degree were the land-grant colleges. No courses in household economics were offered, however, at any of the Seven Sister schools at this time, although Teachers College at Columbia University did open its domestic-science course to Barnard women.[8]

The eastern women's colleges, in fact, which had earlier defended the higher education of women on the ground that it would enhance the "womanly virtues," now led the protest against differentiation in education according to sex. Learning as a preparation for a life career was narrow and self-interested, according to this opinion, and imposed a sordid, utilitarian calculus into the cherished "joyous irresponsibility" of college life. Many refused to concede, furthermore, that the traditional liberal-arts curriculum did not prepare students adequately for life.[9] As a result, the major concession to vocationalism at women's colleges before 1920 turned out to be simply the establishment of campus employment bureaus, intercollegiate vocational offices, periodic employment conferences, and the like. Nevertheless, women's colleges told students that a liberal-arts education devoted primarily to the purpose of culture and mental growth need not be irrelevant to occupational choices. "The college is not and never will be a vocational school" asserted Wellesley College, "if by that you mean a school which instructs in the special technicalities of special jobs." But it was still a true "vocational school" in that its ideal, " 'the supreme development and unfolding of every power and faculty', includes the foundations for business and professional careers as well as home life for its graduates" (*The Liberal Arts as Vocational Training* 1924, p.). The college curriculum, for example, included courses in history and government for the prospective lawyer, courses in science for the future doctor, and courses in economics and statistics for the business woman. Even Latin and mathematics might prove useful in some future employment, these colleges insisted.

The fate of vocational education at many coeducational state universities offers an interesting comparison to the situation at the eastern women's colleges. Because these institutions conceptualized their mandate as service to the state, vocational training was early recognized as an appropriate curriculum direction, even where women were concerned. Although the ideal of liberal culture was thus much less emphasized at these schools than the ideals of public service and vocational preparation, a so-called natural segregation of the sexes caused women to predominate in culture courses like literature and humanities, almost to the exclusion of men, whereas courses that enrolled large numbers of men, such as political science, were not elected by women. Graduate colleges of engineering, law, commerce, agriculture, and medicine were essentially men's schools, although officially open to women, whereas preprofessional courses or graduate institutes in home economics and domestic science were taken only by women. State administrators thought that this division according to the "natural fitness" of men and women was desirable, but in a significant sense it illustrated that the differences between coeducational and separate schooling for women were not always as real as they seemed (Van Hise 1908; Olin 1909).

Ongoing historical research into patterns of higher education of women during this period suggests the possibility that similar sex-segregated curricula existed at private coeducational universities as well as at publicly supported ones. Florence Howe's (1981) research on women at Stanford and Lynn Gordon's (1980) work on women at the Universities of Chicago and California reveal the existence of different conceptions of educational missions regarding male and female students as well as of sex-segregated extracurricular activities. At Stanford Howe found that the education of women was to be equal to that of men—"varied only as nature dictates." In practice, this meant that while men were educated to fit them for usefulness in life and thus offered a specialized, technical curriculum, women were to be educated for motherhood. The result was that women became a second sex on the Stanford campus; invisible, ignored, their presence and significance at Stanford blurred and ambivalent (Howe 1981). At the University of California at Berkeley, where by 1894 women comprised almost one-third of the undergraduate body, Gordon found that ideals of sexual distinctiveness also excluded and set women aside. Divided by class, the sorority system, and the lack of central residence facilities, Berkeley's female students remained on the sidelines (Gordon 1980). At the University of Chicago separatist ideals worked far better in the students' behalf because of a strong support network consisting of a large contingent of female graduate students, a small but cohesive group of female faculty committed to the expansion of opportunities for women students, and the highly visible presence and support of feminist reformers and women's groups in Chicago, a major center of feminist activity. The idea of special education for women, however, was promoted through a Department of Home Economics within the School of Education, as well as through a separate Department of Household Administration under the direction of Marion Talbot, dean of women. Although the Department of Home Economics emphasized technical skills provided in such courses as cooking, sewing, crafts, and basket-weaving, primarily in the interest of providing career opportunities for women in fields other than teaching, Talbot and her associate Sophonisba Breckinridge stressed the intellectual and social-reformist aspects of household administration. Talbot herself gave a seminar on sanitary science that focused on the scientific aspects of that subject. Breckinridge offered courses such as women and the law, and the economic, legal, and social characteristics and possibilities of the family. Other courses were given in chemistry, biology, and other social and natural sciences. Eventually, Chicago's School of Social Service Administration took over many concerns of the Department of Household Administration, which closed its doors when Talbot retired in 1925 (Gordon 1980).

The models suggested by Howe and Gordon—women as separate but equal at Chicago, and women as an invisible second sex at the masculine-dominated Stanford and Berkeley—may apply to other coeducational campuses, but further research into the specific details of curricula and student life is necessary to sort out which colleges during which periods of time adapted or rejected elements of these patterns. Similarly, we need to know which kinds of models existed at which women's schools—were culture and service as the mainspring of liberal education substantially altered by other emphases at specific schools? Both Florence Howe and Patricia Ann Palmieri (1981a) suggest, for example, that at least during a certain period Wellesley provided a woman-centered model of education, one that incorporated women's experience into the curriculum and that allowed women to participate fully in campus life, providing them with faculty role models and options for activity both within and outside of traditional womanly spheres. [See Antler (1980) for a discussion of the post graduate lives of the Wellesley College class of 1897.] (Howe 1981; Palmieri 1981b). Whether such a model took root at most of the other women's schools in the East as well as the Midwest, the West, and the South also needs to be explored.

Transition or Decline: Higher Education for Women, 1890–1920

Even after 1920, the primary purpose of higher education appears to have remained the provision of general culture to students. But despite this continuity of purpose, significant changes had occurred that had the effect of transforming earlier ideals of higher education for women. First, there had been a great change in the motivation of college women themselves. Now that college for women had been legitimated, students went to college with few of those soul-stirrings common to the pioneer college women. Women now attended college not necessarily because of a passionate desire for education or to prove their intellectual equality with men, but often simply because of a desire for "the college life." As Patricia Graham has suggested, "unlike the nineteenth century's prescriptive behavior for women, the twentieth century's was not in conflict with college attendance. In fact, undergraduate study was either consistent with or irrelevant to it. . . . College had begun to play the role that high school had in the lives of women at the turn of the century, for many simply a pleasant interlude on the way to growing up" (Graham 1978, pp. 770–771).

College women's concern with social activism was also modified during this period. After 1920, interest in social service and political action peaked significantly, reflecting a concomitant decline in Progressive social reform. A new trend of positive identification with marriage and maternity came to characterize women students. Whereas approximately half the graduates of women's colleges remained single before 1920, after that time college women preferred to become wives and mothers, generally eschewing the career path. This was a consequence not only of the fact that the student population had broadened and become more representative of the middle-class values of mass democracy (Chafe 1972; Graham 1978) but of the general shift in feminist goals and the so-called decline of feminism itself after the achievement of suffrage. During the period 1920–1960, college-educated women married earlier, bore larger families, and turned their attention wholeheartedly to childrearing, directed by the professional guidance and scientific advice of a new group of "experts" in psychology and sociology. Surveys consistently showed that few of these women had clear vocational goals while in college. Most attended college to obtain a general cultural education, for the prestige, or for the social life. More than two-thirds of students married, most immediately after graduation (one survey found that 15 percent of women married before graduation). Most had their first child within a year or two after school (Chafe 1972, Shosteck n.d.). Women may have thought they were being educated to the ways of modernity and progressive social thought, as did the members of Mary McCarthy's Vassar "group," but beneath the gloss of competence and vision with which some of them emerged lay a fundamental conservatism rooted in traditional ideas about women's place. It is not surprising that while Mabel Newcomer (1959) and others who pioneered in the writing of women's educational history saw this history as one long progressive, utopian movement, those who came after her—among them, Jessie Bernard (1964), Jill Conway (1974), and Patricia Graham (1978)—were far more critical about the achievements of women's education during this period of domesticity *recidivus* (Patricia Palmieri 1981b). Whether their paradigm of progress followed by decline needs further revision—refocusing, for example, on the continuities in curricula and campus life experienced by female students as well as upon changing expectations regarding career and marriage—must await the results of further research into the mid-twentieth-century era, a period that so far has been of only negligible interest to scholars of women's education.[10]

Indeed, several innovations in women's education were fashioned during this period, but as yet we know very little about the full range of such programs. Two experimental schools, Bennington and Sarah Lawrence, were established, for example, in the late 1920s and early 1930s. Each reaffirmed the traditional liberal-arts focus of women's education but one that emphasized artistic as well as academic preparation and the social and ethical, rather than simply methodological, aspects of social science (Jencks and Riesman 1968). Also important was Vassar's Institute of Euthenics, which opened in 1924 after the receipt of a gift of $500 from Mrs. Minnie Blodgett. The institute provided an interdisciplinary program for undergraduates consisting of courses such as child hygiene, nutrition, home nursing, parenthood, and household technology as well as a summer institute for alumnae. Though the undergraduate euthenics program continued until the 1950s, only a handful of Vassar students majored in it, and the institute seems generally to have been scorned by the majority of Vassar's faculty, who believed that the idea of educating women for careers in homemaking represented a step backward for women's education.[11] At Smith the Institute for the Coordination of Women's Interests had an even shorter life (1925–1931). Though not an undergraduate program, its aim was to develop methods and programs to enable college-educated women to pursue part-time careers while marrying and raising children.[12] Vassar's experiment in special education for homemaking does not seem to have been actively pursued by the established women's colleges, yet over the next few decades many schools did broaden their range of courses. The Simmons College plan of professional education, for example, combining "the liberal, the vocational and the homemaking arts," attracted a different population of students than those who attended the Seven Sister schools. For the Simmons students special training for future careers was desirable. Critical of the standard liberal-arts colleges for women that stressed the "inner or intellectual life" at the expense of practical skills, Simmons attempted to unite the vocational-professional and the liberal disciplines in one program, emphasizing new opportunities for women in such fields as "science, industry, business, retailing, publishing, library science, home economics, nursing and social work" (Beatley 1955). By the 1960s many other women's colleges, in addition to offering standard liberal-arts majors, offered some kind of preprofessional program for credit. Courses relating to premed, prelaw, and preteaching were offered at many women's schools. Secretarial courses were provided at some (Hollins), as well as courses in medical technology (Mills), applied art and music (Manhattanville), child development (Scripps), and business, drama, art, and nursing (Skidmore) (Women's College Board 1963). At the large number of Catholic women's schools a focus on values, which translated into a curricular concern with the issues of peace and justice and with preparation for careers in religious institutions, was dominant.[13]

As this survey of changing educational ideals concerning women has demonstrated, expectations regarding college women are much influenced by goals and institutions of the broader society. Such a connection to the culture at large is evidenced as well by pronounced shifts in the enrollments of women in colleges and universities over the last half century. The proportion of women enrolled in postsecondary education rose briefly during the 1920s and 1930s, then experienced a sharp decline in the late 1940s due to the large number of returning veterans entering colleges. The proportion of women attending college rose again in the 1960s (Giele 1978). If we look at figures regarding the attainment of bachelors' degrees, we find that sex ratios have been relatively stable over the period 1930–1970, fluctuating between a low of 45 percent female and a high of 51 percent (Adkins 1975). (For a more detailed analysis of these trends, see chapter 3 of this book.)

Enrollment and degree figures relating to specific educational programs show great variability according to sex. Over this mid-century period, women continued to flock to courses in humanities and education, while men remained more interested in the sciences, politics, economics, and preprofessional training of various kinds. The proportion of women getting bachelors' degrees in sex-segregated programs in education, the humanities, and the arts remained high. In 1970, for example, women constituted 99 percent of persons receiving bachelors' degrees in home economics; 93 percent of those in nursing, therapy, and dental hygiene; 92 percent of those obtaining elementary-education degrees; 86 percent of those in library science; and 79 percent of those in social work and in Western European languages and literature. On the other hand, in that year women constituted only 1 percent of persons obtaining degrees in chemical-material engineering, 3 percent in agriculture, 5 percent in earth sciences, 6 percent in law, and 7 percent in physics (Adkins 1975, p. 146).

Thus, while on the whole, the proportion of women as undergraduates has increased slightly since 1960, sexual differentiation along the lines of separate but equal appears to remain the norm (Adkins 1975). At each successive stage of higher education, furthermore, at least until the early 1970s, the pattern of differentiation by sex intensifies. In every field and in every type of institution, there were relatively fewer women graduate and professional students than at lower levels (Carnegie Commission 1973). An equally serious problem is the small number of women serving as faculty and administrators at institutions of higher learning; indeed, the number of female educators declined both in absolute numbers and proportions since the watershed years of the 1920s (Bernard 1964; Graham 1978). Though cultural factors relating to women's career expectations have influenced this trend, discrimination in relation to hiring and promotion remains a significant barrier to women's achievement in education. Without strong female role models and in the absence of a female academic-mentoring system, the aspirations and options of women undergraduates will remain unnecessarily limited.

Contemporary Trends in Women's Higher Education

Although problems relating to sexual differentiation and discrimination remain troubling, significant changes in the content and delivery of higher education for women students have begun to be perceived, a product in part of the academic revolution of the 1960s, but most important, of the feminist movement of the last decade and a half. The advent of women's studies has altered traditional ideas about curricula for women, as for the first time attention is focused on women's experiences in culture, history, and society.[14] Beginning in 1970, women's-studies programs were developed at many institutions to provide a wide range of courses about women. The courses given reflected a dual perspective: some were offered at the introductory level, usually from an interdisciplinary perspective; others were specialized courses offered within the framework of traditional disciplines. In 1980, women's studies programs were offered in over three-hundred academic institutions, accounting for about twenty-thousand courses nationwide (Bennetts 1980; Hook 1980). Originally, specialized courses offered under Women's Studies included primarily those in history, literature, and sociology, disciplines that led the way in the reappraisal of women's past. Over the course of the decade, fields like psychology, anthropology, education, political science, and the law became well-represented in women's studies curricula (Howe 1977). Today, depending upon institutional resources, courses are offered in virtually every academic area. In addition to those listed above, courses focusing on women's experiences and contributions are increasingly offered in such fields as biology, philosophy, religion, economics, art history, and public policy. Indeed, the framework of some of these disciplines has been markedly altered by the new knowledge and methodologies developed by and about women. First indications suggest that the perceptions and attitudes of women students have also been altered by this women-centered approach to knowledge.

Although women students remain disproportionately concerned with the issue of juggling family and career after completion of their training, recent studies show that women's expectations about their futures are changing in important ways. A survey of Smith College graduates (Bennetts 1979), for example, showed that while 66 percent of alumnae of the class of 1949 ended their education after college graduation, only 27 percent of the class of 1969 did so. Further, more than 50 percent of the 1949 alumnae waited until their children were in school before taking paying jobs, while only 1 percent of the class of 1969 did so. A survey of the 1980 graduates of Harvard and Radcliffe reflected an even more dramatic change in women's career decisions. Again, though women were taking issues of marriage and family into consideration in making their plans to a greater extent than men were doing, the career choices made by graduates of both sexes were remarkably similar. For the first time since statistics on vocational choices had been kept by the college, the gap between the percentages of Harvard-Radcliffe students selecting careers in traditionally male-dominated fields of business, medicine, and law had virtually closed (Radcliffe College 1981).

Women's studies and the feminist movement generally have thus had a positive effect on the attitudes of college women and on their educational goals and plans, an outcome reflected in the new competencies and intense determination exhibited by recent alumnae. Nevertheless, many problems remain. Discrimination against women in the academy exists on many levels, both toward students, faculty, and administrators. Rising vocational expectations and the merging of career aspirations of women and men have created not only new options but new anxieties as well, as college women seek to fulfill the manifold roles that have opened to them. Despite these problems, college women today seem to be rejecting the model of domesticity without gainful employment that characterized the majority of educated women after 1920. Many are delaying marriage and childbearing (or reject-ing them entirely) in order to pursue nascent career objectives.

This revolutionary change in women's behavior and values, in com-bination with new demographic configurations, will make undergraduate women an increasingly significant force within higher education in the next decades. As the baby boom of the 1950s and 1960s traverses the academy, administrators must plan for a reduced population of eighteen-year-olds behind them. Institutions of higher learning, anticipating series shortfalls in enrollments, are aggressively seeking out new populations to fill empty classroom seats. Even the most elite private colleges are now recruiting women. Furthermore, as the aging population swells and the number of workers relative to the population at large decreases, it is likely that women will receive powerful inducements to enter the labor market. These factors suggest that in the near future we can anticipate greater numbers of women competing in higher education and an enhanced concern with preparation for work and career on their part.

As a consequence, barriers within higher education that have previously blocked the fulfillment of women's aspirations in all fields—even the so-called masculine ones—may be reduced. Thus the debate between liberal arts and specialized vocational education for women as well as men takes on a new relevance. The challenge to educators is to redefine the content of higher education for women in innovative ways that will preserve the finest values of women's traditional education yet which will provide them with the knowledge and skills to allow them to take full advantage of the new opportunities available to them. Changing cultural attitudes and new social and demographic trends may provide the impetus to reevaluate the domi-nant patterns of sexual differentiation within higher education, opening to women as well as to men areas of study that have previously been closed. As the women's-studies approach spreads to institutions not now offering a wide range of women-centered courses and becomes further integrated as well into the general curriculum, undergraduate women may find new sources of support and strength as they shape their futures.

Historians of education can play a major role in reevaluating women's past and in helping college women construct a framework for the future. What is needed is research that focuses on all the varied aspects of women's educational experience over time. To date, scholarship has tended to emphasize the contributions of college founders and administrators at the expense of students themselves and even of faculty. Most attention, further-more, has been given to women at the elite eastern women's schools, partic-ularly in the late nineteenth century, neglecting women at small, coeduca-tional midwestern colleges, Roman Catholic women's colleges, southern women's colleges, black women's colleges, state universities, and land-grant universities. Scholars need to address many questions concerning the role of women students in all these specific institutions: what were their backgrounds and origins, their expectations, their routes of access to higher education, their courses of study, their extracurricular activities and their post-graduate experiences? How, ultimately, did college affect their lives and their choices?[15] Much has been accomplished in recent years in helping us understand the experiences of previous generations of college women, but as Patricia Albjerg Graham put it some years ago in outlining an agenda for research on the history of women in higher education, there is still "so much to do" (Graham 1975).

Notes

1. The development of women's higher education in the late nineteenth century has usually been interpreted from the vantage point of the founders and administrators who organized women's colleges during this time—that is, from the top down. The benevolent intentions of these leaders assumed institutional form during this period, so the analysis goes, and gradually a clientele for their educational innovations was located. The process, however, ought also to be examined from the perspective of the clients' own aspirations, for higher education was extremely significant in the effort of many women in the late nineteenth century to redefine women's sphere.

A complete and incisive history of higher education for women in the United States remains to be written. Standard works, though somewhat dated, on women's education include Willystine Goodsell, *The Education of Women* (New York: MacMillan, 1924); Mabel Newcomer, *A Century of Higher Education for American Women* (New York: Harper Brothers, 1959); Helen R. Olin, *The Women of a State University* (New York: G.P. Putnam's, 1909); Thomas Woody, *A History of Women's Education in the United States,* 2 vols. (New York: Science Press, 1929). For more recent approaches to the problems of women's education, see Patricia Albjerg Graham, "So Much to Do: Guides for Historical Research on Women in Higher Education," *Teachers' College Record* 76 (1975):461–486; and Graham, "Expansion and Exclusion: A History of Women in American Higher Education," *Signs* 3 (1978):759–773; Jill K. Conway, "Perspectives on the History of Women's Education in the United States," *History of Education Quarterly* 14 (1974):1–12; M. Jennifer Brown, "The Role of Women as Thinkers: Interpretations of the Effects of Women in Higher Education in Late Nineteenth-Century America," paper presented at the Third Berkshire Conference on the History of Women, Bryn Mawr College, Bryn Mawr, Pennsylvania, June 1976; Roberta Frankfort, *Collegiate Women: Domesticity and Career in Turn-of-the-Century America* (New

York: New York University Press, 1977); Charlotte Williams Conable, *Women at Cornell: The Myth of Equal Education* (Ithaca, N.Y.: Cornell University Press, 1977). For a popular account of the Seven Sister women's colleges, see Elaine Kendall, *Peculiar Institutions: An Informal History of the Seven Sister Colleges* (New York: G.P. Putnam's Sons, 1975).

2. On the founding of the eastern women's colleges, see Elizabeth Deering Hanscom and Helen French Greene, *Sophia Smith and the Beginnings of Smith College, Based upon the Narrative by John Morton Greene* (Northampton, Mass.: Smith College, 1925); Clark L. Seelye, *The Early History of Smith College* (Boston: Houghton Mifflin, 1923); Smith College, *Celebration of the Quarter Century* (Cambridge, Mass.: Riverside Press, 1900); Arthur C. Cole, *A Hundred Years of Mount Holyoke College, The Evolution of an Educational Ideal* (New Haven, Conn.: Yale University Press, 1940); Cornelia Meigs, *What Makes a College? A History of Bryn Mawr* (New York: MacMillan, 1956); Alice Duer Miller and Susan Myers, *Barnard College: The First Fifty Years* (New York: Columbia University Press, 1939); Annie Nathan Meyer, *Barnard Beginnings* (Boston: Houghton Mifflin, 1935); Marian Churchill White, *A History of Barnard College* (New York: Columbia University Press, 1954); Florence Converse, *Wellesley College: A Chronical of the Years, 1875-1938* (Wellesley, Mass.: Hathaway House Bookshop, 1939); Jean Glasscock, ed. *Wellesley College 1875-1975: A Century of Women* (Wellesley, Mass.: Wellesley College, 1975); David McCord, *An Acre for Education: Being Notes on the History of Radcliffe College,* Cambridge, Mass.: Crimson Printing Co., 1958.

3. On the development of the university after the Civil War, see Richard Hofstadter, "The Revolution in Higher Education," in Arthur M. Schlesinger, Jr., and Morton White, eds., *Paths of American Thought* (Boston: Houghton Mifflin, 1961).

4. To ensure that women remained healthy throughout their college stay, the association recommended the introduction of a scientific course of physical education, the provision of an adequately equipped gymnasiam, and a course on hygiene, sanitation, and athletics, as well as the appointment of a competent female instuctor of physical education and a resident physician. Special attention was to be paid to correct problems of inadequate ventilation and sanitation in dormitory and classroom facilities. See Marion Talbot, *The Education of Women* (Chicago: University of Chicago Press, 1910); Goodsell (1924); and Newcomer (1959).

For a discussion of medical views on higher education in England, see Joan N. Burstyn, "Education and Sex: The Medical Case Against Higher Education for Women in England, 1870-1900," *Proceedings of the American Philosophical Society,* April 1973. On the hostility of medical men to women generally, see Carroll Smith-Rosenberg and Charles Rosenberg, "The Female Animal: Medical and Biological Views of Woman and Her

Role in Nineteenth Century American," *Journal of American History* 60 (1973):332–356.

5. On the disciplinary goals of men's colleges in the early nineteenth century, see Lawrence Vesey, *The Emergence of the American University* (Chicago: University of Chicago Press, 1965); and Brubacher and Rudy (1958).

6. For a discussion of educational reform, and the elective system, see Frederic Rudolph, *The American College and University: A History* (New York: Knopf, 1962); Brubacher and Rudy (1958, pp. 101–115); Vesey, *Emergence of the American University,* pp. 81–120; D.E. Phillips, "The Elective System in American Colleges," *Pedagogical Seminary* 8 (1901): 206–230; and A.P. Brigham, "Present Status of the Elective System in American Colleges," *Educational Review* 14 (1897):360–369; Oscar and Mary Handlin, *The American College and American Culture: Socialization as a Function of Higher Education* (New York: McGraw-Hill, 1970). Burton Bledstein states that the university became a "professional service institution" during this period. See Burton Bledstein, *The Culture of Professionalism* (New York: Norton, 1976).

7. On the crusading nature of educated women during this period, see especially Jill Conway, "Women Reformers and American Culture 1870–1930," *Journal of Social History* 5 (1971):164–177; and "Jane Addams: An American Heroine," in Robert Jay Lifton, ed., *The Woman in America* (Boston: Beacon Press, 1967).

8. On the home-economics movement see Journal of Home Economics, "The Home Economics Movement in the United States," *Journal of Home Economics* 3 (1911):331–341; Ellen Cope, "Home Economics," *Pedagogical Seminary* 21 (1914):2; "Mrs. Ellen Richards: Her Relation to the Lake Placid Conference on Home Economics," *Journal of Home Economics* 3 (1911):351–352; and R.H. Jesse, "The Position of Household Economics in the Academic Curricula," *Publications of the Association of Collegiate Alumnae* 3 (1905):24–29.

9. For a more detailed examination of this argument, see Joyce Antler, "The Educated Woman and Professionalization: The Struggle for a New Feminine Identity, 1890–1920" (Ph.D. diss., State University of New York at Stony Brook, 1977).

10. Patricia Ann Palmieri's insightful remarks on the historiography of women and higher education offer further suggestions about past and present directions of research in this area (Palmieri 1981b).

Two scholars are currently preparing comprehensive histories of women in higher education. Barbara Miller Solomon of Harvard University is completing a book on the changing meaning of liberal education for American women from the late colonial period to the present. Florence Howe of the State University of New York, College at Old Westbury, is also at work on a book on patterns of higher education for women at women's colleges and at coeducational universities.

11. Vassar's Institute of Euthenics was the subject of Debra Hermman's paper, "Victims of Equal Education: On the Failure of the Vassar Experiment in Women's Education, 1861–1924," and of Rebecca Mitchell and Ben Harris's paper, "Euthenics at Vassar College: Educating the Scientific Homemaker," (Papers presented at the Fifth Berkshire Conference on the History of Women, Vassar College, June 1981).

12. Several individuals are currently at work on studies of the Smith Institute. See, for example, Judy Jolley Johraz, "The Institute for the Coordination of Women's Interests: A Solution to the Either/Or Issue?," (Fifth Berkshire Conference on the History of Women, Vassar College, June 1981).

13. I am grateful to Marion Kilson of Emmanuel College, Boston, for her helpful comments on the educational traditions of Catholic women's schools.

14. I would like to thank Patricia Albjerg Graham, Barbara Miller Solomon, and Patricia Ann Palmieri for their insights concerning future directions for research on the higher education of women.

15. For an early but incisive analysis of the role of women's studies, see Barbara Sicherman, "The Invisible Woman: The Case for Women's Studies," in W. Todd Furniss and Patricia Albjerg Graham, eds., *Women in Higher Education* (Washington, D.C.: American Council on Education, 1974).

Bibliography

Adams, Elizabeth Kemper. "The Vocational Opportunities of the College of Liberal Arts." *Journal of the Association of Collegiate Alumnae* 5 (1912):256–266.

Adkins, Douglas L. *The Great American Degree Machine: An Economic Analysis of the Human Resource Output of Higher Education.* Berkeley, Calif.: Carnegie Commission on Higher Education, 1975.

Antler, Joyce. " 'After College, What?' New Graduates and the Family Claim." *American Quarterly* 32 (1980):409–434.

Beatley, Bancroft. *Another Look at Women's Education.* Boston: Simmons College, 1955.

Bennetts, Leslie. "The Changing Attitudes of Smith Graduates." *The New York Times,* 30 July 1979.

————. "Women's Viewpoints Gain Respect in Academe." *The New York Times,* 2 December 1980.

Bernard, Jessie. *Academic Women.* University Park: Pennsylvania State University, 1964.

Blatch, Stanton Harriet, and Lutz, A. *Challenging Years: The Memoirs of Harriet Stanton Blatch*. New York: G.P. Putnam's Sons, 1940.

Brubacher, John S., and Rudy, Willis. *Higher Education in Transition: An American History, 1636–1956*. New York: Harper and Row, 1958.

Carnegie Commission on Higher Education. *Opportunities for Women in Higher Education*. New York: McGraw-Hill, 1973.

Chafe, William Henry. *The American Woman: Her Changing Social, Economic, and Political Roles, 1920–1970*. New York: Oxford University Press, 1972.

Clarke, Edward H. *Sex in Education; or a Fair Chance for the Girls*. Boston: James R. Osgood and Co., 1873. Reprint. New York: Arno Press, 1972.

Conway, Jill K. "Perspectives on the History of Women's Education in the United States." *History of Education Quarterly* 14 (1974):1–12.

Eliot, Charles W. "Women's Education—A Forecast." *Publications of the Association of Collegiate Alumnae* 3 (1908):101–105.

Folks, Gertrude H. "Through the Campus Gates: Student Interest in Social Questions." *Vassar Quarterly* 2 (1916):51–53.

Giele, Janet Zollinger. *Women and the Future: Changing Sex Roles in Modern America*. New York: Free Press, 1978.

Gilman, Charlotte Perkins. *Women and Economics*. Boston: Small, Maynard and Co., 1898.

Glasscock, Jean, ed. *Wellesley College 1875–1975: A Century of Women*. Wellesley, Mass.: Wellesley College, 1975.

Goodsell, Willystine. *The Education of Women*. New York: MacMillan, 1924.

Gordon, Lynn. "Women with Missions: Varieties of College Life in the Progressive Era." Ph.D. diss., University of Chicago, 1980.

Graham, Patricia Albjerg. "So Much to Do: Guides for Historical Research on Women in Higher Education." *Teachers' College Record* 76 (1975):461–486.

———. "Expansion and Exclusion: A History of Women in American Higher Education." *Signs* 3 (1978):759–773.

Hall, G. Stanley. *Adolescence: Its Psychology and Its Relations to Physiology, Anthropology, Sociology, Sex, Crime, Religion and Education*. New York: D. Appleton and Co., 1904.

Hook, Janet. "Women's Studies Win Growing Support in Fight for Academic Legitimacy." *Chronicle of Higher Education*, 8 September 1980.

Howe, Florence. *Seven Years Later: Women's Studies Programs in 1976*. Washington, D.C.: National Advisory Council on Women's Educational Programs, 1977.

———. "Ideology at Wellesley and Stanford." Paper presented at the Fifth Berkshire Conference on the History of Women, Vassar College, June 1981.

Howes, Ethel P. "Accepting the Universe." *Atlantic Monthly* 129 (1922): 444–453.

Jacobi, Mary Putnam. "The Higher Education of Women." Letter to the Editor, *Medical News* 66 (1890):75–77.

Jencks, Christopher, and Riesman, David. *The Academic Revolution.* New York: Doubleday, 1968.

Journal of Home Economics. "The Home Economics Movement in the United States." *Journal of Home Economics* 3 (1911):331–341.

Lasch, Christopher. *The New Radicalism in America.* New York: Vintage, 1965.

The Liberal Arts as Vocational Training. Pamphlet prepared by Bryn Mawr, Holyoke, Radcliffe, Smith, Vassar, Wellesley. New York, 1924.

McHale, Kathryn. "The Changing College." *Goucher Alumnae Quarterly* 13 (1934):3–7.

Marbury, Frances Tomlin. "The Social Life of Vassar Students." *The Vassar Miscellany* (1915):3–39.

Marks, Jeannette. *Life and Letters of Mary Emma Wooley.* Washington, D.C.: Public Affairs Press, 1955.

Mills, Herbert E. "Changing Interests of College Women." *Vassar Quarterly* 14 (1929):79–87.

Newcomer, Mabel. *A Century of Higher Education for American Women.* New York: Harper Brothers, 1959.

Olin, Helen R. *The Women of a State University.* New York: G.P. Putnam's Sons, 1909.

Palmer, Edith St. Clair. "The Second Intercollegiate Conference on Vocational Opportunities for Women." *Education* 38 (1918):557–560.

Palmieri, Patricia Ann. "In Adamless Eden: A Social Portrait of the Academic Community at Wellesley College 1875–1920." Ph.D. diss., Harvard University, 1981a.

———. Comment on the Session "The Vassar Experience, 1865–1925." The Fifth Berkshire Conference on the History of Women. Vassar College, 1981b.

Radcliffe College. "Women's Career Goals More Like Men's." *Second Century: Radcliffe News,* June 1981, p. 14.

Robinson, Mabel Louise. "The Curriculum of the Women's College." *Bureau of Education Bulletin,* (Department of Interior), 1918, 6, n.p.

Shosteck, Robert. *Five Thousand Women College Graduates Report: Findings of a National Survey of the Social and Economic Status of Women Graduates of Liberal Arts Colleges of 1946–1949.* Washington, D.C.: B'nai B'rith Vocational Bureau, n.d.

Smith, Mary Roberts. "Shall the College Curriculum be Modified for Women?" *Publications of the Association of Collegiate Alumnae* 3 (1908):1–15.

Talbot, Marion, and Rosenbery, Lois Kimball. *The History of the American Association of University Women.* Boston: Houghton Mifflin, 1931.

Thomas, M. Carey. "Education of Women." In N.M. Butler, ed., *Monographs on Education in the United States,* no. 7. Albany, N.Y.: J.B. Lyon Company, 1900.

———. "Educated Women in the Twentieth Century." Address to General Federation of Women's Clubs, St. Louis. Bryn Mawr, Pa.: Bryn Mawr College, Thomas Papers (newsclipping), 1903.

———. Address at College Evening of the 38th Annual Convention of the National American Suffrage Association. Baltimore, Md., 8 February 1906, p. 30. Bryn Mawr, Pa.: Bryn Mawr College, Thomas Papers.

———. "Present Tendencies in Women's College and University Education." *Publications of the Association of Collegiate Alumnae* 3 (1908):n.p.

Van Hise, Charles. "Educational Tendencies in State Universities." *Publications of the Association of Collegiate Alumnae* 17 (1908):31–44.

Van Kleeck, Mary. "What Alumnae Are Doing: Some Facts and Some Theories About Women's Work." *Smith Alumnae Quarterly* (1911): 75–83.

Women's College Board. *Handbook of Information About Women's Colleges, 1962–63.* Chicago: Women's College Board, 1963.

Woody, Thomas. *A History of Women's Education in the United States,* 2 vols. New York: Science Press, 1929.

3

Recent Trends in the Higher Education of Women

Barbara Heyns and
Joyce Adair Bird

During the last decade, higher education has confronted numerous changes and, to judge from the commentators, endured numerous persisting crises. Enrollments have ceased to climb and in recent years show evidence of decline. The only sector of higher education that has expanded in terms of both students and institutions since the mid-1970s is the public two-year college. Access to universities, particularly the most prestigious institutions, remains a highly publicized issue, as the legal battles waged by Bakke and by DeFunis attest. The confidence of academics has been profoundly shaken by the financial pinch and the steadily worsening job market for scholars, especially those in the humanities.

How have these changes affected the status of women in higher education? Can one discern trends that augur well or ill for sexual equality? In this chapter we will attempt to document and interpret patterns of change in both matriculation and graduation, in both the causes and consequences of higher education. The bulk of the chapter focuses on undergraduate education, although trends in postgraduate work are reviewed as well. Demographic trends that have a bearing on college attendance will be examined and the effects of programs for nontraditional students will be explored, albeit in a somewhat speculative way. A dominant theme throughout is that higher education has become more nontraditional, in terms of curriculum, the continuity and phasing of attendance, and the characteristics of the student body. Insofar as women comprise one of the groups conventionally underrepresented on campus, such developments bode well. Insofar as the composition of college students approximates a broader cross section of the population, greater equality of access is promoted. This chapter aims to assess the recent changes in higher education on one particular group: women.

The first section provides some background on enrollment trends for young cohorts of college students in recent years and presents evidence regarding changes in the sex composition over time. The next section pursues the question of access by comparing the determinants of college going in 1960 with those observed in the early 1970s. Next, three shorter sections summarize other trends in higher education that suggest a growing convergence between male and female students in the purposes of schooling, in the subject matter studied, and in the degrees earned. The final section attempts to integrate the trends for women with those observed for specific age and racial groups. Since higher education has become more accessible to many sorts of nontraditional students, it behooves us to examine the patterns of entry for nonwhites and for mature women in order to assess changes in a broader context.

Changes in Enrollment, by Sex

The last forty years have witnessed a phenomenal growth in higher education. In 1940 only 15 percent of 18- to 21-year-olds were enrolled in college; numerically, enrollments totaled less than 1.5 million students. During the next two decades, the rate of increase in college enrollments as a proportion of this age group was about 1.3 percent annually, bringing the total proportion enrolled to over one-third of the age cohort by 1960 (Trow 1961). Prior to the mid-1950s, enrollment gains were fueled by the return and reentry of veterans. Males constituted the major source of growth, while the proportion of women in colleges and universities lagged behind (Wolf 1977). Between 1950 and 1970 the growth in college enrollments was essentially parallel for males and females; although males were overrepresented among college students, the age-specific rates of entry for men and women were quite similar.

These patterns are clearly shown in figure 3-1, which depicts the trends in college enrollment for the two youngest cohorts, those aged 18-19 and those 20-24, for the period between 1950 and 1978. As the data clearly indicate, the proportion of each age group enrolled in college increased steadily between 1950 and 1970, with roughly equal gains for males and females. Since 1970, and most dramatically since 1975, enrollments have tended to level off or drop, and to drop much more sharply for males than for females. The absolute number of women enrolled continued to increase through 1977, although at a slower pace.

There are several explanations for the trends portrayed in figure 3-1. College enrollments are typically drawn from the population of recent high-school graduates. The proportion of students graduating and hence qualified to pursue postsecondary education seems to have reached a ceiling. Throughout the 1950s and 1960s graduation rates increased both both sexes. There has been little change since 1970, however. This fact, coupled with the decline in the number of children born during the 1960s, implies a shrinking pool of college recruits.

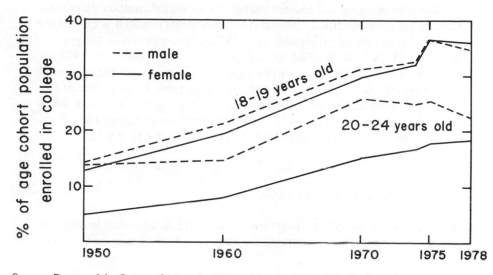

Sources: Bureau of the Census, *Current Population Reports,* "School Enrollment —Social and Economic Characteristics of Students: October 1975," Series P-20, no. 303 (Washington, D.C.: U.S. Government Printing Office, 1976); Bureau of the Census, *Current Population Reports,* "School Enrollment—Social and Economic Characteristics of Students: October 1978," Series P-20, no. 335 (Washington, D.C.: U.S. Government Printing Office, 1979); Robin Vair Wolf, "The Value Change Theory of Female Educational Participation and Professional Employment: A Critique in the Light of the Evidence" (Ph.D. diss., University of California at Berkeley, 1977).

Figure 3-1. Percentage of Age-Cohort Population Enrolled in College, by Sex, 1950 to 1978

The convergence of enrollment rates for men and women is chiefly due to the declining propensity for young men to be enrolled, rather than to increases in the enrollment rate for women of these ages. One plausible explanation for the male decline is that male enrollments are no longer inflated by the Vietnam War. This conflict seems to have induced a rather large proportion of young males to remain in college in order to receive draft deferments, as well as encouraged others to return to college after a tour of duty by using GI benefits. These factors have ceased to have much influence on college going in 1978, resulting in the decline in male enrollments (Suter 1980). A portion of the increase in female college enrollments can be attributed to changes in marital status and family formation. Later age at marriage and postponed childbearing, as well as an increased rate of marital dissolution, apparently have promoted higher levels of both college attendance and labor-force participation among young women. Whatever the reasons, the conclusion remains: there has been a substantial increase in equality of access to higher education by sex since 1970, and this is unlikely to be a transient phenomenon.

The data in figure 3-2 present changes in the sexual composition of students in a slightly modified fashion. Among students enrolled in college the sex ratio has narrowed perceptibly since 1950. Three-quarters of the population aged 21-24 and enrolled in college in 1950 were male. By 1978 the majority of students in the youngest ages were women, and for successive age groups the sex differential has narrowed over time. In 1978 women represented 49.9 percent of all college students, irrespective of age. The fall of 1979 may well have marked the historic moment in which the absolute number of women on campus exceeded that of men for the first time.

The Determinants of College Going

Enrollment data provide an overview of the patterns of access by sex, but they do not enable one to examine the causes. A recurring issue regarding

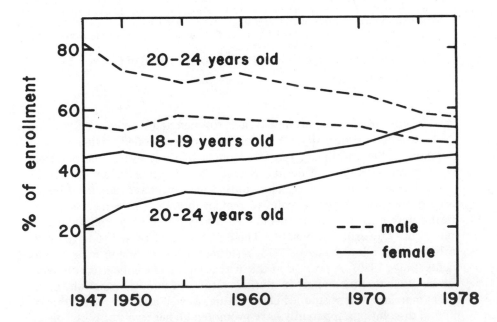

Sources: Bureau of the Census, *Current Population Reports,* "School Enrollment—Social and Economic Characteristics of Students: October 1975," Series P-20, no. 303 (Washington, D.C.: U.S. Government Printing Office, 1976); Bureau of the Census, *Current Population Reports,* "School Enrollment—Social and Economic Characteristics of Students: October 1978," Series P-20, no. 335 (Washington, D.C.: U.S. Government Printing Office, 1979).

Figure 3-2. Sex Composition of College Enrollment, by Sex and Age, 1947 to 1978

access to college concerns the probabilities of attending based on the background and personal characteristics of students. We know that an individual's educational attainment over the course of a lifetime depends on socioeconomic status and ability and that the relative importance of these factors has changed very little during this century (Featherman and Hauser 1976). Estimating the trends for the determinants of college attendance is more difficult, however, since the requisite data are not readily available. Ideally, one would want to follow a national sample of students from high school through college, examining the causes of enrollment and withdrawal at each stage.

Two longitudinal studies carried out in the last twenty years have attempted this task. They are worth scrutinizing in order to establish trends, if only in a somewhat crude fashion. For this analysis we will rely on the published reanalysis of the Project Talent Survey data by Jencks and Brown (1975), originally collected in 1960; and the National Longitudinal Survey (NLS) of 1972, analyzed by Thomas, Alexander, and Eckland (1979).

Table 3-1 presents the two summary equations that seem most relevant. The dependent variable in both studies is likelihood of attending college within the first two years after high school.[1] For each example, college attendance is regressed on sex, race, social-class background, academic achievement, performance in school in terms of grades or class rank, and curriculum assignment. Additionally, Project Talent included the number of siblings and college plans in the specification. The standardized coefficients can be interpreted as the net importance of each of the factors entered, once the effects of the others have been controlled.

The effects of most of the coefficients are strikingly similar between the two points in time. The net effect of sex, or maleness in this case, is almost identical in 1972–1973 to the estimated effect on college attendance in 1963 or 1964, the years when the Project Talent cohort would have entered college; the very small decline associated with the relative advantage of being a male is not significant in these samples. Once social-class background, achievement, race, grades in school, and curriculum or plans are controlled, males retain a very slight advantage in college going. The race effect is negative in both years, although not significantly so in 1960. This suggests that when one controls for the combined effects of class and academic advantages, blacks tend to pursue higher education at a higher rate than do whites.

In both 1960 and 1972 the social-class background of students was the most important factor associated with college attendance, and the magnitude of this effect does not seem to have declined. In both years it is more important than tested ability, race, or sex. The slight increase in the power of ability or achievement to predict college attendance may reflect a secular increase in the importance of test scores, or it may only reflect the fact that the NLS administered the tests in the twelfth grade, rather than the ninth.

Table 3-1
Comparison of Standardized Regression Equations Predicting
College Attendance, 1960 and 1972

Independent Variables	Project Talent Survey 1960	National Longitudinal Survey (NLS) 1972
Sex[a]	.066	.062
Race	− .025	− .115
SES[b]	.193	.194
Siblings	− .061	—
Achievement[c]	.150	.166
Grades[d]	.078	.119
Curriculum[e]	.134	.300
College plans	.291	—
R^2	.425	.329
(N)	(2,042)	(12,024)

Sources: (Project Talent Survey): Christopher S. Jencks and Marsha D. Brown, "Effects of High Schools on Their Students," *Harvard Educational Review* 45 (1975):299, copyright © 1975 by President and Fellows of Harvard College. Used with permission.; (National Longitudinal Survey): Gail E. Thomas, Karl L. Alexander, and Bruce K. Eckland, "Access to Higher Education: The Importance of Race, Sex, Social Class and Academic Credentials," *School Review* 87 (February 1979): 133–156.

[a]Sex and race were defined as dummy variables in both studies, although the coding scheme was modified by the present authors so as to have consistent signs. Males in this case are coded 1.0, as are whites. In the NLS study all ethnic groups were excluded except whites and blacks; in the Project Talent analysis, all nonblack respondents were classified as white.

[b]In the 1960 survey SES is a composite measure created by the Project Talent staff. It is based on father's occupation; father's education; mother's education; family income; the presence of books, appliances, television sets, and radios in the home; the value of the home; and whether the child had a private room. The SES variable used in 1972 is a sheaf coefficient and includes the effects of father's and mother's education, father's occupational status, and a household-item index.

[c]The achievement measure used in the 1960 survey was a composite of four ninth-grade tests: Reading Comprehension, Arithmetic Reasoning, Vocabulary, and Social Studies Information. The NLS measure was a linear composite of four standardized tests, weighted equally: vocabulary, reading, letter groups, and mathematics, taken in grade 12.

[d]Grades in Project Talent were the self-reported grades of ninth graders in academic subjects. NLS obtained a class rank in deciles, from school records.

[e]Curriculum is defined identically for both samples as 1.0 if college preparatory and 0 otherwise.

The net effects of the other variables are more difficult to interpret; class rank in the twelfth grade as used by Thomas, Alexander, and Eckland (1979) is probably a more telling criterion for college admission than self-reported grades in the fall of the ninth grade, which were used by Jencks and Brown (1975). The inclusion of college plans seems to be the major reason for the larger explained variance in the Project Talent equations. Since plans are quite highly related to curriculum placement among high-school seniors, the net effects for curriculum would be more similar in the two years if plans were included in the 1972 equation.

These two surveys contain the only national data on the relative importance of background factors and school experiences on college attendance. Given the fact that they are based on different samples of schools with different sources of potential bias and attrition, the similarity of effects is noteworthy. Had the equations differed inexplicably, it would have been necessary to conclude that either the determinants of college going had changed or that the two samples were not comparable. The similarity of effects is reassuring and encourages a somewhat bolder interpretation. It seems likely that the factors predictive of college attendance in the early 1960s have persisted for a decade or more; with the exception of an increase in black enrollments, the strength and relative importance of background variables appear largely unchanged. Although the requisite data are not available, it seems likely that the determinants of college going for males and females have remained quite similar, despite the increases in female enrollments.

Trends in Sexual Equality within Institutions

As we have seen, equal access to higher education for men and women has very nearly been accomplished during the last decade, at least among the youngest cohorts. Although the determinants of college going appear quite stable, colleges and universities have recruited and absorbed an increasing number of female and other nontraditional students. Equal access is not, however, the only criterion of sexual equality in higher education. It seems pertinent to inquire as to the extent that men and women are obtaining similar treatment and training, have similar or comparable goals, and are able to use educational institutions to realize these goals in a similar manner.

Compelling evidence on such questions is difficult to find. We know that women are slightly less likely than men to be enrolled in private institutions rather than public ones,[2] and that women are more likely to be in two-year rather than four-year institutions.[3] Women are more likely to be enrolled for degree credit than men, and they have retained this advantage despite increases in the proportion of students not receiving degree credit.[4] Men and women are also more likely to study in the same institutions; there has been an increase in the number of coeducational institutions during the last decade and, correspondingly, a precipitous decline in enrollments at single-sex colleges.[5] These changes in the institutional composition of higher education are common to both men and women; taken together, they do not reveal substantial disparities in educational experience by gender.

Several trends in the educational experience of the sexes are worth examining in greater detail. Each contributes to the general conclusion that sexual equality within institutions has increased and that the traditional differences between male and female college students have declined. As we shall see, major fields of study are less sex typed, the proportions of students attending part time have converged, and advanced degrees are more equally distributed between men and women. These trends suggest, although they do not prove, that sex is declining in importance as a factor in the educational experience of students.

Changes in Fields of Study

By and large, more college students in the 1970s are majoring in applied fields, which promise more immediate vocational payoffs, than was true in the mid-1960s. Virtually all the traditional liberal arts and the physical sciences have declined in popularity relative to business or commerce, vocational programs, computer sciences, and similar fields (Bureau of the Census 1976a).

This trend is evident for both male and female students. More relevant to our purpose, however, is the fact that there is an increasing similarity between males and females in the choice of major. In 1966 one out of every three women (33.2 percent) was enrolled in education while only one in six (17.0 percent) was studying math, statistics, engineering, or the biological and physical sciences. By 1974 one woman in five (20.1 percent) was majoring in one of these traditionally male fields. Education, in contrast, was only slightly more popular than math and the sciences, with 21.6 percent. Among men, one in three (32.5 percent majored in math, science, and related fields in 1966; eight years later, only 21.4 percent of the male college students were in these fields. Male enrollments in education declined between 1966 and 1974, from 9.5 percent to 6.5 percent of all male students, but this reduction was not as large as the corresponding decline among women.[6] As table 3-2 makes clear, the traditional fields of concentration for women, such as education and the humanities, have declined in enrollments primarily because of changes in the patterns of choice by women. The disparity between the sexes in field of study had declined in most fields, implying a general convergence of interests and perhaps in vocational plans as well.

As a summary measure of these trends, the index of dissimilarity can be calculated for 1966 and 1974. In 1966 one-third of all college students would

Table 3–2
Field of Study among College Students, 14–34, Percentage Distribution by Sex, 1966 and 1974

	1966		1974	
Major Fields	Women	Men	Women	Men
Agriculture/forestry	0.1	1.9	0.4	1.8
Biological sciences/health	11.7	9.0	16.6	9.7
Business/commerce	8.9	18.4	11.2	19.1
Education	33.2	9.7	21.6	6.5
Engineering	0.4	14.1	0.7	7.8
Humanities	13.8	8.2	9.0	6.4
Math/statistics	3.8	4.0	1.9	1.9
Physical sciences	1.1	5.4	.9	2.0
Social sciences	10.6	10.8	8.8	8.7
Other	5.5	9.0	17.7	25.0
Don't know/not reported	11.0	9.4	11.3	11.0
Totals	99.9	100.1	100.1	99.9

Source: Bureau of the Census, *Current Population Reports,* "Major Field of Study of College Students: October 1974," Series P-20, no. 289 (Washington, D.C.: U.S. Government Printing Office, 1976).

have had to shift major fields in order to produce an identical distribution for males and females. In 1974 reallocating one-quarter of the students (24.9 percent) would be sufficient to produce identical distributions of males and females across major fields. College majors, much like college enrollment, are decreasingly dependent on students' gender. It seems likely that sexual segregation in courses and lecture halls has declined within institutions, just as it has between them.

Changes in the Timing and Time Commitments of Study

Traditionally, women have graduated from high school and begun college at slightly younger ages than men. Hence, the average educational attainment is higher for women than for men when they are in their teens, although males tend to surpass females in accumulated years of schooling in their twenties.[7] Although rates of college attrition differ little by sex (Summerskill 1962; Spady 1970; Astin 1972; Tinto 1975; Peng, Ashburn and Dunteman 1977; Pantages and Creedon 1978:), women generally have been less likely to return to school in order to complete a degree. As Astin (1972) noted, women are more likely to complete a baccalaureate on schedule but less likely to complete one altogether.

Women, to a greater extent than men, study on a part-time basis. Indeed, this fact often has been interpreted as an indicator that they were less serious about their studies than were men.

The most recent data strongly suggest these assessments may be out of date. There have been substantial increases in college enrollments among older women, who are beginning or reentering higher education (Tittle and Denker 1977). Although there are not as yet sufficiently large numbers to change the aggregate levels of attainment reached by women, the trends clearly point in this direction.

Second, part-time study has become a more common way to earn a college degree in recent years, irrespective of sex. In 1970 16.0 percent of all males and 19.2 percent of all females were enrolled part time. By 1978 this had risen to 24.1 percent for males and to 26.7 percent for females. The trend in part-time study is confounded by the fact that enrollments have increased disproportionately in junior and community colleges, and the majority of part-time students attend these institutions. One might expect that the recent influx of mature women returning to school would also inflate the proportions studying part time, since these students are likely to have competing family obligations.

In point of fact aggregate rates of part-time enrollment disguise a very interesting trend that emerges when one compares two-year colleges with four-year institutions. Table 3-3 presents the proportion of students enrolled full time, by sex and by type of program, for the years 1970-1978. The largest decline in the proportion attending full time has occurred in the two-year colleges; the tendency among students at four-year colleges has fluctuated much less. Moreover, in the four-year colleges, sex differences tend to be small and inconsistent over time. Little if any trend in male and female part-time enrollments exists. In contrast, the decline in the percentage enrolled full time in two-year colleges has been much steeper for men than for women. Between 1975-1977, women were actually less likely to be studying part time than were men, reversing the commonplace assumptions.

Table 3-3 clearly demonstrates that while part-time study has become more common for both men and women, the sharper decline in male full-time attendance has led to a convergence in the sex-specific full-time rates.

Changes in the Degrees Received for Study

The trends toward greater sexual equality in access, field of study, and time committed to school are further reinforced by the increased likelihood that women will enter graduate study and receive advanced degrees (Feldman

Table 3-3
**Proportion of Students Attending Full Time, by Sex and Type of
Institution, 1970-1978, for Undergraduate College Students Aged 14-34**

Date	Two-Year Colleges		Four-Year Colleges	
	Men	Women	Men	Women
1970	72.5	65.4	88.3	87.6
1971	66.8	63.7	85.8	87.8
1972	68.4	61.7	86.1	88.1
1973	62.2	60.0	86.6	88.0
1974	60.5	58.7	84.6	84.4
1975	60.2	62.5	85.3	85.1
1976	57.7	59.8	84.4	85.3
1977	54.3	55.0	84.1	83.4
1978	55.9	53.6	85.5	83.7

Source: Bureau of the Census, "School Enrollment—Social and Economic Characteristics of Students: October 1978," Series P-20, no. 335 (Washington, D.C.: U.S. Government Printing Office, 1979).

1974). The changes in the percentage of degrees earned by women has been dramatic in recent years. Between 1965 and 1977, the number of degrees awarded to women more than doubled, from 255,000 to 594,000. Although women are disproportionately concentrated among those receiving bachelor's and master's degrees, the largest *proportional* increases have occurred at the higher degree levels. The proportion of doctorates received by women doubled during the last decade, while the number of first-professional degrees conferred on women more than tripled.

These observations are revealed by the data in table 3-4. Since 1965, there have been gains in both the number and the proportion of women receiving degrees. Moreover, these trends show little sign of decreasing in the next few years, if current patterns of graduate study persist.

Nontraditional Students

White males, entering college at approximately age 18 directly after high-school graduation, represent the traditional student in higher education. Women, as a group, are characterized as nontraditional students. As we have seen, the data suggest that we are nearing the end of a historical period in higher education. The traditional student is no longer dominant numerically; the use of masculine pronouns to refer to *the* college student is less

Table 3-4
Percentage of Bachelor's and Higher Degrees Earned by Women,
1964-1965, 1969-1970, and 1974-1980

School Year	Bachelor's Degree	Master's Degree	Doctor's Degree	First Professional
1964-1965	42.4	33.8	10.8	3.5
1969-1970	43.1	39.7	13.3	5.0
1974-1975	45.3	44.8	21.3	12.4
1975-1976	45.5	46.3	22.9	14.0
1976-1977	46.1	47.1	24.3	18.6
1977-1978	47.1	48.3	26.4	21.5
1978-1979	47.7	49.0	28.0	23.5
1979-1980	49.0	49.4	29.5	24.9

Sources: W. Vance Grant and Leo J. Eiden, *Digest of Education Statistics, 1980* (Washington, D.C.: National Center for Education Statistics, 1980); W. Vance Grant and George C. Lind, *Digest of Education Statistics, 1977-78* (Washington, D.C.: National Center for Education Statistics, 1978); W. Vance Grant and George C. Lind, *Digest of Education Statistics, 1979* (Washington, D.C.: National Center for Education Statistics, 1979); National Center for Education Statistics, "Earned Degrees Conferred, 1975-1976" (Washington, D.C.: U.S. Government Printing Office, 1978); National Center for Education Statistics, *Digest of Education Statistics, 1981;* National Center for Education Statistics, *Digest of Education Statistics, 1982* (Washington, D.C.: U.S. Government Printing Office, forthcoming).

descriptive than sexist. Overall, men are still slightly more represented in colleges and universities than are women, but the trend toward convergence in male and female enrollments is clear, particularly among the young. Since 1975, roughly equal proportions of the 18 to 19-year-old female and male populations have been enrolling in college. The imbalance in overall enrollments is declining and arguably reflects merely a time lag that might be expected during a period of change. Encouraging as these trends are, we should guard against complacency. First of all, female rates and trends of enrollment differ considerably among subpopulations. There are striking differences, for example, between white and nonwhite female enrollments, both at any given point in time and in the patterns in growth. Moreover, within each subpopulation enrollment rates vary according to family and employment status; these factors have traditionally constrained educational attainment for members of either sex, but they have had an especially limiting potential for women.

Second, the effects of sex, race, family status, and employment status on college enrollments vary according to age. Although we have entered a new era in higher education, a time when the chances of going to college immediately after high school are nearly equal for women and men, the majority of the women in the population graduated from high school before

1970 and are now coping with the fact and consequences of their earlier nontraditional-student status. Furthermore, the older the student, the more indelible is this status; students over the age of 35 continue to constitute only a small fraction of total enrollments, regardless of sex.

Finally, the trend toward equality in higher educational participation is most visible in public two-year colleges, the least traditional sector of higher education. The growth in junior colleges, along with the increase in public four-year institutions, has widened the gates of higher education for large numbers of nontraditional students. We suspect, however, that the proliferation of public institutions, in altering the institutional composition of higher education, represents an impressive component of the total change in enrollment patterns. For in spite of greater equality in enrollments, the most prestigious schools remain the preserve of the most traditional students, in terms of sex, race, and age. Insofar as these schools offer a different or better quality of education, we must be concerned about the representativeness of the student body.

In response to changing patterns of enrollment, the college curriculum has become less traditional. A wide array of programs has appeared to meet the needs and demands of nontraditional students. Counseling and tutorial programs, special admissions criteria, new curricula, and financial-aid packages are often tailored with a particular type of nontraditional student in mind. Moreover, recruitment has tended to focus on select target populations, such as minority students and reentry women. The impact of these diverse efforts will be described by contrasting the enrollment patterns of nontraditional students.

First, white and nonwhite representation is compared and rates of gain in enrollments among 16- to 34-year-olds, by sex and race, are described.[8] Next, these data are reexamined according to age, comparing the trends among younger students with those found for students 35 and older. The comparisons in this section will focus on the period from 1970 to 1975; where data are available, however, longer-range trends will be reported.[9]

Nontraditional Students: The Case of Race

Between 1960 and 1975 the gains in proportionate enrollment for women in the 16–34-year-old population were quite similar to the gains made by nonwhites of the same age. Gains (or losses) over the next three years, however, were so dissimilar between these groups that by 1978, nonwhite proportionate enrollment had surpassed that of females (see table 3–5). Over the entire eighteen-year period, nonwhite proportionate enrollment had jumped by 281 percent, while female representation had increased by 183 percent. As a result of these disparate growth rates, the gap between nonwhite and white

Table 3-5
Percentage of Population, 16–34, Enrolled in College, by Sex and Race, 1960, 1970, 1975, and 1978

	Percentage Enrolled		Difference, 1970-1960	Percentage Enrolled, 1975	Difference, 1975-1970	Difference, 1975-1960	Percentage Enrolled, 1978	Difference, 1978-1975	Total Difference, 1978-1960
	1960	1970							
Sex Populations									
Male	8.6	14.9	+6.3	16.9	+2.0	+8.3	15.2	−1.7	+6.6
Female	4.7	10.0	+5.3	13.0	+3.0	+8.3	13.3	+0.3	+8.6
Race Populations									
White	7.1	13.1	+6.0	15.1	+2.0	+8.0	14.3	−0.8	+7.2
Nonwhite	3.6	8.1	+4.5	13.4	+5.3	+9.8	13.7	+0.3	+10.1
Total population	6.6	12.4	+5.8	14.9	+2.5	+8.3	14.2	−0.7	+7.6

Sources: Bureau of the Census, *1960 Census of the Population*, "School Enrollment," Subject Reports PC(2)-5A (Washington, D.C.: U.S. Government Printing Office, 1964); Bureau of the Census, *1970 Census of the Population*, "School Enrollment," Subject Reports PC(2)-5A (Washington, D.C.: U.S. Government Printing Office, 1974); Bureau of the Census, *Current Population Reports*, "School Enrollment—Social and Economic Characteristics of Students: October 1975," Series P-20, no. 303 (Washington, D.C.: U.S. Government Printing Office, 1976); Bureau of the Census, *Current Population Reports*, "School Enrollment—Social and Economic Characteristics of Students: October 1978," Series P-20, no. 335 (Washington, D.C.: U.S. Government Printing Office, 1979).

enrollments narrowed more than the gap between males and females, as shown by the ratio changes presented in table 3-6. As figure 3-3 clearly depicts, however, the greatest inequality was between white males and white females, and the least between white and nonwhite women.

By 1978 none of these differences was very large; each traditional to nontraditional comparison evidences a considerable narrowing of gaps. The sharp plunge downward of white male enrollments after 1975 contributed heavily to convergence; nevertheless, while the representation of 16-34-year-old white women, nonwhite women, and nonwhite men approached quality, white men continued to be disproportionately represented in 1978.

The patterns and timing of growth for each population were more dissimilar than were the overall effects. Table 3-7 compares and summarizes the average annual changes in proportionate enrollments for three periods between 1960 and 1978. The annual growth rate for women remained fairly constant between 1960-1970 and 1970-1975 and it continued during the fol-

Table 3-6
Ratios of Proportionate Enrollments: Traditional to Nontraditional Populations, 16-34, 1960, 1970, 1975, and 1978

	Enrollment Ratios			
	1960	1970	1975	1978
Sex populations				
White male to white female	1.88	1.52	1.32	1.16
Nonwhite male to nonwhite female	1.24	1.16	1.11	1.05
Total male to total female	1.83	1.49	1.30	1.14
Race populations				
White male to nonwhite male	2.24	1.82	1.29	1.09
White female to nonwhite female	1.48	1.39	0.92	0.99
Total white to total nonwhite	1.97	1.62	1.13	1.04

Sources: Bureau of the Census, *1960 Census of the Population,* "School Enrollment," Subject Reports PC(2)-5A (Washington, D.C.: U.S. Government Printing Office, 1964); Bureau of the Census, *1970 Census of the Population,* "School Enrollment," Subject Reports PC(2)-5A (Washington, D.C.: U.S. Government Printing Office, 1974); Bureau of the Census, *Current Population Reports,* "School Enrollment—Social and Economic Characteristics of Students: October 1975," Series P-20, no. 303 (Washington, D.C.: U.S. Government Printing Office, 1976); Bureau of the Census, *Current Population Reports,* "School Enrollment—Social and Economic Characteristics of Students: October 1978." Series P-20, no. 335 (Washington, D.C.: U.S. Government Printing Office, 1979).

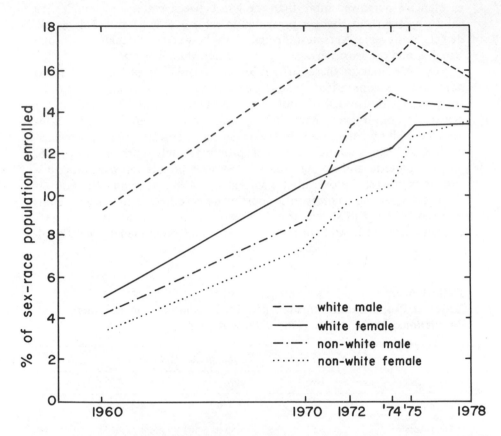

Sources: Bureau of the Census, *1960 Census of Population,* "School Enrollment," Subject Reports PC(2)-5A (Washington, D.C.: U.S. Government Printing Office, 1964); Bureau of the Census, *Current Population Reports,* "Social and Economic Characteristics of Students: October 1972," Series P-20, no. 260 (Washington, D.C.: U.S. Government Printing Office, 1974); Bureau of the Census, *1970 Census of the Population,* "School Enrollment," Subject Reports PC(2)-5A (Washington, D.C.: U.S. Government Printing Office, 1974); Bureau of the Census, *Current Population Reports,* "School Enrollment—Social and Economic Characteristics of Students: October 1974," Series P-20, no. 286 (Washington, D.C.: U.S. Government Printing Office, 1975); Bureau of the Census, *Current Population Reports,* "School Enrollment—Social and Economic Characteristics of Students: October 1975," Series P-20, no. 303 (Washington, D.C.: U.S. Government Printing Office, 1976); Bureau of the Census, *Current Population Reports,* "School Enrollment—Social and Economic Characteristics of Students: October 1978," Series P-20, no. 335 (Washington, D.C.: U.S. Government Printing Office, 1979).

Figure 3–3. Percentage of Population 16 to 34 Years Old Enrolled in College, by Sex and Race, 1960 to 1978 (Selected Years)

lowing three-year period, only at a much slower pace. Among males, however, each period shows a decline over the preceding period. Nonwhite annual increases between 1970 and 1975 were twice as rapid as during the

Table 3–7

Average Annual Amount of Change in Proportionate College Enrollments for the 16- to 34-Year-Old Population, 1960–1970, 1970–1975, and 1975–1978

	Average Annual Change in Proportion Enrolled		
	1970–1960	*1975–1970*	*1978–1975*
Sex populations			
Male	+0.63	+0.40	−0.57
Female	+0.53	+0.60	+0.10
Race populations			
White	+0.60	+0.40	−0.27
Nonwhite	+0.45	+1.06	+0.10
Sex-Race populations			
White male	+0.66	+0.30	−0.63
White female	+0.55	+0.54	+0.07
Nonwhite male	+0.46	+1.10	−0.03
Nonwhite female	+0.42	+1.06	+0.20

Source: Bureau of the Census, *1960 Census of the Population,* "School Enrollment," Subject Reports PC(2)-5A (Washington, D.C.: U.S. Government Printing Office, 1964); Bureau of the Census, *1970 Census of the Population,* "School Enrollment," Subject Reports PC(2)-5A (Washington, D.C.: U.S. Government Printing Office, 1974); Bureau of the Census, *Current Population Reports,* "School Enrollment—Social and Economic Characteristics of Students: October 1975," Series P-20, no. 303 (Washington, D.C.: U.S. Government Printing Office, 1976); Bureau of the Census, *Current Population Reports,* "School Enrollment—Social and Economic Characteristics of Students: October 1978," Series P-20, no. 335 (Washington, D.C.: U.S. Government Printing Office, 1979).

preceding ten years, whereas the reverse pattern is observed for whites. Between 1975 and 1978 the average annual increase in enrollment rate continued to be higher for nonwhite than for white women. The overall loss in annual enrollment for males was mostly due to declining white male enrollment, as nonwhite male representation maintained near stability.

One factor undoubtedly contributing to the rapid increase in the nonwhite rate of enrollment is the expansion of the nonwhite pool of college eligibles. In 1970 the percentage of high-school dropouts in the 14–34-year-old black population was nearly double that of whites (30.0 percent, 15.2 percent).[10] By 1977 the ratio of black to white dropouts decreased to 1.6 (20.4 percent to 12.7 percent). In comparison, the ratio of female to male dropout rates remained at about 1.1 over the same period. Thus, there was a marked change in the relative sizes of the white and nonwhite pools of persons eligible for college, but the relationship between the pools of males and females remained stable. The trends in proportionate college enrollments appear to reflect this difference.

In sum, overall racial differences in college enrollments among the 16–34-year-old population have narrowed considerably and, among women, whites and nonwhites were equally likely to be enrolled in college in 1978. Sex differences in enrollment are more persistent. Although in absolute numbers more nonwhite women are enrolled than nonwhite men, the 1975 gap in proportionate enrollment has persisted to the most recent date. The sex gap among whites, although somewhat narrowed, is greater than among nonwhites, and there has been a leveling off of gains in proportionate enrollments for both white females and white males.

Nontraditional Students: The Case of Age

The changing age composition of the college population is one of the most frequently noted trends in higher education. In 1972 28 percent of all college students were over twenty-five (Grant and Lind 1978); by 1978 the proportion had risen to 34.7 percent (Bureau of the Census 1979a). In 1972 60.7 percent of these students were male; by 1978 52 percent were women. Although mature or reentry students are still found on campuses in relatively small numbers, age is an important criterion for measuring college access for nontraditional groups.

Between 1940 and 1970 the largest proportionate growth in *school* enrollment occurred among the population 30 years of age or older.[11] The proportionate enrollment of women between the ages of 30 and 34 increased during this period by 675 percent. The increase among men of this age was even greater. In 1940 equally low proportions of men and women were attending school—4 out of 1,000 persons in the male and female populations of this age were engaged in some type of regular schooling. By 1970 male enrollments had soared from 4 to 53 out of 1,000, while the increase in women's participation reached 31 out of 1,000 (Wolf 1977, p. 176). The person over 34 years of age is even less represented in educational institutions. In 1940 only 1.5 women, and fewer than 1 man (0.8), out of 1,000 of the respective populations were enrolled in school. During the following thirty years the representation of men over 35 increased by 1,135 percent, more than double the 533 percent growth among the corresponding female population. These unequal increases resulted in approximately equal proportionate enrollments by 1970, when 9.5 women and 9.9 men of 1,000 in each population were enrolled in school (Wolf 1977).

The trends by age and sex mirror those observed for younger students in that sex differences have narrowed and overall growth rate has declined. The upturn in college enrollments was roughly similar for males and females between 1970 and 1975. The rapid rate of growth, as shown in figure 3–4 slowed considerably after 1975, largely due to a drop in proportion-

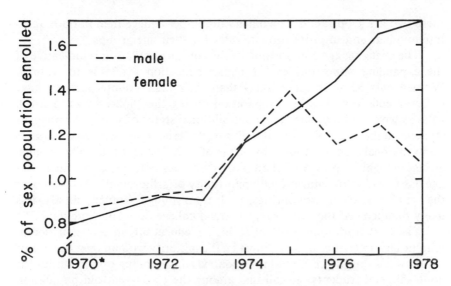

Sources: Bureau of the Census, *Current Population Reports,* "Social and Economic Characteristics of Students: October 1972," Series P-20, no. 260 (Washington, D.C.: U.S. Govern-
ment Printing Office, 1974); Bureau of the Census, *Current Population Reports,* "Social and
Economic Characteristics of Students: October 1973," Series P-20, no. 272 (Washington,
D.C.: U.S. Government Printing Office, 1974); Bureau of the Census, *Current Population
Reports,* "School Enrollment—Social and Economic Characteristics of Students: October
1974," Series P-20, no. 286 (Washington, D.C.: U.S. Government Printing Office, 1975);
Bureau of the Census, *Current Population Reports,* "School Enrollment—Social and Eco-
nomic Characteristics of Students: October 1975," Series P-20, no. 303 (Washington, D.C.:
U.S. Government Printing Office, 1976); Bureau of the Census, *Statistical Abstract of the
U.S.: 1976* (Washington, D.C.: U.S. Government Printing Office, 1976); Bureau of the Census, *Statistical Abstract of the U.S.: 1978* (Washington, D.C.: U.S. Government Printing Of-
fice, 1978); Bureau of the Census, *Current Population Reports,* "School Enrollment—Social
and Economic Characteristics of Students: October 1978," Series P-20, no. 335 (Washington,
D.C.: U.S. Government Printing Office, 1979); Bureau of the Census, *Current Population
Reports,* "Estimates of the Population of the United States, by Age, Sex, and Race: 1976 to
1978," Series P-25, no. 800 (Washington, D.C.: U.S. Government Printing Office, 1979);
Robin Vair Wolf, "The Value Change Theory of Female Educational Participation and Pro-
fessional Employment: A Critique in the Light of the Evidence" (Ph.D. diss., University of
California, Berkeley, 1977).

Figure 3-4. Percentage of Population 35 Years Old and Over Enrolled in
College, by Sex, 1970, 1972–1978

ate enrollment among older males. Among older women, both the absolute
number of college students and the proportion of older women enrolled
continued to increase, but more slowly.

By 1978 the total enrollment of students 35 years and older was 1.3 million, of which 65 percent, or 845,000, were women. The secular increase in
female college attendance has equalized the number of students attending
college *only* among students under 20 and among students 35 or over. For

these two age groups college women outnumber college men in both absolute numbers and in proportionate rates for their age groups.

The changing age composition of the college population is indicative of the expanding opportunities for higher education available to women. Women over 35 were more likely than their male counterparts to have deferred college and career preparation during the 1960s, so as to fulfill roles as wives and mothers. The nontraditional status of younger women as students in the past, by virtue of their sex, underlies older women's status as nontraditional students today, by virtue of age. The fact that older women are more highly represented than older men does not, however, mean that age has no effect on educational opportunity or achievement. Women over the age of 34 years are not only less likely than younger women, but also less likely than men of the same age, to attend college on a full-time basis.[12]

The least traditional student in higher education, in terms of demographic characteristics at least, must be the minority woman over the age of 35. How has this group fared in the context of expanding opportunities for nontraditional students? Recall that among the 16–34-year-old population we observed a change in the rank order of proportionate enrollments between nonwhite and white women, with nonwhite females overtaking white females in terms of the proportion of the population in college. Among the older population, a similar reversal occurred. In 1973 white female proportionate enrollment was less than 10 percent greater than in 1970; over the same period of enrollment rate of nonwhite females had increased by 41 percent (figure 3–5).

Data by race and sex for persons over 35 are not available, unfortunately, for the years since 1975. The observable patterns, however, suggest that reentry women have been disproportionately nonwhite, but that the largest gains in enrollment among the older populations have been made by nonwhite males. To be sure, minorities traditionally have been excluded from higher education regardless of aspirations or qualifications, so it is not surprising to find greater proportions of nonwhite females and males taking advantage of delayed educational opportunity. Nonwhite female rates of enrollment, however, have moved ahead of white female rates in every age group.

One plausible explanation of these findings is that minority recruitment efforts tend to be planned and mobilized separately from efforts to recruit women; moreover, recruitment programs for minorities have a longer history and are more vigorous than those for women. Some support for this interpretation is found in a recent survey of special programs for female and minority students[13] (Atelsek and Gomberg 1978). Out of the total number of institutions in the sample (579), only 15.2 percent reported having a special recruitment or admissions program for women, whereas 37.5 percent had at least one such program for minorities. Of the 266 sample institutions

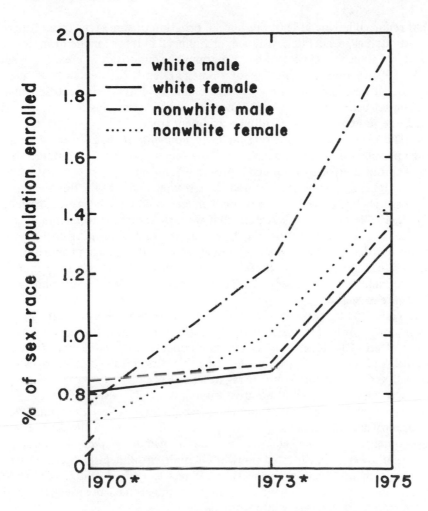

Sources: Bureau of the Census, *Current Population Reports,* "Social and Economic Characteristics of Students: October 1973," Series P-20, no. 272 (Washington, D.C.: U.S. Govern-
ment Printing Office, 1974); Bureau of the Census, *1970 Census of the Population,* "School
Enrollment," Subject Reports PC(2)-5A (Washington, D.C.: U.S. Government Printing
Office, 1974); Bureau of the Census, *Current Population Reports,* "School Enrollment—
Social and Economic Characteristics of Students: October 1975," Series P-20, no. 303 (Wash-
ington, D.C.: U.S. Government Printing Office, 1976); Bureau of the Census, *Statistical
Abstract of the U.S.: 1976* (Washington, D.C.: U.S. Government Printing Office, 1976);
Bureau of the Census, *Current Population Reports,* "School Enrollment—Social and Eco-
nomic Characteristics of Students: October 1978," Series P-20, no. 335 (Washington, D.C.:
U.S. Government Printing Office, 1979); Robin Vair Wolf, "The Value Change Theory of
Female Educational Participation and Professional Employment: A Critique in the Light of
the Evidence" (Ph.D. diss., University of California, Berkeley, 1977).

Figure 3–5. Percentage of Population 35 Years Old and Over Enrolled in
College, by Race and Sex, 1970, 1973, and 1975

that reported having at least one special program of some type (recruitment or admissions, academic assistance, or financial aid) for female or minority graduate students, 93 percent had programs for minorities whereas less than half had programs specifically for women. Even if the demand for more education were growing at the same rate among all types of nontraditional students, such differential recruitment emphasis within institutions would lead one to expect corresponding enrollment trends.

The high ratio of nonwhite males to nonwhite females in the 35-and-over population is quite unexpected. One might rather have expected that the combined efforts of women's programs and minority programs would have heightened the impact for nonwhite women and that the double liability historically endured by nonwhite women would have been transformed into a double asset. To the extent that we may assume enrollments reflect institutional recruitment efforts, however, the higher proportion of nonwhite females over white females, together with the higher proportion of nonwhite males over nonwhite females, indicates stronger effects by minority programs than those designed for women alone, at least where older students are concerned. The trend of an increasing gap between older nonwhite males and females between 1970 and 1975, a period of vigorous recruitment by minority programs, leads us to suspect that recruitment has had a one-sided effect. One is led to the unhappy conclusion that the net effect of women's programs on enrollment during this period is negligible, for white as well as for nonwhite women, regardless of age.

There are, however, alternative explanations. The especially large gap between nonwhite males and nonwhite females may reflect the tenacity of traditional sex roles among the older population. Perhaps white couples are less committed to traditional sex roles than nonwhite couples. It is possible also that lower than expected nonwhite female enrollment is due to family or employment situations presenting barriers to college going. Nonwhite women are more likely to have children, to be the primary breadwinner, and to be employed than are white women.

Conclusions

This chapter has endeavored to summarize recent trends in the higher education of women. As we have seen, the data suggest a remarkable convergence in rates of college going between males and females. Women in their late teens and women over 35 are more likely to be enrolled than males at these ages. Moreover, the evidence on sexual equality within institutions yields a similar portrait. College majors, the proportion enrolled full time, and the number of degrees earned support the general conclusion that the disparity in access between men and women is decreasing. If one were to hazard a prediction, the 1980s may be the decade in which gender no longer influences college enrollment or educational attainment.

These trends must be viewed in the context of the general increase in nontraditional enrollments. Racial gaps, to an even greater extent than sexual ones, have narrowed during the last two decades. Within racial categories, sex differences have tended to persist. In certain cases, such as enrollment for older nonwhite women, they have increased; among whites and younger nonwhites, however, the enrollment gaps between men and women are decisively narrower.

The bulk of this analysis has been descriptive. Although possible explanations have been suggested in passing, the demographic trends alone cannot account for the changing patterns of enrollment. Marital status and childbearing, for example, have been greater obstacles to postsecondary schooling among women than among men, and these differences persist. Enrollment rates for wives and mothers, however, have increased more than those for single women. In 1960, 55.2 percent of all women aged 16–34 lived with a spouse and children; in 1970, 48.7 percent did so. Marriage and childbearing, though, apparently constituted a less serious obstacle than before. In 1960 only seven mothers in a thousand attended college. In 1970 nearly twenty-two did so. The probabilities of women combining parenthood and higher education are greater than ever before.

The most intriguing explanation for the increase in sexual equality in colleges and universities lies outside the control of colleges and universities. Several authors have ventured to explain the declining enrollments in higher education as a response to changes in the labor market. The demand for educated labor has not kept abreast of the supply in recent years. The rate of return to investments in higher education, calculated as the relative earnings of college graduates compared to high-school graduates, has declined during the last decade (Freeman 1976). This has been less true for women than for men however. As a report of the Task Force on Education and Employment of the National Academy of Education noted, "The ratio of median income of male college graduates to that of male high school graduates declined somewhat between 1969 and 1975. For women, the ratio was higher in 1975 than in 1969 and far above its 1949 level" (National Academy of Education 1979, pp. 4–5).

Such trends suggest that the economic benefits of college training for new women graduates have never been greater, and that one can project a narrowing of the income gap between educated men and women in the near future. The trends toward increasing sexual equality can be found not only in schools but in the labor market as a whole. Although one hesitates to be prematurely optimistic, these trends support the inference that sexual equality has increased quite generally, and that the gains observed will prove to be enduring.

Notes

1. The dependent variables in the two studies are similar but not identical. Jencks and Brown allot some importance to any postsecondary training, whereas Thomas and her associates treat vocational training after high school as if it represented no further schooling.

2. In 1977, 79.6 percent of all women college students attended a public college or university, while 77.3 percent of all men did so (Grant and Lind 1979).

3. In 1977, 29.0 percent of all undergraduate men and 31.2 percent of all undergraduate women were enrolled in two-year institutions (Bureau of the Census 1979a).

4. In 1970, 92.8 percent of women and 91.9 percent of all men enrolled in college were earning degree credit. In 1977 the proportions were virtually equal, with 87.0 percent of the women and 86.9 percent of the men enrolled for degree credit (Grant and Lind 1978).

5. The proportion of all institutions that were coeducational in 1945, 1955, 1965, and 1975 were, respectively: 70.5 percent, 75.2 percent, 76.5 percent, and, most recently, 91.0 percent (Grant and Lind 1977).

6. Although more recent data on college majors cannot be obtained for a comparable sample, it seems likely that the decline in proportions of students opting to study education has continued. The American Council on Education has published the results of annual surveys on *The American Freshman: National Norms* every year since 1969. In 1975, 1976, and 1977, 15.3 percent, 14.3 percent, and 13.6 percent of the women chose education as their probable major field of study. For males in these years the comparable percentages were 4.6 percent, 4.5 percent, and 3.8 percent (Grant and Lind 1977; 1978; 1979).

7. One source of this disparity is the fact that males graduate from high school at a later age, on average, than do females. More males acquire a diploma by passing a high-school equivalency exam, often while in the armed forces (Suter 1980).

8. The use of these broad categories of race is constrained by the data available. In 1970 the U.S. Bureau of the Census classified college enrollment data according to white, black, and Spanish-speaking populations; in 1975, however, the broader categories of white and nonwhite were used. To allow comparisons between these two years, we calculated the nonwhite enrollments for 1970 as the difference between total and white enrollments.

9. The traditionally low representation among college enrollments by those 35 and over underlay a major difficulty in our attempt to discern long-range trends. Prior to 1972, *college* enrollment data for this population are not available. However, pre-1970 data on *school* enrollments, which include but do not differentiate between college and other schooling, are available

for the older sector of the population and will be presented to illustrate general educational growth patterns.

10. Data on dropout rates for the black population are not wholly satisfactory for explaining higher college enrollments among the nonwhite population. As blacks comprise the majority of the nonwhite population, however, an approximation of the effect may be inferred. In 1970, among the 16 to 34-year-old nonwhite population, 88.5 percent was black. (Bureau of the Census 1974c).

11. As noted above, college enrollment data were not reported for the population 35 and over until 1972; overall school enrollment data are available, however, and are useful in this discussion as they set the outside limits on college enrollment during this early period, and they provide a sense of relative enrollments for males and females.

12. For example, in 1972, the following percentages of college students were cnrolled full time (Bureau of the Census 1974a):

Age	Male	Female
18–21	92.4	91.2
22–24	72.6	49.8
25–34	43.1	28.6
35 and over	21.4	12.9

13. The study investigated programs for graduate students only in colleges and universities awarding a professional degree, doctorate, or some other degree beyond the master's, and consequently the findings do not provide direct evidence of differential recruitment or support for undergraduates. Nevertheless, we suspect the findings are suggestive of the more general recruitment emphasis in higher education.

Bibliography

Astin, Alexander, W. "College Projects: A National Profile." Washington, D.C.: American Council on Education, 1972.

Atelsek, Frank, J., and Gomberg, Irene L. *Special Programs for Female and Minority Graduate Students.* Higher Education Panel Reports no. 41. Washington, D.C.: American Council on Education, 1978.

Bureau of the Census. *1960 Census of the Population.* "School Enrollment." Subject Reports PC(2)-5A. Washington, D.C.: U.S. Government Printing Office, 1964.

———. *Current Population Reports.* "Social and Economic Characteristics of Students: October 1972." Series P-20, no. 260. Washington, D.C.: U.S. Government Printing Office, 1974a.

————. *Current Population Reports.* "Social and Economic Characteristics of Students: October 1973." Series P-20, no. 272. Washington, D.C.: U.S. Government Printing Office, 1974b.

————. *1970 Census of the Population.* "School Enrollment." Subject Reports PC(2)-5A. Washington, D.C.: U.S. Government Printing Office, 1974c.

————. *Current Population Reports.* "School Enrollment—Social and Economic Characteristics of Students: October 1974." Series P-20, no. 286. Washington, D.C.: U.S. Government Printing Office, 1975a.

————. *Current Population Reports.* "Estimates of the Population of the United States by Age, Sex and Race: 1970 to 1975." Series P-25, no. 614. Washington, D.C.: U.S. Government Printing Office, 1975b.

————. *Current Population Reports.* "Major Field of Study of College Students: October 1974." Series P-20, no. 289. Washington, D.C.: U.S. Government Printing Office, February 1976a.

————. *Current Population Reports.* "School Enrollment—Social and Economic Characteristics of Students: October 1975." Series P-20, no. 303. Washington, D.C.: U.S. Government Printing Office, 1976b.

————. *Statistical Abstract of the U.S.: 1976.* Washington, D.C.: U.S. Government Printing Office, 1976c.

————. *Statistical Abstract of the U.S.: 1978.* Washington, D.C.: U.S. Government Printing Office, 1978.

————. *Current Population Reports.* "School Enrollment—Social and Economic Characteristics of Students: October 1978." Series P-20, no. 335. Washington, D.C.: U.S. Government Printing Office, 1979a.

————. *Current Population Reports.* "Estimates of the Population of the United States, by Age, Sex, and Race: 1976 to 1978." Series P-25, no. 800. Washington, D.C.: U.S. Government Printing Office, 1979b.

Featherman, David L., and Hauser, Robert M. "Sexual Inequalities and Socioeconomic Achievement in the U.S., 1962–1973. *American Sociological Review* 41 (1976):462–483.

Feldman, Saul D. *Escape from the Doll's House: Women in Graduate and Professional School Education.* New York: McGraw-Hill, 1974.

Freeman, R.B. *The Overeducated American.* New York: Academic Press, 1976.

Grant, W. Vance, and Eiden, Leo J. *Digest of Education Statistics, 1980.* Washington, D.C.: National Center for Education Statistics, 1980.

Grant, W. Vance, and Lind, C. George. *Digest of Education Statistics, 1976.* Washington, D.C.: National Center for Education Statistics, 1977.

————. *Digest of Education Statistics, 1977–78.* Washington, D.C.: National Center for Education Statistics, 1978.

————. *Digest of Education Statistics, 1979*. Washington, D.C.: National Center for Education Statistics, 1979.

Jencks, Christopher S., and Brown, Marsha D. "Effects of High Schools on Their Students." *Harvard Educational Review* 45 (1975):273–324.

National Academy of Education. *Education for Employment: Knowledge for Action*. A Report of the Task Force on Education and Employment. Washington, D.C.: Acropolis Books, 1979.

National Center for Education Statistics. "Earned Degrees Conferred, 1975–1976." Washington, D.C.: U.S. Government Printing Office, 1978.

————. *Digest of Education Statistics, 1981*. Washington, D.C.: U.S. Government Printing Office, 1981.

————. *Digest of Education Statistics, 1982*. Washington, D.C.: U.S. Government Printing Office, forthcoming.

Pantages, Timothy J., and Creedon, Carol F. "Studies of College Attrition: 1950–1975." *Review of Educational Research* 48 (1978):49–101.

Peng, Samuel S.; Ashburn, Elizabeth A.; and Dunteman, George H. *Withdrawal from Institutions of Higher Education*. National Longitudinal Study Sponsored Reports. National Center for Education Statistics. Washington, D.C.: U.S. Government Printing Office, 1977.

Spady, William G. "Dropouts from Higher Education: An Interdisciplinary Review and Synthesis." *Interchange* 1 (1970):64–85.

Summerskill, J. "Dropouts from College." In N. Sanford, ed., *The American College*. New York: Wiley, 1962.

Suter, Larry E. "Elementary and Secondary School Progression, High School Graduation, and College Entrance of the American Population: 1950–1978." In A. Kerckhoff, ed., *Longitudinal Perspectives in Educational Attainment*, vol. 1. Greenwich, Conn.: JAI Press, 1980.

Thomas, Gail E.; Alexander, Karl L.; and Eckland, Bruce K. "Access to Higher Education: The Importance of Race, Sex, Social Class and Academic Credentials." *School Review* 87 (1979):133–156.

Tinto, Vincent. "Dropout from Higher Education: A Theoretical Synthesis of Recent Research." *Review of Educational Research* 45 (1975): 89–125.

Tittle, Carol Kehr, and Denker, Elenor Rubin. "Re-entry Women: A Selective Review of the Educational Process, Career Choice, and Interest Measurement." *Review of Educational Research* 47 (1977):531–584.

Trow, Martin. "The Second Transformation of American Secondary Education." *International Journal of Comparative Sociology* 1–2 (1961): 144–166.

Wolf, Robin Vair. "The Value Change Theory of Female Educational Participation and Professional Employment: A Critique in the Light of the Evidence." Ph.D. diss., University of California, Berkeley, 1977.

**Part II
The Precollege Years: Issues
of Access and Selection**

Mapping the Road to Academe: A Review of Research on Women, Men, and the College-Selection Process

Katherine H. Hanson and
Larry H. Litten

The college-attendance decision and college-selection processes have been the focus of basic social research from a variety of fields for at least three decades. Sociologists have focused on these phenomena as part of their studies of social stratification, occupational achievement, and various types of mobility (Alexander and Eckland 1974; Sewell and Shah 1967; Thomas 1977). Economists have examined these processes because they involve large numbers of people making economic decisions and the processes are affected by public policy (Radner and Miller, 1975; Nolfi et al. 1978). Psychologists have been interested in the effects that these processes have on psychological development and individual mental health (Sacks et al. 1978). Marketing theorists have used the college-selection process to study family decision making and information processing in consumer decisions (Wright and Kriewall 1979). Decision theorists have studied these processes because they represent "non-routine, unique decisions of major consequence to the decision-maker" (Lewis and Morrison 1975; Berl, Lewis, and Morrison 1976).

More recently, an applied-research tradition has emerged that focuses on college attendance and selection from two perspectives. Educators and consumer advocates have sought information about these processes that will permit or promote more effective consumer decision making (Starr 1978). College administrators have sought a better understanding of these processes in order to establish recruitment policies and implement more effective recruitment practices (Larkin 1979). This latter set of concerns has been fueled by the bleak prospects posed by impending declines in the number of traditional-age college students and by the heightening of institutional competition that this implies.

Elizabeth Cogan and Susan Silverstein contributed invaluable research assistance in this project.

Reference to sex similarities and differences regarding college attendance and selection is scattered throughout these various bodies of research; there is great variation in the amount and kind of attention given to these phenomena, however. Concern with sex patterns is frequently incidental to other principal analytic foci, and patterns related to race or ethnic groups have had similar marginal treatment. We have not located good theory to tie these findings together, even though sex differences in these processes relate to fundamental social phenomena and have direct implications for public policy and institutional behavior.

This chapter, based on recent research, presents some evidence about how the college-selection process is conducted and experienced by women and by men. We were looking for behavioral or self-reported similarities and differences between the sexes as clues to: (1) how the sexes differ in their psychological orientations (for example, different values) and therefore how they might desire or deserve differential treatment during college recruitment and admissions processes (either to preserve or to eradicate differences, depending on the nature of the difference and one's philosophical perspective), or (2) how the sexes *are treated* differently during college-selection and admissions processes by persons or by institutions with which they interact. The question of historical limitations to past research on the college-selection process is also of concern. The civil-rights and women's movements certainly have altered our cultural milieu in recent years. There have been significant changes in federal policy relating to education—particularly the great increases in student financial aid and, more recently, in legislation and regulations prohibiting sex discrimination. Thus it can be questioned whether earlier research findings concerning the decision to attend college, the process of college selection, or the institutional admissions practices are applicable to contemporary social conditions.

A Model of the College-Attendance and College-Selection Process

The college-attendance and -selection process is actually a series of complex, interacting processes. Lewis and Morrison (1975) have identified as many as thirteen activities that occur in various sequences in the course of selecting a college, with some of the steps being repeated several times. Figure 4–1 shows a greatly simplified model of the college-selection process. (We have maintained a schematic distinction between the two parallel, but interrelated processes of applications for admissions and for financial aid; all students go through the former, but not the latter).

This chapter will focus primarily on Stage Two and Stage Three: The Exploratory Stage and the Application/Matriculation Stage. The attention

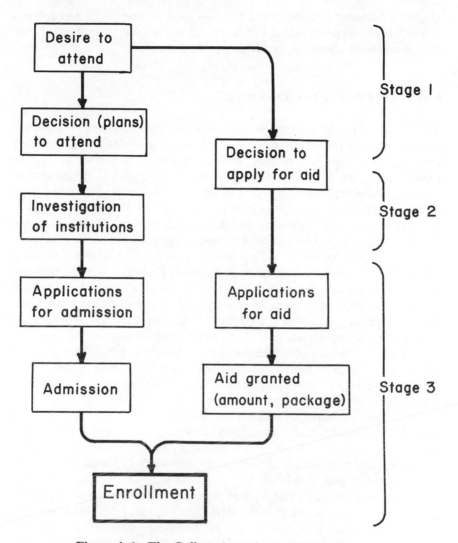

Figure 4-1. The College Attendance/Choice Process

given to Stage One will be confined to the benefits that men and women seek from college attendance. This restricted emphasis is due in part to space limitations. It is also due to the dated nature of much of the literature on college plans and the sociological models that include sex as one of the predictors of college attendance or educational attainment.[1] The focus is on the traditional college applicant—recent high-school graduates—because that is the authors' sphere of research for the Consortium on Financing

Higher Education (COFHE) and the literature is best developed for this group.[2] Both the professional literature and the authors' unpublished consortial and institutional research have been drawn on.

Stage One: Deciding to Go to College

The relationships of self-esteem and self-assessment to college aspirations are not well understood but there is some interesting evidence of past differences between men and women. Astin, Harway, and McNamara (1976) report that in the 1972 National Longitudinal Study (NLS), 75 percent of the women reported that they were capable of college work, but only 45 percent were planning to attend college (a difference of 30 percent).[3] Slightly fewer men perceived themselves capable of college work (72 percent), but they revealed a discrepancy of only 17 percentage points in plans to obtain a bachelor's degree or higher (55 percent) (Astin, Harway, and McNamara, 1976). The Cooperative Institutional Research Programs (CIRP) national surveys of college freshmen in 1971 and 1976 provide some additional evidence of self-esteem problems for women.[4] Close to half of the women and the men rate themselves "above average" in academic ability. Women are 8 to 10 percentage points less likely than men to rate themselves "above average" in intellectual self-confidence and in leadership ability. The sexes show almost equal propensities to rate themselves highly on writing ability, but women are about 15 percentage points less likely than men to rate themselves highly on mathematical ability (Astin et al. 1971; 1976).

The complex factor of socioeconomic status (SES) appears to have an important role throughout the extended college-selection process. Not only does SES appear to be an important factor in the determination of college aspirations and attendance for both sexes (Medsker and Trent, 1965; Christensen, Melder, and Weisbrod, 1972), but, as is discussed later, SES may differentially affect men and women at several points in the college-selection process. Bengelsdorf (1974), Astin, Harway, and McNamara (1976) and a private market-research study of the college-selection decisions of eastern women all noted that women from minority and from low-income, blue-collar families are most likely to be concerned with the costs of attendance.[5] Froomkin (1970) reported that women are more likely than men to receive their principal financial support from their parents. For low-income families (with incomes under $5,000) he found only one-third of the men had 75 percent or more of their college expenses paid for by their families, whereas nearly half of the women had the same percentage paid by their families. Because of this greater financial dependence, women may be more vulnerable to parental influence in the choice of a college than men are. These patterns need additional study with new data; increases in aid may have freed women from such dependence and parental influence.

The evidence on benefits that people seek from college attendance comes principally from two types of data: (1) responses given to questions such as "how important were the following reasons in deciding to go to college?," and (2) reports of the kinds of characteristics that students seek in colleges and the aspects of college that are important in the college-selection process. In response to the first type of question, men and women tend to give slightly different answers. Most of the available evidence comes from the CIRP annual surveys of college freshmen (Astin et al. 1971, 1976, 1978); other evidence of this sort comes from the NLS as reported by Astin, Harway, and McNamara 1976. Table 4-1 shows that among the twelve reasons listed in the CIRP questionnaire, women were consistently more likely than men to indicate intrinsic educational objectives (for example, to gain a general education and appreciation of ideas, to become a more cultured person, and to learn more about "my interests" or "things") and social/educational objectives (for example, to meet new and interesting people); men were more likely than women to enter college in order "to be able to make more money," although the benefit of "getting a better job" was sought by approximately equal proportions of both sexes. Out of the twelve items on the CIRP questionnaire, only one shows substantial sex differences in the changes observed during the decade of the 1970s. In 1971 39 percent of the male freshmen reported that "graduate school preparation" was an important reason for attending college compared with only 29 percent of the women. In 1978 44 percent of both sexes cited this as an important benefit of college attendance.

In reporting on reasons for choosing the school in which they enrolled women were more likely than men in the CIRP survey to cite "special education programs offered" and "the college has a good academic reputation." There is also some evidence that women are more likely to have a better idea of what they want to major in. In a Response Analysis Corporation survey of Scholastic Aptitude Test (SAT) takers in 1977 (Response Analysis Corporation 1978), a higher percentage of women than men had a "definite idea" about what they wished to major in (36 percent versus 25 percent); similar results were obtained in a study of the senior class of 1975 in California (University of California 1978). It is noteworthy that women are slightly more likely to have more specific educational objectives than men and at the same time are also slightly more likely to be open to general educational development.

Other evidence gained from studies of the college-selection process indicates that in addition to a greater concern for some of the intellectual aspects of college, women also tend to show a greater interest in questions of location. The meaning of this concern is unclear; it is often interpreted as women's interests in staying in close touch with home, although there is the counter-evidence from the CIRP surveys that men and women are equally likely to be enrolled in institutions over five-hundred miles from home (Astin et al. 1971, 1976, 1978). Lewis and Morrison (1975) examined both race and sex patterns regarding concerns about college. They report that

Table 4-1
Reasons for Going to College and Selecting a College

A. Very important reasons in deciding to go to college.

	1971			1976			1978		
	Male (%)	Female (%)	Difference, Male-Female (%)	Male (%)	Female (%)	Difference, Male-Female (%)	Male (%)	Female (%)	Difference, Male-Female (%)
Contribute more to my community	15	23	−8	—	—	—	—	—	—
Get a better job	70	77	−7	72	70	2	75	76	−1
General education	53	67	−14	58	71	−13	62	75	−13
Improve reading/study skills	22	23	−1	33	38	−5	35	40	−5
Become more cultured person	25	34	−9	27	39	−12	29	39	−10
Make more money	57	42	15	60	48	12	66	55	11
Learn more about my interests[a]/things[b]	65	74	−9	68	79	−11	69	79	−10
Meet new/interesting people	36	55	−19	45	62	−17	48	65	−17
Graduate-school preparation	39	29	10	44	43	1	44	44	0
Parents wanted me to go	22	24	−2	29	30	−1	27	30	−3
Could not find a job	—	—	—	6	6	0	4	5	−1
Get away from home	—	—	—	8	10	−2	7	9	−2
Nothing better to do	2	2	0	3	2	+1	2	2	0

B. Very important in selecting college where enrolled (partial listing)

	1971			1976			1978		
	Male (%)	Female (%)	Difference, Male-Female (%)	Male (%)	Female (%)	Difference, Male-Female (%)	Male (%)	Female (%)	Difference, Male-Female (%)
College has a good reputation	35	38	−3	46	55	−9	47	54	−8
Special Education Programs offered	30	36	−6	25	36	−11	21	30	−9

Sources: Alexander Astin et al., *The American Freshman: National Norms for Fall 1971* (Washington, D.C.: American Council on Education, 1971); Alexander Astin et al., *The American Freshman: National Norms for Fall 1976* (Los Angeles: Cooperative Institutional Research Program (CIRP), Laboratory for Research in Higher Education, University of California, Los Angeles, 1976); Alexander Astin et al., *The American Freshman: National Norms for Fall 1978* (Los Angeles: Cooperative Institutional Research Program (CIRP), Laboratory for Research in Higher Education, University of California, Los Angeles, 1978).

[a]1971
[b]1976, 1978.

white females were most likely to be concerned about geographic location in selecting a school; while males reported most interest in educational/curricular aspects of the college. Both female and male blacks more frequently expressed concern about admissions phenomena (chances of acceptance, and so forth) and the cost of attendance. They also report that for all blacks and for while males none of the top ten schools being considered was out of state; in contrast, however, five of the schools most frequently mentioned by white women were out of state.

In some market research conducted at Carleton College, it was found that among its accepted applicants, ratings of Carleton's "geographic location" were more powerful predictors of matriculation for women than for men; on the other hand, the rating of "urban-rural location" was a stronger predictor for men (Litten 1978b). In a question asking what could make Carleton more attractive, locational considerations were somewhat more predominant in the responses of female nonmatriculants than among the responses given by their male counterparts (Litten 1978a).

Brush (1976) reports that in two studies of female students who selected small colleges, the importance of location has shifted over a twenty-year period. In 1955 it was fifth out of fourteen reasons for selecting the college; in 1974 it was second out of twenty-nine reasons for selecting the college (academic program quality was first both years). The classified market study found that 50 percent of the women surveyed (and their parents) wanted a college within one-hundred miles of home and that 100 percent preferred to have the college be no farther than five-hundred miles from home. The study notes that concern about location was greater among blue-collar and minority families. The importance of location for women is not well understood, given the fragmentary, ambiguous findings to date.

A minor exception to findings on the sex-related importance of location comes from the study of 144 Pittsburgh students reported by Lewis and Morrison (1975). They reported that women were *equally* likely to be concerned about the following types of attributes in selecting a college: Physical/spatial (location), social, educational/curricular, and admissions (including costs); men showed greatest concern with educational/curricular aspects among these types, followed by cost of attendance. Even though location was not more important than other factors for women in this sample, it was relatively more important for women than for men.

Stage Two: Investigating Colleges

Sources of Information and Advice about Colleges

The principal sources of information cited by high-school students are college catalogs and other recruiting brochures, high-school counselors, parents, peers, and other friends. The way in which these sources are used

and their relative importance to the choice of college have been the subject
of a number of surveys. The literature shows that the use and importance of
these sources does vary somewhat by sex and though there have been significant shifts in the rank importance of these sources to all students over the
past twenty years, the sex differences are still apparent.

Various researchers have consistently reported over the past two
decades that parents are among the most important sources of information,
particularly as sources of first information, and as one of the most influential sources (Kerr 1962; Davis 1977–1978; University of California 1978,
1980; Chapman 1981). Astin, Harway, and McNamara (1976) present data
from Project TALENT that show parents and friends tied as people with
whom students discussed their post-high-school plans at least three times.[6]
Men tended to consult with their fathers, women with their mothers. Analysis of 1972 NLS data showed women more dependent on parents than men,
but it also showed that 93 percent of women ranked self-dependence as an
important factor. Men and women both ranked the importance of teachers
and counselors lower in 1972 than in 1960. The 1978 private market-
research survey of women showed parents were still an important factor.
Sixty percent of the women said their parents influenced their choice of college. An interesting note to this fact is that only 48 percent of the parents of
the women in this study thought they were influential in their daughters'
decisions.[7] (The study also reported that 97 percent of parents were pleased
with their daughter's choice of college.)

If parents are as influential as the students report they are, and if the
greater financial dependence of women on their parents makes women more
vulnerable to parental opinions than men, data from Project SCOPE (Tillery 1973) may explain in part some of the past sex discrepancies in attendance rates.[8] He reports that 42 percent of the women in these samples from
the late 1960s reported that their parents had college aspirations for them,
versus 59 percent of the men (averages for his four state reports). Recent
changes in enrollment patterns may reflect changes in parental attitudes (or
financial-aid developments may have liberated women from persisting
parental attitudes). Froomkin's (1970) analysis reports that SES is an
important component in the parental-influence factor. He showed that 98
percent of college-educated mothers wanted their sons to attend college
while only 73 percent of mothers who had eight years of education or less
wanted their sons to attend college. More interesting is the impact of the
SES factor on their daughters; the college-educated mothers were nearly
identical in their aspirations for their daughters (97 percent), but of those
with eight years of education or less only 60 percent wanted their daughters
to go to college.

Friends and peers are also an important source of information for students. These "significant others" as they are designated by Thomas (1977)
have a greater influence on the NLS sample of men than on women in the
college-decision process. The private market-research study reported that 42

percent of the women cited friends as an important source of information. This same study noted a negative correlation between influence by peers and a student's favorable opinion of women's colleges. Lewis and Morrison (1975) indicate that their women were more likely than men to consult with peers and their men were more likely to consult with counselors.

Counselors are viewed by the students as a good source of information, but recent research also shows that many students of both sexes do not consider their counselors to be an important influence in their choice of college. In the Project TALENT survey analyzed by Astin, Harway, and McNamara (1976), 51 percent of men and 46 percent of women high-school students said they discussed college plans with their counselors two or more times during their senior year. In this study, Astin and her colleagues report from 1972 NLS data that an equal percentage of men and women (9 percent) reported counselors as having an important influence on their post-high-school plans. The private market-research study surveyed both female students and their school counselors. Again, the women downgraded the relative importance of counselors as major influences in their selection process. Only 7 percent said counselors were a big factor; on the other hand, 65 percent of the counselors interviewed perceived themselves to be an important factor.

Much of the ambiguity in findings regarding counselors may be due to the way in which counselors function and the way the question has been posed. Guidance counselors may serve as gatekeepers—suggesting or *failing to suggest* colleges—but they may not be influential in the final selection. Survey questions often relate to the latter phenomenon.

Lewis and Morrison (1975) report different information-seeking patterns by sex and race combinations. Overall, black males consulted more sources of information, followed by white females, black females, and white males in that order. Only white males reported parents as one of the top five generators of information (this is *incidence* of information provision, not *influence* of information provided).

Information Obtained and Sought about Colleges

As we have noted, the college-selection process involves both students as information seekers and applicants and institutions that provide information and admit applicants. Some data are available as a result of studies of the sources of information *made available* to students. These have focused on the content and use of traditional guidance materials as they pertain to men and women. Less information is available on what kinds of information students actively *seek* as they move through the several steps of the college-decision process. Although there is considerable sentiment that students need more information, especially if counseling is available to help them use it, there is also some opinion that the marginal benefit of more information would not equal the cost and that a more *selective* flow of information tailored to the specific needs of individuals or groups should be our goal.

Research about information *sought* by students has primarily focused on surveys of high-school seniors or college freshmen regarding what information about colleges is or was important to them in making their selection of colleges. Very little research has been conducted in this area, especially in testing the hypothesis that males and females might desire different information about colleges before making their decisions to apply to or to enroll in specific institutions. In the most extensive studies to date on these issues, sponsored by the Fund for the Improvement of Postsecondary Education (Lenning and Cooper 1978), no tabulations of the results were made by sex.[9]

In a study of high-ability students [combined Preliminary Scholastic Aptitude Tests (PSATs) of 100 or above] and their parents in six metropolitan areas around the United States, researchers in a cooperative project conducted by Carleton College and The College Board asked what kinds of information students and their parents wanted to know about the colleges to which they or their children would apply (Litten, Jahoda, and Morris 1980). A statistically significant sex difference was found for only one of the twenty-five kinds of information listed on the questionnaire: women were more likely than men to rate information on residential life as "very important" (49 percent versus 37 percent). A number of sex differences were found in the parents survey, however. In view of the possibly greater influence of parents on women than on men, these differences are noteworthy. Parents of daughters were slightly more likely to exhibit a concern about social atmosphere and the setting of a college than parents of sons. There were also interesting parent/child sex interactions. Parents of sons were more interested than parents of daughters in information about graduate-school acceptance rates, but this phenomenon was particularly true for the mothers who responded to the survey. Mothers of sons, mothers of daughters, and fathers of sons were almost equally interested in career-related information about colleges; fathers of female college-bound students were considerably less likely than the other three groups to be interested in this kind of information.

Timing of the Application/Selection Process

Another aspect of the college-selection process that has been found to vary by sex is that of timing. There are limited data on the differences in the timing of the various decision points in the Lewis and Morrison (1975) longitudinal survey in which students were interviewed twice a month throughout their senior year. They found that while most women and men in their sample tend to start seriously on the college information-gathering process at about the same time (early in their senior year), the women in the study completed this stage in the process earlier than the men. Astin also reports evidence from earlier studies that students who begin to plan for college before their senior year (as early as ninth grade) were more likly to go on to college, and that this was particularly true for women (Astin, Harway, and McNamara 1976).

Lewis and Morrison (1975) also looked at the timing of submissions of applications by sex, but they found that on the average women submitted their first application only seven days earlier than did men. In their sample women used early-decision applications more frequently than men, especially among the 40 percent of the female sample that were from private women's schools (only 27 percent of the men were from private schools).

A survey of early-decision applicants for the class of 1983 at a sample of the COFHE institutions also showed that a greater percentage of women tend to apply for early action. In nine out of ten schools a greater percentage of the female applicants were early-action applicants than of the men and the differences were slight at the tenth school (early applicant-men exceeded women by 0.3 percent).

The timing phenomenon raises questions of whether women's behavior is due to the greater certainties that are indicated by other data (for example, plans regarding major), to more orderliness, or to insecurities as indicated by lower academic self-confidence.

Stage Three: Application, Admission, and Matriculation

Types of Institutions Chosen

The college-selection process begins once a student has made the essential decision to pursue a postsecondary education (and for some a desire to attend a particular college may be instrumental in deciding to go to college); it ends with the decision to enroll in a particular institution. CIRP data tell us that most students apply to only a small number of colleges (three or less) and about three-quarters of them are accepted and enroll in their "first choice" institutions (Astin et al. 1971, 1976, 1978).

Many of the studies that have examined participation in higher education by sex have also given some attention to the types of institutions chosen. Evidence of sex preferences between private and public institutions is inconclusive. Bob (1977), in a survey of Kansas students (no date given), indicates that women tended to enroll in private institutions more than men, but states that her findings "do not agree with previous research which found more males attending private four-year colleges and public two-year colleges." A survey of the graduating class of 1975 in California indicates virtually no sex differences (4 percent of both sexes in "privates"; 2 percent males and 3 percent females in undifferentiated "out-of-state") (University of California 1978). The Higher Education General Information Survey (HEGIS) data indicate that between 1970 and 1977, the proportion of first-time male students who were in public institutions rose from 73 to 75 percent; female proportions in public institutions rose from 71 to 74 percent (United States Office of Education 1971; National Center for Education Statistics 1979).

Somewhat more extensive data are available on preferences for four-year versus two-year institutions. Trent and Medsker (1968) found that in their sample from the 1950s, women were more likely than men to choose four-year colleges (46 percent versus 37 percent), and that men were the more likely to enter junior colleges (38 percent of the men; 34 percent of the women) and universities (25 percent of the men; 20 percent of the women). HEGIS data from the 1970s show that at the beginning of the decade these patterns persisted, but they had shifted toward identical sex patterns seven years later.

Astin, Harway, and McNamara (1976, p. 30) report from 1973 HEGIS data that women are "concentrated in smaller, less selective, and less affluent institutions." Radner and Miller (1975) developed one of the economic models that gives major attention to sex as a variable from the Project SCOPE data base. They report that sex does not contribute to the prediction of demand for higher education beyond the predictive power of cost, income, ability, and college selectivity. However, Radner and Miller (1975, pp. 53–54) report that "taking account of sex would somewhat improve the predictions of the distribution of demand among [Institutions of Higher Education]. In particular it would appear that [Institutions of Higher Education] with low selectivity and high and medium costs are relatively less attractive to males than the model would predict and relatively more attractive to females." They note that these institutions that are relatively more attractive to women are mainly private. They also observe that junior colleges are more attractive to men, and less attractive to women, than their model would predict.

Leonard Ramist (1978) has analyzed where students who took SAT tests in 1976 sent their test scores, made applications, were admitted, were enrolled, and persisted throughout the freshman year. We should stress that the population is not SAT-takers as a whole, but those students who sent their scores sent them to a particular set of primarily small institutions.[10] Although the relative magnitudes are not known, nor what proportion of the relevant prospective student pools are accounted for, it is worth noting that women in Ramist's sample are more likely than men to follow an initial interest in a selective school with an application. It would be interesting and useful for the design of counseling programs to know whether these patterns regarding selective schools represent more realistic early self-appraisals by women (leading to fewer false starts and better follow-through) or an early failure of self-esteem or ambition. The marked preference for small schools exhibited by women early in the application process would also be worth understanding better—is it an appreciation of the presumed direct benefits of small colleges or a failure of nerve regarding larger institutions?

In a paper entitled, "What Type of College do Career-Salient Women Choose—Coeducational or Women's?," Lentz (1977) reports on the importance of career and how career-related concerns affected college choice for women at coed and single-sex colleges. Her study indicates that women in single-sex colleges are more likely to be career-oriented and more likely to report that career-related factors influenced their college choice than their peers in coeducational institutions. Since she did not study the college choices of career-salient high-school students, however, her research does not answer the question posed by the title of her paper.

Using data collected in a longitudinal study of a high-school senior class of 1955, a period in which men were considerably more likely than women to continue to college, Alexander and Eckland (1974) examined the relationships between various background and secondary-school characteristics and the selectivity of the college attended. For men, higher family income (as measured by a proxy variable, family possessions), higher ability (or high-school performance when it was added to the equation), and higher socioeconomic status of their secondary school's student body all contributed to a greater propensity to enroll in a more selective school. For women, family income and ability were important in determining the selectivity of the college attended, with income playing a larger role for women than for men. Socioeconomic composition of high school did not affect women's propensity to enroll in more selective schools.

Alexander and Eckland (1974) acknowledge that these findings do not illuminate fully the phenomenon with which they are concerned. No evidence is available regarding whether the observed differences were due to differentials in propensities of students from, say, higher status levels as opposed to lower, to apply to more selective schools, to be admitted preferentially by selective schools, or for such students to be more likely to accept offers of admission (for financial reasons or otherwise). The type of analysis that Alexander and Eckland (1974) used does not permit examination of interactive effects between two variables like ability and income (simply because they did not use interaction terms in their equation) nor threshold effects (for example, are there certain income levels for women below which selective college attendance is highly unlikely?). The latter kind of finding, where it exists, can contribute most to the design of targeted programmatic measures to alter existing patterns. The Carleton/College Board 6-Market Study found that parents showed no difference on the basis of their child's sex in their propensity to list a first-choice college that was out of state. The first-choice colleges listed for sons tended to be more selective than those listed for daughters, however. This discrepancy was especially pronounced when mothers had filled out the questionnaires (Litten, Jahoda, and Morris 1980).

COFHE data obtained through the Admissions Testing Program of The College Board show that thirty highly selective schools, including five women's colleges, are less likely to receive applications from women in the higher levels of verbal ability than from men in the same test score categories.[11] Although there has been a recent shift in the COFHE data base, table 4–2 suggests that these differential application rates have become more pronounced in the uppermost strata and that the discrepancy is more severe the higher the test scores. Although COFHE membership changed once during this period, data from the Ivy League institutions, a group whose composition did not change, exhibit this increased sex difference in the probability of application at approximately the same historical point as in the larger group: the difference between the sexes increased by almost 50 percent for the 750–800 range in 1976, and by 69 percent in 1977 for the 700–749 range.

Institutional Admissions Processes

So far, the decision to attend college and the type of college chosen have been treated as acts of the individual influenced by personal attributes and environment. The college-enrollment process, however, is a two-way action—students apply to schools and schools admit students. The behavior of schools could differentially affect men and women.

In one of the most widely known studies that addresses the possibility of differential institutional treatment of men and women in the admissions process, Cross (1971, 1974) cites data from *The College Handbook* of 1969, which she interprets as "blatant examples of discrimination at the under-graduate level where many people still insist it does not exist" (1974, p. 34). The evidence that she cites comes from two different colleges where greater proportions of men than women applicants are accepted at various levels of ability and high-school performance. The data that she presents led her to conclude that women who take the trouble to compute their chances would certainly get the message that they must be better qualified than men to gain admission to the selective four-year liberal-arts college illustrated. Further calculations on the data presented by Cross indicate that both schools were predominately male, a fact that probably would not have escaped women who took the trouble to make the suggested computations. Although institutional discrimination cannot be ruled out, two cases do not provide sufficient evidence of a pervasive problem. This is particularly true in an era when men's colleges were in the process of going coeducational in phases.

Table 4-2
Percentage of SAT-Taking Population in Each Verbal SAT Range Who Apply to a COFHE School

Verbal SAT	1974[a]		1975[a]		1976[a]		1976[b]		1977[b]		1978[b]	
	Male	Female	Male	Female	Male	Female	Male	Female	Male	Female	Male	Female
750–800	59	51	63	58	64	49	71	55	86	67	87	70
700–749	47	39	49	41	48	40	53	44	67	49	68	55
650–699	34	27	38	29	37	24	42	32	51	36	52	39
	Male/Female Difference		Male/Female Difference		Male/Female Difference		Male/Female Difference		Male/Female Difference		Male/Female Difference	
750–800	8		5		15		16		19		17	
700–749	8		8		8		9		18		13	
650–699	7		9		8		10		15		13	
600–649	6		7		6		8		11		10	

[a]Twenty-three COFHE institutions.
[b]Thirty COFHE institutions.

Some of these schools had departments that were traditionally male (for example, engineering); women were not as inclined to enter these fields in those days as they are now. Most of these schools lacked the traditionally women's departments (for example, nursing and education).[12]

Among other efforts to detect discrimination against women in the admissions process, Walster, Cleary, and Clifford (1970) sent bogus applications to 240 randomly selected schools, with systematic alterations of the sex, ability, and race data on the applications. They did not find any evidence of overall sex or race discrimination; they did, however, report lower acceptance rates for women with low rank and test scores. They conclude that "since, in the actual high school populations, there are more students, both male and female, at the lowest of our ability levels than at the higher levels, it is clear that *overall* women are discriminated against in college admission" (Walster, Cleary, and Clifford, 1970, p. 237). Unfortunately, it is not so clear, since women are known generally to have higher class ranks than men. By assigning equal ranks and scores to their "low ability" men and women, the researchers probably put their female "applicants" at a relative disadvantage by making them comparatively weaker among the authentic women applicants to each college than were their men.

Astin, Harway, and McNamara (1976) examined the acceptance rates or enrollment composition by sex for eight schools in light of their stated admissions criteria and concluded that women are disadvantaged in their applications to technical schools because they constitute a small percentage of the enrollments ("because of the strong emphasis on mathematics and science"). They also conclude that in the single four-year college that provided them with fairly complete information, it was "curious that women fared so badly, in terms of proportions of applicants accepted." The data that they report do not seem to support their conclusions, however, since in four of the five schools at this college a greater proportion of women applicants was accepted than male applicants and in the remaining school the acceptance ratios were 76 percent for females and 78 percent for males.

In the study conducted by Astin, Harway, and McNamara (1976), high-ability students' application and acceptance patterns were examined for a national sample of freshmen in 1975. They found that "at each [selectivity] level, a higher proportion of women than of men were accepted" (Astin, Harway, and McNamara, 1976, p. 143). They conclude that this "confirms, in part, the findings of Walster, Cleary, and Clifford (1970) . . . that is, higher ability women [such as the women in this sample, who were enrolled in selective institutions] fare well in college admissions. If sex discrimination occurs, it is probably among less able students" (Astin, Harway, and McNamara, 1976, p. 143). This is not very strong evidence of discrimination. Roby (1973), on the other hand, cites a number of instances in the early 1970s where restricted scholarship funds were more available to men than to women.

Some evidence collected for the COFHE institutions indicates that in the interest of classes with equal sex ratios, and in the face of the lower propensity of high-ability women to apply to these selective schools, women may enjoy favored status in their admissions processes (table 4–3). Excluding the women's colleges and the Ivy League institutions that include a number of male institutions that are still in the process of becoming completely coeducational, we find that in the small COFHE colleges women are somewhat more likely to be accepted at most ranges of Verbal SAT scores than are men, and in the universities women are more likely to be admitted than men by small amounts of one half of the comparisons. These figures also show the instability of such data—a problem that is acute when dealing with the small numbers of institutional-applicant pools.

Future Directions

In spite of the considerable amount of scholarly attention that college-attendance and -selection processes have received and the extensive reviews such

Table 4–3
Admission Ratios in Selected COFHE Schools
(percent)

	Small Colleges			
	1977		1978	
Verbal Score	Male	Female	Male	Female
750–800	63	73	77	69
700–749	59	59	59	63
650–699	50	56	49	50
600–649	44	47	42	44
	Universities			
	1977		1978	
Verbal Score	Male	Female	Male	Female
750–800	79	82	83	84
700–749	74	73	78	76
650–699	69	68	72	74
600–649	63	63	67	69

Note: *Admission ratio* represents number of accepted students divided by number of applicants. The survey excludes women's colleges and Ivy League schools.

as that by Astin, Harway, and McNamara (1976), we do not yet have an adequate, comprehensive model or understanding of the college atten-dance/selection process, particularly as it exists for men and women in con-temporary society. There is a clear need to bring together the sociological, psychological, economic, and institutional market-research traditions and to develop models that illuminate individual and family information-seek-ing and decision-making processes leading to college attendance and selec-tion, and to study the effects of social and economic conditions on these processes.

The 1980 replication of the National Longitudinal Study ("High School and Beyond") will provide an invaluable opportunity to document the shifts in patterns of educational aspirations and plans—although as this review is being written, the debate is in progress over the relative substantive costs and benefits of obtaining directly comparable data versus some sub-stantive or analytical improvements in the items.

The costs of mounting such a national effort are substantial enough to dictate a relatively infrequent effort. An alternative is emerging, however, which could provide some reasonable approximations to a national effort. State-level information systems are being developed at the National Center for Higher Education Management Systems that may well include surveys of educational aspirations, intentions, and attainment. Since aspiration-attainment linkages are among the most important measures of frustra-tion—and therefore a principal indicator of possible institutional or system-atic discrimination— it is important that researchers push for the develop-ment of data bases through which these issues can be examined.

Another recent and rich, but relatively inaccessible, source of informa-tion on the college-selection process is developing with the emergence of extensive marketing-research activity by colleges and universities. These studies focus directly on how students and those who influence them pro-ceed to learn about colleges, evaluate them, and select a college to attend. Again, surprisingly, this research often does not examine sex differences in the phenomena with which it deals. (One researcher at a public institution that has conducted and published some of the most extensive work of this sort confessed that while they were interested in the sex issues, as a public institution they felt that they could not develop any marketing plans based on sex differences, so they did not even analyze their data by sex.)

As new data bases are developed, researchers will have no shortage of questions pressing for more definitive answers. A number of lines of inquiry have been suggested in this chapter. The highest priority should be given to research that could lead to equality of the sexes in achieving their potential through higher education. Now that the participation rates of women and men have approached parity, the focus should be on the quality of educa-tion and the factors that will encourage women to apply to high-quality programs in numbers proportional to their ability. A few more questions that ought to have high priority in a comprehensive research agenda follow.

1. What information do high-school students want or need (as compared to what they get from counselors and colleges), and what information can they use effectively?
    a. How do women and men differ in their information needs?
    b. Why do they differ and how are men and women changing?
2. What are the basic sex differences in student values and expected benefits from a college education?
3. What is the relative importance of factors that influence the college-selection process, and what importance should each factor have in order to make the process effective from a personal and societal perspective?
    a. How does economic/social climate influence these phenomena?
    b. How do parents and important others influence these phenomena?
    c. How do internal psychological factors influence these phenomena?
    d. How does institutional behavior influence these phenomena?
    e. How do these processes and the reasons for choices vary by sex?
4. From the institution's point of view, how can we explain why (and how) some institutions have greater success than others in finding and maintaining an appropriate student applicant and matriculant population?

Some of the less developed research approaches need to be exploited, particularly those related to the information-seeking and decision-making aspects of the college-selection process. We need many more of the contributions of psychology, social psychology, anthropology, and the small groups/family structure research traditions in sociology. We also need to nurture norms of sharing that will permit academic market research to contribute directly to our scientific understanding of college-selection processes. Open inquiry is an essential quality of academic life that is currently being compromised as colleges conduct market research in the face of mounting enrollment pressures.

We suspect that a multidisciplinary approach will be the most fruitful and will be necessary to build successfully the base of information that will be needed by institutional planners, college marketers, and counselors of students. Research regarding the presence of sex discrimination is certainly needed but we suggest that it be reformulated with great care to avoid both the weaknesses of design and interpretation that have plagued earlier studies. Research on sex differences will be essential, but it will also have to relate to philosophical discussions of whether observed differences should be accommodated, nurtured, or eradicated in order to serve the best interests of individuals and society.

Notes

1. Alexander and Eckland (1974), producers of some of the most elaborate of these models in the mid 1970s (using data from the 1950s) conclude that: "Future work in this general area, particularly on sex differences, also should be sensitive to historical changes in the processes discussed in this report. We strongly suspect that samples drawn in more recent years may not show as marked sex effects as exhibited here" (Alexander and Eckland 1974, p. 680).

2. COFHE is a consortium of thirty independent selective, relatively high-priced colleges and universities. COFHE conducts admissions and financial-aid research for its members and provides information to them regarding developments in these areas.

3. The NLS was a longitudinal survey of high-school students first studied in 1972 and resurveyed throughout the following decade; it is being replicated currently with the senior class of 1980, parents, and sophomores in a project titled, "High School and Beyond."

4. CIRP surveys have been conducted annually by the American Council on Education since 1966 (in cooperation with UCLA since 1973). See Astin et al. (1971, 1976, 1978).

5. At several points we will cite this classified document because it was a study that specifically focused on the college-selection processes of women. Permission was sought to refer to it by name and sponsor, but it was denied; we were given permission to cite from it anonymously. The practice of confidential research in academic market analysis is becoming a serious obstacle to scholars of higher education and social processes (Litten 1980, 1981). This particular study was conducted by a market-research firm for a women's college and consisted of over one-thousand personal interviews with students in states within a triangle formed by Virginia, Massachusetts, and Illinois.

6. Project TALENT was a national survey of high-school students that was initiated in 1960 and followed the students one, five, and eleven years later.

7. On the other hand, one of the authors had a female college-senior research assistant who once confided "when you asked me in the post-admission survey who had influenced my selection decision as a high school senior, I never realized how much my parents had influenced me by what they said . . . and by what they *didn't* say."

8. Project SCOPE was a longitudinal survey of high-school seniors and sophomores initiated in 1966; it had eighty-thousand subjects from California, Illinois, Massachusetts, and North Carolina.

9. This information comes from a personal communication from Oscar Lenning, National Center for Higher Education Management Systems. Reprinted with permission.

10. A "large" school in Ramist's sample has an entering class of at least five-hundred, and only 30 percent of his schools were "large." Ramist's purpose in his paper was to compare the recruitment patterns of types of institutions for purposes of institutional self-assessment of their programs through comparative benchmarks. His analysis was performed only for students who sent test scores to one of 251 colleges that participated fully in the Admissions Testing Program that follows students from test-score submission through the freshman year. Ramist describes his sample of institutions according to categories of size, selectivity, and geographic base (national, regional), but he does not indicate type of control, location, or type of college (for example, private, liberal arts, comprehensive university). Although Ramist's paper indicates that he is reporting the presence of various types of students in the application pools of colleges, in a telephone conversation he stated that his relative percentages for the sexes (and other groups) are based on their presence in the population and that our interpretation of his data is legitimate.

Also, since Ramist does not provide numbers (just statements like "men have higher yields than women") and since reported preferences at successive stages do not adjust for the effects of differential preferences exhibited at earlier stages in the application process, the conclusions are at best suggestive.

Ramist reports that men are more likely than women to send their test scores to colleges that draw at least one quarter of their score reports from outside the College Board region in which they are located ("national colleges"). Men are substantially more likely than women to evidence interest in national, selective colleges; women send their scores more frequently than men to very small, unselective colleges, both national and state colleges, and to small regional colleges (Ramist does not differentiate by type of control). These findings compliment Astin's conclusions based on student-body compositions. Information used with permission.

11. These schools constitute 66 percent of the thirty-five schools listed as "most selective" by Cass and Birnbaum (1977), plus six schools listed as "highly selective" and one that is "very selective."

12. At the time this paper was first written we contacted Cross to find out the identity of these two colleges. She could not recall them. Subsequent sleuthing on our part through the *College Handbook* located the two colleges. Our speculations did not apply to these cases, but we have not been able to locate personnel at the two institutions who can explain why the acceptance-rate discrepancies existed in 1969. Discrimination can neither be ruled out nor very convincingly demonstrated. It is all history, however, since both colleges have equal acceptance rates for the two sexes today. The principal lesson from this exercise is the need to explore more thoroughly alternative explanations and to document discrimination when such charges are made.

Bibliography

Alexander, Karl L., and Eckland, Bruce K. "Sex Differences in the Educational Attainment Process." *American Sociological Review* 39 (1974): 668–682.

Astin, Alexander et al. *The American Freshman: National Norms for Fall 1971.* Washington, D.C.: American Council on Education, 1971.

———. *The American Freshman: National Norms for Fall 1976.* Los Angeles: Cooperative Institutional Research Program (CIRP), Laboratory for Research in Higher Education, University of California, Los Angeles, 1976.

———. *The American Freshman: National Norms for Fall 1978.* Los Angeles: Cooperative Institutional Research Program (CIRP), Laboratory for Research in Higher Education, University of California, Los Angeles, 1978.

Astin, Helen S.; Harway, Michele; and McNamara, Patricia. *Sex Discrimination in Education: Access to Postsecondary Education,* vol. 1. Washington, D.C.: National Center for Education Statistics, Education Division, U.S. Department of Health, Education and Welfare, 1976.

Bengelsdorf, Winnie. *Women's Stake in Low Tuition.* Washington, D.C.: American Association of State Colleges and Universities, 1974.

Berl, Janet; Lewis, Gordon; and Morrison, Sue. "Applying Models of Choice to the Problems of College Selection." In J. Carroll and J. Payne, eds., *Cognition and Social Behavior.* New York: Lawrence Erlbaum Associates, 1976.

Bob, Sharon. "The Myth of Equality: Financial Support for Males and Females." *Journal of College Student Personnel* (1977):235–238.

Brush, Lorelie R. "Choosing a Women's College." *College and University* (1976):360–367.

Cass, James, and Birnbaum, Max. *Comparative Guide to American Colleges.* New York: Harper and Row, 1977.

Chapman, David. "A Model of Student College Choice." *Journal of Higher Education* 52 (1981):490–505.

Christensen, Sandra; Melder, John; and Weisbrod, Burton. "Factors Affecting College Attendance." Madison, Wisconsin: Institute for Research on Poverty, University of Wisconsin, 1972.

Cross, K. Patricia. *Beyond the Open Door.* San Francisco: Jossey-Bass, 1971.

———. "The Woman Student." In W. Todd Furniss and Patricia A. Graham, eds., *Women in Higher Education.* Washington, D.C.: American Council on Education, 1974.

Davis, J. "Parents: The Hidden Resource." *College Board Review,* (1977–1978):25–29.

Froomkin, Joseph. *Aspirations, Enrollments, and Resources.* Washington,

D.C.: Office of Education, U.S. Department of Health, Education, and Welfare, 1970.

Kerr, W.D. "Student Perceptions of Counselor Role in the College Decision." *Personnel and Guidance Journal* 41 (1962):337–342.

Larkin, Paul G. "Market Research Methods for Improving College Responsiveness." In John Lucas, ed., *Developing a Total Marketing Plan.* New Directions for Institutional Research, no. 21. San Francisco: Jossey-Bass, 1979.

Lenning, Oscar T., and Cooper, Edward M. *Guidebook for Colleges and Universities: Presenting Information to Prospective Students.* Boulder, Colo.: National Center for Higher Education Management Systems, 1978.

Lentz, Linda P. "What Type of College do Career-Salient Women Choose—Coeducational or Women's?" Paper for the American Educational Research Association, April 1977.

Lewis, Gordon H., and Morrison, Sue. "A Longitudinal Study of College Selection." Technical Report no. 2. School of Urban and Public Affairs, Carnegie-Mellon, Pittsburgh, Pa., 1975.

Litten, Larry. "More Reflections from the Applicant Pool." Carleton College, Northfield, Minn., 1978a.

———. "Sharpened Reflections: A Reliability Report on Applicant/ Matriculant Research at Carleton—1976 and 1977." Carleton College, Northfield, Minn., 1978b.

———. "Marketing Higher Education: A Reappraisal." In *Marketing in College Admissions: A Broadening of Perspectives.* New York: College Entrance Examination Board, 1980.

———. "Avoiding and Stemming Abuses in Academic Marketing." *College and University* 56 (1981):105–122.

Litten, Larry; Jahoda, Ellen; and Morris, Darrell. "His Mother's Son and Her Father's Daughter: Parents, Children and the Marketing of Colleges." Paper for the Middle Atlantic Assembly of The College Board, Philadelphia, Pa., 1980.

Medsker, Leland, and Trent, James. "The Influence of Different Types of Public Higher Education Institutions on College Attendance from Varying Socioeconomic and Ability Levels." Cooperative Research Project Report no. 438, University of California, Berkeley, 1965.

National Center for Education Statistics. *Fall Enrollments in Higher Education, 1977.* Washington, D.C.: National Center for Education Statistics, 1979.

Nolfi, George J.; Fuller, Winship C.; Corazzini, Arthur J.; Epstein, William H.; Freeman, Richard B.; Manski, Charles F.; Nelson, Valerie I.; and Wise, David A. *Experiences of Recent High School Graduates.* Lexington, Mass.: Lexington Books, D.C. Heath and Company, 1978.

Radner, Roy, and Miller, Leonard. *Demand and Supply in U.S. Higher Education.* New York: McGraw-Hill, 1975.

Ramist, Leonard. "Admissions—Yield and Persistence Analysis." Paper for the Association for Institutional Research Annual Forum, Houston, Texas, May 1978.

Response Analysis Corporation. *High School Students View the SAT and College Admissions Process.* Princeton, N.J.: Response Analysis Corporation for the College Board, 1978.

Roby, Pamela. "Institutional Barriers to Women Students in Higher Education." In Alice Rossi and Ann Calderwood, eds., *Academic Women on the Move.* New York: Russell Sage Foundation, 1973.

Sacks, Herbert S., et al. *Hurdles: The Admissions Dilemma in American Higher Education.* New York: Atheneum, 1978.

Sewell, William H., and Shah, Vimal P. "Socio-Economic Status, Intelligence and the Attainment of Higher Education." *Sociology of Education* 40 (1967):1–23.

Starr, Joan. *Inside Information: A Handbook on Better Information for Student Choice.* Washington, D.C.: American Association for Higher Education, 1978.

Thomas, Gail E. "Race and Sex Effects on Access to College." Report No. 229. Center for Social Organization of Schools, The Johns Hopkins University, Baltimore, Md., 1977.

Tillery, Dale. *Distribution and Differentiation of Youth: A Study of Transition from School to College.* Cambridge, Mass.: Ballinger, 1973.

Trent, James W., and Medsker, Leland L. *Beyond High School.* San Francisco: Jossey-Bass, 1968.

United States Office of Education. *Opening Fall Enrollments, 1970.* Washington, D.C.: U.S. Office of Education, Department of Health, Education, and Welfare, 1971.

University of California. Office of Outreach Services. *Beyond High School Graduation: Who Goes to College.* Berkeley, Calif.: University of California, Berkeley, 1978.

————. Office of the Academic President. *Factors Affecting Student Choice.* Report of the Task Group of the Undergraduate Enrollment Study. Berkeley, Calif.: University of California, 1980.

Walster, Elaine; Cleary, T. Anne; and Clifford, Margaret M. "Research Note: The Effect of Race and Sex on College Admission." *Sociology of Education* 44 (1970):237–244.

Wright, Peter, and Kriewall, Maryanna. "State-of-Mind Effects on Predictions of College Choices from Derived and Reported Utility Functions." Graduate School of Business, Stanford University, and Graduate School of Business, University of Santa Clara, August 1979.

5

Sex Bias in Aptitude and Achievement Tests Used in Higher Education

Marlaine E. Lockheed

Recent interest in bias in testing has prompted numerous inquiries regarding the nature of test bias and the evidence of its extent in tests used for selection and evaluation in higher education. Two general types of bias have been identified: bias in the language or orientation of a test and bias in the validity of a test. The purpose of this paper is to review the evidence for sex bias in standardized tests used in higher education and to determine the extent and impact of such sex bias.

Bias may be defined from both social and psychometric points of view. The psychometric literature on test bias is extensive and cannot be reviewed here.[1] It is important to point out, however, the statistical nature of psychometric bias. According to Jensen (1980, p. 375), psychometric bias refers to "systematic errors in the *predictive validity* or the *construct validity* of test scores of individuals that are associated with the individual's group membership." Psychometric bias, therefore, may be defined as "a set of statistical attributes conjointly of a given test and two or more specified subpopulations" (Jensen 1980, p. 375).

Social bias, on the other hand, is unrelated to the psychometric properties of the test. Social bias refers to aspects of a test, the test process, or the interpretation of a test that may be identified without reference to individual test scores and may be considered inherently unfair, whether or not the test scores of individuals are affected by the presence of such bias. Evidence of psychometric bias is frequently used to uncover or identify social bias, and evidence of social bias is frequently claimed to account for psychometric bias, but the two are distinct.

A third form of bias, situational bias, refers to aspects of the test situation or measurement process that may bias the test score. Situational bias will not be discussed in this paper.

Support for the preparation of this paper was provided by the Division of Educational Research and Evaluation of the Educational Testing Service. The conclusions of the paper do not necessarily represent the views or policies of the Educational Testing Service. The author is indebted to Karen Jensen Finkelstein for valuable research assistance and to Miriam Godshalk for editorial assistance.

99

Sex bias in tests includes social bias and psychometric bias, both of which have been studied empirically. Situational bias in tests has been largely ignored in empirical studies of sex bias. To differentiate social sex bias from psychometric sex bias, the terms *gender bias* and *psychometric bias* will be used.

This chapter is organized as follows: first, empirical studies of gender bias will be reviewed; second, empirical studies of psychometric sex bias will be reviewed; third, studies relating gender bias to psychometric sex bias will be considered. A summary of the published studies of sex bias in tests used in higher education is presented in table 5-1.

Review of Empirical Studies of Gender Bias

Gender bias is an aspect of a test that formally or informally acknowledges, reinforces, and communicates cultural beliefs about sex differences in abilities, interests, or personal characteristics. This type of bias appears in the language of the test and has been referred to elsewhere as "facial bias" by Cole (1978), "content bias" by Dwyer (1976), and simply "sex bias" by Tittle (1974). Gender bias is the opposite of sex fairness or gender balance, which calls for an equal representation of males and females and of their interests or likes in tests. Gender balance implies that the language of the test and of the test items be balanced with respect to references to males and females, that the status of males and females within the test and its items be balanced or equal, that socially determined interests or talents of males and females be equally represented, and that sex stereotypes be absent (Lockheed 1974).

Empirical studies of gender bias conducted over the past decade show a decline in such bias since it was first identified. This decline is generally attributed to greater sensitivity on the part of test developers. For example, procedural guidelines for test development at Educational Testing Service (1979, p. 25), drafted in the mid-1970s and put into final form in 1979, state that "no item in any test should include words, phrases or description that is generally regarded as biased, sexist or racist (e.g. demeaning modifiers and stereotypes)." Test developers are also encouraged to include "material reflecting the cultural background and contributions of women, minorities and other subgroups" (Educational Testing Service 1979, p. 24). Comparable guidelines were developed by most test publishers in the late 1970s.

The decline in gender bias in tests is demonstrated by changes in three indicators of such bias: the gender ratio in tests or test items; the extent of sex stereotypes in the depiction of individuals in tests or test items; and the degree to which the content of the test or of the test items may be considered sex stereotyped. Each of these indicators will be discussed separately in the following sections.

Table 5–1
Empirical Studies of Gender Bias and Psychometric Sex Bias in Aptitude and Achievement Tests Used in Higher Education

Study	Test Date	Male N	Female N	Item N	Gender-Bias Variable	Evidence of Gender Bias	Psychometric-Bias Variable	Evidence of Psychometric Bias
ATP Achievement Test in Psychics (Wheeler and Harris 1980)	December 1978	802	710	75	None	None	$|D_i| \geq 1.25$ s.d. of D	On total test: 72 items easier for males; 1 item easier for females; 7 items relatively easiest for males; 7 items relatively easiest for females
							Items omitted	22 items omitted by twice as high a proportion of women as men (including 5 items identified as relatively easiest for males); 3 items omitted by higher proportion of males (including 2 items identified as relatively easiest for females)

Table 5-1 continued

Study	Test Date	Male N	Female N	Item N	Gender-Bias Variable	Evidence of Gender Bias	Psychometric-Bias Variable	Evidence of Psychometric Bias
							Speededness: percentage of examinees completing last item	54.3 percent of males and 48.0 percent of females
							Speededness: percentage of examinees completing 75 percent of the items on the test	98.9 percent of males and 98.7 percent of females
Graduate Record Examination, Quantitative (Donlon, Hicks, and Wallmark 1980)	December 1974	1,720	1,735	55	None	None	$D_i \geq 1.5$ s.d. of D	ps not provided; 4 items relatively easiest for males; 5 items relatively easiest for females
Graduate Record Examination, Quantitative (Wild and Durso 1979) (black examinees)	December 1976	615	1,125	55	None	None	Speededness: percentage of examinees completing last item	43.9 percent of males and 44.1 percent of females in 20-minute session; 40.3 percent of males and

	Graduate Record Examination, Quantitative (Wild and Durso 1979) (white examinees)		
	December 1976	2,915	2,825
		55	
		None	None
Percentage of items omitted			43.0 percent of females in 30-minute session
Percentage of items omitted			8.6 percent items omitted by males and 9.4 percent items omitted by females in 20-minute session, 9.70 percent items omitted by males and 9.9 percent items omitted by females in 30-minute session
Speededness: percentage of examinees completing test item			58.2 percent of males and 48.6 percent of females in 20-minute session; 64.2 percent of males and 48.9 percent of females in 30-minute session

Table 5-1 continued

Study	Test Date	Male N	Female N	Item N	Gender-Bias Variable	Evidence of Gender Bias	Psychometric-Bias Variable	Evidence of Psychometric Bias
							Percentage of items omitted	4.5 percent items omitted by males and 7.5 percent items omitted by females in 20-minute session. 4.2 percent items omitted by males and 7.2 percent items omitted by females in 30-minute session
Graduate Record Examination, Verbal (Donlon, Hicks, and Wallmark 1980) (reading items)	December 1974	1,720	1,735	40	None	None	$|D_i| \geq 1.5$ s.d. of D	p not provided; 3 items relatively easiest for males; 3 items relatively easiest for females
Graduate Record Examinations, Verbal (Wild and Durso 1979) (reading items; black examinees)	December 1976	560	1,085	40	None	None	Percentage of items omitted	2.8 percent items omitted by males and 2.4 percent items omitted by females in 20-minute

Test	Date					Speededness: percentage of examinees completing last item	Percentage of items omitted
Graduate Record Examination, Verbal (Wild and Durso 1979) (reading items; white examinees)	December 1976	2,930	2,825	40	None	None	58.6 percent of males and 62.5 percent of females in 20-minute session; 60.0 percent of males and 56.9 percent of females in 30-minute session	1.3 percent items omitted by males and 1.5 percent items omitted by females in 20-minute session; 1.4 percent items omitted by males and 1.4 percent items omitted by females in 30-minute session

session; 1.3 percent items omitted by males and 1.4 percent items omitted by females in 30-minute session

Table 5-1 continued

Study	Test Date	Male N	Female N	Item N	Gender-Bias Variable	Evidence of Gender Bias	Psychometric-Bias Variable	Evidence of Psychometric Bias
							Speededness: percentage of examinees completing last item	83 percent males and 82.6 percent females in 20-minute session; 84.2 percent males and 82.6 percent females in 30-minute session
Graduate Record Examination, Verbal (Donlon, Hicks, Wallmark 1980) (vocabulary items)	December 1974	1,720	1,735	50	None	None	$|D_i| \geq 1.5$ s.d. of D	p not provided; 2 items relatively easiest for male; 3 items relatively easiest for female
Graduate Record Examination, Verbal (Wild and Durso 1979) (vocabulary items, black examinees)	December 1976	560	1,085	55	None	None	Speededness: percentage of examinees completing last item	44.4 percent of males and 55.3 percent females in 20-minute session; 49.1 percent males and 56.1 percent females in 30-minute session

	Date						Percentage of items omitted	Speededness: percentage of examinees completing last item
Graduate Record Examination, Verbal (Wild and Durso 1979) (vocabulary items, white examinees)	December 1976	1,976	2,825	55	None	None	13.5 percent of items omitted by males and 11.9 percent of items omitted by females in 20-minute session; 12.5 percent of items omitted by males and 11.9 percent of items omitted by females in 30-minute session	65.6 percent males and 68.7 percent females in 20-minute session; 68.1 percent males and 67.3 percent females in 30-minute session

Table 5-1 continued

Study	Test Date	Male N	Female N	Item N	Gender-Bias Variable	Evidence of Gender Bias	Psychometric-Bias Variable	Evidence of Psychometric Bias
							Percentage of items omitted	11.3 percent of items omitted by males and 10.7 percent of items omitted by females in 20-minute session; 11.4 percent of items omitted by males and 10.4 percent of items omitted by females in 30-minute session
Scholastic Aptitude Test, Mathematics, (Donlon 1973)	May 1964	55,717	47,082	60	None	None	Differences in percentage passing $p > \pm .07$	29 items easier for males; 0 items easier for females
Scholastic Aptitude Test, Mathematics,	April 1975	1,000	1,000	60	None	None	$|D_i| \geq 1.25$ s.d. of D	5 items relatively easiest for males; 3

(Stern 1978) (black examinees)							items relatively easiest for females
Scholastic Aptitude Test, Mathematics (Stern 1978) (white examinees)	April 1975	1,000	60	None	None	$|D_i| \geq 1.25$ s.d. of D	4 items relatively easiest for males; 2 items relatively easiest for females
Scholastic Aptitude Test, Mathematics (Strassberg-Rosenberg and Donlon 1975)	April 1974	1,000	60	Gender ratio	In 12 "real world" items, the gender ratio = 2.25	$|D_i| \geq 1.5$ s.d. of D	59 items easier for males; 1 item easier for females. On total test: 3 items relatively easiest for males; 3 items relatively easiest for females. On regular math: 3 items relatively easiest for male; 2 items relatively easiest for females. On data sufficiency 2 items favored females

Table 5-1 continued

Study	Test Date	Male N	Female N	Item N	Gender-Bias Variable	Evidence of Gender Bias	Psychometric-Bias Variable	Evidence of Psychometric Bias
Scholastic Aptitude Test, Verbal (Coffman 1961)	March 1954	370	370	60	Judgments about item difficulty	7 items judged easier for males; 10 judged easier for females; 43 judged neutral	Adjusted difference in percentage passing: $\phi > \pm 1.96$; $p < .05$	6/7 "male" items easier for males; 8/10 "female" items easier for females
Scholastic Aptitude Test, Verbal (Donlon 1973)	May 1964	55,717	47,083	90	None	None	Difference in percentage passing: $p \geq \pm .07$	8 items easier for males; 11 items for females
Scholastic Aptitude Test, Verbal (Stern 1978) (black examinees)	April 1975	1,000	1,000	85	None	None	Relatively easiest items for each sex $\|D_i\| \geq 1.25$ s.d. of D	3 items relatively easiest for males; 6 items relatively easiest for females;
Scholastic Aptitude Test, Verbal (Stern 1978) (white examinees)	April 1975	1,000	1,000	85	None	None	Relatively easiest items for each sex $\|D_i\| \geq 1.25$ s.d. of D	7 items relatively easiest for males; 10 items relatively easiest for females

Test	Date				Gender ratio	Relatively easiest items for each sex	
Scholastic Aptitude Test, Verbal (Strassberg-Rosenberg and Donlon 1975)	April 1975	1,000	1,000	90	1.75 male references to each female reference	$|D_i| \geq 1.5$ s.d. of D	p not provided; 9 items relatively easiest for males; 3 items relatively easiest for females. No relationship between gender ratio and item difficulty
Test of Standard Written English (Stern 1978) (black examinees)	April 1975	1,000	1,000	50	None	$|D_i| \geq 1.25$ s.d. of D	1 item relatively easiest for males; 3 items relatively easiest for females
Test of Standard Written English (Stern 1978) (white examinees)	April 1975	1,000	1,000	50	None	$|D_i| \geq 1.25$ s.d. of D	2 items relatively easiest for males; 3 items relatively easiest for females

Gender Ratio

Gender ratio is the relative distribution of references to males and females in the language of the test; this may be computed by item or over the test as a whole. A gender ratio of 1.0 would be gender balanced. The first published investigation of the occurrence of male and female references in tests was conducted by Tittle, McCarthy, and Steckler (1974). They studied nine series of standardized tests of academic achievement, including twenty-nine different test batteries, published between 1964 and 1970, that were used for elementary- and secondary-school assessment. Within each test all references to males and females were counted. Of the tests examined, all but one contained a greater number of male references than of female references. The male-female ratio of references within tests—the gender ratio—ranged from 14.11 to 0.86. In only eight of the twenty-nine test batteries that were examined was the gender ratio less than 2.0. Thus, in the majority of the tests there were 100 percent to 700 percent more references to males than to females. The older the age group was for whom the test was written, the higher was the gender ratio. These findings were confirmed at the item level by Donlon, Ekstrom, Lockheed, and Harris (1977), who replicated the Tittle, McCarthy, and Steckler (1974) study with four nationally administered elementary and secondary tests published after 1965. The range of item gender ratios across tests and subtests was 26.5 to 1.57.

In 1973 Lockheed conducted a similar investigation of the gender ratio in eight major college and graduate-school entrance examinations (Lockheed 1974). Gender imbalance was found within these tests at the item level. Items were coded according to whether they contained no sex reference, male-only sex reference, female-only sex reference, or both male and female sex reference. The ratio of male-only items to female-only items ranged from 16.0 to 2.0. Of the 1,220 items coded, only 22 contained references to *both* men and women. Seventy-five percent of all the items contained no sex reference, but of the remaining 25 percent, more than four-fifths were male-only items.

Improvement in gender ratios occurred during the 1970s both in tests used for elementary- and secondary-school assessment and in those used for higher-education admissions. For example, Jensen and Beck (1978) compared gender ratios in the 1970 Metropolitan Achievement Test with those in the 1978 edition. In 1970 the range of the gender ratio over five levels of the test was from 4.11 to 0.86; by 1978 this range was 1.91 to 0.87. Gender balance, therefore, was found in this particular test by 1978. In tests used in higher education, Strassberg-Rosenberg and Donlon (1975) examined gender ratios in the 1974 version of the Scholastic Aptitude Test-Verbal. The gender ratio was computed as 1.75, indicating a considerably more gender-balanced test than the 1970 version reviewed earlier (Lockheed 1974).

Sex-Role Stereotypes

Gender bias is also indicated by sex differences in how the male and female actors are portrayed within items. In their study of sex-role stereotypes in achievement tests, Tittle, McCarthy, and Steckler (1974, p. 78) reported that "women are portrayed almost exclusively as homemakers or in the pursuit of hobbies." Furthermore, they (Tittle, McCarthy, and Steckler 1974, p. 22) reported that "some items imply that the majority of professions are closed to women." In the investigation of the college and graduate-school admissions tests that Lockheed conducted in 1973, the relative status of males and females within an item was coded (Lockheed 1974). Of the 22 items (out of 1,220) that contained both a male and a female actor, ten items portrayed the men and women as equal in status; the remaining twelve items showed the men as being of higher status than the women. No item on any of the eight tests portrayed a women in a higher status position than a man—for example, as a female principal with a male teacher or a female lawyer with a male client. Typically, females were referred to as mothers, teachers, secretaries, or wives. Males were referred to as lawyers, managers, principals, superintendents, doctors, or other professionals.

In the study conducted by Donlon et al. (1977), male roles, female roles, and neutral roles were coded separately. The identification of particular roles as female, male, or neutral was made according to the percentages of females and males found actively engaged in each of these roles as documented by Occupational Characteristics, 1970 Census of Population, and other sources. In the tests and subtests studied, the average number of "male roles" per item ranged from 2.14 to 0.0 and of "females roles" ranged from 2.22 to 0.08. Although the sex of the role taker was recorded, these data were not analyzed.

Interests

Another indicator of gender bias is the use of tradition or stereotyped male or female interests or skills in the item context. For example, a mathematical-operations question may be posed in the context of counting marbles or counting dolls. Few studies of gender bias in tests have addressed this issue directly, although this general area of concern, which may be considered the cultural relevance of a test, has been covered widely as it relates to the issue of minority representation on tests (Quirk and Medley 1972; Linn 1973). Coffman's (1961) early study of sex bias in the verbal section of the SAT did, however, address this issue. Judgments were made concerning which of the sixty test items would favor men, which would favor women, and which would be neutral. As Coffman (1961, p. 123) noted, "of the seven items judged to be easier for men, one involved mechanical knowledge, . . . [o]ne involved knowledge of the vocabulary of business and five involved understanding of science. . . . Of the ten items judged to be easier for women, nine involved words which might be categorized as describing feelings or personality characteristics. . . . The other item judged to be easier for women was a sentence completion item dealing with . . . 'the arts'.'' No other published empirical study of standardized tests has, a priori, evaluated items for sex stereotypes in interest or skills. Instead, most empirical studies have observed sex differences in performance and then reviewed the content of the items where the differences were most acute. Although this procedure may accurately describe the content of items showing sex-differentiated performance, it does not permit an independent assessment of the test content for gender bias.

Review of Empirical Studies of Psychometric Sex Bias

Psychometric bias is the obverse of validity. As Cole (1978, p. 4) noted, "The notion of test bias appearing most frequently in the literature of the last decade is the notion that a test is biased if it measures different things in different groups." The source of such bias may come from the measure, the measurement process, or the interpretation of the results. Generally speaking, the question of bias is raised whenever the bivariate distributions of test scores differ from one group to another. Bias may be considered to fall under three rubrics corresponding to the three categories of validity identified by the *APA Standards for Educational and Psychological Tests* (1974). These three categories of psychometric validity are construct validity, content validity, and criterion-related validity. These terms have been defined as follows: "Construct validity refers to the degree to which scores on a measure permit inferences about underlying traits. . . . Content validity usually refers to the degree to which a measure captures a program objective (or objectives). . . . Criterion-related validity refers to the degree to which scores on a measure relate to scores on an external criterion (Anderson et al. 1975, pp. 459–461).

Bias may be assessed in total tests, subtests, and items. Much has been written about the assessment of psychometric bias. In general, content validity is measured by observing the items and observing how well they sample representatively some domain of tasks, whereas the measurement of construct validity and criterion-related validity depends upon correlations. Such bias, therefore, may be present when the pattern of correlations differs between groups. Construct validity will not be discussed in this book.

Total Test Bias

Empirical studies of psychometric bias in aptitude tests used for college admissions have focused on the ability of the tests to predict academic performance. Sex differences in the correlations between test scores and grades have been observed since the earliest reported studies of the college-admissions tests. In 1932, for example, Brigham published *A Study of Error: A Summary and Evaluation of Methods Used in Six Years of Study of the Scholastic Aptitude Test of the College Entrance Examination Board*. In this study he reported that the correlations between scholastic-aptitude test scores and freshmen grades for men at men's colleges differed from those correlations for women at women's colleges: the correlations for women were lower than those for men. More recently, however, Seashore (1962) summarized several studies that concluded that women's grades at coeducational colleges were more accurately predicted by tests than were men's. These conclusions were reiterated by Cole (1973), who, in her analysis of data from students enrolled in nineteen American coeducational colleges, found that standardized test scores and high-school grades predicted women's first-term grades better than men's first-term grades.

The main rationale for examining the predictive validity of a test, however, is its use for selection purposes. Selection is itself subject to bias. Several models of selection bias have been identified and applied to male-female selection. The models of selection bias and evidence of fairness in using each are as follows:

1. The traditional regression model, where test bias refers either to over prediction or to underprediction of criterion measures for different populations when a single regression equation is used. This method has been found to be biased against women (American Council on Testing 1973; Wild 1977).
2. The subjective regression model, in which a constant is added to minority-group scores to increase the probability of minority-group selection according to the regression model (Darlington 1977). No empirical test of this model has been reported.
3. The equal-risk model, where all persons who have the same probability of being successful on a criterion measure are selected (Einhorn and Bass 1971). According to this model, the use of either separate or combined male-female regression equations has been found to be fair but impractical (American Council on Testing 1973).
4. The constant-ratio model, where selection by group is made in proportion to that group's success on the test (Thorndike 1971), was found to be unfair to men (American Council on Testing 1973).
5. The conditional-probability model, in which the probability of being selected is contingent upon achieving a satisfactory criterion score and is not related to group membership (Cole 1973), was also found to be unfair to men (American Council on Testing 1973).
6. The threshold-utilty model (Petersen and Novick 1976), in which "the institution selecting the students must determine the degree of preference, or utilities, for each group. If the utilities are the same for

male and female groups, the model is the same as the equal risk model''
(Wild and Dwyer 1978, pp. 4–5). No empirical test of this model has
been reported.

Other indicators of test bias are test speededness and omit patterns.
Many tests are constructed on the assumption that the majority of test
takers will have the opportunity to try most of the items. If subpopulations
differ on how many items in a test are reached, then the test may be considered biased against the group that reached the fewer items. Speededness was
examined by Wild and Durso (1980) in a study of the effects of testing time
on the verbal and quantitative scores of men and women who reported
scores on the December 1976 administration of the Graduate Record Examination. They found that increasing the testing time did not affect performance differences between men and women on this test.

In a similar study of men and women who reported scores on the
December 1978 Admissions Testing Program (ATP) Physics Achievement
Test, Wheeler and Harris (1981) reported little difference between the sexes
in the number of items actually reached on the test. Patterns of items
omitted on this test, however, showed marked sex differences; women were
more likely to omit items, particularly items early on in the test, than were
men. They (Wheeler and Harris 1981, p. 25) also noted that ''this omit pattern on the early items in the test might indicate that some female candidates
are experiencing a higher level of test anxiety than male candidates.''

Item Bias

Bias in a test item is most often indicated by item statistics, such as p-values,
deltas, item-total correlations, and, more recently, item-characteristic
curves based on Birnbaum's three-parameter logistic model (Lord 1977);
one parameter (Rasch) models (Wright, Mead, and Draba 1976) or grouped
empirical-item response curves (Scheuneman 1979). Of these identification
procedures, the p-values and delta approaches have generally been used in
empirical studies of sex bias. The p-value is the percentage of the test takers
who pass an item. This value may be transformed into ϕ, or 2 arcsin $\sqrt{p}$, or
into Δ, which is defined as $4z + 13$ where z is a normal deviate corresponding to $1 - p$. In either case, it may be considered an index of item difficulty.
If an item is more difficult for one group than another, it may or may not be
biased; if the correlation between one group's score on an item and some
other criterion—usually the total test—is not the same as that of the other
group, the item again may or may not be biased. The item also may or may
not be biased if distracters operate differently for one group than for
another.[2]

Numerous studies of item bias have been conducted, generally in the process of constructing tests, particularly when the intent of the test developer has been to produce a test that gives equivalent results for males and females. Current studies of sex bias at the item level are integrally linked to efforts to determine the effects of test content on sex differences in performance. Only some of these studies have actually examined the effects of gender bias on performance. These will be reviewed in the following section.

Review of Empirical Studies of the Relationship between Gender Bias and Psychometric Bias

Studies of sex bias in items have taken two approaches:

1. Those that measure gender bias and psychometric bias separately and then correlate these measures (the experimental or quasi-experimental prospective studies);
2. Those that measure psychometric bias only, and then examine the characteristics of items for which psychometric bias emerges (the retrospective studies).

Prospective Studies

The earliest studies relating gender bias to sex differences in item difficulty were experimental studies that employed few subjects and studied fewer items. In 1959 Milton, for example, reported a study that examined the relative performance of twenty-four undergraduate men and twenty-four undergraduate women on a mathematics test having ten "feminine" items and ten "masculine" items. Although the men solved more problems than did the women, Milton (1959, p. 706) noted that "the difference between the scores of men and women was reduced when the problems were stated with content appropriate to the feminine role." These findings, however, were *not* supported in a subsequent partial replication by Hoffman and Maier (1966). More recently, Graf and Riddle (1972) found that although the "masculinity" or "femininity" of a problem did not affect the subjects' performance on the item, the gender bias of the item did affect speededness for females. Female subjects solved a yardage problem in two-thirds the time it took them to solve a stocks problem.

Studies of the relationship between gender bias and psychometric bias in nationally administered ability tests for higher education are few. Although three quasi-experimental studies of the effects of gender bias on performance have been identified, only two of them examined tests used for higher education. Studying data for college-bound students of 1954, Coffman (1961) examined items on the SAT-Verbal aptitude test for gender bias and made predictions as to which items would favor men and which would favor women. The items were judged for the traditional interests or skills of men and women. Fourteen of the sixteen predictions based on these judgments were confirmed. Of the nine items concerning mechanical knowledge, science, or business that were judged to be easier for men, eight actually were easier for male test takers. Of the ten items concerning personal feelings or personality characteristics that were judged easier for women, nine were actually easier for female test takers. In a more recent study of college-bound students, Strassberg-Rosenberg and Donlon (1975, p. 14) found that although the SAT-Verbal test was generally stereotypical, "reference to male or female characters and pronoun usage did not seem to influence either the delta value or bias index (D-value) of the individual verbal items." In a study of gender bias effects on sex differences in performance on achievement tests, however, Donlon et al. (1977) did find an effect. Girls in the fifth, eighth, and ninth grades performed better than boys on test items in which female characters equaled or outnumbered male characters.

Retrospective Studies

Retrospective studies of the relationship between gender bias and psychometric bias appear relatively frequently in the literature, and they dominate the body of current research. Retrospective studies suffer from two problems. First, the indicator of psychometric bias most often used is the delta plot or D-value, which is a measure "based on item performance relative to other items, not on absolute differences between the sexes" (Strassberg-Rosenberg and Donlon 1975, p. 20). Therefore, items identified by this statistic as "favoring" females may nonetheless be answered correctly more often by males. Second, these retrospective studies are often flawed in design. In retrospective studies what is known is the dependent variable—in this case, the relative difficulty of the item for males and females—and what the research seeks to identify are the determinants of these sex differences in performance. The determination of which items are differentially difficult for males and females is made by the application of somewhat arbitrary criterion to the difficulty measure. By choosing different criteria, different numbers of discriminating items may be identified. The criterion, however, is frequently set so that the discriminating items constitute less than 10 percent of the items on the test. Since these studies typically examine *only* the identified discriminating items and ignore the remaining items, they suffer from incomplete designs.

The first retrospective study was conducted by Donlon (1973), who examined sex differences in item performance for the 103,275 persons who took the Scholastic Aptitude Test in May 1964. Items for which the women's performance was statistically superior to the men's and items for which the men's performance was statistically superior to the women's were located and examined for gender bias. Of the ninety verbal items on the test, eight items showed a minimum of a 7 percent male superiority in performance and eleven items showed like female superiority. Seven of the eight items favoring males were coded as having scientific or "practical affairs" content; eight of the eleven items favoring females were coded as having human relations, humanities, or aesthetic-philosophical content. Of the sixty mathematical items on the test, twenty-nine showed a minimum of a 7 percent male superiority in performance, whereas none showed as similar female superiority; on two items female performance was 2 percent better than male performance. The items that were the easiest for men dealt with so-called real-world topics, and the two items that were easiest for women included a laundry problem and an algebra problem. On eighteen other algebra problems, however, the male performance exceeded that of the females.

Two years later, Strassberg-Rosenberg and Donlon (1975) reexamined the 1974 SAT for psychometric bias. The measure used was delta plots, in which item difficulties (deltas) for males and females were plotted on a single graph, and outliers were identified from the major axis of the elliptical plot for the highly correlated delta values. The use of this statistic makes it difficult to compare the item performance (p-values) for males and females, even though delta is based upon a transformation of p. The delta, moreover, leads to ambiguities in the interpretation of findings since it compares item difficulty within subpopulations, not between subpopulations. For the verbal part of the SAT, Strassberg-Rosenberg and Donlon (1975) identified twelve out of ninety items as *outliers*—items for which the difficulty index (delta) for males was different from that for females. Of these outliers, nine were the easiest for males and three were the easiest for females. The easiest items for males were on topics related to science and practical affairs; the easiest items for females were on topics related to aesthetics and philosophy. Inspection of the delta plots for this test also showed that not only were these items relatively the easiest for each sex, they were also absolutely easier in comparison with the other sex. Thus, although the SAT-Verbal exhibited no sex differences overall, if the twenty-four aesthetic-philosophical and human-relations items had been matched in number to equal the thirty science and practical-affairs items, the women's SAT-Verbal scores might have been substantially higher than the men's scores. The mathematics component of the 1974 SAT covered three domains of mathematics—geometry, algebra, and arithmetic—and included several miscellaneous items. With one exception, men outperformed women on all mathematics items. The delta-plot technique identified five outliers "favoring" men and two outliers "favoring" women. The items easiest for men covered geometry and arithmetic, whereas the items easiest for women covered algebra (Strassberg-Rosenberg and Donlon 1975).

A third retrospective study of gender bias and psychometric bias was conducted by Stern (1978), who examined the item and test scores of 1,000 black males, 1,000 black females, 1,000 white males, and 1,000 white females who reported scores for the April 1975 SAT administration. The four sample groups were matched according to their performance on a short test of verbal ability. Performance analyses of the SAT-Verbal and SAT-Mathematics tests and of the Test of Standard Written English (TSWE) were reported. Overall, males outperformed females on the mathematical items, and females outperformed males on the TSWE items; white females outperformed white males on the SAT-Verbal items. The three SAT-Verbal items easiest for black females covered aesthetics and science, and the three SAT-Verbal items easiest for black males covered science and the world of practical affairs. Six of the seven items easiest for white females covered aesthetics and human relationships, and six of the seven items easiest for white males covered science and the world of practical affairs. On the SAT-Mathematics test, geometry items and quantitative comparison items were more difficult for white females; no other content factors were related to sex differences in item difficulty. On the TSWE, sentence-correction items were more difficult for white males than were usage items.

The language of the summary in a fourth retrospective study conducted by Donlon, Hicks, and Wallmark (1980), examplifies how the delta could be misinterpreted by a nonstatistical reader. Donlon, Hicks, and Wallmark (1980) studied the performance of 1,720 white males and 1,735 white females who took the Graduate Record Examination (GRE) aptitude test in 1974. Overall, few sex differences in either vocabulary or reading were found; males outperformed females on the mathematics section. The delta plots for the mathematics section showed only one item out of fifty-five on which females actually outperformed males but showed nine items considered to be outliers. The authors noted that of the nine mathematical outliers, "five outliers were relatively favorable to females, four to males" (Donlon, Hicks, and Wallmark 1980, p. 16), and they concluded that the test "is not overly unfair to one of the sexes" (Donlon, Hicks, and Wallmark 1980, p. 19). The reader who is unfamiliar with the interpretation of the delta—that is, that a delta-plot analysis is designed to identify the relatively easier items for each comparison group—might erroneously conclude that there were, on this test, five items on which women outperformed men, four items on which men outperformed women, and on the rest of the items the two sexes performed about equally. This would be an inaccurate interpretation of the delta.

A fifth retrospective study by Wheeler and Harris (1981) examined the performance of 710 females and 802 males who took the ATP Physics test in December 1978. From test statistics and delta plots, it was clear that on seventy-two of the seventy-five items of the test, males outperformed females. Using delta-plot analysis, the authors identified the seven items that were "relatively easier for males," compared with other items and the seven items that were "relatively easier for females." However, no content area was identified as being relatively easier for males or females, based on this analysis. This study also utilized several other indicators of psychometric bias, including percentage passing, item discrimination, speededness, omits, and error analysis. The latter three analyses provided evidence for bias and suggested that some aspect of the measurement process may have inhibited female performance. Women were less likely than men to complete the entire test and were more likely to omit items, particularly the first ten items. Error analysis also revealed sex differences that indicated that the females did not understand basic concepts whereas the males "knew too much." Both test anxiety and lack of physics-related experience may have contributed to the observed differences.

Conclusion

This chapter has reviewed the empirical evidence regarding bias in standardized aptitude and achievement tests used in higher education are biased. Two forms of bias, gender bias and psychometric bias, were described and evidence for each examined. The major findings of this review of studies of sex bias are as follows:

1. The majority of studies of sex bias in tests used in higher education are psychometric studies of item bias; this was the case in 90 percent of the twenty data bases examined.
2. In those few (3) studies that did examine gender bias, there was no conclusive evidence that gender bias was related to psychometric bias or to sex differences in performance. For two tests it was found that the gender ratio, an indicator of gender bias, favored males, and for one test it was found that items whose content was judged to favor females outnumbered items whose content was judged to favor males.
3. Only three studies were found that examined both gender bias and psychometric bias; one found a relationship between gender bias and sex differences in performance, but the others did not.
4. The majority of items on tests used in higher education are not psychometrically sex biased. Of the 970 items that were analyzed in the data bases reviewed in this paper, 163 (16.8 percent) showed a sex-by-item interaction.

The recent popular concern about sex bias in testing has been prompted, first, by an interest in identifying the factors related to the observed differences between men and women in their performance on some tests and, second, by an interest in fairness. The interest in fairness gave rise to many empirical studies of gender bias in elementary and secondary achievement tests; these studies were published in the early part of the 1970s. A similar interest in fairness did not generate an empirical literature regarding tests used in higher education. Rather, the tests used in higher education were scrutinized for psychometric item bias, while procedures were set in place to guarantee sex-fair tests.

Little progress was made in identifying the factors related to observed sex differences in performance. Although a number of psychometric item-bias studies were conducted, the number of items identified as biased were so few that few consistent patterns of content differences related to performance differences emerged. In some studies claims were made that male examinees perform better than female examinees on "real-world" spatial problems and female examinees outperform male examinees on "social relations" or algebra problems. The evidence for these claims is slight, however, and the vast majority of items on which no sex differences in performance were observed were never examined for content. Moreover, the designs of many of these studies were incomplete, making it impossible to assess the effect of content factors on sex differences in performance accurately.

Because indicators of psychometric sex bias have differed between studies, comparison is difficult. An important change has been the change from studying differences in performance directly to studying relative differences in performance. This approach diverts attention from the actual performance of male and female examinees on a given item, which is a more appropriate indicator to use when attempting to predict differences in performance from differences in item content.

The item-bias studies, however, provide a rich body of data for exploring sex differences in performance. One finding that emerged consistently from these studies was the substantial performance differences between male and female examinees on tests of mathematics and science. Out of 135 math and science items for which performance data were available, men outperformed women on 131 items; women outperformed men on two items. By comparison, on 150 verbal items for which performance data were available, men outperformed women on only 14 items, whereas women outperformed men on 19 items. There is very little evidence to link this sex difference in performance to gender bias in the language of the test; beyond that, mathematics and science items are typically neutral in tone. On the other hand, these performance differences should not be interpreted as evidence of innate sex differences in mathematics or science abilities.

Such differences have been substantially reduced when men and women with equivalent training and experience have been compared (Dewolf 1981; Wheeler and Harris 1981). In all probability with women generally taking fewer or easier courses in mathematics and science, the experience of the examinee population on which the data are based is itself sex differentiated.

Notes

1. Excellent discussions of bias may be found in Robert L. Linn, "Fair Test Use in Selection," *Review of Educational Research* 43, (1973):139-161; Robert L. Linn, "In Search of Fair Selection Procedures," *Journal of Educational Measurement* 13 (1976):53-58; and Lee J. Cronbach, "Five Decades of Public Controversy over Mental Testing," *American Psychologist* 30 (1975):1-14; the most extensive treatment may be found in Arthur R. Jensen, *Bias in Mental Testing* (New York: Free Press, 1980).

2. It is not within the scope of this paper to discuss item-bias indicators more extensively. For an excellent review of many of these indicators, the reader should consult William H. Angoff, "Use of Difficulty and Discrimination Indices for Detecting Item Bias," Ronald A. Berk, ed., *Handbook of Methods for Detecting Test Bias,* forthcoming.

Bibliography

American Council on Testing. "Assessing Students on the Way to College." American Council on Education Technical Report. *ACT Publications,* no. 1, Iowa City: American Council on Testing, 1973.

American Psychological Association. *Standards for Educational and Psychological Tests.* Washington, D.C.: American Psychological Association, 1974.

Anderson, Scarvia B.; Ball, Samuel; Murphy, Richard T. and Associates. *Encyclopedia of Educational Evaluation.* San Francisco: Jossey-Bass, 1975.

Angoff, William H. "Use of Difficulty and Discrimination Indices for Detecting Item Bias." In Ronald A. Berk, ed., *Handbook of Methods for Detecting Test Bias,* forthcoming.

Brigham, Carl C. *A Study of Error.* New York: College Entrance Examination Board, 1932.

Coffman, William E. "Sex Differences in Responses to Items in an Aptitude Test." *Eighteenth Yearbook, National Council on Measurement in Education* (1961):117-124.

Cole, Nancy S. "A Model for Fairness in Selection." Paper presented at the meeting of the American Educational Research Association, New Orleans, 25 February–1 March 1973.

————. "Approaches to Examining Bias in Achievement Test Items." *Newsnotes of the Association for Measurement and Evaluation in Guidance* 13 (1978):4.

Cronbach, Lee J. "Five Decades of Public Controversy over Mental Testing." *American Psychologist* 30 (1975):1–4.

Darlington, R.B. "Another Look at Culture Fairness." *Journal of Educational Measurement* 8 (1971):71–82.

Dewolf, Virginia A. "High School Mathematics Preparation and Sex Differences in Quantitative Abilities." *Psychology of Women Quarterly* 5 (1980):555–567.

Donlon, Thomas F. "Content Factors in Sex Difference on Test Questions." ETS Research Memorandum 73–28. Princeton, N.J.: Educational Testing Service, 1973.

Donlon, Thomas F.; Ekstrom, Ruth B.; Lockheed, Marlaine; and Harris, Abigail. "Performance Consequences of Sex Bias in the Content of Major Achievement Batteries." ETS Progress Report 77–11. Princeton, N.J.: Educational Testing Service, 1977.

Donlon, Thomas F.; Hicks, Marilyn M.; and Wallmark, Madeline M. "Sex Differences in Item Responses on the Graduate Record Examination." *Applied Psychological Measurement* 4 (1980):9–20.

Dwyer, Carol Ann. "Test Content in Mathematics and Science: The Consideration of Sex." Paper presented at the meeting of the American Educational Research Association, San Francisco, April 1976.

Educational Testing Service. "Principles, Policies and Procedural Guidelines Regarding ETS Products and Services." Princeton, N.J.: Educational Testing Service, 1 February 1979.

Einhorn, H.J., and Bass, A.R. "Methodological Considerations Relevant to Discrimination in Employment Testing." *Psychological Bulletin* 75 (1971):261–269.

Graf, Richard G., and Riddle, Jeanne C. "Sex Differences in Problem-solving as a Function of Problem Context." *The Journal of Educational Research* 65 (1972):451–452.

Hoffman, Richard L., and Maier, Norman R.F. "Social Factors Influencing Problem-solving in Women." *Journal of Personality and Social Psychology* 4 (1966):382–390.

Jensen, Arthur R. *Bias in Mental Testing.* New York: Free Press, 1980.

Jensen, Marjane, and Beck, Michael D. "Gender Balance Analysis of the Metropolitan Achievement Tests, 1978 Edition." Paper presented at the meeting of the National Council on Measurement in Education, Toronto, Canada, 28 March, 1978.

Linn, Robert L. "Fair Test Use in Selection." *Review of Educational Research* 43 (1973):139–161.

————. "In Search of Fair Selection Procedures." *Journal of Educational Measurement* 13 (1976):53–58.

Lockheed, Marlaine E. "Sex Bias in Educational Testing: A Sociologist's Perspective." Paper presented at the International Symposium on Educational Testing, The Hague, Netherlands, July 1973. Princeton, N.J.: Educational Testing Service, 1974.

Lord, Frederick M. "Practical Applications of Item Characteristic Curve Theory." ETS Research Memorandum 77–3. Princeton, N.J.: Educational Testing Service, 1977.

Milton, G.A. "Sex Differences in Problem Solving as a Function of Role Appropriateness of the Problem Content." *Psychological Reports* 5 (1959):705–708.

Petersen, N.S., and Novick, M.R. "An Evaluation of Some Models for Culture-fair Selection." *Journal of Educational Measurement* 13 (1976):3–29.

Quirk, Thomas J., and Medley, Donald M. "Race and Subject-Matter Influences on Performance on General Education Items of the National Teacher Examinations." ETS Research Bulletin 72–43. Princeton, N.J.: Educational Testing Service, 1972.

Scheuneman, Janice D. "A Method of Assessing Bias in Test Items." *Journal of Educational Measurement* 16 (1979):143–152.

Seashore, Harold G. "Women are More Predictable than Men." *Journal of Counseling Psychology* 9 (1962):261–270.

Stern, June. "College Board Item Bias Study of the Scholastic Aptitude Test and the Test of Standard Written English Form XSA 2/E4." ETS Statistical Report 78–56. Princeton, N.J.: Educational Testing Service, June 1978.

Strassberg-Rosenberg, Barbara, and Donlon, Thomas F. "Content Influences on Sex Differences in Performance on Aptitude Tests." Paper presented at the meeting of the National Council on Measurement in Education, Toronto, Canada, 28 March 1975.

Thorndike, Robert L. "Concepts of Culture-fairness." *Journal of Educational Measurement* 8 (1971):63–70.

Tittle, Carole K. "Women and Educational Testing: A Selective Review of the Research Literature and Testing Practices." New York: The Ford Foundation Division of Education and Research, 1974.

Tittle, Carole, K.; McCarthy, Karen; and Steckler, Jane F. "Women and Educational Testing." Princeton, N.J.: Educational Testing Service, 1974.

Wheeler, Patricia, and Harris, Abigail. "Comparison of Male and Female Performance on the ATP Physics Test," College Board Report 81–4. New York: The College Board, 1981.

Wild, Cheryl L. "Statistical Issues Raised by Title IX Requirements on Admission Procedures." *Journal of National Association of Women Deans, Administrators, and Counselors* 40 (1977):53–56.

Wild, Cheryl, and Durso, Robin. "Effect and Increased Test-taking Time on Test Scores by Ethnic Group, Age, and Sex." In *Psychometrics for Educational Debates*. ed. L.J. Th. Van derKamp, D.N.M. deGruitjer and W.F. Languak. New York: Wiley, 1980.

Wild, Cheryl, and Dwyer, Carol A. "Sex Bias in Selection." ETS Research Memorandum 78-1. Princeton, N.J.: Educational Testing Service, 1978.

Wright, B.D.: Mead, R.J.; and Draba, R.E. "Detecting and Correcting Test Item Bias with a Logistic Response Model." Research Monograph no. 22. Chicago: University of Chicago, Department of Education Statistical Laboratory, 1976.

6

Sex Differences in the Significance of Economic Resources for Choosing and Attending a College

Rachel A. Rosenfeld and
James C. Hearn

Statement of the Problem

In the past few years, the historic gaps between men and women in attending college have steadily narrowed and in some cases disappeared (see Heyns and Bird, chapter 3 in this volume for a description of these changes). Substantial differences, however, still exist with respect to the *particulars* of college choices. Women trail men in their rates of full-time enrollment and enrollment in private institutions (National Center for Education Statistics 1979) and in their rates of enrollment in four-year as opposed to two-year institutions (National Center for Education Statistics 1980; Astin 1978). In addition, there is evidence that men are slightly more likely than women to enroll in higher cost, larger, more selective, and farther-from-home institutions (Astin 1978; National Center for Education Statistics 1980).

These findings suggest that it is now more important to analyze the determinants and implications of gender differences in specific college choices than to focus an analysis solely on differences in the decision whether to attend college at all. This issue of choice is relevant even beyond college to the extent that the degree, experiences, and prestige provided by one's educational institution affect one's later educational and occupational opportunity and attainment. Some research on this subject has suggested that the effects of specific college characteristics on eventual success are trivial or nonexistent (see Alwin 1974; Trusheim and Crouse 1980), but there is also a substantial research literature suggestive of such effects in highly specified models (see Weisbrod and Karpoff 1968; Solmon 1975; Wachtel 1975; Tinto 1980; Anderson 1981). If people's educational and occupational careers consist of a sequence of moves through a series of positions, each offering a given probability of further educational or occupa-

We would like to thank the Spencer Foundation, American College Testing Program, National Opinion Research Center, and NIMH grant 5-732 MH 15163-02 for support of this research; Pamela Perun for her comments; Michael Tierney and Alexander Astin for their suggestions with respect to use of the data; and Lorayn Olson for her assistance in processing the data.

tional advancement within a given time frame, then evidence that women are making educational choices that are less articulated with future advancement opportunities than the choices of men (for example, two-year colleges, nonprestigious institutions) and less productive of swift, orderly advancement (for example, part-time enrollment status) indicates a need for research on sex differences in the college-choice process, both to explain these choices and as background for understanding gender inequality in later attainment.

One possible explanation for sex differences in institutional-choice patterns is a disparity between men and women in the economic resources available for financing postsecondary education. Financial support can come from several sources: (1) from the student and his or her parents come the various elements of the family contribution including parents' resources, student employment (summer or part time), and student savings; and (2) from the school and various other private and public sources come the elements of the aid package including college work-study employment, private loans, state or federally subsidized loans, academic-scholarship grants, and need-based grants (private, state, or federal). Our focus in this chapter is on the role played by these financial factors at various stages in the college-choice process. (Hanson and Litten discuss this process in chapter 4). After an overview of the nature of the choice process by sex, we address empirically three central questions: (1) Are there sex differences in the role of parents' economic resources in the initial stages of the college-choice process? (2) Do men and women react differently in their final college choice to various kinds of financing arrangements? (3) Do women receive inferior financial-aid packages compared with those of men?

In explaining initial choices, we pay particular attention to findings in other research that socioeconomic background plays a larger role in the educational aspirations and attainment of girls whereas boys, ability is relatively more important (Sewell and Shah 1967; Alexander and Eckland 1974; Hout and Morgan 1975; Rosen and Aneshensel 1978). It may well be that these findings, as they relate to postsecondary attendance, result not only from more traditional early sex-role stereotyping in the lower socioeconomic strata but also from significant economic constraints on high-school girls, for example, greater willingness of parents to fund males' higher-education aspirations, awareness on the part of high-school girls of their lower part-time and vacation job earnings, and the fears of girls from lower-income families that less postsecondary financial aid will be available to them than to boys. Evidence supplied by Litten, Jahoda, and Morris (1980), Haven and Horch (1972), Rossi and Calderwood (1973), and Abramson (1975) suggest that these are indeed reasonable hypotheses.

These findings may apply to the specific college-choice process as well as to the *general* attainment process. We therefore assess here sex differences in the role of socioeconomic background in constraining the kinds of colleges chosen by males and females. Our aim is to determine whether young women in their college choices are more burdened by their socioeconomic background than young men. If so, this would provide an explanation for the aforementioned sex differences in favor of boys in the kinds of institutions attended.

In the analysis of the second central question, we carry over these same themes into our analysis of the choice of a college to attend from among several at which one has been accepted. Here, we hypothesize that, for the reasons just cited, women will be more sensitive than men to the financial characteristics associated with each favored institution, such as costs and grants-in-aid. Two sources of indirect evidence supporting this hypothesis are students' attitudinal reports of the factors behind their college-going behaviors and empirical analyses of the relationships between choice behaviors, student characteristics, environments, and institutional characteristics. Freshmen women have historically been more likely than freshmen men to report concerns about financing their higher education.[1] With respect to actual behavior, Carroll (1977) found women's enrollment to be more responsive than men's to levels of grant awards; Bishop (1977) found larger effects on college attendance for women than men for tuition, fees, travel, and room and board expenses; and Dresch and Waldenberg (1978) found women more sensitive to economic and labor-market conditions in their attendance decisions.

In the third part of the analysis, we examine whether there is a difference in the kinds of aid packages presented to males and females at the institutions they have chosen to attend. This analysis may be viewed as examining the borderline between college choice and the reality of college attendance itself, since students are usually only partly aware of their aid packages when they make their final choices between institutions, becoming fully informed only in the weeks or days immediately preceding or following their arrival on campus (Willett 1976). Past research on aid packaging has found women relying more on their parents' financial contributions than men and receiving somewhat less financial aid (Haven and Horch 1972; Bob 1977; Davis 1977). A more recent study for the Department of Education (Deane, Miller, and Dellefield 1980) revealed no major differences in aid distributions for men and women, suggesting a trend toward equity that may be indirectly upheld by Barbara Heyns' finding that college men and women's reported rates of financial dependence on parental contributions apparently have become effectively equal after years of greater dependence being reported by women.[2] Unfortunately, none of this research has fully answered the questions of whether men and women from similar socioeconomic and educational backgrounds in similar institutional settings are receiving similar financial-aid packages. The intent of our third analysis is to address that issue more directly.

In examining these three central issues, we have taken the research traditions comprehensively reviewed by Hanson and Litten in chapter 4 of this book as a starting point. These analysts urge in the conclusion of their overview of college-choice research that high priority be given to uncovering factors encouraging women to apply to and attend high-quality institutions in numbers proportionate to their ability, the goal being "equality of the sexes in achieving their potential for higher education." The objective of the research reported in this chapter is to focus on one factor possibly affecting whether women reach their potential, that of the availability of economic resources.

Data

The present study employed "the SISFAP-A 11th–12th Grade Freshmen Longitudinal File," which consists of data for a nationally representative group of 1975 college freshmen who had (1) taken the Preliminary Scholastic Aptitude Test (PSAT) as high-school juniors in 1973–1974, (2) taken the American College Testing Program Assessment (ACT) or the Scholastic Aptitude Test (SAT) as high-school seniors in 1974–1975, and (3) completed the Cooperative Institutional Research Program (CIRP) survey instrument as college freshmen in the fall of 1975. Individual student case data from these three sources were matched by Alexander Astin and his associates at the Higher Education Research Institute. Their methods of data gathering, the SISFAP-A data set itself, and the results of their subsequent study of college-choice processes are described in detail in Astin (1978).

SISFAP-A is the most recent nationally representative longitudinal data base to include extensive data on student ability, student characteristics other than ability, and institutional characteristics other than type and control.[3] It may have some sample bias toward more knowledgeable, better-prepared students, because of the requirement that students in the sample by PSAT- and ACT- or SAT-takers. In some schools, *all* students, regardless of future plans, are required to take the PSAT, whereas in others only the most motivated students (such as those seeking National Merit Scholarships) take it. Overall, of all entering 1975 freshmen, 67.4 percent of the men and 68.5 percent of the women had taken the PSAT; 46.5 percent of the men and 48.6 percent of the women had taken the ACT; and 69.2 percent and 72.4 percent of the men and women had taken the SAT (Astin, King, and Richardson 1975). Further, results from analysis of our data are not generalizable to the increasing numbers of students entering college as adults with full-time work and family experience behind them (National Center for Education Statistics 1980). Nevertheless, these college-choice data are a unique resource not only because of their comprehensive, longitudinal nature but also because of their timing: it was in 1975 that among the eighteen and nineteen-year-old population women for the first time exceeded men in rates of college enrollment (see Heyns and Bird in chapter 3 of this book).

For our secondary analysis of the SISFAP-A data, we drew a random sample of 2978 men and 3150 women from the over 115,000 cases in the data base. For the descriptive analyses presented here, Astin's (1978) across-students, across-institutions weighting procedure was employed to counter the underrepresentation problems previously mentioned. These weights, however, were available for only a subset of the schools in the sample. The weighted *N*s were deflated to the true sample size for performing the significance tests for the descriptive data. For the multivariate, correlational elements of the analysis, weights were not employed, since heavily weighted outlier cases could seriously limit the validity of the results. Because of the missing value considerations, the actual sample sizes vary somewhat across the descriptive and multivariate analyses.

College Choice and Student and Family Characteristics

All the students in our sample had taken the PSAT test in the eleventh grade. Although they might not yet have decided on a particular college— or even decided for sure they would go in school after high school— they at least were making some initial moves toward applying for college. In the eleventh grade, the students probably had only vague ideas, if any, about chances that a particular institution would choose them and about the chances that they would receive financial aid. Their early choices would be made in the context of what they knew about themselves and their parents' attitudes and financial situation. As Tierney (1980, p. 17) puts it, "The initial 'screening' of colleges takes place long before students know whether or not they have been admitted, much less the amount of financial aid they might be offered. Thus, most federal and state policies which are oriented toward providing equality of opportunity . . . are not even relevant at this stage. . . ." In this section we give an overview of the choice process for men and women and then look at the ways in which student and family characteristics affect the nature of the students' early choices in comparison with the nature of the schools they actually enter in 1975.

General research on the college-choice process has concluded that most students finally apply to only a small number of colleges, often only one (Jackson 1977, 1978). Sending out an application, however, does not necessarily mean that other schools were not considered. By the middle of twelfth grade, a student may have already sifted through various matches of his or her abilities and needs and institutions' offerings and criteria (Russick and Olson 1976). Here we can look at students' choices as early as eleventh grade, when some students are just beginning to sift through their options.

Table 6–1 shows the number of colleges that students listed when taking the PSAT (with a maximum of two), the number of colleges to which they had their SAT or ACT scores sent, and the number of schools other than the one attended to which they actually applied. The women are more likely than the men to have some choice in the eleventh grade (and in fact list more choices than men), but to have sent their scores and to have submitted applications to fewer schools (see also Hanson and Litten in chapter 4 of this book for a discussion of other findings suggesting that women narrow their choices faster than men). Notice that for both men and women, the most frequent number of ACT-SAT scores sent out is three. A student is allowed to send out up to three sets of scores free. On additional scores there is a small charge. It could be that women (and their families) are less ready to incur the extra fee, although only around 10 percent of either sex send out more than three scores, and the difference by sex is small. But regressions on the numbers of schools listed or applications sent (tables not shown) did not support this hypothesis.

Not only do women seem to have made choices earlier and from a smaller choice set than men (at least after eleventh grade), but also their choices seem to be more realistic. In looking at the same data from which we took our sample, Astin (1978, p. 44) notes that ''men are somewhat less successful than women in implementing their early choices. . . .'' In our subsample of the data, 39.9 percent of the women and 37.4 percent of the men were also accepted at the college they preferred as a first alternative to the one they entered, and 76.4 percent of the women as compared with 74.4 percent of the men were attending their first-choice college in 1975. These differences, however, are not statistically significant.

Hanson and Litten (chapter 4) and Heyns and Bird (chapter 3), among others, have commented upon the differences in the types of colleges women and men attend at the end of this choice process. In this chapter, we look at the types of schools women and men are considering even before they make their decisions to enter a particular school. If women experience greater economic constraints in choosing a college, we would expect women to choose college options that cost less—less selective, two year rather than four year, closer to home, and with lower tuition and fees. In table 6–2 the means for various aspects of first-choice schools in eleventh and twelfth grade are shown for men and women, as well as the characteristics of the schools people actually attended.

As table 6–2 shows, women tend from eleventh grade on to choose schools that are less selective (Astin and Henson 1977), closer to home, two year rather than four year, private and small rather than public and big. At

Table 6–1
Overview of Choice Process

	Number of Schools					
	0	1	2	3	4 or More	Total N
Number of schools listed on PSAT, eleventh grade (%)						
Men	46.8	17.3	35.9**			2,221
Women	39.1	16.5	44.4			2,197
Number of schools listed on SAT-ACT, twelfth grade (%)						
Men	14.2	6.8	13.7	52.7	12.6**	2,221
Women	14.6	8.3	19.4	47.5	10.2	2,197
Number of other colleges to which applied (%)						
Men	40.0	19.4	16.4	12.7	11.5**	2,221
Women	44.1	22.0	18.3	7.5	8.0	2,197
Choice of college attending in 1975	First	Second	Less than second			
Total percentages						
Men	74.4	18.9	6.7			2,221
Women	76.4	13.1	5.5			2,197

**Distributions different by sex at $p < .01$.

Table 6–2
**Mean Characteristics of Women's and Men's College Choices, Eleventh Grade—
1975 College Entry**

Characteristic	Eleventh Grade First Choice[a]	Twelfth Grade First Choice	1975 College Entry
Tuition and fees[b]			
Women	107.93	108.40	87.29
	(84.87)	(80.17)	(71.32)
Men	105.31	104.17	87.42
	(89.17)	(84.27)	(69.80)
Selectivity[c]			
Women	99.18**	98.99**	94.35**
	(13.01)	(12.41)	(12.77)
Men	104.14	101.92	94.46
	(14.47)	(13.35)	(13.90)
Distance from home[d]			
Women	209.04	181.30**	148.12
	(412.45)	(402.15)	(330.95)
Men	236.09	224.63	159.68
	(396.69)	(420.29)	(314.58)
Two-year—four-year—percentage four-year			
Women	89.4	84.2	63.3
Men	90.5	86.4	61.3
Public/private—percentage public			
Women	64.5**	62.7**	75.2
Men	69.7	68.3	77.0
Size[e]			
Women	6.69**	6.23**	5.96
	(1.68)	(1.86)	(1.81)
Men	6.90	6.62	6.01
	(1.60)	(1.76)	(1.82)

Note: Standard deviations in parentheses.

**Means different by sex at $p < .01$.

[a]Data are based only on cases with some choice in a given year.

[b]Tuition and fees are divided by 10 and rounded to three digits: $100 = $1,000.

[c]Selectivity is average SAT (verbal + math) score for entering students. ACT composites were converted into SAT scores. These averages are divided by 10.

[d]Distance is calculated from home and school zip codes. Where a home zip code was missing, this variable has no value.

[e]Size is coded as enrollment: less than 250 = 1; 250–499 = 2; 500–999 = 3; 1,000–1,499 = 4; 1,500–1,999 = 5; 2,000–4,999 = 6; 5,000–9,999 = 7; 10,000–19,999 = 8; 20,000 or more = 9.

the same time, they are not selecting schools with lower tuition and fees. The comparisons here differ somewhat from those of Heyns and Bird and others (for example, Frankel and Gerald 1980), probably because of the restriction of this sample to traditional students who were preparing for college as early as the eleventh grade.[4] Overall, the differences between men and women seem to decrease over time. By the time these students were entering college, the only significant difference between the men and the women was in the selectivity of the school attended. These averages across time, of course, are based only on those cases where a person had some choice at a given stage, and there were differences by sex in the timing and number of choices. But even where men and women with choices in both eleventh and twelfth grade were compared (not shown), the pattern present in table 6-2 persists—women and men seem to lower their expectations over time as far as the type of school they wish to attend, and the divergence between men and women decreases. Women who expressed choices in both eleventh and twelfth grade entered schools that differed significantly from those of men in their distance from home as well as in their selectivity.

Looking at average characteristics of college choices by sex does not illuminate the process behind these choices. We suspect that the variables accounting for the type of school selected have different relative importance for women than for men. A general finding with respect to college entrance is that ability is relatively more important than family background for men as compared with women (Sewell and Shah 1967; Alexander and Eckland 1974; Thomas, Alexander, and Eckland 1979). In using data on a cohort of freshmen older than ours, Karabel and Astin (1975) found that sex differences in selectivity of college entered persisted even after controlling for ability and family background, but they did not pursue the differences by sex in the effects of these variables. Other research suggests that there are differences by sex in the effects of ability and socioeconomic status (SES) on type of college attended, similar to those on college attendance. Alexander and Eckland (1977, p. 181), using data from a longitudinal study of people first surveyed as high-school sophomores in 1955 found "individual status origins are much more strongly implicated in the sorting of women among colleges than is the case with men." Further, although academic class standing was a significant predictor of selectivity of college for both men and women, it had a stronger effect for men.

The greater importance of family resources for women suggests that indeed their family's financial situation (as well as perhaps general attitudes toward the education of women that vary with income) is more crucial for whether and where they will go to school. Here we are able to see how family socioeconomic backgound and student characteristics affect the types of schools chosen by men and women as they move through high school. We will look at how these two sets of variables predict over time two aspects of a college choice: tuition and fees, and selectivity. These two characteristics are intercorrelated about .5, but represent different dimensions of an institution. Tuition and fees are the most obvious economic aspect—what it costs to attend without financial aid. Selectivity roughly represents the intellectual climate of a school. It is a variable that probably has been most studied with respect to its later returns in the form of income and occupational status (Solmon 1975; Alexander and Eckland 1977, Trusheim and Crouse 1980). The results of these regressions are shown in tables 6-3 and 6-4. Distance is also important, potentially modifying the economic aspect of college attendance: a school's distance from home can modify costs if the student is able to save on room and board by living at home. We also ran regressions on distance, but we do not show these results since the patterns are basically the same with respect to the other variables— selectivity and tuition and fees—and the amount of variance explained very low (2-6 percent).[5]

For both men and women, socioeconomic background (as measured by race, parental income, mother's education, father's education, and number of dependent siblings) adds relatively small absolute additional explained variance once measures of ability and aspirations [grade-point average (GPA), test scores, highest degree planned] have been included. Overall, one is able to predict the selectivity and the tuition and fees of a student's choice more fully at the time they actually enter college than earlier. The differences by sex in the two tables are consistent with earlier findings by Alexander and Eckland (1977) with respect to the selectivity of the colleges chosen by an earlier cohort of freshmen, although perhaps less strong. Family-background variables explain somewhat greater additional variance for women than for men, and a greater range of the socioeconomic background variables are significant (net of all other variables in the equation) for explaining women's as compared with men's choices. For both men and women, parental income and race are significant in explaining selectivity, but after the eleventh grade, parental education is more important for women. With respect to tuition and fees, parents' education and race, as well as income, are important especially for women's early choices, whereas the effects of race are larger for women than men in predicting the tuition and fees at the college they entered in 1975. Socioeconomic background seems more important for the choices of women than for men, although this is more than simply an income effect. As Litten and Hanson suggest, the greater financial dependence of women on their parents may make them more subject to the influence of the parents' values and aspirations for them.

Choosing between Schools at Which Accepted

The last section examined the overall progression of college choices and how family and student characteristics differed by sex in their relative im-

Table 6-3
Effects of Student Characteristics and Family Background on Tuition and Fees of Students' Choice, Eleventh Grade, College Attendance, by Sex
(metric coefficients, standard errors in parentheses)

	Eleventh Grade First Choice		Twelfth Grade First Choice		School Entered, 1975	
	Women	*Men*	*Women*	*Men*	*Women*	*Men*
GPA[a]	-4.12	-.12	-3.12	-2.88	-.05	1.78
	(2.95)	(3.40)	(2.28)	(2.31)	(1.47)	(1.49)
Average Test Score[b]	1.66**	1.19**	2.06**	2.06**	2.07**	1.51**
	(.32)	(.37)	(.26)	(.27)	(.24)	(.25)
Highest degree planned[c]	15.99**	30.32**	17.54**	22.04**	19.09**	17.82**
	(4.87)	(5.94)	(3.95)	(4.50)	(3.58)	(4.29)
Race[d]	9.04	-10.11	16.28**	5.42	22.69**	15.89
	(9.00)	(13.80)	(7.62)	(10.57)	(6.89)	(9.72)
Parents' income[e]	.81**	.30	.50*	.56*	.91**	.83**
	(.29)	(.34)	(.23)	(.27)	(.13)	(.15)
Mother's education[f]	3.08	-1.20	11.42**	7.56	7.11	5.85
	(5.19)	(6.06)	(4.21)	(4.75)	(3.80)	(4.22)
Father's education[f]	16.66**	8.98	11.07**	-.68	3.75	-.10
	(5.65)	(6.55)	(4.55)	(5.17)	(4.03)	(4.51)
Dependent siblings[g]	-.48	1.45	1.07	1.47	-.26	-.05
	(1.55)	(1.80)	(1.22)	(1.40)	(1.10)	(1.24)
Constant	-12.44	.94	-50.80	-29.10	-62.91	-36.65
R^2						
Total equation	.08	.06	.09	.07	.11	.08

Table 6-3 continued

	Eleventh Grade First Choice		Twelfth Grade First Choice		School Entered, 1975	
	Women	*Men*	*Women*	*Men*	*Women*	*Men*
R^2 continued With only student variables.	.05	.05	.07	.07	.08	.06
N	1,371	1,216	1,961	1,914	2,282	2,194

*.01 ≤ p < .05.

**p < .01.

[a]GPA: For 1975 this is average high-school grades, 8 = A, A+; 7 = A−; 6 = B+; 5 = B; 4 = B−; 3 = C+; 2 = C; 1 = D. For twelfth grade it is coded 7 = 3.5–4.0; 6 = 3.0–3.4; 5 = 2.5–2.9; 4 = 2.0–2.4; 3 = 1.5–1.9; 2 = 1.0–1.4; 1 = 0.5–0.9. For eleventh grade it is 7 = A; 6 = A−, B+; 5 = B; 4 = B−; 3 = C; 2 = C−, D; 1 = 0.

Test score: For 1975 and twelfth grade, this is average SAT verbal and math score (or ACT scores converted to SAT), divided by 10; for eleventh grade, this is average verbal and math PSAT score, divided by 10.

[c]Highest degree planned: For 1975, highest degree indicated on Entering Freshmen Questionnaire; for twelfth grade, SAT or ACT response; for eleventh grade, twelfth grade plans: 1 = B.A. or less; 2 = more than a B.A.

[d]Race: 2 = black; 1 = nonblack, from 1975 questionnaire.

[e]Parents' income: in 1,000s, coded at midpoints of categories: For 1975, from the entering freshmen questionnaire, 1.5, 3.5, 5.0, 7.0, 9.0, 11.2, 13.8, 17.5, 22.5, 27.5, 32.5, 37.5, 45.0, and 60.0; for eleventh and twelfth grades, from SAT or ACT questionnaire, 1.5, 4.5, 6.75, 8.25, 10.5, 13.5, 17.5, 30.0.

[f]Parents' education: From the 1975 questionnaire, 1 = no college education; 2 = some college.

[g]Number of brothers and sisters dependent on parents (SAT) or under 21 (ACT): 1 = none; 2 = 1; 3 = 2; 4 = 3; 5 = 4; 6 = 5; 7 = 6+.

Table 6-4
Effects of Student Characteristics and Family Background on Selectivity of Students' Choice, Eleventh Grade, College Attendance, by Sex
(metric coefficients, standard error in parentheses)

	Eleventh Grade First Choice		Twelfth Grade First Choice		School Entered, 1975	
	Women	*Men*	*Women*	*Men*	*Women*	*Men*
GPA[a]	.28	1.09*	.39	1.35**	.73**	1.15**
	(.42)	(.45)	(.31)	(.29)	(.20)	(.18)
Average test score[b]	.36**	.29**	.51**	.48**	.54**	.56**
	(.04)	(.05)	(.04)	(.03)	(.03)	(.03)
Highest degree planned[c]	3.01**	3.82**	3.59**	2.80**	3.22**	2.37**
	(.69)	(.79)	(.55)	(.57)	(.48)	(.52)
Race[d]	-7.18**	-7.19**	-5.62**	-4.72**	-4.96**	-5.90**
	(1.28)	(1.83)	(1.05)	(1.35)	(.92)	(1.18)
Parents' income[e]	.19**	.21**	.15**	.13**	.10**	.12**
	(.04)	(.05)	(.03)	(.03)	(.02)	(.02)
Mother's education[f]	1.88*	.27	2.42**	1.49*	1.57*	.96
	(.74)	(.80)	(.58)	(.60)	(.51)	(.51)
Father's education[f]	.73	1.89*	.66	1.25	1.49*	.78
	(.81)	(.87)	(.63)	(.66)	(.06)	(.55)
Dependent siblings[g]	-.13	.37	-.13	-.01	.03	-.04
	(.22)	(.24)	(.17)	(.18)	(.18)	(.15)
Constant	80.67	79.95	69.81	67.80	63.97	65.54
R^2						
Total equation	.22	.19	.28	.28	.33	.37
With only student characteristics	.16	.14	.23	.25	.29	.33
N	1,371	1,216	1,961	1,914	2,282	2,194

*.01 < p < .05.
**p < .01.
[a-g]See notes to table 6-3.

portance in affecting choice of type of school. In this section, we consider
the situation where at least two schools have accepted a student and possibly
made offers of financial aid. How then does a student react to the different
offers? What discriminates between the school a student eventually attends
and the others that accepted him or her? In particular, what part do tuition
and fees and an offer of financial aid play, and does this role differ for
women and men? We expect cost of the school and its aid offer to make a
difference for both men and women (Jackson 1977; Davis and van Dusen
1978; Hyde 1978; Nolfi et al. 1978; Tierney 1979) but to have somewhat
more importance for women than for men (Bishop 1977; Carroll 1977).

The attitudes expressed by our sample do suggest that women are more
sensitive to the financial aspects of higher education. Women have greater
concern than men about financing their education: for 16.7 percent of the
women this is a major concern, whereas this is true for only 10.3 percent of
the men. For 33.0 percent of the women as compared with 41 percent of the
men there is no concern about financing their education. Men may have
more backup resources—in the form of wages for summer and part-time
school-year work, than do women. Indeed, the men more than the women
plan to rely on their own resources for financing their education and so may
be less responsive to a particular college's offer. For example, almost 25
percent of the men but less than 15 percent of the women expected to earn
$500 or over from part-time work during the 1975 school year. In the
reasons men and women give for choosing their college on the 1975 questionnaire, there is no significant difference by sex in the importance of an
offer of financial aid. But more women (25.4 percent) as compared with
men (22.4 percent) said low tuition was very important. Women were also
more likely than men to say that being able to live at home was very important (11.3 percent versus 9.5 percent), another reason that is potentially
economic. At the same time, women were more likely than men to give the
reputation of the school as very important for their choice (49.2 percent versus 46.1 percent). By examining actual choices in a multivariate framework,
it is possible to look more closely at the relative importance of these aspects
of the schools between which choice will be made.

This analysis is shown in table 6–5, where the unit of analysis is the
university or college. Students were asked in the 1975 freshman questionnaire to which colleges, other than the one they were entering, they had applied for admission and whether they were accepted there. Every student
who was accepted by at least one other school contributes two sets of observations to the data for the analysis in this section: that for the school he or
she actually entered in 1975 (its tuition and fees, financial aid offer, its
distance from home, its selectivity, and so forth) and that for the first alternative (its tuition and fees, financial-aid offer, and so forth). The dependent
variable is thus whether a school is the one entered or not.

Table 6-5
Choosing between College Offers, by Sex
(metric coefficients, standard errors in parentheses)

University Characteristics	Choices of Women		Choices of Men	
	(a)	*(b)*	*(a)*	*(b)*
Amount of financial aid offered:				
Grants	.00001**	.00001**	.00008**	.00008**
	(.00001)	(.00001)	(.00001)	(.00001)
Loans	.0002**	.0002**	.00016**	.00016**
	(.00002)	(.00002)	(.00002)	(.00002)
Student work study	.0002**	.0002**	.00011**	.0001*
	(.00006)	(.00006)	(.00005)	(.00005)
Tuition and fees (divided by 10)		−.0009**	−.0014**	−.0014**
		(.0003)	(.0003)	(.0003)
Selectivity (divided by 10)		.003**	.004**	.005**
		(.001)	(.0010)	(.001)
Distance from home		−.00005	−.00005**	−.00005*
		(.00003)	(.0002)	(.00002)
Public (= 1)/ private (=2)		.15**	.20**	.17**
		(.05)	(.048)	(.053)
Two-year (= 1)/ four-year (= 2)		.08	.10**	.08
		(.04)	(.045)	(.05)
Student-faculty ratio[a]		−.002	−.02**	−.02*
		(.007)	(.005)	(.007)
Size of school[b]		.008		−.01
		(.009)		(.009)
Percentage women enrolled[c]		.02**		.010
		(.008)		(.010)
Constant	.43	−.19	−.07	−.06
R^2	.088	.095	.075	.076
N		2,613		2,419

Note: Dependent variable = 1 if the school was the one entered in 1975, 0 if it was the student's first preferred alternative and the student had been accepted there.

*.01 < p ≤ .05.

**p < .01.

[a]Student-faculty ratio: 1 = less than 10 to 1; 2 = 10–12 to 1; 3 = 13–15 to 1; 4 = 16–18 to 1; 5 = 19–21 to 1; 6 = 22–24 to 1; 7 = 25–27 to 1; 8 = 28–30 to 1; 9 = more than 30 to 1.

[b]Size: 1 = less than 250 students; 2 = 250–499; 3 = 500–999; 4 = 1,000–1,499; 5 = 1,500–1,999; 6 = 2,000–4,999; 7 = 5,000–9,999; 8 = 10,000–19,999; 9 = greater than 19,999.

[c]Percentage women: 1 = 0; 2 = 1–9; 3 = 10–24; 4 = 25–44; 5 = 45–54; 6 = 55–74; 7 = 75–90; 8 = 91–99; 9 = 100.

The results in table 6–5 are broadly consistent with other research: higher financial-aid offers increase the likelihood that a student will attend a given college and higher tuition and fees, all things being equal, decrease the likelihood of matriculation. The full equations for women and men (shown in the columns labeled *(b)* look very similar. Indeed, the coefficients for the various kinds of aid do not differ significantly by sex, whereas the coefficient for tuition and fees has a significantly greater depressing effect on men's choice. In looking at the full model, however, the contribution of each variable to predicting the dependent variable net of *all* the other variables in the equation must be evaluated. Another way to approach the problem of predicting which school a student will choose is by finding the most parsimonious model, by trying to find a "best" model. This can be done by step-wise regression. In column *(a)* the results are presented from a forward-inclusion procedure, where variables are added one at a time, and at each step the variable explaining the greatest amount of variance left unexplained by the previously included variables is entered.[6] When variables are brought in only until the last variable is significant at maximum at the .05 level, the equation for women includes *only* the aid variables, whereas the equation for men includes a much greater range of institutional variables—financial aid is offered and tuition and fees, but also student-faculty ratio, selectivity, and so forth. In the context of this analysis, then, an offer of financial aid is more critical for the choices women make between schools. These results suggest an extension of earlier results on the timing of men and women's choices. It may be that women make an earlier choice, weighing in *these* choices educational environment as well as cost (as conditioned by their ability and SES), whereas men wait to narrow their choice set using noneconomic criteria until much later in the choice process.

Sex Differences in the Distribution and Packaging of Financial Aid

This section examines in more detail the type of aid package given to students by the schools they actually enter. The type of aid package can have an effect on whether a student *continues* in college. As was discussed previously, research to date has not systematically addressed the question of whether men and women from similar backgrounds in similar institutions receive similar financial-aid awards and packages. Instead, the focus has been on the overall distribution of aid for men and women, regardless of their own characteristics and those of the institutions they choose. This section begins with descriptive findings of the kind frequently presented in previous analyses of aid equity, then presents findings on aid distribution that are based on more extensive controls for the differing backgrounds and institutional choices of men and women.

Table 6-6 presents the descriptive data on the distribution of financial aid among males and females. The results are consistent with recent research finding no difference in grant allotments to men and women (Deane et al. 1980), but they suggest women may be somewhat more likely to finance their education by loans than men. The descriptive results also suggest women may rely more on work-study aid than men in their aid packages, but when they do receive work-study aid, men get the higher-paying jobs.

Table 6-6 also reveals that the women in our sample as a whole received significantly more aid than the men. Other analysis we undertook found, in keeping with earlier studies, that they expected greater parental contributions than men. On the surface, these two findings seem to indicate a rather rosy picture for college women, but it should be remembered that women's advantage in aid outlays tended to come in the form of claims on future earnings rather than claims on their time as undergraduates (that is, in loans rather than work-study jobs). To the extent that work-study programs are educationally rewarding, this result seems to suggest some delayed-reaction inequity in aid disbursements: after college, women face not only lower earnings futures but also higher debt burdens.[7]

The conclusions derived from table 6-6 are valid insofar as they refer to the postsecondary financing patterns of men and women as a whole. The issue of women receiving more and greater college loans than men is indeed a legitimate social concern. But for a number of reasons, conclusions about sex discrimination based on these data alone must be very tentative. Although men and women in our sample differed significantly in neither parental income nor the costs of the institutions they attended, we did find enough sex differences in attendance patterns and individual characteristics to suggest caution in interpreting the purely descriptive data of table 6-6. Until one examines the distribution of aid while holding constant the interrelationships in institutional choices among ability, costs, socioeconomic background, and other factors, it is not justifiable to speak of inequities.

Accordingly, we ran multiple regressions using a wide range of student and institutional characteristics to predict (1) parental contribution, (2) the size of the total aid package, (3) the amount of grants, (4) the nonburdening proportion of the aid package (that is, the proportion in grants), (5) the amount of loans, and (6) the returnable portion of the aid package (that is, the proportion taken up by loans). For the first two dependent variables, we ran regressions for all students and for aided students alone, while in the other regressions only aided students were examined. Included as independent variables were all variables legitimately affecting aid distribution (for example, parental income, tuition and fees, dependency status, ability), plus two variables reflecting potential discrimination (sex and race).

Sex was included as an independent variable in these regressions, rather than used as a basis for separating the sample, because aid distribution is essentially a treatment rather than a complex choice process. In other words, our interest here is not in how the two sexes differ in *weighting* various factors in deciding on an institution, but rather in *whether or not* institutional-aid officers and parents consider sex in and of itself as a uniquely relevant factor in dispersing funds for postsecondary attendance.

Table 6-7 presents the results of the financing regressions. The results for parental contribution suggest that parents do indeed contribute more to a daughter's postsecondary education than to a son's, just as suggested by the descriptive analysis, even under similar institutional and personal conditions. This pattern supports much of the literature reviewed earlier and is probably partially due to a perception of parents that college women earn less during summers than men and thus need more parental support to live as comfortable as college men. Further, greater proportions of the men in our samples state that they are financially independent. Higher parental contributions, however, may also be a response to underawarding of women by aid officers and need-analysis systems: the results of the total aid regression for aided students suggest the size of the aid package of women receiving aid tends to be smaller than that of similarly situated men. In addition, regressions for the amount of grant aid and the amount of loan aid showed women receiving less such aid than similarly situated men. It is of interest that the proportional analyses for grants and loans revealed no significant sex differences in the composition of the aid packages of men and women, but the significant sex differences in the total and component *amounts* of those packages suggest that greater parental-support patterns may be a necessity for college women.

The contrast between these regression results and the descriptive results is instructive. Earlier, we found women somewhat more likely to get work-study and loan aid than men, less likely to get the higher paying work-study jobs among work-study students, and *overall* getting somewhat more loans, work-study, and total aid than men. The analyses of table 6-7 put these findings in the context of the different backgrounds and institutional choices of men and women. Under similar conditions, women tend to receive *less* total aid than men, *smaller* grant awards, and *smaller* loan awards. These differences are not major, but they are significant, and fit logically with a pattern of women expecting, needing, and receiving greater parental contributions. The contrasts in the two sets of results for this section point to the complexity of the issue of aid inequity. Because of the difficult methodological and philosophical issues involved in addressing this concern (Hyde 1979), straightforward conclusions about aid inequity may be impossible, but our results present sex differences that are suggestive, albeit not incontrovertible or inarguable, evidence of such inequity.[8]

The regression results otherwise presented few surprises. Race was a significant factor in limiting parental contribution and enlarging grant aid,

Table 6-7
Distributions, by Sex, of Financial-Aid Awards

	Mean for Those Receiving This Kind of Aid		Percentage Receiving This Kind of Aid		Mean for All Students		Mean for All Students with Aid	
	Men	Women	Men	Women	Men (N = 2,221)	Women (N = 2,196)	Men (N = 963)	Women (N = 1,014)
Grants	$1,031 N = 815 (950.9)	$1,056 N = 833 (916.3)	37	38	$379 (760.7)	$400 (762.1)	$756 (883.9)	$709 (788.4)
Loans	1,095 N = 331 (845.0)	1,118 N = 397 (747.6)	15	18*	163 (508.4)	202* (534.6)	315 (626.2)	376* (638.9)
Work-study	674 N = 156 (621.8)	567* N = 234 (421.8)	7	11*	47 (238.2)	60 (222.1)	96 (317.2)	127* (266.9)
Total aid	—	—	43	46	589 (1,053.7)	663* (1,058.1)	1,359 (1,191.2)	1,435[a] (1,147.4)

Note: Standard errors in parentheses.

*Difference in means by sex of $p < .05$.

[a]Total aid is larger than the sum of the parts listed here because of other (minor) sources of aid.

Table 6–7
Regression Analysis of Individual Financing Patterns
(standard errors in parentheses)

	Parental Contribution, All Students[a]		Parental Contribution, Aided Students[b]		Size of Total Aid Package, All Students[a]		Size of Total Aid Package, Aided Students[b]	
	Metric Coefficient	*Standardized Coefficient*	*Metric Coefficient*	*Standardized Coefficient*	*Metric Coefficient*	*Standardized Coefficient*	*Metric Coefficient*	*Standardized Coefficient*
Sex	.23	.07 (.04)**	.25	.08 (.05)**	−51.6	−0.02 (30.2)	−175.6	−.07 (47.0)**
Race	−.56	.07 (.08)**	−.36	−.07 (.09)**	533.7	.11 (63.7)**	404.9	.10 (83.0)**
Average test score	.33	.00 (.00)	.49	.00 (.00)	7.9	0.07 (2.0)**	11.5	.10 (3.0)**
GPA	−.48	−.04 (.02)**	−.16	−.01 (.02)	76.0	0.10 (11.6)**	10.5	.01 (19.0)
Full-time status	.80	.00 (.31)	.24	.00 (.46)	143.7	.01 (221.3)	340.5	.01 (405.6)
Residence on campus	.76	.18 (.05)**	.55	.14 (.07)**	281.4	.10 (37.0)**	429.0	.14 (58.5)**
Financial independence	−1.08	−.18 (.07)**	−.75	−.15 (.09)**	284.8	.07 (50.4)**	424.5	.11 (74.5)**

Dependent siblings	−.14	−.12 (.01)**	−.14	−.15 (.02)**	75.	.10 (9.2)**	62.8	.08 (14.1)**
Parents' income	.46	.40 (.00)**	.60	.41 (.00)**	−30.9	−.39 (1.0)**	−26.9	−.23 (2.3)**
Tuition and fees	.52	.28 (.00)**	.36	.21 (.00)**	2.8	.22 (.34)	4.3	.32 (.49)**
Private control	−.36	−.10 (.08)**	−.75	−.02 (.10)	289.4	.13 (58.0)**	169.0	.07 (84.3)*
Constant	2.90		1.36		−2,001.7		−1,885.64	
R^2	.38		.34		.29		.23	

Note: Coding is as follows: Sex: 2 = female; 1 = male. Race: 2 = black. 1 = nonblack. Test scores: average of SAT equivalent for Math and Verbal. GPA: 8 = A, A+; 7 = A−; 6 = B+; 5 = B; 4 = B−; 3 = C+; 2 = C; 1 = D. Full-time status: 2 = full time; 1 = part-time. Residence: 2 = not with parents or other relations; 1 = with parents or other relatives. Financial independence: 2 = independence of parents; 1 = dependent on parents. Dependent siblings: 1. = none; 2 = 1; 3 = 2; 4 = 3; 5 = 4; 6 = 5; 7 = 6+. Parents' income: recoded to midpoints of categories in thousands of dollars, values equal to 1.5, 3.5, 5.0, 7.0, 9.0, 11.2, 13.8, 17.5, 22.5, 27.5, 32.5, 37.5, 45.0, and 60.0. Tuition and fees: total tuition and fees divided by 10 and rounded. Private control: 2 = private; 1 = public. Parental contribution: 1 = 0; 2 = $1–$499; 3 = $500–999; 4 = $1,000–1,999; 5 = $2,000–4,000; 6 = over $4,000.

*.01 ≤ p ≤ .05.

**p ≤ .01.

[a]Sample is all students (N = 4,608).
[b]Sample is all aided students (N = 2,317)

Table 6–7 continued

	Amounts of Grants		Percentage of Total Aid Package in Grants[b]		Amounts of Loans[b]		Percentage of Package in Loans[b]	
	Metric Coefficient	Standardized Coefficient	Metric Coefficient	Standardized Coefficient	Metric Coefficient	Standardized Coefficient	Metric Coefficient	Standardized Coefficient
Sex	−123.8	−.06 (40.7)**	.59	.01 (1.65)	−61.1	−.05 (27.4)*	1.9	−.03 (1.5)
Race	447.5	.13 (71.8)**	11.6	.09 (2.9)**	−104.1	−.05 (48.4)*	−10.3	−.09 (2.6)**
Average test score	16.0	.16 (2.6)**	.50	.13 (.11)**	−6.2	−.10 (1.8)**	−.43	−.13 (.10)**
GPA	53.2	.07 (16.4)**	2.8	.10 (.67)**	−38.2	−.08 (11.1)**	−2.1	−.09 (.60)**
Full-time status	204.3	.01 (350.8)	7.5	.01 (14.3)	90.4	.01 (236.7)	11.7	.02 (12.8)
Residence on campus	189.6	.07 (50.6)**	−8.5	−.09 (2.1)**	177.5	.11 (34.1)**	5.1	.06 (1.8)**
Financial independence	329.0	.10 (64.4)**	2.12	.02 (2.6)	31.1	.01 (43.5)	−2.29	−.02 (2.3)

Dependent siblings	40.6	.06 (12.2)**	-.82	-.03 (.49)	11.4	.03 (8.2)	.31	.01 (.44)
Parents' income	-24.04	-.24 (2.0)**	-.92	-.02 (.08)	-.30	-.00 (1.3)	.18	.05 (.07)*
Tuition and fees	2.4	.21 (.42)	-.36	-.08 (.17)*	2.1	.29 (.29)**	.70	.18 (.02)**
Private control	144.7	.07 (73.0)*	-1.3	-.02 (3.0)	-65.3	-.05 (49.2)	-5.6	-.08 (2.7)*
Constant	-1,905.28		19.92		409.15		37.67	
R^2	.18		.05		.08		.04	

Note: Coding is as follows: Sex: 2 = female; 1 = male. Race: 2 = black; 1 = nonblack. Test scores: average of SAT equivalent for Math and Verbal. GPA: 8 = A, A+; 7 = A-; 6 = B+; 5 = B; 4 = B-; 3 = C+; 2 = C; 1 = D. Full-time status: 2 = full time; 1 = part-time. Residence: 2 = not with parents or other relations; 1 = with parents or other relatives. Financial independence: 2 = independent of parents; 1 = dependent on parents. Dependent siblings: 1 = none; 2 = 1; 3 = 2; 4 = 3; 5 = 4; 6 = 5; 7 = 6+. Parents' income: recoded to midpoints of categories in thousands of dollars, values equal to 1.5, 3.5, 5.0, 7.0, 9.0, 11.2, 13.8, 17.5, 22.5, 27.5, 32.5, 37.5, 45.0, and 60.0. Tuition and fees: total tuition and fees divided by 10 and rounded. Private control: 2 = private; 1 = public. Parental contribution: 1 = 0; 2 = $1-$499; 3 = $500-999; 4 = $1,000-1,999; 5 = $2,000 - $4,000; 6 = over $4,000.

*.01 ≤ p ≤ .05.

**p ≤ .01.

[a]Sample is all students (N = 4,608).
[b]Sample is all aided students (N = 2,317)

a pattern probably due to the assets of black students' families being lower than those of white students' families with comparable incomes. The analyses for proportions of aid packages in loans and in grants were rather weak in explained variance, suggesting measurement error, a random component in packaging, attention by aid officers to student characteristics not included in the present model, or substantial institution-by-institution differences in packaging philosophies. Support for the latter explanation has recently been provided by Deane et al. (1980).

Conclusion

This chapter has investigated the extent to which men and women differ in their choice of colleges, especially with respect to the importance of economic factors in this choice process, and the extent to which colleges differentially package aid for men and women. Research has shown various ways in which, in the past, the economics of attending college have differed by sex. In predictions of college attendance socioeconomic background has played a relatively more important role for women, whereas ability has been relatively more important for men. There have been charges of discrimination against women in the awarding of financial aid, especially before Title IX (for example, Bob 1977), and it has been consistently shown that women rely more heavily than men on their parents' resources. These differences could reflect the position of women in the world of work. While in school, they earn less than their male peers and so have lower earnings during the summers and during the term with which to finance their education. They are less likely to be independent of their parents for the same reason. Parents and funding agencies may have been unwilling to give large amounts of aid to women since they have assumed that the returns to a college education are lower for women as compared with men, given the nature of the jobs women hold and their interrupted employment.

At a time when college attendance rates no longer differ greatly by sex, we have turned to the study of potential differences in the selection of a particular school. For men at least, the nature of school attended can have payoffs even beyond that of the years spent in school. The different options, though, have different costs, and the same sorts of barriers that earlier reduced the attendance of women at *any* college could be acting to sort them into the lower cost, less prestigious schools.

We consistently found some evidence of economic barriers to choice. Women formed their choices earlier than men, seeming to consider a safer range of schools. To some extent, the women in our sample chose lower-cost options. Socioeconomic background seemed to play a slightly more important role for women than for men in the type of choices they made—and not parents' income per se, but other aspects of SES such as parental education. Perhaps it is the values within the home that are important in a woman's choosing a higher-cost, higher-selectivity school. In choosing between schools, offers of aid were more crucial for women than for men. As far as receiving aid from the school they eventually attend, women received aid packages similar in composition but smaller than those of comparable men. Further, despite the greater constraint of SES on women as compared with men, parents of given SES contributed more to their daughters than to sons with similar ability and attending similar schools.

Although there is some evidence of economic (and socioeconomic) barriers to women's choice of college, the evidence is admittedly weak. It may be that we have chosen to look at the selection process at a time when men and women are converging in the ways in which they make their choices— studies with data on earlier cohorts seem to have gotten stronger results. Legislation such as Title IX has forced the institutions themselves to treat men and women equally—and some of those who have seen discrimination against women students in the past have also offered evidence of decreasing differences in things such as aid packages now (Bob 1979). The women's movement could have influenced the attitudes of both women students and their parents with respect to the value of getting not just a college education, but a good college education. On the other hand, women do not seem to have less worry about financing their college education, as one can see by comparing the responses to the question about financial concern with financing education across the years on the National Norms for Entering Freshmen. Women still earn less on the jobs they hold while in high school (Lewin-Epstein 1981) and while they are in college (Carnegie Commission 1979). The economic returns to college, though, have been rising from women, perhaps because of changes in women's career commitment and labor-force attachment. In choosing a college, too, "getting a good job" was actually a major reason for a significantly greater proportion of the women in our sample than of the men, as was "couldn't get a job." Although Alexander and Eckland (1977), with data on a cohort almost twenty years ahead of ours, did not find the payoffs from attending a highly selective college for women as they had for men, as women move into positions formerly held exclusively by men, their academic credentials may actually become more important for them than for men. For women to meet their rising expectations, college—and a good college—may be increasingly important. Obviously, trends in sex differences in college choice, the determinants of choice, and the outcomes of choice, need to be monitored.

Careers, though, are determined by more than the choice of a college. There are choices to be made within school: of major, or continuance. Despite some reduction in sex stereotyping of majors (see Heyns and Bird in chapter 3 of this book) differences persist, and it is here, within their major departments, that students are prepared for graduate school and careers (see Hearn and Olzak in chapter 12 of this book). Further, Hearn and Olzak show women were likely to choose a vocationally relevant major, consistent with our women's sample's emphasis on the importance of getting a good job. The type of major could even affect receipt of financial aid. All this urges continued attention, while examining sex differences in educational opportunities to the links between women's education and their work in the occupational structure and home.

Our results are limited to a group of traditional students. As Steiger and Kimball (1978) and Heyns and Bird show, more nontraditional women students are attending college—older, married, or previously married women, some of whom are preparing to support themselves or make necessary contributions to family income in times of high inflation. Although age and family status may be lower barriers to higher education for women than before, they may still be barriers to choice of a particular institution. Family responsibilities limit the geographical range within which one can look for a college. Being part time and being married can reduce the amount of financial aid to which one is entitled. Further, the expenses involved in going to college for a mother may include child care, which raises the net cost of attendance to her. Again, the links between schooling and women's work and family life cycles must be held in mind. In talking about equality between the sexes in educational opportunity, one cannot ignore the world beyond the college walls. Conversely, study of the college-choice process is of value not only in its own right, but also for an understanding of inequality in the labor market and family.

Notes

1. From Barbara Heyns's unpublished summarization of data from the National Center of Education Statistics (NCES) and the Cooperative Institutional Research Program, available for this chapter via a personal communication to the first author. Information used with permission.

2. Ibid.

3. The most similar recently gathered data sets are: (1) the 1980 High School and Beyond data, soon to be released to the public, (2) the 1978–1979 data base recently prepared by Applied Management Sciences, Inc. for the Department of Education's major study of financial-aid practices nationwide, and (c) the yearly Cooperative Institutional Research Program survey conducted by the Higher Education Research Institute and the American Council on Education. Data base (1) will contain an inadequate range of institutional characteristics of choices for the present study as well as surveying students *before* they have graduated from high school. Later waves will, however, be a valuable source of information if institutional

characteristics are added to the data base. Data base (2) does not include any indicators of students' tested ability or commitment to college and has a limited range of nonfinancial institutional indicators. Data base (3) is recent and contains a wealth of indicators of relevant student characteristics (the 1975–1976 version of the CIRP questionnaire was an element of the matching process that created the SISFAP-A data base), but it contains no indicators of students' tested ability, fewer questions on early choice, and an inadequate set of institutional indicators. For the task at hand, the SISFAP-A data base is the optimal choice.

4. Different weighting schemes also yield results closer to those found elsewhere. Our unweighted results do show women selecting schools with lower tuition and fees, significantly so in 1975. Astin (1978), using a somewhat different weighting scheme, which we were not able to reproduce, also found women choosing schools with lower average tuition and fees than those chosen by men. Our weighted results on other characteristics correspond well to Astin's. We believe that the weighting scheme we use generally corrects problems of representativeness of the sample.

5. Sometimes when estimating regressions on correlated dependent variables, one wants to use the method of "seemingly unrelated regressions," which allows one to make corrections for the intercorrelation (Zellner 1962). In the case where all the independent variables for the regressions on the separate dependent variables are the same, as here, there is no correction needed and doing the regressions separately is exactly the same as doing "seemingly unrelated regressions."

6. See Draper and Smith (1966) for a discussion of other inclusions criteria. Different procedures can lead to different "best" equations.

7. Some authors have suggested that the unequal long-term burdens of college loans on men and women students might be addressed by providing women with fewer loans or more favorable loan terms, compared with men (Froomkin 1974).

8. An attempt was made to supplement the regression analysis by way of examining the interaction of sex and parental income in explaining financing variations. The hypothesis was that income might play an especially powerful role in women's financing patterns, given the attainment and choice evidence discussed earlier in this chapter. A product interaction term for sex and income nevertheless did not add significantly to the R^2 in any of the eight regressions of table 6–6.

Bibliography

Abramson, J. *The Invisible Woman: Discrimination in the Academic Profession.* San Francisco: Jossey-Bass, 1975.

Alexander, K.L., and Eckland, B.K. "Sex Differences in the Educational Attainment Process." *American Sociological Review* 39 (1974): 668–682.

————. "High School Context and College Selectivity: Institutional Constraints in Educational Stratification." *Social Forces* 56 (1977): 166–188.

Alwin, Duane. "College Effects on Educational and Occupational Attainments." *American Sociological Review* 39 (1974):210–223.

Anderson, Kristine L. "Post High School Experiences and College Attrition." *Sociology of Education* 54 (1981):1–15.

Astin, Alexander. "Final Report, SISFAP-Study A: The Impact of Student Financial Aid Programs on Student Choice." Report prepared for the U.S. Office of Education under contract 300–75–0382. Los Angeles: Higher Education Research Institute, 1978.

Astin, Alexander, et al. *The American Freshman: National Norms for Fall 1975.* Los Angeles: Cooperative Institutional Research Program, 1975.

Astin, H.; Harway, M.; and McNamara, P. *Sex Discrimination in Education,* vols. I and II. Washington, D.C.: National Center for Education Statistics, U.S. Government Printing Office, 1976.

Astin, Alexander, and Henson, James. "New Measures of College Selectivity." *Research in Higher Education* 6 (1977):1–9.

Bishop, John. "The Impact of Public Policy on the College Attendance of Women." Paper presented at the American Economic Association meetings, New York, 1977.

Bob, Sharon. "The Myth of Equality: Financial Support for Males and Females." *Journal of College Student Personnel* 18 (May 1977): 235–238.

————. "Women and Financing Higher Education." Paper presented at the Research Conference on Educational Environments and the Undergraduate Woman, Wellesley College, September 1979.

Carnegie Commission on Higher Education. *Next Steps for the 1980's in Student Financial Aid: A Fourth Alternative.* San Francisco: Jossey-Bass, 1979.

Carroll, S.J. *The Enrollment Effects of Federal Student Aid Policies.* Santa Monica, Calif.: Rand Corporation, 1977.

Davis, Jerry S. "Paying for College Costs: Does the Student's Sex Make a Difference?" *Journal of Student Financial Aid* 7 (1977):22–34.

Davis, Jerry S., and Van Dusen, W.D. *Guide to the Literature of Student Financial Aid.* New York: College Scholarship Service, 1978.

Deane, Robert; Smith, M.; Miller, S.; and Dellefield, W. "Study of Program Management Procedures in the Campus Based and Basic Grant Program (G-129)." In *Who Gets Financial Assistance, How Much, and Why?* Report to Department of Education Office of Program Evaluation. Silver Springs, Md.: Applied Management Sciences, 1980.

Draper, Norman, and Smith, Harry. *Applied Regression Analysis.* New York: Wiley, 1966.

Dresch, S.P., and Waldenberg, A.L. "Labor Market Incentives, Intellectual Competence, and College Attendance." Paper presented at the Annual Meeting of the American Association for the Advancement of Science, Washington, D.C., 1978.

Frankel, Martin, and Gerald, Debra. "Women Enrollments in College, Degrees Conferred to Women: A Historical and Future Perspective." Paper presented at the American Educational Research Association Meeting, Boston, 1980.

Froomkin, J. *Study of the Advantages and Disadvantages of Student Loans to Women.* Washington, D.C.: Joseph Froomkin, Inc., 1974.

Haven, E.W., and Horch, D.H. *How College Students Finance Their Educations.* Princeton, N.J.: College Scholarship Service of the College Entrance Examination Board, 1972.

Hout, M., and Morgan, W.R. "Race and Sex Variations in the Causes of Expected Attainments of High School Seniors." *American Journal of Sociology* 81 (1975):364-394.

Hyde, William. "The Effects of Tuition and Financial Aid on Access and Choice in Postsecondary Education." *Papers in Education Finance #1.* Denver, Colo.: Education Finance Center, Education Commission of the States, 1978.

————. "The Equity of the Distribution of Student Financial Aid." Report no. F79-2, Education Finance Center, Education Commission of the States. Denver, Colo.: Education Center of the States, 1979.

Jackson, Gregory A. "Financial Aid to Students and the Demand for Postsecondary Education." Ed.D. diss., Graduate School of Education, Harvard University, 1977.

————. "Financial Aid and Student Enrollment." *Journal of Higher Education,* 49 (1978):548-574.

Karabel, Jerome, and Astin, Alexander. "Social Class, Academic Ability, and College 'Quality'." *Social Forces* 53 (March 1975):381-398.

Lewin-Epstein, Noah. "Youth Employment During High School." Report to the National Center for Education Statistics, Department of Education. Chicago: National Opinion Reserach Center, 1981.

Litten, Larry; Jahoda, Ellen; and Morris, Darrell. "His Mother's Son and Her Father's Daughter: Parents, Children and Marketing of Colleges." Unpublished manuscript, Carleton College, 1980.

National Center for Education Statistics. *Digest of Education Statistics, 1979.* Washington, D.C.: U.S. Government Printing Office, 1979.

————. *The Condition of Education*. 1980 Edition. Washington, D.C.: U.S. Government Printing Office, 1980.

Nolfi, George, J.; Fuller, Winship C.; Corazzini, Arthur J.; Epstein, William H.; Freeman, Richard B.; Manski, Charles F.; Valerie I.; and Wise, David A. *Experiences of Recent High School Graduates*. Lexington, Mass.: Lexington Books, D.C. Heath and Company, 1978.

Rosen, B.C., and Aneshensel, Carol S. "Sex Differences in the Educational-Occupational Expectation Process." *Social Forces* 57 (1978): 164–186.

Rossi, A.S., and Calderwood, A., eds. *Academic Women on the Move*. New York: Russell Sage Foundation, 1973.

Russick, Bert, and Olson, Paul. In *Choice or Chance: Planning for Independent College Marketing and Retention*. St. Paul, Minn.: Northwest Area Foundation, 1976.

Sewell, William, and Shah, Vimal. "Socioeconomic Status, Intelligence, and Attainment of Higher Education." *Sociology of Education* 40 (1967):1–23.

Solmon, L. "The Definition of College Quality and Its Impact on Earnings." *Explorations in Economic Research* 2 (1975):537–588.

Steiger, Joann, and Kimball, Barbara. "Financial Aid for Lifelong Learning: The Special Case of Women." *School Review* 86 (1978):398–409.

Thomas, Gail; Alexander, Karl; and Eckland, Bruce. "Access to Higher Education: The Importance of Race, Sex, and Social Class. *School Review* 87 (1979):133–156.

Tierney, M.L. "The Impact of Financial Aid on Public/Private Postsecondary Education: Some Policy Implications." Paper presented to the Association for the Study of Higher Education, Washington, D.C., 1979.

————. "Student College Choice Sets: Toward an Empirical Characterization." Paper presented to the Association for the Study of Higher Education, Washington, D.C., 1980.

Tinto, Vincent. "College Origins and Patterns of Status Attainment." *Sociology of Work Occupations* 7 (1980):457–486.

Trusheim, D., and Crouse, J. "Effects of College Prestige on Men's Occupational Status and Earnings." Paper presented at the Annual Meeting of the American Educational Research Association, Boston, April 1980.

Wachtel, Paul. "The Effect of School Quality on Achievement, Attainment Levels, and Lifetime Earnings." *Explorations in Economic Research* 2 (1975):502–536.

Weisbrod, B.A., and Karpoff, P. "Monetary Returns to College Education, Student Ability, and College Quality." *Review of Economics and Statistics* 50 (1968):491–497.

Willett, Sandra. "Information on Federal Student Assistance: Its Availability, Price, and Other Unfinished Business." Unpublished manuscript, Kennedy School of Public Policy, Harvard University, 1976.

Zellner, Arnold. "An Efficient Method of Estimating Seemingly Unrelated Regressions and Tests for Aggregation Bias." *Journal of the American Statistical Association* 57 (1962):348-368.

**Part III
The College Experience:
Issues of Growth and Change**

7

Epistemology and Agency in the Development of Undergraduate Women

Blythe Clinchy and
Claire Zimmerman

For the past several years we have been studying the intellectual and ethical development of Wellesley College women. The project has two objectives: to describe in detail the cognitive development of women during the college years and to translate that description into suggestions for liberal-arts education for women. Our research grew out of William Perry's (1968, 1970, 1981) work at Harvard. On the basis of a longitudinal study of Harvard undergraduates, largely male, Perry suggested that students move through an invariant sequence of epistemological positions, each new position reflecting a more complex conception of knowledge, truth, and value. The sequence begins with simplistic notions of absolute right and wrong (*dualism:* positions 1 and 2), moving through a stage in which opinions are seen as equally valid personal truths (*multiplism:* position 3), and ending with the view that knowledge is contextual, that is, that truth must be evaluated within a frame of reference (*contextualism:* positions 4 and 5).[1] Further development consists of the evolution of *commitment*.

Students who are reasoning at the most advanced contextual level (position 5) assume that all thought is contingent upon context. No thought can be stripped bare of its frame of reference. Facile distinctions between fact and interpretation of fact disappear. The person grasps that there is no factual meaning without a context, that all mental acts are interpretive. For the first time, students are able to compare frames of reference, to assess various conclusions in terms of the assumptions on which they are based and the quality of the arguments from assumption to conclusion. They are now aware of the irreducible subjectivity in all judgments but also of the possibility of making sensible judgments.

This chapter is an expanded version of a paper presented by Blythe Clinchy at the Research Conference on Educational Environments and the Undergraduate Woman, Wellesley College, September 1979. The research on which this chapter is based has been supported by the Andrew W. Mellon Foundation, the Spencer Foundation, Proctor and Gamble, and Wellesley College.

161

Epistemological positions are assumed to act as cognitive structures that shape the students' understanding of events. Undergraduates at different positions, listening to the same lecture, will hear different lectures. A dualistic student listening to a lecture on the Soviet intervention in Afghanistan thinks the teacher is revealing the truth about why the Soviet Union has intervened. A multiplistic student thinks the teacher is expressing a personal opinion about the intervention and she asks herself whether she agrees or disagrees that these are the real reasons for the intervention. The teacher's words carry no particular authority. A contextualist knows there are many different perspectives on the intervention issue. She knows there is no single truth about it, and she knows that understanding the issue does not mean trading personal opinions about it. She assumes the teacher also knows these things. A contextualist sees the teacher as trying to enrich his or her own understanding by explaining the issue from a variety of perspectives. For example, what is the relationship between the intervention and current unrest in the Moslem world? the oil crisis? the Soviet Union's past history of military activity in Europe? the Cold War of the 1950s? Since the Contextualist understands that the problem is infinitely complex, she automatically generates for herself other perspectives as she listens to the teacher. She assumes that she and the teacher are trying to do the same thing, to understand the issue better by illuminating some of its many complexities.

Our own work began as an attempt to test Perry's model on a sample of undergraduate women similar to Perry's subjects in aspects other than gender. We are using a modified longitudinal-sequential research design.[2] During each of the last four years, we have interviewed a random sample of twenty to twenty-five first-year students at Wellesley. Each student is reinterviewed annually during her stay at the college. Each interview lasts from one to two hours and is taped and transcribed. We now have 235 interviews with 90 women in this core sample. In addition, we have drawn supplementary samples for various special purposes.

Perry used an unstructured interview. Ours is semistructured: the student reads and discusses written statements that purport to be quotations from college students, and the interviewer is trained to probe the student's responses. The written statements and the probes are designed to elicit material that can be scored for epistemological position, using criteria we have developed. We developed the criteria because we found Perry's descriptions of the positions too sparse and imprecise for adequate coding. Although we are still coding and analyzing the data, preliminary quantitative analysis of data from a longitudinal subsample, based on these criteria, shows development proceeding by small but significant steps from year to year, with very little skipping of positions and almost no regression. Since these results would be predicted by cognitive-developmental theory, they provide some construct validity for our version of the scheme. [See Parker (1978) for reports of other research based on Perry's scheme.]

Our version is largely a fuller and more precise articulation of Perry's, but there are real divergences at some points. We describe our reconstruction of the scheme elsewhere (Clinchy and Zimmerman, forthcoming). Differences between Perry's scheme and ours may be due to sex differences in the samples upon which the schemes are based, but they may not, since Perry's research and ours differ in many other respects as well: sex of interviewers, sex of coders, type of interview, time and place of testing, among others. We have not yet studied men using our interview schedule and scoring criteria. This chapter is concerned only with the growth of young women and, in particular, with vicissitudes in the development of *agency,* the capacity to decide and to act and to trust one's decisions and actions. Many factors affect a person's ability to decide and to act. One of them is epistemology. The person's assumptions about knowledge, truth, and value affect the degree to which she can be an active agent. This chapter describes the interplay between epistemology and agency as we see it in the course of development during the college years. We will focus on positions 3 and 4, the middle positions on the epistemological scale, comprising the transition from dualism to contextualism. These are the positions at which most undergraduates seem to spend most of the college years. The quotations come from interviews we have collected.

Positions 1 and 2: Dualism

At the early positions in Perry's scheme reasoning is dualistic. The world is seen as divided into two poles; at one pole is we-right-good, and at the other is other-wrong-bad. There are absolute truths, known to authorities. Although people do disagree on some issues, and some people appear to be uncertain about some matters, one can count on qualified experts to agree on the single right answer to any question.

There is power in this position. The student can take a stand, make a judgment, express real conviction. For perhaps the last time in her life, she knows she is right. In this sense, she is active. But of course she is profoundly passive, too. The stands she takes are not really hers; they were dispensed by a benign authority. She cannot originate ideas, and she cannot evaluate them. At this position the student is truly a subordinate.

We shall not dwell on this position, since we are concerned here with undergraduates, and researchers have found this reasoning to be rare among college students. Only one of the college women we have interviewed showed any evidence of simple dualistic thinking—a native-American freshman reared on a reservation. Even in a sample of high-school sophomores

(Clinchy, Lief, and Young 1977), we found only a few examples of dualistic thinking.

Position 3: Multiplism

At the next step in development a rapidly expanding grey area invades the black-and-white universe of dualism. The student recognizes that in some areas uncertainty and diversity of opinion are legitimate. On some issues (for example, the causes of cancer) multiplicity is merely a "temporary fuzziness in Authority's domain" (Perry, 1970, p. 97); someday the experts will have the facts. The right-wrong criterion is not threatened, and faith in Authority remains intact. Most of our younger students and some of our older ones perceive science this way.

But in other areas diversity of opinion is perceived as permanent, and it is *intrinsic:* to some questions there are no right answers, and there never will be. Most of our younger students perceive the humanities this way. Someday someone will demonstrate the true cause of cancer; no one will ever demonstrate the true meaning of *Billy Budd.* In domains of intrinsic multiplicity there is a change in the nature of truth. Absolute truth will never exist, and Authority is dethroned. The student abandons the right-wrong criterion in favor of the doctrine of subjective validity; there are no wrong opinions; "everyone's opinion is right to herself." "Anyone's interpretation is valid, if that's the way they see it. . . . I mean, nobody can tell you that your opinion is wrong, you know."

This position brings an increase in activity. Believing that she has a right to her view and free from the threat of wrongness, the student can think anything she likes, and she can risk expressing her opinions. For the first time, students report, they feel that their own opinions *matter,* to themselves and to others—even to teachers: "He cares what *I* think. I didn't think anybody cared what I thought." And teachers let you think anything you want.

This new freedom is coupled with responsibility. No longer a mere receptacle for Authority's wisdom, the student must decide upon her own truths. But both the freedom and the responsibility are tempered. Position 3 opinions are not active constructions; they are ready-made reactions. They are more like feelings than thoughts: "I usually find that when ideas are being tossed around I'm usually more akin to one than another. I don't know—my opinions are just sort of there a lot of times." The interviewer asks a student how she assesses the theories presented in a psychology course. "Well, with me it's almost more a matter of liking one more than another. . . . I mean, I happen to agree with or identify more with one kind of theory."

People are not responsible for their opinions. Opinions are accidents of personal history: "I happen to think killing is wrong. That's how I was brought up." Paradoxically, although espousing ardently the right to freedom of opinion, Position 3 believes that opinions are determined, rather than chosen. Thus, one is absolutely free to hold values that are utterly determined. "I don't think anyone can say that things are right, or wrong. It's purely a matter of individual decision whether you do something or somebody decides to do the same thing. I was brought up differently than they were; I've got a different set of values." Superficially an individualist, Position 3 is quite conventional: "I just kind of feel whether things are right or wrong. I think my ideas about it are mostly like norms."

At an earlier position when *we, right,* and *good* were inextricably bound, the student had faith in the intrinsic value of her beliefs. At Position 3 this claim is abandoned. Beliefs are simply "individual preferences." I can say that I like a poem; I cannot say the poem is good. "To me, what makes one poem better than another one is that I can get something from it as a person. . . . That says nothing about the poem itself. I mean, I have no authority. But just for me a good poem will be one I can relate to, just on a personal basis." I may remain a Christian at Position 3, as at Position 2, but I will argue not that Christianity is right but simply that I believe it; it is right for me. The self-righteousness of Position 2 is replaced by humility.

This humility emerges from an important epistemological insight. The student sees that she has no direct access to absolute truth, that she perceives the world through a particular frame, and that that frame is only one of a variety of possible frames: "I can say I *think* a poem is good. I can't say the poem is good." Opinions are right only within a particular frame. My opinions are right from my own personal perspective—they are right for me—but they have no validity apart from that perspective. I can expect others to respect my opinions, out of respect for my person, but I do not expect others to be affected by my ideas; my ideas have no power.

Nor can I judge—or even comprehend—another's opinions, because I am a prisoner of my own personal perspective. I cannot change my frame, and I cannot enter another frame. Since judgments can be made only within frames, and since I cannot transcend my own frame, I cannot legitimately evaluate another's actions or beliefs. I am free only to disagree. For the dualist, views with which one disagrees are wrong; one consigns non-Christians to outer darkness as other-wrong-bad. At position 3 the student distinguishes between validity and agreement. Given two interpretations of a story, a sophomore comments:

> There's a probability that I would like one more than another. I would agree with one more than another. There are certain things that would appeal to me that wouldn't appeal to you, or certain things I had seen in the

story that you hadn't seen, and the one that most closely matched up my interpretation would be, probably, the one I'd like a little more. But I wouldn't condemn the other one. I—I—I would let it—I would let it alone. I wouldn't say it was wrong. I'd just say that I agree more with this one.

We tried to test the limits of position 3's tolerance by asking students whether they believed Hitler was wrong. Would they say they simply disagreed with Hitler? The question arouses considerable conflict at position 3. The conflict is between the student's strong intuition that genocide is wrong, not only for her, but absolutely wrong, and her equally strong view that it is wrong to judge. Hitler was wrong, but it is wrong to call him wrong. In their opinion he was very wrong, but the criterion of subjective validity says that if Hitler felt he was right, then genocide was right for him and that one should not inflict one's opinion on Hitler. The following excerpt illustrates position 3's struggles with the question:

Well, from my point of view I would say that what Hitler did was morally *terrible*. I mean from most people's views. **Uh-huh.** Because, well, just take into consideration everything that he did. Killing everybody just because he wanted to have this perfect race, and nothing, human life didn't have any value to him, it was just [long pause]. . . . Are you asking me if what he did was morally right or wrong? **Yeah.** Well, I would say it would be morally wrong from my point of view. I mean, he was insane anyway, so—[little laugh]. . . . Well . . . there were people who were following him and they thought it was right, too. So I can't speak for them 'cause they obviously felt—they—they went right along with him in his campaign. . . . OK, then, for them they were right, then, I guess. They—it's terrible to say that, but—um—they were doing what they thought was right, even though I think it's wrong, and I think the majority of the world probably would agree that it's wrong. And it seemed to me that, well, these people, though they thought at the time that they were doing it right . . . didn't—after, afterward—didn't a lot of them say that they'd been brain-washed or that they [pause]. . . . **Was he right or was he wrong? He believed he was right, so was he therefore?** No. 'Cause I'm looking at it from my point of view. But if you asked Hitler, he would say "yes." You can't, see, there's no absolute. It depends on your frame of reference, and I would say no. What all of them did was terrible, it was wrong, morally wrong. **But**—Then there's the other side of the story. If you asked them, they would say it's right. So is **there a way to decide whether you're right or he's right?** I guess. If you asked, if you took a poll [laughter] of the whole world, the majority wins.

When pushed, most students, like this one, settle for consensus as a criterion. A sophomore:

"It's sort of been a popular judgment that what he did was wrong, and, um, you know that's pretty much, uh, um, considered unanimously to be wrong.

The interviewer persists: "Would you say that Hitler was right or wrong?"

> I don't know, wrong. [Softly, hesitantly] Yes. Exterminating a whole lot of people is not generally considered to be a good thing. And—uh—inflicting his opinion on them. . . . No doubt it was right to him, but—um—in the long run, it wasn't too popular.

The student may turn to popular opinion for her moral values, but on some issues she is forced to make her own judgments. The norms will not tell her what to do with her life. Left to herself the student at position 3 would remain a spectator. Confronted by a multitude of possible mates, values, and vocations, she watches, she listens; she does not act. She simply exposes herself (a persistent phrase at position 3) to the passing parade and waits for some item in the parade to turn her on. The student, of course, does not control the spectacle; she is at the mercy of its managers. If the career-services office does not bring to the campus recruiters from advertising, she will never know about advertising. If she cannot fit in an art course, she will never know anything about art.

The spectator's thinking is essentially magical. She assumes that, if she stays open, some meaningful choice will emerge. One student describes herself as "kind of floating around," waiting for a vocation, "and I wish it would descend on me pretty fast." Another says, "I think something will just hit me, some ideology or something will sort of stick to me." Another, a freshman, beginning to question parental prohibitions against premarital sex, assumes the issue will resolve itself: "It's just going to be that if it occurs that way, I'm just going to let it rise." (Senior year, still at position 3, she gave birth to an illegitimate child.)[3]

The problem, in part, is cognitive incompetence. Although one is free to choose, one has no means of choosing. As Keniston (1960) has said, adolescents may experience freedom as oppressive when they have no criteria for choosing among alternatives. The world has become much more complex, and the student has no tools for reducing the complexity. The peer culture seems to support the students' passivity. Everyone remains open to everyone else. Arguments are frowned upon. An atmosphere of bland acceptance pervades the residence hall.

It is different in the classroom. Professors, it turns out, are not so open. The following scenario is typical. A student, delighted that "he cares what *I* think" and assuming that "we're all allowed to read into *Hamlet* anything we want," dashes off a paper expressing her sincere personal opinions about *Hamlet*. She receives a C−. What went wrong? The student concludes that teachers are "biased," stuck within their own perspectives, unable to entertain other points of view. After all, the student herself can conceive of no criterion for judgment apart from the illegitimate one of agreement; what other grounds could the teacher have? Teachers should accept her opinions. Teachers who reject her opinions fail to make the distinction the student has made between agreement and validity.

> One thing that really gets me angry is, um, when you write a piece of writing, and a teacher will look at it and say, "This is not good." And I don't like getting grades on something I've written, because I don't think they have any criteria to judge it. . . . I've written a lot of poetry . . . How can you grade something like that? You really can't. I mean, it's just a matter of personal taste. Some people might like the poem; some people might not. . . . It would really get me angry when, um, you write something that's very subjective—I don't see how someone can just say, "Well, this is good, and this is bad. . . ." You do get some teachers who, if you disagree with them, forget it. You get an F. That's what happened to me, so I can vouch for that.

Perry reports that some of his students dig in their heels at this position, continuing to assert that "they" have no right to judge. Very few of ours do. The frequency of position 3 reasoning seems to drop gradually from about 40 percent in freshman year to about 5 percent in senior year.[4] Teachers should not judge, but they do. The student realizes that if she is to survive in this environment, she had better figure out what it is "they" want. At the next level of development—we call it position 4A—she is preoccupied with this task.

Position 4A: Contextualism Foreseen

Position 4 marks the end of the student's brief emancipation from authority. A period of alienation and subordination sets in. We think the sophomore slump takes place about there. At position 4 the student becomes two people. In the real world she can continue to operate at Position 3; she can be herself and express freely those opinions which are right for her. But in the classroom she cannot. There, her task, as one sophomore puts it, is to "find out what the guy wants and give it to him."

The student may begin by writing papers that are slavish imitations of her teacher's views: "It's safer if I repeat exactly what she said." But this is not always possible, nor does it seem to be what is wanted. One of Perry's students reports that insight achieved at this level: "It's not *what* they want you to think. It's the *way* they want you to think."

It is somewhat less degrading to be told how to think than to be told what to think. But only somewhat. Students at this position believe that each teacher has an arbitrary, idiosyncratic way of thinking. The professors' approaches have no objective value; they are simply styles. Teachers try to inflict their personal styles on students. Many students feel angry and helpless.

> It's a case of writing a paper to please a teacher, and if that's academic prostitution, okay, but I mean, everybody has to play the game if they want to go through it. I've a paper that would have gotten me an A last year in a course would get me a D now. . . . There's nothing I can do about it. . . . Last year a girl was talking about an English professor. She'd written her first paper, and it was totally her own work. I mean, she hadn't quoted anything and hadn't used examples or anything, and she got a C−. The next paper, she quoted a few lines from the book. She got a C+. Her last paper was 50 percent quotes—I mean, really ridiculous—and she got an A! And other teachers say, "I don't want any of this quotation. I don't want to see it." Last year I was in a course where the teacher started out the course by saying, "All right, I feel that the papers that contain the most quotations and references to the book are closest to the truth, therefore are the best papers." So I figured, okay, lots of quotes, fine. That's the way, and it worked. I mean, they were good papers, but they were still the way the teacher wanted them written. And it turned out I got a very good grade in the course, but this year, if I tried that—[pause] I have tried it, and it doesn't work. Maybe it's wrong to try and extend something that works in a novel course to a poetry course. But still [pause]. The style the teacher likes is different. And unless you change your style, you're going to keep getting hurt, you know.

Many of our students do find themselves thinking as their teachers do, and it scares them. A freshman:

> After exposing yourself to a person twice a week for over an hour you do kind of begin to think the way they do. I mean, each professor has his own way of looking at a problem or analyzing something. You start to adopt that yourself. I have a professor who's convincing us of something gradually, and he gives us a little bit more each week, and the way he puts it in front of us is so forceful that you just couldn't help but swallow it, even though you don't really want to.

The student feels she has lost her own voice and is beginning to speak in teachers' voices.

> Sometimes you have to sacrifice. If you really want a good grade, and you know what the teacher wants, sometimes you have to sacrifice your own thoughts.

And,

> I've been forced to write what somebody wants to hear, and that upsets me very much. I've written the first paper, say, in a course, and read some of my friends' papers and seen sort of what they wanted or how you should go

about it and written a second paper and just handed all that to them and gotten, "Oh, wonderful! This is good!." And been upset, because maybe it's not exactly what I really wanted to write.

In time the student begins to perceive similarity among teachers' demands. Most teachers do not insist that you ape their styles; they ask only that you produce reasons for your opinions. Students seem to regard this request as legitimate, but it is clear they also find it rather unreal. Writing a paper in the humanities, a student says, is "an exercise in presenting an opinion and backing it up." In the student's eyes the plausibility of the argument has nothing to do with the validity of the conclusion. Reasons are manufactured to convince teachers; they do not convince the student herself: "Your opinion might be just as valid as mine; mine might just be better backed." The student continues to resist the suggestion that one interpretation could be better than another. A sophomore:

> I don't think you can say that any interpretation is better than any other one. It can be argued better. Or it may have more insight. But everyone's entitled to their opinion, you know. If more thought goes into one interpretation, you might say that it is qualitatively better, but not necessarily. . . . I just don't think "better" is a good word. **What would you call it?** I—I can't think of a word that would really describe it.

The frequent use of the term *backing* is instructive. Students at this position do not use reason to *construct* their opinions. Reasoning is added on in support of intuitive reactions, "to prove what you feel." The student takes a position that is simply "there" (the residue of her experience), or she selects one that appeals to her.
She then looks for backing.

> Well, what you do is, you look at the material you have for writing the paper, and probably you'll get conflicting views, different authors, and you decide which one you think you like, and you get as much information that supports the opinion as you can. You look at different options, and whatever appeals to you—I mean, you don't have to sit down and analyze anything. If you find yourself sort of leaning one direction, then that's the side you take. The evaluation is very—it's sort of a gut reaction. It just comes naturally.

Sometimes the student has no gut reaction. She has no position, but she is forced to argue a position. It is an empty exercise.

> I write good papers when I try, but it's not something I enjoy doing. It still seems to me like I'm bullshitting. I can write a good paper, and someday I may learn to write one that I like, that is not just bullshit. But I still feel it's

somewhat pointless. You do it, and you get your grade, but it hasn't proved anything to me. The problem comes in that I don't feel terribly strongly about one point of view, but it seems to make more sense. It would be easier to write the paper supporting it in this direction than the other one. Because there's more facts to be used. So I write about that. And it's not one of my deep-founded beliefs, but it writes the paper.

Because the student cannot yet use reason to construct an opinion, she would prefer to present a list of pros and cons, but teachers force her to decide. She feels they force her to lie.

I wrote a couple of papers freshman year which were really a mess, because a question was posed, and I didn't think the question was either right or wrong. So I showed the arguments for both sides, and the professor said, "No, no, no, you can't do this. You have to pick one side or the other and then argue it. You can't just say that they're both right and they're both wrong, 'cause that's—that just isn't the way you're supposed to write a paper." So I said, Okay, you know. All right. So the next time he gave us another question to write a paper on, and again I felt that there were arguments that could be posed for both sides. And I wrote them all down side-by-side and I tried to decide which one had more arguments in favor of it. And then I wrote it as if I felt that this statement was totally true, and that the other was totally false. I didn't really feel that way.

There is a split here between the person and the product. The person is not really in her papers. This is alienating, but it is also useful. Teachers criticize your arguments, but they do not attack your personal opinions. Since your argument has little to do with you—is impersonal—teachers' criticisms are not so devastating. The student can begin to discern that there are impersonal criteria for judging. Conclusions may be equally valid, but arguments are more or less valid. Being forced to take a stand in papers when you "don't feel that way" is also alienating, but useful. Students at higher positions tell us that they think they had more practice in decision making in academics than in personal life. In their personal lives they were allowed to drift; in the academic life they were forced to make deliberate decisions and support them.

Seventy percent of our students move beyond position 4A by junior year, 80 percent by senior year. A few get stuck at 4A. They feel powerless.

I really need to learn to think by myself. I read a book and nothing goes through my head—only the plot you know. . . . I'm not creative and I'm not insightful in most things—like even in daily life, like I don't see what I'm gonna say is gonna have an effect on somebody. I just don't think about it. . . . I don't know, I really . . . it's something I've never learned to do—to really think things out. I . . . I'm just like a machine: I put things into my head and I bring them out again. I memorize things and that's what

I'm good for! That's how come I got here! I have this computer type mind that you put equations in there and they come out the other end, and I'm not good at anything creative, or anything that takes real . . . thought!!

Position 4B: Limited Contextualism

At the next step—position 4B in our scheme—the student learns that what "they" want is complex, contextual reasoning, and she learns how to deliver it. She learns to evaluate arguments in terms of formal criteria supplied by the discipline—the degree to which an interpretation hangs together, for example, or the degree to which it embraces the complexity of the text. Although these criteria are formal, they do not refer merely to disembodied form, divorced from substance. The substance of an opinion *is* its structure. Opinions are constructions, and some constructions are better than others.

This is an important step. Opinions are no longer equally valid. I can make judgments about other people's opinions, and they can make judgments about mine. These judgments need not be personal, and they need not be arbitrary. There are still no bad people, but there are bad arguments. And I can spot them: I have acquired analytic tools that make rational criticism possible. I am no longer at the mercy of every high-sounding text I encounter. And my own opinions are not mere accidents of socialization. I construct them, and I am responsible for them. If I construct them well, they have value. They have value not just to me and not just because they are mine, but because they meet certain objective, impersonal standards.

Position 4B is the modal position at junior year in the sample we have studied. The sophomore slump behind them, most of these juniors are heavily involved in academic tasks. They describe their growing academic competence as a source of pleasure and power:

> It does give you a sense of confidence to know that you can deal with new material and be confident with it, and you can know how to analyze it—go through it and think about it in a very rational, organized way.

At position 4B the student is no longer a prisoner of her own personal perspective. Indeed, she now believes that it is obligatory to transcend that perspective. One must try to enter other frames.

> It's hard to look at things in a different way. But if someone confronts me with something that I would have a first inclination to say no, you shouldn't do that. That's really bad. Um, I'd try to look at it in terms of, of the way *they* look at it, to get a different perspective of other things. And I think that's the best way of being objective, is to try to look at it from a different, a different perspective. And I think that's important.

It is important. Earlier, the student's awareness of context led to paralysis in judgment. She knew that the meaning and value of a phenomenon depended upon the context in which it occurred, but she believed she could not transcend the context of her own immediate experience. "How can I judge Hitler? I wasn't there." Now, the student believes she can get "there," or close to it. She cannot get inside Hitler's head, but she can acquire knowledge of the historical context, and she can use that knowledge to increase her understanding of the phenomenon of Nazism.

The women we have interviewed speak of this contextual reasoning in a different key from that used by Perry's male subjects. The men sound aggressive; they use contextual reasoning to attack problems. The women sound receptive. They say that in analyzing a text they must leave their own minds behind and enter the author's mind.

> If I'm reading the author I try to think as the author does. Until I finish the whole thing. And then I go back and reflect on it and then I decide, uh, what points I agree with and disagree with. But as I'm going along I try not to bias—it's hard but I try not to bias the train of thought with my own impressions. I try to just pretend that I'm the author. I try to really just put myself in that person's place and why is it that they believe this way.

But receptivity should not be confused with passivity. This is an active receptivity. The student is not gullible; but is critical.

> When you're reading a theorist and you want to criticize them, you can't just criticize him from your own perspective. You have to understand where he was writing and what, what situation—maybe he was just—trying to justify his historical position, and you have to think of that kind of thing.

The teacher is no longer perceived as Svengali. One can enter the teacher's mind, now, without fear of losing one's own.

> I try to—to understand what a professor's opinion is. It sometimes helps your papers to write in their mode of thought. It doesn't mean that you're totally accepting what they're saying, but you understand better if you really attempt to get into it, rather than just refusing it from the very beginning, and saying I disagree. So I usually try to understand what they're saying by trying to think in the way they do. And I really don't think that's a cop-out, you know, writing what the professor wants, because I think [pause] well, a lot of times you don't realize until the end of a course what direction the professor is really trying to go, what they're trying to show you. So I think that it's really important to try and do that. They can help you think in a certain way, but then you've got to fit that into a larger whole and decide if that's really the way you want to . . . I suppose some people would see it as playing a game, or giving the teacher what he/she wants; I don't really look upon it that way. I think it's valuable to really

attempt to see something in somebody else's way or to try to really, honestly grasp the point they're trying to make.

The student who reaches position 4B has achieved considerable intellectual skill. She is able and knows she is able to construct convincing arguments. She can enlarge her own understanding through the powers of her own mind. All this brings with it an increasing sense of agency. It is interesting to note that this is an agency rooted in *communion:* The student is now in imaginative contact with other minds. She has escaped the lonely isolation of position 3. For women, the development of contextual reasoning appears to be embedded in the interpersonal. In this respect, our view of epistemological development in women is similar to other psychologists' constructions of feminine development in other domains: for example, Gilligan's (1977, 1978, 1979) and Gilligan and Murphy's (1979) views on moral development and the views of Chodorow (1978), Carlson (1972), and others on personality development.

At position 4B agency is largely confined to the academic domain. The student conducts most of her arguments on paper. She exercises her new powers of contextualism as a sort of vocational skill, useful in school but irrelevant to real life.

Many of our 4B seniors say that they wish they could go on being students forever. Many are very good students. Our data indicate that achievement of position 4B is necessary and sufficient for high academic achievement in this setting. Many fear (with reason, we think) that their competence is merely academic. They have little confidence in their capacity to function effectively outside school. Too many young women are graduated from college in this condition, about 40 percent of our sample.[5]

Position 5: Contextualism

At position 4B the student assumed that contextual reasoning was necessary in dealing with certain issues. But she did not yet assume that *all* issues, *all* questions demand this approach; she did not see its relevance or use it spontaneously in many areas of her thinking. For example, when she thought about a newspaper article, a film, her future life, her family, her friends, herself, her thinking was still more multiplistic than contextual. She tended to react to such things intuitively.

At position 5 she takes for granted that *all* areas of life require a contextual approach, and no matter what the situation, she spontaneously constructs a variety of interpretations and evaluations. Whether the question is the future of genetic cloning or the future of her relationship with a particular man, the answer is always "it depends." Both questions require examination from a variety of perspectives. The capacity for detachment that appears at this position helps the student to achieve a measure of control in her personal life.

> What Wellesley has given me is not just four years of facts, but this analyzation process. I use it in everything, now. I don't think it can be separated from me at this point, I really feel as though this way is now *me,* you know, is now a part of me. It's very important in the way I think now. It gives me the ability even in personal problems to stand back and say, "Why am I feeling this?." To—to be a little more rational, I guess, not just to—to plunge in without trying to see beyond the immediate problem, you know, but the relationship of the problem to the other things around it. It gives me a sense of perspective, I guess, is what it is.

A student reports that courses in philosophy have changed her behavior in "personal life." She is no longer at the mercy of impulse.

> It becomes more objective, like a third person, in yourself. I find that when I get upset or angry and I start to blow my top at someone or something, it's like one part of me can say, "My God, look at yourself." And it's very clearly aware of what's happening, while this other part of me is ranting and raving. I can see myself more clearly, what I'm doing, and what the implications of that are.

Earlier, the student suspected that complexity was an academic artifice. Teachers presented complex problems "to get you to think." Now she knows that complexity is real. The knowledge is comforting. Earlier, when she found it hard to figure something out, she asked, "Are things really this complex, or am I stupid?." Things really are this complex, and she is not stupid. In fact the simple has now become suspect.

> A questioning attitude has now become so much a part of us that it's unconsciously applied to other things, and you're no longer looking for simple answers. If you're out in the "real world," and a simple answer is presented to you, you start to think, "Wait a minute," and you start looking for another side to it because it can't be that simple, it can't be that easy.

It is no longer necessary to rely on others' interpretations. Indeed, it is no longer possible. One can and must make meaning for one's self. Given the nature of truth, all opinions are qualified. But this is as true of others' opinions as of one's own. Knowledge is no longer received from on high. One uses information from others to construct one's own knowledge. This is all anyone can do. At position 3 the student thought that her views—at least in some domains—were as good as anyone's. At position 4 this sense of equality was replaced by a posture of subordination to authority. At position 5 students once more see themselves as having equal access to knowledge. There are no sacred texts, no high priests. There are only colleagues. The following quotation, from an interview scored at position 5, illustrates the confidence that comes with colleagueship:

> I have a right. I'm just as much a part of things as everyone else. And therefore what I have to say is just as important as what everyone else has to say. And therefore, I'm going to say them. So that's confidence. You know that what you have is necessary. It's there. It should be there.

Out of context, this quotation, asserting the right to one's own opinion, could be seen as position 3. We see position 3 epistemology as imbalanced in the direction of right and position 4 epistemology as imbalanced in the direction of responsibility. Position 5, as we see it, integrates the right to construct one's own knowledge with the responsibility to construct it in a careful, contextual fashion.

At position 3 one is free to hold convictions instilled through socialization. At position 5 one becomes capable of *metathinking,* of thinking about one's thought. The self and its cognitions are no longer given or fixed. One can construct and reconstruct one's subjective world. Because one can break set—look at old situations in new ways—one can devise new solutions, create new opportunities. Metathinking confers real agency.

But metathinking also leads to indecision. Here, again, position 5 sounds like position 3, unable to make up her mind. Women at position 5 often fear that they have regressed, seniors say they have become as wishy-washy as they were freshman year. But position 3's wishy-washiness was relatively passive and reactive. At position 5 it is the activity of contextual reasoning that makes one wishy-washy.

> I think I really learned how to reason things through and how to analyze here. . . . I've found myself beginning to take more factors into account before deciding opinions. . . . I used to have more or less absolute morals. I would think something was right or I would think that it was wrong. And then I've changed my way of thinking so that I can see arguments on both sides more and I weigh the factors very carefully before I decide, and so, usually it's hard to take a firm stand on anything then. I mean maybe I'll refine this process of whatever it is, to the point where I can take more definitive stands. But right now, it's funny because I don't seem to be making any kind of definite judgments one way or the other on anything . . . I usually find myself caught somewhere in the middle. I can see it in interpretations of literature, I can see it in interpretations of history. In Psych. too, deciding whose theories you're going to accept and whose theories you're going to reject. . . . I used to be absolutely against abortion, anything you could say about it, I would be against it. For various reasons, this and this and this and this. And then being here, just being in this environment I guess, I started thinking more about it, thinking more in terms of it's your

own body, when exactly does life begin, etc., etc., and so now I've kind of refined my view of it and redefined my values about it. . . . I still don't think it's right but now I also don't think it's wrong. It's more in the middle. . . . I wish I could just make up my mind on some things though. . . . I find myself consciously making decisions now more than before. Before I would kind of just do things . . . And now even with the smallest little things you have to make decisions about what you're going to do. Whether it's "I am going to Cambridge on Saturday" or "I am going to stay here and do work." And you think about it more, you know, little tiny things. . . . Little things become big.

And the big things seem utterly insurmountable—things like "What shall I do with my life?." Perry describes the dilemma.

> If one comes to look upon all knowing and all valuing as contingent on context, and if one is then confronted with an infinite universe of potential contexts for truth and care, one is threatened with loss of identity. From one context to another what one will see as true and what one will care about will be discontinuous; one will not know who "I" am. [Perry 1968, p. 134]

During the early stages of position 5, the student is too busy exploring and expanding her intellectual competence and the world it reveals to her to worry about issues of identity and commitment. But gradually the exercise of skill becomes more habitual and less exhilarating, the revelations less novel and more expectable. And the student begins to worry about her own place in this contextual world. The need is partly imposed from without, of course. Society is saying that the moratorium is nearly over; one must soon make real decisions in the real world. But there is also pressure from within. One wants to be something, to believe something, to do something, and one does not know how. As Perry says, toward the end of position 5 the student feels a need for commitment but has no sense of how it might develop within this contextual universe.

Most of the seniors we have studied are at this position. The frenzy they exhibit around issues of life after college occurs in part because their cognitive timetables are at odds with society's timetable. They are unready to make the decisions the world says they must make. In an earlier era, women sometimes took flight into marriage to prolong the moratorium. Now, they may take flight into law school. (What happens then we do not know; we are just beginning to interview alumnae.)

Commitment within Contextualism

It is important to distinguish between *commitment,* as Perry defines it, and everyday meanings of commitment. Perry's commitment refers to an "affirmation" (Perry 1968) of personal choices or values within a contextual universe. That is, the person invests herself in an occupation, in a set of personal values, in relationships with a mate or with friends, understanding fully that reason alone can never justify these investments as the right ones. They are right only within a given context; from other points of view, other occupations, other values, or other relationships would make just as much sense. Nonetheless, the person comes to feel that these decisions and commitments are necessary, that the assumptions of position 5 are not sufficient for the good life, although they are necessary to it.

Some of the seniors whose protocols we have analyzed have moved on to position 6 (Perry's *Commitment Foreseen*) and a few to position 7 (*initial commitment*). Because our understanding of the evolution of commitment is embryonic, we shall not dwell on these positions. At position 5 the student could not make up her mind. At position 6 she may still have trouble making up her mind, but she knows that someday she will. If she cannot decide, she assumes the time is not yet ripe. She is not ashamed of indecision, and she is not frightened by it: indecision is temporary, and it is natural.

> I find it very hard to make decisions. And it used to bother me that I was so indecisive . . . but it doesn't bother me as much anymore . . . It's not that I don't eventually make a decision. It's just that I've seen that there's a lot of sides to something, and I can't just kind of disregard a lot of things that to me are important that I have to think about before I make a decision.

Decisions cannot be forced; they will evolve. This relaxation can be mistaken for the passivity of earlier positions, but the flavor is quite different. At position 3 one waited for the right answer to appear magically from without; now, one waits for an appropriate answer to evolve naturally from within. It is all right to float, so long as one *decides* to float.

> I've decided to give myself the experience of not knowing where I'm going or not knowing what I'm doing. But that's a conscious decision, rather than something I'm finding myself sort of caught in. To be in control of not being in control. . . .

And,

> The more I think about things in advance, the more I have a chance to take control of my life myself and not just let things happen to me. That is valuable. At other times, I would just like things to come as they will come. It's a weighing of spontaneity and control.

Perry says that students at the highest stages of development habitually engage in this sort of weighing of opposites. This was true of his sophisticated male subjects, and it seems to be true of our sophisticated female subjects. It may be that at the highest positions men and women are very similar. Position 3, as it appears in our sample, contains many features that are stereotypically female (for example, intuition, emotion, passivity, and an emphasis upon the personal) and some that are stereotypically masculine (for example, separation and an orientation toward rights). Position 4 contains many features that are stereotypically masculine (for example, objectivity, logic, analysis) and some that are stereotypically feminine (for example, conformity and a search for approval). But the contextual world appears to be androgynous. To act responsibly in such a world requires synthesis of so-called male thesis and so-called female antithesis—of the subjective and objective, of control and spontaneity.

This, perhaps, is agency in its most sophisticated form—at least as it appears during the college years. We know little about the development of agency at higher levels because few students reach these levels during the college years. We hope that as we analyze more data from the sophisticated students we have and from our alumnae sample we will be able to describe further developments more precisely and, perhaps, suggest ways in which colleges might nurture such development more effectively than they do. We believe that too many women graduate from college deficient in the capacity to decide and to act and to trust their decisions and actions. This may be true of men as well but may be more crucial in the case of women, since in the real world the students talk about women are more often rewarded for docility than for agency. If they do not develop agency in college, they may never develop it.

Notes

1. We prefer the term *contextualism* to Perry's *relativism* or *contextual relativism*. The everyday meaning of relativism is close to Perry's *multiplicity* and is, therefore, confusing.

2. This design enables us to make longitudinal, cross-sectional, and time-lag comparisons within the data and thus to separate out effects of age, cohort, and time of measurement. Developmental changes in the individual can thus be distinguished from historical changes in the culture.

3. The reader will notice the sexual connotations of the language used by many of these position 3 students (for example, exposing the self, being turned on, staying open, letting it rise). In a forthcoming paper we discuss the language typically used by women at various epistemological positions in relation to possible unconscious emotional conflicts at these positions.

4. These figures may magnify slightly the decline in position 3 reasoning during the college years. Our attrition rate is low. Few students leave the college permanently, and few who stay have refused continued participation

in the study, but a preliminary look at the data that have been analyzed suggests that both sorts of attrition (leaving the college and leaving the study) occur more frequently among position 3 students than among students at higher positions.

5. We are currently doing an intensive study, funded by the Spencer Foundation, of the 4-5 transition. The aims of this project are to identify (1) small transformations that occur during the transition, and (2) experiences that may promote or inhibit transition. We are pursuing educational implications of the research as Shaughnessy Scholars in 1981-1982 under a program sponsored by the Fund for The Improvement of Post-Secondary Education (FIPSE). In addition, Clinchy is codirector, with Mary Field Belenky, Nancy Goldberger, and Jill Mattuck Tarule, of a two-year project on Education for Women's Development, also supported by FIPSE. In this project about one-hundred-fifty women varying widely in age, ethnic and social background, and educational setting, have been interviewed concerning their educational experiences. The women's developmental status is being assessed along a number of dimensions, including our version of the Perry scheme. The ultimate aim of the project is to contribute to the design of educational environments that will promote development in adolescent and adult women.

Bibliography

Carlson, R. "Understanding Women: Implications for Personality Theory and Research." *Journal of Social Issues* 28 (1972):17-32.

Chodorow, N. *The Reproduction of Mothering.* Berkeley: University of California Press, 1978.

Clinchy, B.; Lief, J.; and Young, P. "Epistemological and Moral Development in Girls from a Traditional and a Progressive High School." *Journal of Educational Psychology* 69 (1977):337-343.

Clinchy, B. and Zimmerman, C. *Cognitive Development in College Women,* forthcoming.

Gilligan, C. "In a Different Voice: Women's Conceptions of Self and Morality." *Harvard Educational Review* 47 (1977):481-517.

————. "Moral Development in the College Years." In A. Chickering, ed., *The Future American College.* San Francisco: Jossey-Bass, 1978.

————. Women's Place in Man's Life Cycle. *Harvard Educational Review* 49 (1979):431-446.

Gilligan, C., and Murphy, M. "The Philosopher and the Dilemma of the Fact: Evidence for Continuing Development from Adolescence to Adulthood." In D. Kuhn, ed., *Intellectual Development Beyond Childhood.* San Francisco: Jossey-Bass, 1979.

Keniston, K. *The Uncommitted*. New York: Harcourt, Brace, and World, 1960.

Parker, C., ed., *Encouraging Development in College Students*. Minneapolis: University of Minnesota Press, 1978.

Perry, W. *Patterns of Development in Thought and Values of Students in a Liberal Arts College: A Validation of a Scheme*. Washington, D.C.: U.S. Department of Health, Education and Welfare, 1968.

―――. *Forms of Intellectual and Ethical Development in the College Years*. New York: Holt, Rinehart, and Winston, 1970.

―――. "Cognitive and Ethical Growth: The Making of Meaning." In A. Chickering, ed., *The Modern American College*. San Francisco: Jossey-Bass, 1981.

8 Social Psychology Looks at but Does Not See the Undergraduate Woman

Sumru Erkut

Broadly stated, social psychology is the study of individuals in a social context. One may be tempted to conclude that undergraduate women (individuals) in colleges and universities (social context) would be subject matter par excellence for social psychologists. Such is not the case, however. Although social psychologists have not necessarily avoided looking at undergraduate women as subjects in their studies, they have definitely not researched their needs, concerns, experiences, or their general development. There are three reasons for this neglect. One has to do with the scope of mainstream social-psychological research. The second reason is the lack of a theoretical perspective for studying women in higher-education settings. The third reason is the limitations of social psychology's methodological tools.

Social psychologists who have done research in higher education have often employed surveys to gather their data and relied on regression-based techniques to analyze their results. More often than not, such methods are identified with sociological and even educational research. Consequently, social psychologists who do survey research on higher education often publish in sociology or education journals because not only their research focus but their methods fall outside mainstream social psychology. In fact, the only book on higher education that identifies itself with the discipline of social psychology in its title, *College and Student: Selected Readings in the Social Psychology of Higher Education* (Feldman 1972a), contains not a single study that was previously published in a social-psychology journal.

Scope of Mainstream Social Psychology

Mainstream social psychology, what House (1977) refers to as psychological social psychology, emphasizes hypothesis testing over descriptive research. Social psychologists study the behavioral response of individuals to a social stimulus that is perceived to be theoretically relevant to the behavior in question. The object of the research is to see if individuals think, act, or feel differently as a function of the social stimulus to which they have been exposed. The emphasis on hypothesis testing is characteristic of both experimental laboratory research and the more applied research in social psychology.[1]

The emphasis on hypothesis testing as opposed to descriptive research has definite implications for the social-psychological study of the undergraduate woman. The few, primarily hypothesis-testing studies that happen to employ female undergraduates as subjects have been thoroughly integrated into the mainstream of social-psychological literature. Two such works stand out: Newcomb's Bennington College study (1943) with its follow-up twenty years later (Newcomb, Koenig, Flacks, and Warwick 1967) and the Siegels' study of Stanford women in residence halls (Siegel and Siegel 1957). These two studies have been widely reprinted. Not only are they well known to most social psychologists, but their inclusion in the prestigious readers commissioned by the Society for the Study of Social Issues (Newcomb and Hartley 1947; Swanson, Newcomb, and Hartley 1952; Maccoby, Newcomb, and Hartley 1958; Proshansky and Seidenberg 1965) has helped define the subject matter of social psychology.

The popularity of Newcomb's and the Seigels's studies contrasts sharply with social psychologists' total neglect of two other studies of undergraduate women. These have also been conducted by prominent social psychologists: Nevitt Sanford headed the Vassar studies (1956) and Lois Murphy headed the Sarah Lawrence studies (Murphy and Raushenbush 1960). The reason for this neglect is that the Vassar and Sarah Lawrence studies are primarily descriptive. They focus on the experience and development of young women at these two highly distinctive college environments. As such, mainstream social psychologists consider these works to be in the realm of educational psychology or personality development but not social psychology.

Mainstream Social Psychological Research on the
Undergraduate Woman

That undergraduate women were looked at but not seen is very much evident in the mainstream research of Newcomb and the Siegels. Newcomb's study of Bennington College women (1943) was never presented in the social-psychological literature as a study of undergraduate women. Rather, it was presented as a test of the hypothesis that reference groups play an important role in attitude change (1947; 1952). Newcomb found that Bennington women, most of whom were from fairly conservative Republican backgrounds, became more liberal in their political-economic outlook with each successive year of residence at Bennington. The attitude change was most pronounced for women who were well integrated into life at Bennington and who were popular and were aware of Bennington's liberal norms. The shift in attitude from conservative to liberal did not occur for women who were not well adjusted to life at Bennington but maintained their primary loyalties to their parents. Thus, those who took the Bennington community as a reference group became more liberal in attitude toward public issues. Those who did not remained conservative. The Siegel's (1957) study can be considered a sequel to Newcomb's. Through a clever field experiment, the Siegels were able to test whether membership groups, in addition to reference groups, have an effect on attitude change. They initially measured the attitudes of twenty-eight freshman women who shared the same membership group (residence in a freshman dormitory) and the same reference group (as expressed by a preference to live in the high status row houses during the sophomore year). Of these women, nine drew lots with sufficiently large numbers to qualify them to move into the prestigious housing. Consequently, during the sophomore year, nine women had the same membership and reference group, the other nineteen had divergent membership and reference groups in that they were now living in nonrow housing. At the end of the sophomore year, all twenty-eight women indicated preferences for the following year's housing; they also filled out an attitude questionnaire. All nine row-house women chose to remain in row housing. These women showed the least change in attitudes. Eleven women currently living in non-row housing applied for row housing for the following year. These women showed some change in attitudes. This finding indicates that membership in nonrow housing, even though their reference group was still the row houses, affected their attitudes. The most attitude change occurred among the eight women who expressed a desire to remain in nonrow housing. They had come to take the imposed, initially nonpreferred membership groups as their reference group. Thus, the Siegels' study shows that membership groups that diverge from reference groups can affect attitudes, if not to the extent that is produced when membership and reference groups coincide.

Just as Newcomb did not present his research as a study of women at Bennington College, the Siegels never presented their experiment as an investigation of undergraduate women. Indeed, Stanford, the university where the study took place, is never identified in their published report. The fact that the subjects were women appears to be a matter of convenience. Women were studied because assignment to women's residence halls at Stanford made it possible to conduct a natural field experiment. That the subjects were women does not seem to have been a factor in Newcomb's study either. In the Bennington follow-up study (Newcomb, Koenig, Flacks, and Warwick 1967), however, we do see some subtle evidence of the recognition that the subjects are women. Newcomb speculates that Bennington graduates who maintained their liberalism over the years were able to do so because they surrounded themselves with liberal reference

groups, most particularly a liberal husband. The lapsed liberals were surrounded by conservative husbands and friends. The few who remained
liberal despite having conservative husbands were active in liberal causes
and thus had extradomestic liberal reference groups. It is curious that
Newcomb does not entertain the possibility that women could persist in
holding an attitude on the basis of a deeply held internal conviction,
without external support.[2] One can only speculate that had Newcomb been
studying males, he would have been more likely to invoke internalized
values as a basis for the persistence of attitudes.

Nonmainstream Social-Psychological Research

Whereas mainstream social psychology has looked at but not seen the
undergraduate women, many researchers with training in social psychology
have studied women in college even if they were not able to publish their
studies as social-psychological research. Two sets of early studies of this
genre stand out. One is a research program sponsored by the Mary Conover
Mellon Foundation at Vassar College of Vassar students and alumnae (see,
for example, Brown 1962; Bushnell 1962; Freedman 1962; see especially
Sanford 1956). The Vassar studies appear to have explored all aspects of
student culture, academic life, intellectual growth, personality change, and
life after college of the women who attended this small, highly selective
liberal-arts college during the 1950s and some who graduated between 1929
and 1935. The second set of studies were conducted at Sarah Lawrence College during the 1930s and 1950s (see Munroe 1944; Murphy and Ladd 1944;
Murphy and Raushenbush 1960). The Sarah Lawrence studies, too, explored all aspects of student culture, academic life, intellectual growth, and
personality development of women who attended this very small, highly
selective liberal-arts college. Both the Vassar and Sarah Lawrence studies
provide rich, detailed data on women undergraduates. Beyond describing
the college experience of women at these two highly atypical, single-sex institutions, however, their results are of limited value.[3] Indeed, the authors
of both the Vassar and the Sarah Lawrence studies are always careful to
point out that their subjects very likely do not represent the typical undergraduate woman.

   The period between the later 1950s and early 1970s has been witness to a
growing number of studies of undergraduate women, sometimes studied
alone, sometimes in comparison with men. For example, Almquist and
Angrist (1970) did a longitudinal study of career salience among 110 women
in the same class in a women's college of a coeducational university. Astin
(1977) carried out longitudinal surveys of some 200,000 college women and
men from a national sample of over 300 institutions of higher education

over a span of nearly fifteen years from 1961 to 1974. Douvan and Kaye (1962) studied high-school students' reasons for seeking higher education and choosing a particular college on a national probability sample of 1925 girls and 1045 boys. When the findings on female undergraduates are compared with results of similar research on male undergraduates we see that some of the impact of college is the same for women and men. As a result of a college education both women and men show a decline in authoritarian attitudes and religious observance and an increase in liberalism (see Freedman 1962; Feldman and Newcomb 1969; Astin 1977). On the other hand, women as a group differ from men as a group when they start college. Astin (1977) shows that some of these differences persist or become more accentuated during the four years in college. Women begin with stronger religious, altruistic, and artistic interests than men. Men begin with stronger business interests, greater hedonism, and higher interpersonal and intellectual self-esteem than women. These initial differences persist throughout the college years. Sex differences in status needs increase in college along with aspirations for high-level degrees because women show sharper declines in these areas during college than do men. Men are more likely to achieve in athletics, publish original writing, and acquire technical or scientific skills. Women are more likely to get married; men are more likely to go on to graduate or professional schools (see Astin 1977, pp. 215, 216). Whereas there is no appreciable sex differences in rates of dropping out of college, women and men differ in the reasons for leaving (Iffert 1957; Pantages and Creedon 1978). Women are more likely to leave because of getting married or getting pregnant; men are more likely to leave because of academic problems.

Women now outnumber men in college enrollments. The sheer weight of their number and the impact of social forces that brought about that increase in women's enrollment in the first place are likely to alter the college experience of women and, for that matter, of men. The 1980s should prove to be an exciting time to study women in college.

Lack of a Theoretical Framework

The scarcity of social-psychological theories for understanding women's development as a result of a college education is another reason why social psychologists have not studied the undergraduate woman. The lack of theories is a serious handicap in that, as previously mentioned, social psychologists are primarily interested in hypothesis-testing research.

The pervasiveness of a masculine bias in social-psychological model building is only partly responsible for the lack of theories for understanding women's development (see, for example, critiques in Horner 1968; Gilligan 1977). The lack is also partly due to the insufficient theoretical attention social psychologists have paid to demographic characteristics. Whereas social psychologists have been eager to incorporate personality theories about individual differences into their research, demographic characteristics such as sex and level of education have been relatively ignored.[4]

The serious study of the psychology of women is still in its infancy. As yet we have no overarching models for interpreting women's development. Some minitheories have been put forth to explain a limited range of women's behaviors. These have been widely incorporated into social-psychological research but with mixed results. For example, Horner's motive to avoid success (1968, 1972) has been extensively tested but problems of measurement and conflicting results have largely discredited the original thesis (see Tressemer, 1974, 1976; Zuckerman and Wheeler, 1975; Shaver, 1976). Sex role orientation and its outgrowth, androgyny (Bem, 1974; Spence and Helmreich, 1978) were acclaimed as a breakthrough for studying both women and men. However, what sex role orientation indices measure has come under serious questioning recently (see Lenney, 1979; Locksley and Colten, 1979; Pedhazur and Tetenbaum 1979).

In lieu of overarching theories there have been attempts to describe women's cognitive, ethical, and moral development (see Clinchy and Zimmerman in chapter 7 of this book, and Gilligan 1977), but these efforts have not yet generated social-psychological research on women. Extending Perry's epistomological and ethical development scheme of development in college to women, Clinchy and Zimmerman describe cognitive development during the college years. This scheme, if it can be extended beyond the traditional college age range, should prove to be a valuable heuristic for studying the impact of a college education on women.

Theorizing about educational attainment has fared even worse than gender in social-psychological research. In the 1950s and 1960s there was interest in education as an independent variable in two different lines of research. On the more psychological side, researchers interested in authoritarian personality investigated whether college education is associated with less dogmatic and more tolerant attitudes (Stern, Stein, and Bloom 1956; Plant 1965; Lehmann, Sinha, and Hartnett 1966; Trent and Medsker 1968). On the more sociological side, Inkeles (Inkeles 1969; Inkeles and Smith 1974) has studied the socialization impact of formal education (see also Dreeben 1968). Today, however, one rarely sees controls for education in social-psychological research, let alone theorizing about its impact.

Because women's attainment of higher education spans quite a few years, the most appropriate theoretical approach toward understanding the impact of a college education would have to incorporate a developmental perspective. In addition to those who graduate from college within four years of finishing high school, many women go back to college after taking time out for raising a family, and many start college after their childbearing years. Thus, the typical undergraduate woman is not necessarily between the ages of seventeen and twenty-one (see Heyns and Bird in chapter 3 of this book). Much of the research on the impact of college does not control for the impact of maturation. In the study of seventeen to twenty-one-year-old undergraduates this is a definite problem in that what occurs as a product of maturation may be misattributed to the impact of college. An even more serious problem arises when studying women in college, many of whom are of an atypical age for traditional undergraduates. It has been suggested that with age comes an increase in variability in growth rate among individuals (see Huston-Stein and Baltes 1976). Thus it is crucial to understand women's development over their life course, not just in the seventeen to twenty-one age range, in order to assess properly the impact of a college education that may come early, on time, late, or intermittently over a large span of years.

In addition to incorporating a developmental perspective, theorizing about women's college experience must take into account a number of issues identified by researchers in the field. Many researchers point to the career versus family dilemma that confronts women—but not men—to interpret the differences in the college experience of women and men. The dilemma is that given the sexual division of labor in most families, the limited and unattractive choices for alternative child care, in addition to a widely shared ideology that women *ought* to be the primary housekeepers and child rearers plus play a supportive role for their husbands, many women find it difficult to commit themselves to the pursuit of a career outside the home. Many women, and most likely many more men, believe that a woman who wishes to have a full family life must give up her aspirations for an outside career. Conversely, women who wish to make commitments to a career cannot have a full family life. Thus, women face the dilemma of choosing between marriage and career.

Until the mid-1970s, most researchers conceptualized and investigated women's college experience as the playing out of the career versus family dilemma. Research on college women showed that the majority of women resolved the dilemma by gearing their college experience and career choices to subordinate career to family (Beardslee and O'Dowd 1962; Douvan and Kaye 1962; Angrist 1972). Women did this by majoring in traditionally feminine fields such as education, nursing, humanities, and social sciences (with the exception of economics). They were likely to drop out of college upon getting married or becoming pregnant. They altered their career aspirations to accommodate their spouses' and children's need. These women prepared for flexible jobs as teachers, nurses, secretaries, jobs which allows for discontinuity. (A women can work full time or part time, continuously or intermittently in these lines of work without too much threat of becoming unemployable.) Women's educational and career planning that is intended to accommodate family needs has been characterized as contingency planning (see Bernard 1981). The contingencies are dictated by getting married or remaining single, husband's job mobility, child-care needs, family financial needs, separation, divorce, or widowhood. It appears women prepare themselves by being ready for a variety of contingencies—being ready to change jobs when husband is transferred, stop working when children are born, work full or part time when there is family financial need. The contingency planning of women is complemented by the men's preparation to be the primary breadwinner to maximize the total welfare of the family. Indeed, contingency planning by women makes sense when there is a primary breadwinner in the family other than the mother.

Recent demographic trends have brought into question the wisdom of women' contingency planning. Today the average woman will spend at least a portion of her life without a primary breadwinner spouse, either through widowhood, divorce, separation, or never having been married. Consequently, the majority of the country's poor are women, especially those among elderly or female-headed families. Thus, it no longer makes economic sense for women to gear their college education to prepare for the traditionally female jobs. More and more women in college are preparing to combine family and career. For example, in a study carried out in 1979 Erkut and Mokros (1981) found that college women who picked a female professor as a role model were most interested in finding out that it is possible to combine a rewarding professional life with a fulfilling family live.

Moreover, the last decade has brought with it a change in ideology that challenges women to prepare for and seek equity in education, work, and social relationships. Many researchers believe that the changes in sex-role ideology are responsible for the recent findings that many women in college plan for continuous careers in which they will combine their career and family roles (Parelius 1975; Safilios-Rothschild 1979). Indeed, women who espouse nontraditional views of their sex role are more likely to have higher educational aspirations, greater career commitment, and aspirations for careers in traditionally male-dominated fields (see Angrist 1972; Lipman-Blumen 1972).

In addition to sex-role ideology, a number of other factors have been isolated as concomitants of a career commitment and choice of nontraditional careers. For example, Hawley (1972) found that women undergraduates who believed significant men in their lives did not hold sex-stereotypic views were more likely to have continuous career plans. On the other hand, those who believed men evaluate behavior on the basis of sex appropriateness were more likely to emphasize marriage over a career. Almquist and Angrist (1970) found that career-salient women were more likely to report being influenced by college faculty and occupational role models than family or peers. The opposite was true of non-career-salient women.

Still another factor that is hypothesized to influence the outcome of a college education is whether the college is coeducational or single sex. Tidball (1973, 1980) demonstrated, using correlational techniques, that women from women's colleges are overrepresented among successful female graduates (success being defined as being listed in *Who's Who of American Women*). Tidball and Kistiakowsky (1976) showed that successful women in the sciences are more likely to have attended women's colleges. The Brown Project (Brown University 1980), which is the report of an investigation of student life in four coeducational and two womens' colleges, indicated that women who attend single-sex colleges have higher self-esteem than women who attend coeducational colleges. Erkut and Mokros (1981) found women at a single-sex liberal arts college to have higher aspirations for advanced degrees than both men and women at five comparable coeducational institutions.[5]

What is needed, then, is a developmental approach to understanding women's experiences in college that takes into consideration recent changes in sex-role ideology, the problems and prospects of combining career with family, and the special needs of female students, which women's colleges may be fulfilling better than coeducational colleges.

Lack of Adequate Research Tools

The third reason why social psychologists have not studied undergraduate women is that most of them are unfamiliar with and distrust research methods other than the tightly controlled experiment. The typical social-psychological study is an experiment in which individuals are randomly assigned to experimental and control groups where the experimental manipulation involves a carefully controlled altering of one aspect of the social environment.[6] Although there exists relatively new, nonexperimental methodology that, in effect, substitutes statistical for experimental controls, social psychologists have been slow in using such methods.

In the study of the impact of a college experience on undergraduate women, the basic issue is how to design a study that can test whether the effect (or impact) obtained was due solely to the undergraduate experience. The ideal design may appear to be an experiment in which a randomly drawn sample of high-school graduates is randomly assigned to two groups, one of which attends college for four years, the other of which does not. The random assignment would ensure that the two groups are identical in all respects except that one group receives the experimental treatment (college) but the other group does not. Since both groups mature during the four years of this study, any differences obtained between the two groups cannot be attributed to maturation. Also since both groups were identical before the college experience (because of random assignment) the effects obtained cannot be due to characteristics individual students bring to college. Thus, the experimental method assures that, if the controls have worked, the obtained effect is due to the college experience.

Unfortunately, such a study cannot be conducted because it is not possible to assign high-school graduates randomly to college and noncollege groups. Moreover, even if it were hypothetically possible to do this, it is not altogether clear what constitutes a noncollege control group. People who do not attend college do a variety of things including getting a job, starting a family, doing odd jobs, or doing nothing special. Clearly, in addition to maturing over four years, noncollege attenders are benefiting from a number of experiences. Similarly, given the variety of college experiences available (community colleges, four-year liberal-arts colleges, universities, single-sex versus coed institutions, private versus public institutions, and so forth), it is not entirely clear what constitutes a college experience. Thus, it is no wonder that social psychologists, with their preference for the experimental method over other methods, have been reluctant to study the impact of college on women, or for that matter on men.

Without a doubt, isolating the effect of a complex experience that takes place over several years—while other changes are also taking place (that is, studying the impact of college)—is not an easy task. Researchers who have undertaken such investigations have had to confront a host of methodological problems. Feldman, one of the few social psychologists interested in studying college impacts, has summarized the methodological issues confronting the researcher of higher education (see Feldman 1972b, 1972c).

The first step is to choose a data-collection strategy that is appropriate for making inferences about events that occur through time. Cross-sectional designs attempt to handle this problem without waiting for the effect of college to take place. Rather, they compare two different groups, one which has gone through the experience and the other which has just begun it. Typically, this would involve comparing freshmen and seniors at one point in time. But there are problems with cross-sectional designs. One problem is the lack of comparability of freshmen and seniors, making it inappropriate to assume that any observed differences are due to the impact of college.[7] A second problem is the lack of comparability of the college experiences of current freshmen and seniors. Because colleges are dynamic institutions, the experiences seniors have had in their four years of college may be different from those current freshmen will be facing. Finally, at a general level, cross-sectional designs do not allow the researcher to disentangle change in the same individual over time from differences among individual rates of change (Baltes and Nesselroade 1973). Because individuals vary in the rate at which they change, comparisons among individuals who are at two different points of development (for example, freshmen and seniors) cannot be taken as evidence for how individuals would change over time. Thus the cross-sectional design does not have much to recommend itself other than economy in time and money.

Another method, the unmatched longitudinal design, involves the study of a sample of freshmen and a sample of seniors four years later without making an effort to see if the same students were studied over time. The unmatched longitudinal design assures that the two groups have the same four years of college experience. The comparability of the two groups, however, is still suspect because of changes in the sample pool due to dropouts and transfers.

The matched longitudinal design where the same freshmen are restudied as seniors overcomes the problems of both the lack of comparability of the two groups and the lack of comparability of the college experience. It is the design most suitable for studying the impact of events over time. But it, too, is not without its shortcomings. Since only the students on whom data can be obtained both as freshmen and seniors are included in the study, the sample is not representative of all college students. The design does not provide information on the college experience of dropouts or transfer students.

All three designs also suffer from another shortcoming in that they focus on students in college. The lack of a noncollege control group against which to test whether any obtained effect was due to maturation or extracollege social forces is not easily overcome. Some researchers have included in their studies noncollege control groups (Plant 1965; Trent and Medsker 1968). As noted, there are problems with choosing a noncollege control group because going or not going to college is not a random but rather a highly selective process. Noncollege and college groups differ on a number of relevant characteristics (for example, socioeconomic status), making comparisons between the two groups difficult.

Feldman (1972b) recommends an indirect approach for testing the alternative hypotheses of the effect of maturation and events outside of college. The indirect approach is based on the assumption that if the college experience has an impact, more years in college will have more of an impact than fewer years in college. Thus, time of exposure to college (measured in quarters, semesters, or years) can be introduced as a control in the study of college impacts. Astin (1977) augments the time of exposure to college variable with controlling for intensity of exposure to college. The latter variable is an indicator of the extent of a student's involvement with the college environment—that is, time and effort spent in activities that relate directly to the college and its programs (for example, living in a residence hall versus commuting, interacting with faculty, joining clubs or honor societies, taking part in extracurricular activities). It is expected that if the college experience does have an impact, students who immerse themselves in college life will be affected more than those who are not so involved.[8]

Choosing a cross-sectional or longitudinal design and various strategies for employing controls are the preliminary problems a researcher faces. Next, a series of issues regarding what to measure must be faced. Longitudinal studies of college impact are typically analyses of change or analyses of college outcomes. Change studies are analogous to the pre-post-measurement designs with which social psychologists are so familiar. Subjects are measured in the beginning of their college careers and then at the end using the same instruments. The differences between the pre and post scores yields the change score. If one is interested in analyzing whether and why given attributes change or remain stable when a person attends college, change scores appear to be the appropriate dependent variable. Using change scores is problematic, however. Change scores tend to be systematically related to any random error in measurement (see Cronbach and Furby 1970). Indeed, because of this problem, Cronbach and Furby recommend using outcome measures rather than change scores. In fact, some aspects of college impact do not lend themselves to change measures, that they are truly college outcomes (for example, graduation or dropping out of college, choice of major, choice of career). Many other college outcomes, such as attitudes, beliefs, or knowledge can be conceptualized either as a change or an outcome. Moreover, outcome variables can be measured in the freshman and senior years as in a pre-post design. Freshmen scores can then be used as one of the predictors of scores obtained when the subjects are seniors (see Astin 1977). Outcome measures overcome the problem posed by correlation of change scores with measurement error if the outcome is obtained only once. However, if pre and post measures on outcome scores are obtained, one encounters the same problem of correlated errors in measurement.

Two types of independent variables are typically incorporated into studies of college impact. One of them is the characteristics students bring to college. These are often measures of demographic characteristics such as age, socioeconomic status, or race; measures of ability such as IQ scores, grades in high school, or SAT scores; or they can be the pre measures of the outcome variables. The reason for incorporating student characteristics into the study as independent variables is to be able to ascertain whether *these* rather than the college experience can better explain college outcomes. The second set of independent variables has to do with operationalizations of the college experience. In studies such as Astin's (1977), where a large number of colleges are studied, a host of variables measuring the college environment (for example, size, selectivity, geographic location, type of control, coed versus single sex) have been employed.

The use of student characteristics and college environment as independent variables in regression analyses have proven to be problematic (see Feldman 1972c) because the two sets of variables are highly correlated. Particular types of students are attracted to particular colleges. Moreover, the type of student body a college attracts is a major factor in creating the college's unique environment. The problem this intercorrelation poses for regression analysis is how to apportion the common variance shared by the two sets of independent variables. Controlling for student variables first would potentially underestimate the true impact of college experience because the common part of the variance would be attributed to student characteristics. Conversely, controlling for college environment first would potentially underestimate the true impact of student variables because the common variance would be attributed to environment variables. One way out of this dilemma is to have a theoretical model that determines the nature of the causal relationships among student, college environment, and college-outcome variables. It is possible to argue that student variables should be controlled first because a student's characteristics are temporally prior to any college experiences she has. On the other hand, one can argue that the college environment exists and draws particular types of students, so the environment variables should be controlled for first. An alternative model to both of these is to conceive of student and college-environment variables as reciprocally influencing each other.

The literature on methodological problems in determining college impacts is full of controversy over which type of variables to control for first and through which type of statistical techniques (see Pugh 1968; Richards 1968; Werts and Watley 1968; Creager 1969; Ward 1969; Astin 1970, 1977). Feldman (1972c) summarizes the controversies over the uses of alternative statistical models and concludes by suggesting that the theoretical questions one asks of the data ought to determine the mode of analysis. Indeed, the lack of formal theorizing has been the major stumbling block in studies of college impacts.

An extension of regression-based techniques, structural-equation models (see Van de Geer 1971; Duncan 1975; Namboodiri, Carter, and Blalock 1975; Heise 1975; Bielby and Hauser 1977; Joreskog 1979), solves many of the problems discussed above (for example, change scores being correlated with errors in measurement in initial scores, how to apportion the shared variances between student input characteristics and college environment, and lack of explicit causal models). What a structural-equation model does can be summarized as follows. The researcher posits assumptions about the causal relationships among a set of theoretically significant variables, thus specifying a causal model. The given set of causal assumptions generates a corresponding set of equations. The solution to these equations gives estimates of the magnitude of causal relationships among the variables. Finally, it allows the researcher to test the validity of the model by assessing the goodness of fit between observed relationships among the variables and those predicted from the estimated parameters.[9]

Structural equation models would appear to be a fruitful approach for achieving statistical controls in naturalistic data on issues that do not lend themselves to experimental controls. The technique has already been successfully applied to exploration of issues related to women's career attainment (Perun 1979); career commitment (Bielby in chapter 14 of this book), family formation (Alexander, Reilly, and Eckland in chapter 15 of this book), and the psychological effects of working conditions on women (Miller, Schooler, Kohn, and Miller 1980). To date no researcher has applied this technique to the study of undergraduate women. No doubt it will soon be employed to explore the impact of college on female undergraduates.

Summary and Conclusions

Social psychologists have conducted many studies in which college women have served as subjects. In these studies, however, the focus has not been on the college experience of women students. Rather women, along with men in college, have been a convenient subject pool. Thus, whereas women have been looked at, the study of their development in college has not made its way into the mainstream of social-psychological literature. In this essay three reasons for this oversight have been cited. These are social psychologists' primary interest in hypothesis testing as opposed to descriptive research, lack of theorizing about women's development in college to generate hypotheses for research, and social psychologists' lack of familiarity with research methods that employ statistical rather than experimental controls.

Nevertheless, many researchers with training in social psychology have done research on women in college, even if they were not able to publish their studies in established social-psychological journals or texts. Some of this research that was carried out in the 1950s, 1960s, and even early 1970s is dated now. Since the mid-1970s, more women of all ages have been going to college and more women of all ages work for pay outside the home. These demographic changes, coupled with a changing sex-role ideology, have altered the classic dilemma facing college women. Now the basic issue facing women is no longer how to choose between family versus career but how to combine family and career. Fresh theorizing that takes into consideration these recent trends is clearly needed for an adequate understanding of women's college experiences. In structural-equation models we now have a statistical tool that more adequately surmounts the difficulties of assessing the impact of college than previously popular methods. The challenge of the 1980s is to begin work on generating theories about the experiences of today's college women. There will be, then, neither reasons nor excuses for not doing first-rate hypothesis-testing research about the undergraduate woman.

Notes

1. An applied focus has been a rich and respected research tradition in the social-psychological literature. In many disciplines applied research is

often more descriptive. However, the applied work that is integrated into the mainstream of social-psychological literature has been either generated by theoretical formulations (for example, Lewin's field theory in relation to changing food habits (Lewin 1943) or has been instrumental in generating theoretical formulation (for example, investigations of helping behavior instigated by the Kitty Genovese murder, which led to theoretical formulations on prosocial behavior by Latané and Darley (1970) and Staub (1978).

2. It is useful to consider Kelman's (1958) theory of the bases of attitudes to clarify Newcomb's subtle deprecation of women. Kelman suggests that the three different bases (or reasons) of holding attitudes have implications of how easily those attitudes can change. (1) Most easy to change are attitudes adopted on the basis of external threats or rewards. When the threat or reward is gone the person no longer complies. (2) The bases of some attitudes are identifying with or desiring to be like an admired person or group. One often takes on the attitudes of loved, admired ones. When that admiration or love is gone, the attitude changes. Kelman suggests reference groups are influential in attitude formation and change because the process of identification with an admired group leads one to take on its attitudes and values. (3) The hardest to change are attitudes based on freely internalized values and beliefs about what is right or good. Kelman suggests that the persistence of internalized attitudes does not depend on having an external source of support such as a reference group. In light of Kelman's theory it could well be that some of the Bennington alumnae who remained liberal over the years did so not because they maintained liberal reference groups but because they had internalized liberalism as a deeply held conviction.

3. These colleges are atypical in the statistical sense in that they are smaller and more selective than the majority of colleges women attend. They both draw their students predominantly from well-to-do eastern families and they were both single-sex institutions during the time the research was conducted.

4. In the social-psychological literature one can find many examples of theoretical formulations concerning various personality variables that are hypothesized to condition or modify individual's responses to social stimuli [for example, see Rotter (1966) on internal versus external control, Friedman and Rosenman (1974) on type A personality]. On the other hand, many studies that control for sex as an independent variable do so without providing a theoretical justification. If significant effects due to sex are obtained, they are often given an ad hoc interpretation based on how the sexes are socialized differently.

5. Whereas these studies strongly suggest that women who attend single-sex colleges are more achieving, because of methodological constraints, we cannot ascertain whether the educationally enhancing effect of women's colleges is due to the nature of the institution or to the type of women who are attracted to single-sex colleges. It is possible, however, to

hypothesize and test what aspects of a women's college are likely to have an educationally enhancing effect on women. For example, the number of women on the faculty (Tidball 1973), the number of women in administration (Stewart and Chester 1980), and supportive professiorial role models (Erkut and Mokros 1981) have been proposed as factors that contribute to the success of women's colleges in educating women. If the needs that are being met by these aspects of education at a women's college can be properly identified, it may be possible, through various reforms, to implement policies to fulfill these needs in both coeducational and women's colleges.

6. This point is borne out by the fact that, of the research published in the three leading social-psychology journals, *Journal of Personality and Social Psychology, Journal of Experimental Social Psychology,* and *Journal of Applied Social Psychology,* laboratory experiments constituted 84 percent, 85 percent, and 63 percent respectively of studies published in 1974 (Helmreich 1975). Moreover, the majority of nonlaboratory experiments were still field experiments.

7. There are at least two reasons why current freshmen and seniors may not be comparable. One is that current seniors when they were freshmen may have been quite a different group than the current freshmen. This could be due to changes in the characteristics of the applicant pool, or changes in admission policies, or to external events in society such as the beginning or ending of a war. The other reason for lack of comparability has to do with losing students because of attrition and gaining them through transfers. Unless the dropout and transfer students are identical to those who remain in college, which we know is not the case (see Lehmann, Sinha, and Hartnett 1966), then the current seniors are not comparable to current freshmen even if they were comparable four years ago.

8. Astin (1977) further recommends using age as a control for maturation. This is based on the assumption that if a particular change is, in part, due to maturation, students who are older when they enter college will be less likely to exhibit that change during college because they will have gone through that change with their own age cohorts. Thus, a negative correlation with age at college entry and change in college is at least partial support for the hypothesis that the change was brought about by maturation.

9. Joreskog and his colleagues (Joreskog and Van Thillo 1973; Joreskog and Sorbom 1978) have designed computer programs, ACOVSM (Joreskog, Van Thillo, and Gruvaeus 1970), COFAMM (Sorbom and Joreskog 1976), and LISREL (Joreskog and Sorbom 1978) to specify, estimate, and test structural-equation models. These programs have been put to use in the sociological research since the 1970s (Mason, Hauser, Kerckhoff, Poss, and Manton, 1976; Bielby, Hauser, and Featherman 1976; Kohn and Schooler 1979). They have been applied to problems in educational research since the late 1970s (for example, Werts and Hilton

1977; Marini and Greenberger 1978). The first studies employing structural-equation models in social-psychological research appeared only in the late 1970s (see Moreland and Zajonc 1979).

Bibliography

Almquist, E., and Angrist, S.S. "Career Salience and Atypicality of Occupational Choice Among College Women." *Journal of Marriage and the Family* 32 (1970):242–249.

Angrist, S.S. "Changes in Women's Work Aspirations During College (Or Work Does Not Equal Career)." *International Journal of Sociology of the Family* 2 (1972):87–97.

Astin, A.W. "The Methodology of Research on College Impact, Part One." *Sociology of Education* 43 (1970):223–254.

———. *Four Critical Years*. San Francisco: Jossey-Bass, 1977.

Baltes, P.B., and Nesselroade, J.R. "The Developmental Analysis of Individual Differences on Multiple Measures." In J.R. Nesselroade and H.W. Reese, eds., *Life-span Developmental Psychology: Methodological Issues*. New York: Academic Press, 1973.

Beardslee, D., and O'Dowd, D. "Students and the Occupational World." In N. Sanford, ed., *The American College*. New York: Wiley, 1962.

Bem, S.L. "The Measurement of Psychological Androgyny." *Journal of Consulting and Clinical Psychology* 42 (1974):155–162.

Bernard, J. "Women's Educational Needs." In A.W. Chickering, ed., *The Modern American College*. San Francisco: Jossey-Bass, 1981.

Bielby, W.T., and Hauser, R.M. "Structural Equation Models." *Annual Review of Sociology* 3 (1977):137–161.

Bielby, W.T.; Hauser, R.M.; and Featherman, D.L. "Response Errors of Nonblack Males in Models of the Stratification Process." In D.J. Aigner and A.S. Goldberger, eds., *Latent Variables in Socioeconomic Models*. Amsterdam: North Holland, 1976.

Brown, D. "Personality, College Environments, and Academic Productivity." In N. Sanford, ed., *The American College*. New York: Wiley, 1962.

Brown University. *Report of the Brown Project*. Providence, R.I.: Brown University, Office of the Provost, 1980.

Bushnell, J.H. "Student Culture at Vassar." In N. Sanford, ed., *The American College*. New York: Wiley, 1962.

Creager, J.A. "On Methods for Analysis of Differential Input and Treatment Effects on Educational Outcomes." Paper presented at the Annual Meeting of the American Educational Research Association, 1969.

Cronbach, L.J., and Furby, L. "How We Should Measure 'Change'—Or Should We?" *Psychological Bulletin* 74 (1970):68–80.

Douvan, E., and Kaye, C. "Motivational Factors in College Entrance." In N. Sanford, ed., *The American College*. New York: Wiley, 1962.

Dreeben, R. *On What Is Learned in Schools*. Reading, Mass.: Addison-Wesley, 1968.

Duncan, O.D. *Introduction to Structural Equation Models*. New York: Academic Press, 1975.

Erkut, S., and Mokros, J.R. "Professors as Models and Mentors for College Students." Working Paper. Wellesley, Mass.: Wellesley College Center for Research on Women, 1981.

Feldman, K.A., ed. *College and Student: Selected Readings in the Social Psychology of Higher Education*. New York: Pergamon Press, 1972a.

———. "Difficulties in Measuring and Interpreting Change and Stability During College." In K.A. Feldman, ed., *College and Student: Selected Readings in the Social Psychology of Higher Education*. New York: Pergamon Press, 1972b.

———. "The Assessment of College Impacts." In K.A. Feldman, ed., *College and Student: Selected Readings in the Social Psychology of Higher Education*. New York: Pergamon Press, 1972c.

Feldman, K.A., and Newcomb, T.M. *The Impact of College on Students*. San Francisco: Jossey-Bass, 1969.

Freedman, M.B. "Studies of College Alumni." In N. Sanford, ed., *The American College*. New York: Wiley, 1962.

Friedman, M., and Rosenman, R.H. *Type A Behavior and Your Heart*. New York: Knopf, 1974.

Gilligan, C. "In a Different Voice: Women's Conception of the Self and Morality." *Harvard Educational Review* 47 (1977):481–517.

Hawley, P. "Perceptions of Male Models of Feminity Related to Career Choice." *Journal of Counseling Psychology* 19 (1972):308–313.

Heise, D.R. *Causal Analysis*. New York: Wiley, 1975.

Helmreich, R. "Applied Social Psychology: The Unfulfilled Promise." *Personality and Social Psychology Bulletin* 1 (1975):548–560.

Horner, M. "Sex Differences in Achievement Motivation and Performance in Competitive and Noncompetitive Situations." Ph.D. Diss. University of Michigan, 1968.

———. "Toward an Understanding of Achievement-Related Conflicts in Women." *Journal of Social Issues* 28 (1972):157–175.

House, J.S. "The Three Faces of Social Psychology." *Sociometry* 40 (1977):161–177.

Huston-Stein, A., and Baltes, P.B. "Theory and Method in Life-span Development Psychology: Implications for Child Development." In H.W.

Reese and L.P. Lipsitt, eds., *Advances in Child Development and Behavior*. New York: Academic Press, 1976.

Iffert, R.E. *Retention and Withdrawal of College Students*. Bulletin 1958. Washington, D.C.: U.S. Government Printing Office, 1957.

Inkeles, A. "Social Structure and Socialization." In D.T. Goslin, ed., *Handbook of Socialization Theory and Research*. Chicago: Rand McNally, 1969.

Inkeles, A., and Smith, D.H. *Becoming Modern*. Cambridge, Mass.: Harvard University Press, 1974.

Joreskog, K.G. "Statistical Estimation of Structural Models in Longitudinal Developmental Investigations." J.R. Nesselroade and P.B. Baltes, eds., *Longitudinal Research in the Study of Behavior and Development*. New York: Academic Press, 1979.

Joreskog, K.G., and Sorbom, D. *LISREL IV—A General Computer Program for Estimation of Linear Structural Equation Systems by Maximum Likelihood Methods*. Chicago: International Education Services, 1978.

Joreskog, K.G., and van Thillo, M. *LISREL—A General Computer Program for Estimating a Linear Structural Equation System Involving Unmeasured Variables*. Research Report 73-75. Uppsala, Sweden: University of Uppsala, 1973.

Joreskog, K.G.; van Thillo, M.; and Gruvacus, G.T. *ACOVSM—A General Computer Program for Analysis of Covariance Structures Including Generalized MANOVA*. Research Bulletin 70-01. Princeton, N.J.: Education Testing Service, 1970.

Kelman, H.C. "Compliance, Identification and Internalization: Three Processes of Attitude Change." *Journal of Conflict Resolution* 2 (1958):51–60.

Kohn, M.L., and Schooler, C. "The Reciprocal Effects of the Substantive Complexity of Work and Intellectual Flexibility: A Longitudinal Assessment." *American Journal of Sociology* 84 (1979):24–52.

Latané, B., and Darley, J.M. *The Unresponsive Bystander: Why Doesn't He Help?* New York: Meredith Corporation, 1970.

Lehmann, I.J.; Sinha, B.K.; and Hartness, R.T. "Changes in Attitudes and Values Associated with College Attendance." *Journal of Educational Psychology* 57 (1966):89–98.

Lenney, E., ed. "Special Issue: Androgyny." *Sex Roles* 5 (1979):Whole issue.

Lewin, K. "Forces Behind Food Habits and Methods of Change." *Bulletin of the National Research Council* 108 (1943):35-65.

Lipman-Blumen, J. "How Ideology Shapes Women's Lives." *Scientific American* 226 (1972):34-42.

Locksley, A., and Colten, M.E. "Psychological Androgyny: A Case of Mistaken Identity?" *Journal of Personality and Social Psychology* 37 (1979):1017–1031.

Maccoby, E.E.; Newcomb, T.M.; and Hartley, E.L., eds., *Readings in Social Psychology*. New York: Holt, Rinehart and Winston, 1958.

Marini, M.M., and Greenberger, E. "Sex Differences in Educational Aspirations and Expectations." *American Educational Research Journal* 15 (1978):67–79.

Mason, W.M.; Hauser, R.M,; Kerckhoff, A.C.; Poss, S.S.; and Manton, K. "Models of Response Error in Student Reports of Parental Socioeconomic Characteristics." In W.H. Sewell; R.M. Hauser; and D.L. Featherman, eds., *Schooling and Achievement in American Society*. New York: Academic Press, 1976.

Miller, J.; Schooler, C.; Kohn, M.L.; and Miller, K. "Women and Work: The Psychological Effects of Occupational Conditions." *American Journal of Sociology* 85 (1980):66–94.

Moreland, R.L., and Zajonc, R.B. "Exposure Effects May Not Depend on Stimulus Recognition." *Journal of Personality and Social Psychology* 37 (1979):1085–1089.

Munroe, R. *Teaching The Individual*. New York: Columbia University Press, 1944.

Murphy, L.B., and Ladd, H. *Emotional Factors in Learning*. Sarah Lawrence College Publications, no. 4. New York: Columbia University Press, 1944.

Murphy, L.B., and Raushenbush, E., eds. *Achievement in the College Years*. New York: Harper, 1960.

Namboodiri, N.K.; Carter, L.F.; and Blalock, H.M., Jr. *Applied Multivariate Analysis and Experimental Designs*. New York: McGraw-Hill, 1975.

Newcomb, T.M. *Personality and Social Change*. New York: Dryden Press, 1943.

———. "Some Patterned Consequences of Membership in a College Community." In T.M. Newcomb and E.L. Hartley, eds., *Readings in Social Psychology*. New York: Holt, 1947.

———. "Attitude Development as a Function of Reference Groups: The Bennington Study." In G.E. Swanson, T.M. Newcomb, and E.L. Hartley, eds., *Readings in Social Psychology*. New York: Holt, 1952.

Newcomb, T.M., and Hartley, E.L., eds., *Readings in Social Psychology*. New York: Holt, 1947.

Newcomb, T.M.; Koenig, K.E., Flacks, R.; and Warwick, D.P. *Persistence and Change: Bennington College and Its Students After Twenty-Five Years*. New York: Wiley, 1967.

Pantages, T.J., and Creedon, C.F. "Studies of College Attrition: 1950–1975." *Review of Educational Research* 48 (1978):49–101.

Parelius, A.P. "Emerging Sex-Role Attitudes, Expectations, and Strains Among College Women." *Journal of Marriage and the Family* 37 (1975):146–153.

Pedhazur, E.J., and Tetenbaum, T.J. "Bem Sex-Role Inventory: A Theoretical and Methodological Critique." *Journal of Personality and Social Psychology* 37 (1979):996–1016.

Perun, P.J. "Academic Women, Productivity, and Status Attainment: A Life Course Model." Working Paper. Wellesley, Mass.: Wellesley College, Center for Research on Women, 1979.

Plant, W.T. "Longitudinal Changes in Intolerance and Authoritarianism for Subjects Differing in Amount of College Education Over Four Years." *Genetic Psychology Monographs* 72 (1965):247–287.

Proshansky, H., and Seidenberg, B. *Basic Studies in Social Psychology.* New York: Holt, 1965.

Pugh, R.C. "Partitioning of Criterion Score Variance Accounted for in Multiple Correlation." *American Educational Research Journal* 5 (1968):639–646.

Richards, J.M., Jr. "Relationships Between an Analytic Model and Some Other Techniques for Evaluating the Effects of College." *School Review* 76 (1968):412–427.

Rotter, J.B. "Generalized Expectancies for Internal Control of Reinforcement." *Psychological Monographs* 80 (1966):whole issue.

Safilios-Rothschild, C. *Sex Role Socialization and Sex Discrimination: A Synthesis and Critique of the Literature.* Washington, D.C.: U.S. Department of Health, Education and Welfare, National Institute of Education, 1979.

Sanford, N., ed. "Personality Development During the College Years." *Journal of Social Issues* 12 (1956):whole issue.

Shaver, P. "Questions Concerning Fear of Success and Its Conceptual Relatives." *Sex Roles* 2 (1976):305–320.

Siegel, A.E., and Siegel, S. "Reference Groups, Membership Groups, and Attitude Change." *Journal of Abnormal and Social Psychology* 55 (1957):360–364.

Sorbom, D., and Joreskog, K.G. *Confirmatory Factor Analysis with Model Modification.* Chicago: International Educational Services, 1976.

Spence, J.R., and Helmreich, R.L. *Masculinity and Femininity: Their Psychological Dimensions, Correlates and Antecedents.* Austin, Texas: University of Texas Press, 1978.

Staub, E. *Positive Social Behavior and Morality: Social and Personal Influences.* New York: Academic Press, 1978.

Stern, G.G.; Stein, M.I.; and Bloom, B.S. *Methods in Personality Assessment.* Glencoe, Ill.: Free Press, 1956.

Stewart, A.J., and Chester, N.L. "Expanding Career Awareness and Options Among Women Undergraduates in Coeducational Institutions."

Mimeographed. Cambridge, Mass.: Radcliffe College, Henry A. Murray Research Center, 1980.

Swanson, G.E.; Newcomb, T.M.; and Hartley, E.L., eds. *Readings in Social Psychology*. New York: Holt, 1952.

Tidball, M.E. "Perspectives on Academic Women and Affirmative Action." *Educational Record* 54 (1973):130–135.

———. "Women's Colleges and Women Achievers Revisited." *Signs* 5 (1980):504–517.

Tidball, M.E., and Kistiakowsky, V. "Baccalaureate Origins of American Scientists and Scholars." *Science* 193 (1976):646–652.

Trent, J.W., and Medsker, L.L. *Beyond High School: A Psychological Study of 10,000 High School Graduates*. San Francisco: Jossey-Bass, 1968.

Tressemer, D. "Fear of Success: Popular But Unproven." *Psychology Today* 7 (1974):82–85.

———. "Do Women Fear Success?" *Signs* 1 (1976):863–874.

Van de Geer, J.P. *Introduction to Multivariate Analysis for the Social Sciences*. San Francisco: Freeman, 1971.

Ward, J.J., Jr. "Partitioning of Variance and Contribution or Importance of a Variable: A Visit to a Graduate Seminar." *American Educational Research Journal* 6 (1969):439–447.

Werts, C.E., and Hilton, T.L. "Intellectual Status and Intellectual Growth, Again." *American Educational Research Journal* 14 (1977):137–146.

Werts, C.E., and Watley, D.J. "Analyzing College Effects: Correlation Vs. Regression." *American Educational Research Journal* 5 (1968): 585–598.

Zuckerman, M., and Wheeler, L. "To Dispel Fantasies About the Fantasy Based Measure of Fear of Success." *Psychological Bulletin* (1975): 932–949.

9

Educational and Career Progress of Chicana and Native-American College Women

Helen S. Astin and
Patricia P. McNamara

Only recently has the study of minority women in higher education emerged as an area of inquiry. Research examining the educational and career development of minority women tends to focus on black women, who comprise a numerically larger group with a longer history of involvement in higher education than either Chicanas or native-American women. Certainly, there are commonalities affecting the academic and occupational aspirations and experiences of many minority women that cut across racial-ethnic differences: for example, limited exposure to women who might serve as role models for achievement in a wide range of career alternatives; poor educational preparation for the demands of college-level work; difficulties in financing a higher education; and treatment based on stereotypic preconceptions about their individual backgrounds, abilities, and goals. But it is equally certain that there are important differences among minority women stemming from the historical experiences of their people, the roles and expectations of women within their culture, and the cultural values and attitudes that are a source of strength and identity to young women.

Much of the literature on Chicanas and American Indians ignores or deals only superficially with the roles, accomplishments, and contributions of women. Anthropological and historical accounts of tribal cultures give scant attention to the role of women within the society. Even when they do, Medicine reports, they often focus on "the bizarre and the spectacular" (1978, p. 34). Recent literature on Chicanas and native-American women reflects a greater interest in the Chicana's role within the family and community and in the native-American woman's role in traditional societies as well as in the physical and mental health of these women, than in their educational and career development. For example, in *La Chicana* (Mirande and Rodriquez 1979) and *Essays on la Mujer* (Sanchez and Martinez Cruz 1977),

The authors contributed equally to the preparation of this chapter and would like to thank Mary Beth Snyder for her assistance. This research is supported in part by a grant from the Ford Foundation.

205

historical discussions of the Chicana's role and position within the family and the larger Chicano community, her image in literature, and her personal development are extensive compared with the brief treatment accorded educational and career-development issues.

To some extent the research and writing that have been published in the past five years or so have sought to refute myths and popular misconceptions about Chicanas and American Indian women and to correct biases and omissions in the literature. Native-American women and Chicanas have been active in this effort to set the record straight—a record written not only primarily by men but also by men from outside the culture—and to gain recognition for the vital contributions that women have made and are making within their communities. The popular stereotypes of native-American women and Chicanas have been a source of particular irritation to contemporary women whose own sense of identity is linked with that of earlier generations of women and who feel the residual effects of these persistent stereotypes in the way people respond to them. Interestingly, these stereotypes present a parallel dichotomy. On the one hand there is the lovely, noble Indian princess, whose principle activity appears to be saving white men's lives, and the beautiful, vivacious senorita, equally unapproachable. On the other hand there is the plain, illiterate, surordinate drudge—the squaw and the pious peasant woman whose principal activities are making tortillas and giving birth. Although some progress has been made, many of the issues that concern native-American women and Chicanas today have yet to be addressed seriously. In a review of the literature on native-American women, Green remarks: "We are blessed to be rid, in their former number and nature, of the deviance studies, rug/pot articles, and puberty-rite descriptions, but we long for work that might be particularly useful to Native American women as well as scholars" (1980, p. 266).

Both Chicanas and Indian women appear to place a high value on their roles as women, preserving and transmitting their culture in the face of pressures toward acculturation and assimilation into the dominant society, and on the extended family structure that characterizes Chicano culture and tribal societies. Indeed, many women feel that role differentiation and maintenance of family solidarity are crucial to cultural survival and to the fight against oppression by the larger society. Nonetheless, these women are also voicing their concerns as women within the Chicano or Indian culture, although their first allegiance is to the causes of their people. Green points out: "For Indian feminists, every women's issue is framed in the larger context of Native American people" (1980, p. 264). Vasquez observes: "Mexican-American women are involved in dual strategies of attaining equity within the context of families and as minority group members in the larger society" (1980, p. 11).

The resources and skills these women acquire through education and employment assist them both in attaining status within their families and communities and in participating in and serving their communities more effectively. Kidwell describes the contributions of college-educated women to Indian communities as "much more significant than their limited numbers might indicate" (1980, p. 84). Baca Zinn's research (1980) suggests that higher educational attainment and labor-force participation among Chicanas are related to more egalitarian family structures: joint decisions were more common among families where both spouses worked.

This chapter describes and examines the characteristics, experiences, and achievements of a sample of Chicanas and native American women who entered college in 1971. These women, who provided information about their personal and academic backgrounds, their aspirations and life goals, and their beliefs and self-concepts when they entered college and eight-and-a-half years later in 1980, are not representative of all Indian and Chicano women who attend college. Nonetheless, the extensive information available for them allows us to begin to explore and attempt to map out a picture of the characteristics and the educational and career development of two groups of women who only relatively recently have begun to participate in higher education in substantial numbers.

Educational Attainment: A National Context

Chicanos and native Americans are among the youngest and fastest-growing populations in the United States. Between the 1970 and 1980 censuses, the "Spanish-origin" population grew 61 percent and the native American population showed a 71-percent increase. This phenomenal growth reflects, to varying degrees, higher birth rates among both populations, immigration by persons of "Spanish origin," and improved census-data collection procedures that provide more reliable counts of both groups than were previously available. An educated estimate, based on 1980 census data, puts the Chicano population about 9 million, accounting for 3.8 percent of the nation's population. The 1980 census counted 1.4 million American Indians, Aleuts, and Eskimos, making up 0.62 percent of the U.S. population. At the time the women in our sample were entering college, 84 percent of the Chicano population was concentrated in two states, California and Texas. Over three-quarters of the Indian population lived west of the Mississippi; almost half were in Arizona, California, New Mexico, and Oklahoma.

National statistics also document the educationally disadvantaged status of both populations. In 1970, the year before our respondents enrolled in college, only about one-quarter (24.2 percent) of Chicanos and one-third (33.3 percent of native Americans aged 25 and above were high-school graduates, compared with over half (54.5 percent) of the white population. The median number of years of school completed by all persons over age 24 was 8.1 for Chicanos, 9.8 for Indians, and 12.1 for whites (1970 census data, reported in Almquist and Wehrle-Einhorn 1978). It should also be noted that these aggregate statistics mask significant differences in educational attainment among Indian tribes and communities and, especially, between more educated urban Indians and their rural counterparts.

The 1970 census found that 4 percent of all native Americans and 4.3 percent of all Chicanos aged 25 or older had attended college for four or more years, compared with 11.8 percent of whites. When these data are reported separately by age cohort, it is evident that younger generations tend to have received more schooling than their elders. However, data on the educational attainments of persons 25–29, collected in 1976, show that 34 percent of white men and 22 percent of white women had completed four or more years of college, whereas among Chicanos only 11 percent of the men and 5 percent of the women had a comparable education, as did 8 percent of American Indian and Alaska native men and 4 percent of the women (U.S. Commission on Civil Rights 1978). The gap in educational attainment between whites and young adults from the Chicano and native-American communities is clearly persistent and significant. Furthermore, women not only have less education than men in each population, but the discrepancies in achievement between the sexes are greater among Chicanos and native Americans than among whites. Who are the women who, unlike the majority of their peers, enter college? What are their aspirations and goals? What impact does their experience in college have on their lives?

Sample and Procedures

The data on Chicano and native-American young adults presented in this chapter are drawn from a longitudinal study conducted by the Higher Education Research Institute and supported by the Ford Foundation. This study followed up some 48,000 students selected from respondents to the 1971 Cooperative Institutional Research Program (CIRP) annual survey of entering college freshmen. The CIRP questionnaire asks respondents to describe their racial-ethnic background by marking all of seven categories that apply, including "American Indian" and "Mexican-American/Chicano." All freshmen at any one of 487 colleges and universities who had checked either of these two categories in 1971—2,533 American Indians and 2,682 Chicanos—were included in the sample for the longitudinal study and were sent follow-up questionnaires in winter 1980.

A random sample of survey nonrespondents was interviewed by telephone to determine if they differed in any significant and systematic way from respondents and to enlarge the number of persons for whom outcome information on educational and occupational status was available. Both the questionnaire and the telephone interview included items designed to verify respondents' primary racial-ethnic identification, since the 1971 survey form permitted multiple responses. Persons identifying themselves as "American Indian or Alaskan Native" on the follow-up survey were asked to write in the name of their tribe, band, or community.

Follow-up information was obtained from 20 percent of the Indian and 23 percent of the Chicano samples. Despite efforts to update the home addresses sample members had provided as freshman, 20 percent of all survey forms were returned as undeliverable. Assuming that undeliverable rates for the Chicano and Indian samples were at least equivalent to that of the total sample, we estimate that outcome data were collected from 25 percent of the Indian sample and 29 percent of the Chicano sample for whom current addresses were available. However, 68 percent of the "Indian" sample follow-up respondents indicated that their primary identification was not Indian, and they were therefore reclassified accordingly.

The following discussion is based on the response of 607 Chicanos, of whom 296 (49 percent) are women, and 230 American Indians, of whom 127 (55 percent) are women. Neither of these samples can or should be construed as representing its respective entering freshman class of 1971. Approximately half of our sample is made up of questionnaire respondents; past experience shows that persons who complete and return such surveys tend to be more "successful" than their nonresponding peers. Thus, even with the inclusion of telephone-interview respondents, the data are likely to be somewhat biased toward profiling a more elite group of students.

Information on respondents' family background, high-school achievements, educational and career goals, and attitudes and values was collected at the time of college entry (1971). Information about their college experience and college outcomes, such as educational attainments and changes in career aspirations, in self-esteem, and in life goals, was collected in 1980 or assessed by comparing 1971 and 1980 responses to identical or similar questions. Comparison data on Chicanos and native American men and on all 1971 freshmen (of whom 92 percent of the men and 91 percent of the women are white) will be introduced throughout the discussion to provide a context for understanding these data on Chicanas and native-American women.

Descriptive Profile

Chicanos and American Indians in our sample were more likely to be first-generation college attenders than were all men and women who entered college in 1971. However, the educational profile of their parents indicates that, overall, they come from more educated families than is typical of the Chicano and, especially, of the Indian populations. To some extent this undoubtedly reflects biases within our sample; yet it also suggests that more educated parents expect and encourage their children to equal or excel their own educational achievements. Just over half (53 percent) of all women and 57 percent of all men who entered college in 1971 reported that their fathers had a high-school education or less, compared with 80 percent of Chicanas, 86 percent of Chicanos, 62 percent of native-American women, and 63 percent of native-American men in our sample. Each group reported lower levels of education for their mothers than their fathers; yet within each population a larger proportion of the women than of the men said that their mothers had attended or graduated from college. Having more educated parents certainly influences one's chances of going to college, and it appears to be especially important for young women.

Larger proportions of the Chicano and Indian students than of all freshmen reported family incomes under $10,000 per year at the time of college entry. Whereas about one-third of all freshmen (34 percent of men and 35 percent of women) estimated their family incomes at less than $10,000 per year, approximately two-thirds of Chicanos (67 percent of men and 66 percent of women), 42 percent of Indian men, and 52 percent of Indian women reported family incomes in this range. Furthermore, 1970 census data indicate that family income must be stretched farther in Chicano and Indian families because of their larger size. An analysis of family size in nine populations ranked Chicanos first, native Americans second, and whites ninth (Almquist and Wehrle-Einhorn 1978).

It is, therefore, not surprising to find that, as entering freshmen, Chicanos and Indians are more likely to express concern about their ability to finance a college education than are freshmen in general. Indian students are somewhat less likely than Chicano students to indicate that finances are a major concern; this may well be attributable to the availability of Bureau of Indian Affairs (BIA) scholarship aid for students with at least one-fourth degree Indian blood. Chicanas and Indian women, like freshmen women in general, tend to report that finances are a major concern somewhat more often than their male peers. This pattern has been ascribed to women undergraduates' greater reliance on parental support and to the fact that, although women are more likely to receive scholarships and loans, men receive more total financial aid (Astin, Harway, and McNamara 1976).

High-School Preparation and Achievement

High-school preparation plays an important role in determining if and where a student may pursue postsecondary education. The majority of both

Chicanos and Indians reported that they had attended public high schools. One-fifth of the Chicanas and 16 percent of the Chicanos had graduated from a private, religious high school. Given that about 72 percent of Chicanos are raised as Catholics, this is not surprising. Interestingly, Indian men were more likely than Indian women to report having attended a private high school—10 percent versus 6 percent, respectively. Unfortunately, our data do not allow us to determine what proportion of the Indian students graduated from federally run as opposed to local high schools.

As is true for the general population of entering freshmen, Chicanas and native-American women had earned much better high school grades than their male counterparts (see table 9–1). For example, 30 percent of Chicanas and 36 percent of Indian women reported a high-school GPA of B+ or better, compared with 19 percent of Chicanos and 25 percent of Indian men. However, the grades reported by Chicanas and Indian women were somewhat lower than those of all freshmen women, of whom 41 percent reported a B+ or better high-school GPA.

High-school grades do not necessarily reflect the quality of preparation received for college. With the exception of reading and, for Chicanos, foreign language, Chicano and Indian freshmen are considerably more likely to express a need for remedial help or tutoring in basic subjects while in college (see table 9–2). Indian men appear to feel better prepared for college-level work than do Indian women and Chicano freshmen of both sexes. Although Chicanos are the group least likely to feel that they will need special help in a foreign language, they are most likely to anticipate the need

Table 9–1
Average High-School Grade Reported by All Freshmen, Chicano Freshmen, and Native-American Freshmen in 1971, by Sex
(percentages)

Average High-School Grade	All Freshmen		Chicanos		Native Americans	
	Men	Women	Men (311)	Women (296)	Men (97)	Women (119)
D	0.9	0.2	1.0	—	1.0	—
C	13.7	5.8	18.5	8.7	12.4	8.4
C+	19.3	10.8	19.8	14.0	12.4	9.2
B−	18.5	13.9	22.8	17.8	23.7	16.0
B	22.4	28.1	19.1	29.4	25.8	30.3
B+	13.8	21.7	11.4	18.9	14.4	24.4
A−, A, or A+	11.3	19.4	7.4	11.2	10.3	11.8

Source: A.W. Astin et al. *The American Freshman: National Norms for Fall 1971* (Washington, D.C.: American Council on Education, 1971). Reprinted with permission.

Table 9-2
Proportion of All Freshmen, Chicano Freshmen, and Native-American Freshmen Who Express a Need for Special Tutoring or Remedial Work in Selected Subjects in 1971, by Sex
(percentages)

Subject	All Freshmen		Chicanos		Native Americans	
	Men	*Women*	*Men (311)*	*Women (296)*	*Men (97)*	*Women (127)*
English	21.0	10.8	33.1	24.3	21.4	17.3
Reading	12.5	8.3	13.8	7.8	8.7	11.0
Mathematics	33.9	38.4	47.9	51.0	38.8	54.3
Social studies	3.4	4.2	7.4	8.8	2.9	11.8
Science	16.1	26.8	29.9	33.4	19.4	37.0
Foreign language	24.2	16.7	12.9	10.5	36.9	20.5

Source: A.W. Astin et al. *The American Freshman: National Norms for Fall 1971* (Washington, D.C.: American Council on Education, 1971). Reprinted with permission.

for assistance with English. All three groups of women feel less well prepared than their male counterparts in mathematics, science, and (to a far lesser degree) social studies. A considerably larger proportion of Chicanas and Indian women than of all freshmen women expect to need help with math and science.

Reasons for Attending College and College Choice

The top-ranking reason for going to college among all three groups of women was "to learn more about things that interest me" (see table 9-3). Chicanas and native-American women endorsed this reason as "very important" with greater frequency than did all freshmen women, and the same pattern is found in the responses of their male counterparts. However, for men this reason ranked second to going to college in order "to be able to get a better job." Among women, job preparation and gaining "a general education and appreciation of ideas" were the second and third most frequently cited reasons for going to college, followed by "to meet new and interesting people."

More Chicanas and native-American women than women in general report that their parents' desire for them to go to college was a very important factor in their decision to continue their education. A larger proportion of native-American women and of Chicanas than of all freshmen women are pursuing a college education in order to be able to contribute more to

Table 9-3
**Proportion of All Freshmen, Chicano Freshmen, and Native-American Freshmen
Rating Selected Reasons for Going to College as "Very Important," by Sex, 1971**
(percentages)

Reason	All Freshmen		Chicanos		Native Americans	
	Men	*Women*	*Men (311)*	*Women (296)*	*Men (103)*	*Women (127)*
My parents wanted me to go.	21.9	24.1	30.5	29.7	28.2	33.9
To be able to contribute more to my community.	15.0	23.1	28.9	31.4	23.3	33.1
To be able to get a better job.	77.0	70.1	82.0	72.6	76.7	64.6
To gain a general education and appreciation of ideas.	53.3	66.8	62.1	74.0	45.6	56.7
To improve my reading and study skills.	21.7	22.7	38.6	43.2	19.4	26.8
There was nothing better to do.	2.2	2.3	1.6	2.7	3.9	7.1
To make me a more cultured person.	24.5	34.0	39.5	48.6	24.3	28.3
To be able to make more money.	57.0	41.5	59.8	45.3	62.1	36.2
To learn more about things that interest me.	64.5	73.9	72.0	83.1	71.8	81.9
To meet new and interesting people.	36.3	55.3	39.5	56.4	43.7	51.2
To prepare myself for graduate or professional school.	38.9	29.3	51.4	47.0	42.7	39.4

Source: A.W. Astin et al. *The American Freshman: National Norms for Fall 1971* (Washington, D.C.: American Council on Education, 1971. Reprinted with permission.

their community. Chicanas and Indian women are also considerably more likely than women in general to report that preparing for graduate or professional school is a very important reason for attending college. Indeed, they cite this reason more frequently than do all men in the freshman class, though less often than do their own male peers. Almost half (47 percent) of the Chicanas and two-fifths (39 percent) of the Indian women hold the long-range goal of seeking advanced training. This high level of aspiration may reflect the small and select nature of our sample; yet it also suggests that the small percentages of college-age Chicanas and Indian women who do attend college have high educational goals.

Overall, the profile of responses to this question suggests that Chicanas are especially attracted to college by a desire for learning and knowledge in and of itself, whereas Indian women see higher education as instrumental and essential to achieving specific goals. Chicanas tend to endorse reasons having to do with gaining a general education and appreciation of ideas, becoming a more cultured person, and improving academic skills more often than do other women, although they also clearly hope and expect a college education to lead to better job opportunities. Indian women show greater interest in learning specifically about things that interest them, in preparing for advanced education, and in enhancing their ability to contribute to their community. Interestingly, native-American women cite the desire for a better job and more money as very important reasons for going to college less often than any other group of respondents.

The Chicanas and native-American women in our sample are atypical of their respective undergraduate peers in terms of the types of higher-education institutions they entered as freshmen. About three-fifths (59 percent) of Chicano full-time freshmen attending college in fall 1972 were enrolled at two-year colleges (Astin 1981); 46 percent of the Chicanas in our sample entered two-year colleges, 35 percent attended four-year colleges, and 19 percent matriculated at universities. Almost half (48 percent) of all native-American full-time freshmen enrolled in higher education in fall 1972 were attending two-year colleges (Astin 1981). Only 13 percent of the Indian women in our sample entered two-year colleges as freshmen, whereas 43 percent attended four-year colleges and another 43 percent universities. Somewhat larger proportions of the Chicanos (52 percent) and American Indian men (24 percent) had enrolled at two-year colleges as freshmen. To a considerable extent, the distribution of our respondents across institutions reflects the difficulty of locating students who matriculate at community colleges after a period of eight years, since public two-year colleges are far less likely to maintain updated address files on alumni. This fact further supports our impression that this sample may not be representative of all undergraduate Chicanos and Indians.

About half (49.7 percent) of all freshmen women attend colleges within a fifty-mile radius of home, whereas 72 percent of Chicanas and 29 percent of the Indian women in our sample had gone to schools this close to home. Indians living on reservations and in rural areas—who made up about 56 percent of the Indian population in 1970, according to census data—often had no access to higher education within a fifty-mile radius of home prior to the establishment of tribally controlled two-year colleges, which had just begun at the time these students entered college. The fact that almost three-quarters of the Chicanas attended college within fifty miles of home—and almost two-fifths (38 percent) within ten miles of home—reflects their enrollment in two-year colleges and the effects of financial constraints on college choice. It also suggests that a desire to attend college near one's family and community may influence the selection of a school. Furthermore, anecdotal information from college-educated Chicanas suggests that some Chicano parents are extremely reluctant to allow their daughters to leave home in order to go to college.

Degree Aspirations and Career Plans

As suggested by our earlier finding that high percentages of these Chicanas and Indian women say they are attending college to prepare for advanced education, a significant proportion of both groups aspired to a graduate or professional degree when they entered college. Just over one-third of all freshmen women (36 percent) and Chicanas (34 percent) and two-fifths (42 percent) of Indian women said that they hoped to earn an advanced degree. Some two-fifths (42 percent) of all freshmen women and Indian women and 46 percent of Chicanas aspired to earning a bachelor's but no higher degree. All three groups of women are less likely than their male peers to report a graduate or professional degree as their ultimate educational goal.

As freshmen, over half the Chicanas and native-American women anticipated that they would major in the arts and humanities, the social sciences, or education (see table 9–4). We find strong sex differences between their choices of a probable major field and those of their male peers. Men express a stronger interest than women in business, engineering, the physical sciences, and prelaw majors. They also tend more often to select a premedical curriculum, although Chicanas do indicate almost as high a level of interest in this field.

Women, on the other hand, express an intention to major in education, the arts and humanities, and nursing much more often than men. Indian women show an especially strong interest in nursing and allied health programs. Chicano students of both sexes seem especially attracted to the social sciences, whereas Indian freshmen appear somewhat more likely to select the biological sciences and the arts and humanities.

Both Chicanas and Indian women tend to gravitate toward traditionally female careers, although they do express an interest in law and medical careers more often than do all freshmen women (see table 9–5). They appear to be attracted to service-oriented and artistic careers with equal or greater frequency than freshmen women in general and to show less interest in business-related occupations. Chicanas aspire to careers as elementary- and secondary-school educators (31 percent) and as social workers (6 percent) more

Table 9–4
Fields Indicated as Their Probable Major, by Chicano Freshmen, and Native-American Freshmen in 1971, by Sex
(percentages)

| | Chicanos | | Native Americans | |
Field	Men (267)	Women (268)	Men (100)	Women (116)
Business	9.7	4.5	11.0	2.6
Engineering	14.2	0.7	12.0	0.9
Biological sciences	2.2	2.2	6.0	3.4
Physical sciences	4.9	2.2	4.0	1.7
Premedical	7.1	5.6	8.0	1.7
Education	7.5	16.4	5.0	19.0
Allied health	3.7	4.1	2.0	8.6
Arts and humanities	6.7	20.5	10.0	24.1
Social sciences	17.6	18.7	9.0	11.2
Prelaw	7.1	0.7	10.0	1.7
Nursing	1.1	4.1	—	11.2
Other	18.0	20.1	23.0	13.8

often than either of the other two groups of women. Nursing, college teaching, and artistic careers appear to be particularly popular among Indian women, compared with the frequency with which these are chosen by their non-Indian peers. Our impression that these women expect to pursue careers is reinforced by the fact that only 0.4 percent of the Chicanas and 1.8 percent of the Indian women in our sample selected "housewife" as their probable future occupation.

Educational Outcomes

We do not have follow-up information on the educational attainments for our entire sample; about one-fifth of the respondents did not provide this information. However, even if we make the worst-case assumption that nonrespondents to this item have not earned a bachelor's degree, we find that about half of the women (50 percent of Indian women and 48 percent of Chicanas) and 46 percent, each, of Chicano and Indian men in our sample have received a bachelor's or higher degree. If we make the best-case assumption that the distribution of degrees among persons who failed to

Table 9-5
Occupations Selected as Their Probable Career, by all Freshmen, Chicano Freshmen, and Native-American Freshmen in 1971, by Sex
(percentages)

Career	All Freshmen		Chicanos		Native Americans	
	Men	Women	Men (254)	Women (256)	Men (90)	Women (114)
Artist (creative/ performing)	4.9	7.2	3.2	8.3	5.6	14.0
Business person	16.1	4.4	10.7	1.6	13.3	1.8
Clergy	1.0	0.2	—	0.4	1.1	—
College teacher	0.8	0.6	2.0	0.8	—	1.8
Doctor (dentist/ physician)	6.4	2.0	5.5	4.7	5.5	5.3
Educator (primary/ secondary)	7.5	24.8	11.1	30.8	7.7	20.2
Engineer	9.7	0.2	11.0	—	10.0	0.9
Farmer/forester	4.8	0.7	3.6	0.4	5.5	—
Health professional	3.8	8.8	4.8	5.6	5.5	7.1
Lawyer	6.8	1.4	8.3	2.7	11.1	2.6
Nurse	0.3	8.6	0.8	4.3	—	11.4
Research scientist	3.3	1.5	2.8	1.2	3.3	1.8
Other	21.7	26.1	26.4	32.5	24.4	27.3
Undecided	12.9	13.5	10.2	7.0	6.7	6.1

Source: A.W. Astin et al. *The American Freshman: National Norms for Fall 1971* (Washington, D.C.: American Council on Education, 1971). Reprinted with permission.

supply this information is parallel to that of respondents, our estimates of baccalaureate completion increase to 59 percent of Chicanas, 64 percent of Indian women, 57 percent of Chicanos, and 58 percent of Indian men. The exact percentage of each group that has completed a baccalaureate undoubtedly falls within the range established by these high and low estimates. Furthermore, even if we choose the most conservative estimates, based on the worst-case analysis, these rates of baccalaureate attainment are higher than those estimated for the total sample of Chicano and Indian freshmen in 1971 who were sent the follow-up survey (see table 9-6).

The higher bachelor's degree attainment rates reported by our respondents are probably explained by their underrepresentation, as freshmen, in the two-year colleges (where, as table 9-6 shows, degree-completion rates are dramatically lower than at other types of institutions) and also by the fact that the achievers are more likely to respond to this kind of survey. Indeed, telephone conversations with nonrespondents indicate that some

Table 9–6
Estimated Bachelor's Degree Completion Rates in 1980 for Whites, Chicanos, and Native Americans Who Entered College in 1971, by Type of Institution
(percentages)

	All Institutions	Universities	Other Four-Year Colleges	Two-Year Colleges
Native Americans	38.6	45.8	58.9	22.5
Chicanos	39.7	62.6	70.4	19.5
Whites	55.6	73.3	72.7	29.0

Source: A.W. Astin et al. *The American Freshman: National Norms for Fall 1971* (Washington, D.C.: American Council on Education, 1971). Reprinted with permission.

survey recipients felt it would be inappropriate to complete the questionnaire because they had dropped out of college. Some believed that the survey had been mailed to them on the mistaken assumption that they had graduated with their freshman class; others simply explained that their college experience had been too brief for our questions to seem relevant.

Given that our respondents disproportionately represent the achievers, the discrepancy between freshman degree aspirations and actual educational attainments after eight years is worth noting. As freshmen, at least four-fifths of these men and women had planned to earn a bachelor's or higher degree. In 1971 only 5 percent of the Chicanas and 6 percent of the Indian women indicated no interest in earning a college degree or certificate. However, at the time of the 1980 survey, 14 percent of the Chicanas and 18 percent of the native-American women reported that they had not received any degree beyond their high-school diploma.

Examining the educational progress of those Chicanas and Indian women for whom both 1971 and 1980 data are available, we find that, among those who aspired to the bachelor's as their highest degree, approximately three-fifths have achieved or exceeded their original degree objective. Of those who aspired to a master's degree as freshmen, about one-fourth have attained their degree goal. Of the Chicana freshmen who aspired to law and medical degrees, one-fifth had earned an advanced professional degree by 1980. None of the native-American women who had similar aspirations as freshmen had received any degree beyond the baccalaureate.

Educational aspirations do change over time. For example, among the women who reported their earned degrees in 1980, four-fifths of the Chicanas and two-thirds of the Indian women who reported no degree plans as freshmen had gone on to earn a vocational certificate, an associate degree, or a bachelor's degree. On the other hand, of the freshmen women who aspired to the doctorate, 30 percent of the Chicanas and one-fourth of the Indian women had yet to earn a bachelor's degree. It is, of course, easier to achieve a modest than an ambitious goal; but the women who set high goals have a higher achievement profile, overall, than do those with lower initial aspirations.

These men and women have not necessarily completed their educational careers. Almost two-fifths of the Chicano men and women, one-third of the Indian women, and one-quarter of the Indian men in our sample reported that they were working toward a postsecondary certificate or degree at the time of the follow-up survey. Some are still pursuing the degree that they cited as their objective when they entered college; others appear to have changed their goal. The only difference between the educational involvements reported by Chicano men and women is that, among those pursuing advanced training, women are more likely to be earning a master's degree, whereas men are more likely to be working toward a professional degree. Indian women, on the other hand, were more likely than Indian men to report that they were still pursuing a degree; and, among those reporting current educational involvements, 45 percent of women and 32 percent of men were in graduate or professional school.

Self-Esteem and Life Goals: Changes over Time

The follow-up questionnaire repeated a self-rating and a life-goals item from the survey that respondents had completed as freshmen in 1971. The self-rating item asks respondents to rate themselves "as compared with the average person your age" on a number of personal traits that measure intellectual and social competencies. The life-goals item assesses individual values and orientations by asking respondents to indicate the personal importance of each goal. We examined changes over time in the self-ratings and life goals of these Chicanas and native-American women.

The number of women rating themselves in the top 10 percent on every trait increased over time, with one exception: Indian women's self-rating on social self-confidence decreased slightly (see table 9-7). Positive changes in college students' self-esteem have been reported before (Astin 1978). However, some questions still remain about the extent to which these changes result from maturation and about whether specific experiences in different institutional environments affect the direction and magnitude of change. We were particularly interested in examining changes in both self-esteem and life goals associated with attendance at different types of institutions.

Table 9–7
Changes in Self-Ratings among Chicanas and Native-American Women, 1971–1980
(percentages)

Personal Trait	Chicanas (N = 195)		Native Americans (N = 65)	
	1971	1980	1971	1980
Academic ability	6.2	13.4	9.2	16.9
Artistic ability	1.0	7.1	6.2	15.4
Drive to achieve	16.8	21.9	13.8	16.9
Leadership ability	5.1	16.3	6.2	9.2
Math ability	2.6	4.6	3.1	4.6
Popularity	2.6	10.7	1.5	4.6
Public-speaking ability	3.1	5.6	—	4.6
Intellectual self-confidence	5.6	11.2	4.6	6.2
Social self-confidence	5.1	13.3	6.2	4.6
Writing ability	1.5	9.7	6.2	9.2

Note: Numbers indicate the percentage rating themselves in the top 10 percent "compared with the average student [of their own] age."

Self-Esteem: Chicanas

On only one of these ten personal traits did more than 6 percent of Chicana freshmen rate themselves in the top 10 percent: drive to achieve (17 percent). The reference group for these women's self-ratings is a peer group from which relatively few young people went on to college. The fact that relatively few Chicana freshmen rate themselves in the top 10 percent on any trait other than drive to achieve suggests that these young women do not see themselves as especially more able than their peers. However, they do feel that their motivation and determination to succeed is stronger than that of their peers, many of whom chose other alternatives than college.

The traits that show the greatest increases in self-esteem over time among Chicanas are: leadership ability (11-percent increase), writing ability, social self-confidence, popularity (8-percent increase each), and academic ability (7-percent increase). College provides young women with new experiences and a new environment in which to exercise and develop social and intellectual skills. In general, self-esteem does increase with age. Nonetheless, the positive changes in social self-confidence and popularity suggest two interpretations: the Chicana high-school student whose academic aspirations set her apart from many of her peers may feel more socially accepted and comfortable in college, where her peers share her academic aspirations and interests. Another possibility is that college introduces Chicanas to persons from different backgrounds, with different interests and experiences, and provides them with opportunities to test and develop their social skills. The increased confidence these women express in their leadership ability suggests that they will indeed assume a participatory role in family decisions and community activities. In addition to an increase in their assessment of their academic ability generally, they also feel that their college experience has specifically strengthened their writing ability, a skill that college students must exercise.

Overall, the self-ratings of Chicanas who went to four-year public and private colleges show the greatest increases in self-concept. Although the self-ratings of women who attended public universities and private four-year colleges show the largest increases in academic ability, the self-ratings on drive to achieve reflect a much more substantial increase in the private four-year colleges than in the public universities. Self-ratings on leadership ability reflect more pronounced gains among women who enrolled in both public and private four-year colleges.

What is it about the institutional environments at these colleges and universities that might explain their differential impacts on Chicanas' self-ratings? Four-year colleges, especially private schools, tend to be smaller in size than public universities and to place more emphasis on teaching undergraduates rather than on graduate training and research. Thus they tend to offer young women more opportunities to participate in academic and extracurricular activities and to assume leadership roles. The data also indicate that many of the Chicanas who attend private four-year colleges are enrolled in Catholic colleges. The increased drive to achieve reflected in the self-ratings of women who attended private four-year colleges may result from a greater emphasis on achievement, more individual attention, and greater exposure to women faculty members who serve as models for achievement at Catholic colleges. The increases in academic self-esteem and intellectual self-confidence reported by these women are probably related to smaller class size as well as to the college characteristics just cited. How then do we account for the increased self-ratings on academic ability among students at public universities? Anecdotal information suggests one possible interpretation: Chicana freshmen accepted at public universities feel considerable anxiety about being academically underprepared and, subsequently, discover that they can and do perform as well as many majority students in this competitive environment. Thus their self-assessments of their academic ability increase.

The self-ratings of Chicanas who attend public colleges and universities show the largest gains in social self-confidence. Because public institutions are both larger than private schools and less likely to place restrictions on student behavior, these women probably have more numerous and varied social experiences. This greater independence, responsibility for their own behavior, and exposure to new social situations leads to enhanced social self-esteem among women attending public institutions.

Compared with their peers attending other types of institutions, Chicana freshmen who enrolled at public two-year colleges had the lowest overall self-ratings. Their self-ratings also reflected the smallest gains in self-esteem over time. Indeed, their self-rating on academic ability shows almost no change over time, although their confidence in their writing skills and math ability did increase.

Self-Esteem: Native-American Women

The freshmen self-ratings of the native-American women tend to be higher, overall, than those of the Chicana freshmen. However, when we compare their self-ratings by type of institution, this discrepancy appears to be explained by the far greater underrepresentation of Indian women in community colleges: in general, freshmen in two-year colleges have lower self-ratings. There are two traits on which more than 6 percent of the Indian freshmen women rated themselves in the top 10 percent: drive to achieve (14 percent) and academic ability (9 percent). Again, the trait on which these women feel most atypical of their peer group is drive to achieve.

The self-ratings that reflect the largest gains over time are: artistic ability (9-percent increase) and academic ability (8-percent increase). Over time, Indian women's self-ratings show smaller increases than those of Chicanas. This is due, in part, to the Indian women's higher self-ratings as freshmen. However, in 1980 the self-ratings of native-American women on self-confidence (social and intellectual), popularity, leadership ability, and drive to achieve were all considerably lower than the comparable self-ratings of Chicanas. All these traits are related to interaction with others and thus reflect, directly or indirectly, confidence in various types of social situations. One possible interpretation for these lower self-ratings among Indian women is found in Ross's (1981) study of Yakima cultural traits that might lead to cultural conflict or misunderstanding between Indian students and their non-Indian college peers, faculty members, and administrators. Many of these traits are common to other Indian tribal cultures and value systems. For example, Ross reports that Yakima children are brought up to maintain quiet and distance in uncertain relationships; to avoid publicly contradicting or arguing with others; to express their own beliefs only among their own people, if at all; to avoid mentioning family problems outside the family; to regain peace of mind by spending time alone on the reservation; and to value mutual assistance and cooperation over competition with others.

Indian students whose behavior and values reflect these cultural traits may be seen by their non-Indian peers as aloof, withdrawn, and uninterested in overtures to friendship. This cultural strain, which is felt but perhaps never recognized, may then lead to less of the interaction that is important to gaining self-confidence. A second possible interpretation of the lower ratings among Indian than Chicano women in 1980 is that Indian women from more strongly traditional reservation-based communities who go to college lose their social niche within their home communities, yet do not fit socially or want to assimilate into the dominant culture.

Because our sample of native-American women is smaller than the Chicana sample, it is difficult to say very much about the extent to which changes in self-esteem are associated with different institutional environments. Generally, the self-ratings of women who enrolled in public universities and private four-year colleges do show more positive increases, as well as changes in a larger variety of traits. The only Indian women who expressed strong confidence in their public-speaking ability in 1980 had attended public universities and private four-year colleges. Women who enrolled in community colleges rated themselves in the top 10 percent on only one trait—artistic ability—as freshmen and on only two traits—artistic ability and leadership ability—in 1980. The Indian women who entered private universities tended, almost without exception, to rate themselves lower in 1980 than they had as entering freshmen.

Life Goals: Chicanas

When they entered college, Chicanas most frequently endorsed two goals as personally essential to themselves: becoming a community leader and raising a family (see table 9-8). Eight years later, in 1980, the two life goals they most often marked "essential" were raising a family and influencing social values. Becoming a community leader was the goal least—rather than most—often indicated as essential in 1980. Some of these goals became more important to Chicanas over time, especially influencing social values and the political structure and, in their personal lives, raising a family and being very well off financially.

Private institutions appeared to have the greatest influence on social and political awareness: the life goals of women who attended private schools showed the largest increases in the desire to influence social values and the political structure. The women who least often endorsed these two goals as essential were those who had attended community colleges. The community-college students were the women for whom raising a family was most important. Public colleges and universities appeared to have the greatest influence on entrepreneurial life goals: the life goals of Chicanas who

Table 9–8
Changes in Life Goals among Chicanas and Native-American Women, 1971–1980
(percentages)

	Chicanas (N = 195)		Native Americans (N = 65)	
Life Goal	1971	1980	1971	1980
Influencing the political structure	1.6	13.1	—	10.8
Influencing social values	6.3	19.3	1.5	15.4
Raising a family	17.5	27.3	18.5	33.8
Being very well off financially	5.2	14.9	6.3	18.8
Becoming a community leader	24.7	4.6	6.2	13.8
Being successful in a business of my own	2.6	8.8	4.6	13.8
Participating in a community-action program	9.3	9.8	9.2	9.2
Becoming involved in programs to clean up the environment	13.0	11.4	4.7	14.1

Note: Numbers indicate the percent rating the personal importance of each goal as "essential."

had attended these institutions showed the largest increase in desire to be very well off financially and successful in a business of one's own.

Life Goals: Native-American Women

Raising a family and participating in a community-action program were the two life goals most often endorsed by freshmen women. Eight years later, raising a family was still the goal most frequently marked "essential," followed by being very well off financially and influencing social values. Every life goal was ranked higher in 1980 than in 1971, with the exception of participating in a community-action program, where the percentage of women rating it essential remained unchanged over time.

As with Chicanas, private institutions appeared to have the greatest influence on the importance Indian women gave to influencing social values and the political structure. Women who had attended private schools also tended to place more importance on raising a family over time, although the life goals of community-college attenders reflect a high valuing of family and financial well-being that is stable over time. Universities, whether public or private, are associated with the largest increases in importance given to being very well off financially, although it is the women at public four-year colleges who most often endorsed this goal as essential in 1971 and in 1980.

Summary and Conclusions

Over 60 percent of both groups of women are first-generation college attenders. The finding that the mothers of these women are somewhat better educated than the mothers of their male counterparts underscores the importance of maternal education as an influence on daughters' aspirations and achievements. Both Chicanas and native-American women tend to come from large, economically disadvantaged families.

Strong parental support and encouragement appear to be especially important facilitators of college attendance among Chicanas and Indian women. However, additional personal factors influenced their decisions to pursue postsecondary education. Chicanas appear to be attracted to college by the idea of learning and gaining new knowledge, whereas native-American women tend to report more instrumental reasons for going to college related to the acquisition of specific skills and preparation for advanced training.

In general, about half of all Chicano and native-American freshmen enroll in community colleges. Although the freshmen enrollment profile of the Indian women in our sample reflects substantial underrepresentation in the public two-year colleges, the Chicanas' enrollment pattern by type of institution comes close to approximating the national statistics. Chicanas' high participation in community colleges reflects financial considerations and possibly a desire or parental pressure to live at home. Over one-third of the Chicana freshmen attended a college within ten miles of home.

As entering freshmen, Chicanas and native-American women express a greater need for help with mathematics and science than do all freshmen women. Moreover, the Chicanas are especially likely to feel that they need help with English; this is understandable since high proportions of Chicanas grow up speaking Spanish at home. Nonetheless, both Chicanas and Indian women have high aspirations and expectations of pursuing not only the bachelor's but also postgraduate degrees. Indeed, three-fifths of those aspiring to a bachelor's degree had received it by 1980. Moreover, one-fourth of those with plans for a master's degree and one-fifth of the Chicanas with plans for professional degrees had already received these post-graduate degrees. However, none of the native-American women who hoped to attain professional degrees had received any degree beyond the baccalaureate. Since one-third of these women reported that they were still working toward a degree, it is likely that more of them will eventually realize their original educational goals.

The occupational plans of Chicana and native-American freshmen are reflected in their choices of major field of study and in their career expectations. Their aspirations tend to be traditional and sex-role stereotyped, as were those of their white counterparts in the early 1970s. However, more Chicanas and native-American women than white women aspired to law and medical degrees.

Over time, the self-esteem of Chicanas and native-American women who attend college increases. Four-year colleges appear to have the strongest positive effect on Chicanas' self-esteem, whereas private four-year colleges and public universities are associated with the largest increases in self-concept among native-American women. Private colleges and universities appear to influence the social and political awareness of both Chicanas and native-American women. Public colleges and universities appear to encourage entrepreneurial aspirations and goals.

The research findings presented in this chapter show that attending college enhances the self-esteem of Chicanas and native-American women, as well as helping them attain their educational and occupational goals. One can only hope that more Chicanas and native-American women will enter college and realize their educational aspirations, thus increasing their own sense of self-worth, their status within their own families, and their ability to serve as leaders and active participants within their communities.

Bibliography

Almquist, E.M., and Wehrle-Einhorn, J.L. "The Doubly Disadvantaged: Minority Women in the Labor Force." In A.H. Stromberg and S. Harkess, eds., *Women Working: Theories and Facts in Perspective.* Palo Alto, Calif.: Mayfield, 1978.

Astin, A.W. *Four Critical Years.* San Francisco: Jossey-Bass, 1978.

————. Final report of the Commission on the Higher Education of Minorities. Unpublished draft report. Los Angeles: Higher Education Research Institute, 1981.

Astin, A.W., et al. *The American Freshman: National Norms for Fall 1971.* Washington, D.C.: American Council on Education, 1971.

Astin, H.S.; Harway, M.; and McNamara, P.P. *Sex Discrimination in Education: Access to Postsecondary Education.* Final report to the Education Division, National Center for Education Statistics, 1976. ERIC document 132 967.

Baca Zinn, M. "Employment and Education of Mexican American Women: The Interplay of Modernity and Ethnicity in Eight Families." *Harvard Educational Review* 50 (1980):45–62.

Green, R. "Native American Women." Reprinted from *Signs: Journal of Women in Culture and Society* 6 (1980):248–267, by permission of The University of Chicago Press.

Kidwell, C.S. "The Status of American Indian Women in Higher Education." In *Conference on the Educational and Occupational Needs of American Indian Women*. Washington, D.C.: Program on Teaching and Learning, National Institute of Education, 1980.

Medicine, B. *The Native American Woman: A Perspective*. Las Cruces, N.M.: ERIC/CRESS, 1978.

Mirande, A., and Rodriquez, E. *La Chicana*. Chicago: University of Chicago Press, 1979.

Ross, K.A. *Cultural Barriers for American Indians: The Experience of the Yakima Indian Nation in Higher Education*. Toppenish, Wa.: Kamiakin Research Institute, forthcoming 1981.

Sanchez, R., and Martinez Cruz, R., eds. *Essays on La Mujer*. Los Angeles: Chicano Studies Center, University of California, 1977.

U.S. Commission on Civil Rights. *Social Indicators of Equality for Minorities and Women*. Washington, D.C.: U.S. Government Printing Office, 1978.

Vasquez, M.J.T. "Power and Influence of the Chicana: A Review of Research Findings." Paper presented at the Annual Meeting of American Psychological Association, Montreal, 1980.

10 Sex Differences in the Impact of College Environments on Black Students

Jacqueline Fleming

There are in existence today about 120 predominantly black colleges and universities located, for the most part, in the South. Together, they currently enroll over 175,000 students. Most of these schools were established or have their origins beginning in 1865, following the close of the Civil War. At that time northern missionaries began large-scale efforts to provide education to freed men so that they could participate fully in society. (Jencks and Riesman 1968; Willie and Edmonds 1978).

Despite a very rocky history during which many of these schools were forced to close and during which attempts were made to prevent them from maintaining their academic (as opposed to vocational) curricula, they are responsible for a number of notable achievements. Most important is the fact that they have assumed the major responsibility for educating the black population. It is estimated that by 1947 over 90 percent of the B.A.'s received by blacks were earned in black schools. Even today, these schools grant a disproportionate share of college degrees. According to Pifer (1973), 85 black schools enroll about 42 percent of the black students in degree-granting colleges but grant 70 percent of the degrees earned by blacks because of the attrition rates at white colleges. The significance of black schools is that they educated students who could not, by law or custom, be educated elsewhere. Today, they still provide a higher-education-experience to many students who would not otherwise receive one for lack of funds or adequate preparation for college. As a consequence of their peculiar evolution, black colleges have been responsible for the creation of a black middle class and for the education of black leaders instrumental in solving the problems of race relations and those most prominant in the political forefront (Gurin and Epps 1975; Mays 1978).

Now, however, black schools are increasingly being challenged to justify their continued existence (McGrath 1965; Jencks and Riesman 1968; Sowell 1972; Boyd 1974). The past accomplishments of these institutions

This research was supported by a grant from the Carnegie Corporation to the United Negro College Fund.

229

notwithstanding, the current mood is that predominantly white institutions are more capable of assuming the responsibility for black education. The particular strengths of black colleges are actually seen as liabilities in that they have direct consequences for the low quality of the student body (Jencks and Riesman 1968). The existence of two sets of schools, existing side by side, duplicating the same services is seen as wasteful (McGrath 1965). Furthermore, the minimal financial resources of black schools means that they can offer only a mediocre academic experience (Jencks and Riesman 1968; Sowell 1972). Thus, there is considerable feeling that black colleges do not do their students justice and that the intellectual responsibility would be better left to predominantly white institutions. Indeed, most black students are already attending white colleges, and despite social isolation they are said to be making a satisfactory adjustment (Boyd 1974).

Although the debate continues, there are few hard data that might inform the issues. There is little comparative research that demonstrates how black students function or develop in black versus white educational environments, or what the relative intellectual consequence are for matriculation in one college environment or the other. Is it the case that black institutions contribute something unique to black education that is unlikely to be duplicated by white institutions now or in the near future? Or, alternatively, is there evidence that the superior resources available to white institutions produce intellectual gains that outweigh whatever benefits may be derived from the predominantly black educational experience?

The research reported in this chapter comes from an intensive four-year, comparative investigation of these issues funded by the Carnegie Corporation (Fleming 1980). The study attempts to determine the differential impact of predominantly black and predominantly white college environments on the functioning of black students. Furthermore, it seeks to determine the differential patterns of adjustment that can be observed at educational institutions with a specific eye toward illuminating those patterns that appear to be a function of the racial composition of the college environment.

Beyond the broad question of what the differences in functioning are among black students in each educational environment is the more pointed question of who gets the most out of each kind of experience. Although black students, on the average, may benefit more in one or the other environment, there must be individual differences such that some individuals may not conform to the general picture. Thus, the specific purpose of this chapter is to determine the degree to which *sex* is associated with the black students' experience in black and white colleges. Sex is, of course, a major variable that is associated with consistent effects in many areas of functioning. Because of major differences in socialization as a function of sex, it has attained the status of a powerful psychological construct that, among other things, is associated with differences in motivational dynamics, coping mechanisms, and professional attainments (Anastasi, 1958; Maccoby and Jacklin, 1974). Within black populations, the issue of sex differences is of particular interest because much has been written on the presumed dominance of black women (Moynihan 1965; Staples 1970; Jackson 1973; Fleming, forthcoming).

Method

Design of the Study

The design of the research involved a comparative, cross-sectional study in which samples of freshmen and seniors were compared in order to determine the differences that could be observed in their functioning. The subjects were approximately 870 black male and female students recruited from seven colleges in the Atlanta, Georgia area (three predominantly black and four predominantly white). The idea in the exploratory year of the research, from which these data come, was to sample students from a cosmopolitan area of the country that attracts many black students to a variety of educational environments. It should be pointed out that all three of the predominantly black schools were private institutions as opposed to only one of the white colleges. Two of the predominantly black schools were single-sex institutions, whereas all of the predominantly white schools were coed. All of the white institutions were considerably wealthier than any of the black schools. It seemed important for this exploratory effort to match students' characteristics, that is, anticipated background and aptitude variables, rather than matching institutional characteristics, since the latter would be a major focus for succeeding years of the study. These considerations should be kept in mind while evaluating the results.

The predominantly black institutions participating in the study were: (1) Morehouse College, a private, male, four-year liberal-arts institution with an enrollment of 1,275; (2) Spelman College, a private, female, liberal-arts school, with an enrollment of 1,155; and (3) Clark College, a private, coed, liberal-arts school with an enrollment of 1,475. The predominantly white institutions were: (1) Emory University, a private liberal-arts school located in Atlanta, with a total college population of 6,995, fifty of whom were black students; (2) Georgia Institute of Technology, a state institution in Atlanta with a primarily engineering curriculum, enrolling an undergraduate population of 6,321, about 400 of whom were black; (3) University of Georgia, a state-supported liberal-arts school located in Athens, Georgia, enrolling 15,047 white and 361 black undergraduates; (4) Georgia College, a public liberal-arts college located in Milledgeville, with a student body of 2,500 white and 350 black students. The sample of 870 students, which included 540 attending black schools (207 males; 333 females) and 330 students attending white colleges (199 females; 131 males) is described in table 10-1. Despite the effort to match background characteristics students in black schools exhibited substantially lower scores on socioeconomic status ($p = .015$) and aptitude test scores ($p = .001$) than counterparts in predominantly white schools.

The data were collected during the five-month period from January through May 1977 while the principal investigator and field staff were on location in Atlanta. Students were recruited from lists made available by the colleges through an initial letter describing the study, and through follow-up phone calls and class announcements. As indicated in table 10-1, the response rate, as a function of those students actually contacted by letter, ranged from 36 percent to 84 percent. Group testing sessions that included from twenty to one hundred students were conducted by one male and one female member of the project staff. Subjects received a lengthy questionnaire that constituted the basic study instrument and were paid $5 for the 3-4 hour session. Permission to obtain transcripts and aptitude test scores was given by 75 percent of the sample.

Instruments

The questionnaire provided assessments of a large number of variables in several content areas. The first of these was background information, and an initial series of questions was asked in order to obtain such relevant information as family composition and prior schooling. In addition, the Hamburger (1971) Socioeconomic Ranging Scale provided a summary measure of socioeconomic status. SAT/ACT scores were used a baseline measure of scholastic aptitude.

In order to allow students to provide a subjective appraisal of their college experiences, the perceived college climate (that is, environmental press) was assessed with the open-ended method used by Stewart (1975) in her longitudinal follow-up of college-educated women, in which responses to the following three questions were content analyzed. First, "What is the single most enjoyable thing you do in college, or the most enjoyable event? In other words, when do things really seem to go well for you? Please, decribe as fully as possible, explaining the significance of this positive aspect of college." Second, "Similarily, what do you think is the most disappointing thing that occurs or that has occurred in college? Please fully describe the significance of this disappointing aspect of college life for you." Finally, "At the present time, how much and in what ways would you say college has influenced or changed you?" A content analysis of

Table 10-1
Subject Population

	Freshman		Seniors		Total	Response Rate (%)
	Males	Females	Males	Females		
Predominantly black colleges						
Morehouse	92		54		146	37
Spelman		102		83	185	46
Clark	39	102	22	46	209	50
Total	131	204	76	129	540	
Predominantly white colleges						
Emory	10	9	1	18	38	84
University of Georgia	25	57	18	25	125	59
Georgia College	7	41	8	22	78	45
Georgia Tech	41	27	21	0	89	36
Total	83	134	48	65	330	

responses yielded twenty-four items. Examples of the best aspects of college were class and learning activities, personal accomplishment, the opposite sex, and instructors. Example items of the worst aspects of college were financial problems, interpersonal tensions with roommates or friends, race-related tensions, and unfairness or favoritism by teachers. Sample items assessing the influence of college were cognitive growth ("I learned a lot"), identify formation ("I found myself"), and coping and survival ("I learned to look out for myself").

In order to direct student attention to a series of specific aspects of the college experience, several scales were provided so that students could rate the nature of their feelings (on a six-point scale from very dissatisfied to very satisfied) on the college experience in general, the college administration, the college faculty, the quality of instruction, other students at the college, and the extent of informal contact with faculty members.

In regard to intellectual and academic adjustment, a series of twenty-one questions were included to probe the nature of students' adjustment to academic life in college. They were not concerned with the specifics of what students were studying (for example, the precise major), but with their feelings about the course of instruction, their degree of satisfaction with their academic performance, their perception of the faculty's responsiveness to their needs, and so on. In essence, then, their degree of subjective involvement and active participation in academic and campus activities was the focus of the investigation. Some specific items involved the students' satisfaction with teaching methods and faculty interest and encouragement in their welfare; others asked if the student had sought assistance from a teacher or administrator in choosing courses or in planning their future. Finally, students were questioned about the extracurricular activities in which they had participated or held leadership positions. In addition, transcripts were obtained for about 75 percent of the total sample (n = 650). Although grade averages were reported on the questionnaires by better than 90 percent of the sample, the potential distortions in self-report data in areas as ego-involving as grades as well as students' inability to report the specific details of their academic histories argued for reliance on official records. From the transcripts, six measures of academic performance were used: overall grade-point average for the most recent semester or quarter available; grade-point average in the major for the most recent semester; cumulative overall grade-point average; cumulative grade-point average in the major; honor status in the most recent semester; and academic probation status in the most recent semester.

Several questionnaire items also pertained to the nature of students' postgraduate plans and aspirations: "Are you seriously planning to go to graduate or professional school after college," and, "If you do not plan to go to graduate school, what are your career plans?" Again, the specific career choice made by students was not the primary focus, but rather the direction and level of their aspirations. From the above questions, a series of twenty variables was extracted, including level of educational aspirations, ratings for SES level of vocational aspirations according to the Hamburger scale, and the choice of male-dominated, neutral, and female-dominated careers. In addition to the information specific to career aspirations, the study included a broader assessment of students' vocational interests. It is now reasonably well established that vocational choices and interests do not have a significance different from or independent of the personality, but that the vocational choice has reliable and important psychological and sociological meanings. A modified version of Holland's Self-Directed Search (1973) was employed to assess vocational-interest patterns. The instrument consists of two hundred yes/no items that assess a person's interests, competencies, and vocational interests. From these items it is possible to characterize people by their resemblance to each of six personality types: *realistic* (mechanical; nonintellectual), *investigative* (scientific and scholarly; nonpersuasive), *artistic* (expressive and original), *social* (liking to help, teach others), *enterprising* (outgoing and aggressive for organizational gain), and *conventional* (clerical and conforming).

In relation to psycho-social adjustment, a series of items assessing sex-role orientation was developed for the purpose of this study in order to determine the extent to which students were oriented toward marriage/family/home as opposed to career, and the extent of perceived conflict or compatibility between the two sets of goals. Sample items were: "How important is it for you to marry"; "At what age would you ideally like to have children"; "How difficult do you think marriage and a family would make it for you to have a full-time career"; and "To what extent will marriage make your career harder?." Six items composing a social-adjustment scale addressed some of the aspects of interpersonal and heterosexual adjustment faced by students in college. The previous literature suggests that the potential significance for the individuals of each of these aspects of social living is such that a poor resolution would generate powerful feelings of loneliness and isolation (Clark and Plotkin 1963; Hedegard and Brown 1969). These questions probed the students' relationship with a roommate (if any), with other students, and with members of the opposite sex. Each item was substantially correlated with a total scale score in the expected direction, which justified treating the items as a coherent scale.

The self-concept measure utilized in the present research was a modification of the Adjective Checklist (Wylie 1974). Subjects were instructed to indicate on a six-point Likert-type scale the extent to which each of thirty-six adjectives (or adjective phrases) described them. The list consists of both positive and negative self-descriptions selected to assess factors such as intelligence, assertiveness, incompetence, introversion, and other directedness. Thus, while this selection of adjectives does not allow a simple dichotomous assessment of good/bad, high/low self-concept, it locates the natures of self descriptions in specific content areas. Five factors were extracted from the thirty-six items defining dimensions of (1) social decorum; (2) incompetence, (3) ambition, (4) fatigue, and (5) extro-intro version.

Four measures of psychological and physical aspects of stress were included in the study because of research evidence that the experience of illness, psychosomatic decease, and general bodily disturbance is not distributed normally in the population but is associated with stressful environmental conditions: the MMPI Hypochondriases Scale (Hathaway and McKinley 1940); the Holmes and Rahe Life Changes Questionnaire (Rahe, McKean, and Arthur 1976); a report of psychosomatic symptoms (Lachman 1972); and an illness report (Hinkle et al. 1958). From the twenty-one items of the Life Changes questionnaires, three factors were extracted assessing academic stress, personal threat, and personal stress.[1]

Three personality scales were also utilized that provide measures of personality orientations particularly relevant to problems facing black students in different learning environments: Social Assertiveness (Rathus 1973); Black Ideology (Ramseur 1975); and Test Anxiety conceived as a fear of failure in motivation research (Mandler and Sarason 1952; Atkinson and Litwin 1960). Factors derived from the items of social-assertiveness and black-ideology scales were also utilized (see notes 2, 3, 10, 11, and 12).

Analysis

Each of the dependent variables derived from the instruments given above was submitted to a one-way analysis of variance with class (freshmen and senior) as the independent variable. Furthermore, each variable was controlled (separately) for the effects of two covariates—socioeconomic status and aptitude test scores. These two background variables are the ones most important in distinguishing students in black versus white colleges and are the two factors most often related to attrition from freshman to senior year (Astin 1975).

The analysis of variance (ANOVA) program in the Statistical Package for the Social Sciences (SPSS) used adjusts for unequal cell sizes. Because of the large number of variables employed, findings are presented only for results at or beyond the .05 level of statistical significance. It was found that significant results for the uncorrected analysis were usually significant across all the corrected analyses as well; thus, all significant uncorrected findings are also considered for interpretation. The analysis of variance procedures employed provides a number of statistically significant differences between independent groups of freshmen and seniors who differ by

sex and college environment. It is not, however, the fact of significant dif-
ferenes between independent groups that is of interest, but the implications
of those differences for developmental change related to the impact of black
or white college environments, and particularly the differential development of males and females in each kind of college environment. Yet the use
of cross-sectional data, so often dictated by the practical problems of field
research, poses certain problems for the interpretation of developmental
change. Although Feldman and Newcomb (1969) find in their review of
many studies of the impact of college environments on student adjustment
that cross-sectional findings parallel those of longitudinal studies in direction and nature, methodological problems still remain (Baltes, Reese, and
Nesselroade 1977; Baltes, Reese, and Lipsitt, 1980). The ever-present
possibility of generational differences between the freshmen and seniors,
changes in admissions procedures, and differences in aptitude and social-
class background make it difficult to insure that statistically significant differences are due solely to the impact of the college environment. Statistical
procedures have been used in this research control for differences in aptitude and social class—two of the most critical influences in attrition; but the
possibility of unknown and uncontrolled factors in the research remains.

The interpretive approach taken in this study, therefore, is that the
nature of freshman-senior differences suggest hypotheses as to the presumed impact of college on black men and women that can be tested in further research. Indeed, plans to confirm these cross-sectional findings in a
larger study with longitudinal data are underway, but the present results
constitute only a first step in the long-term program of research. Thus, in
the results section significant differences for each sex are presented first in
the three areas of investigation, followed by the hypotheses implied by
them.

Results

Sex Differences in the Impact of Predominantly White
Schools on Black Students

In their subjective assessments of the college experience, senior males gave
less positive ratings than freshmen males to their feelings about the college
administration ($p = .002$), to their feelings about the faculty ($p = .036$) and
to their feelings about other students ($p = .016$). On the climate variables,
senior males were less likely to feel that the worst aspect of the college
experience was personal failure in academics ($p = .017$), but more likely to
feel that it had been the lack of institutional support ($p = .035$). They more

often felt that the best aspect of college was student involvement in political or cultural activities (such as demonstrations and art festivals) ($p = .015$).

Much like their male counterparts, senior females gave less positive ratings than did freshman females to their feelings about the administration ($p = .0001$), the faculty ($p = .007$), and other students ($p = .001$). The one significant finding for the best aspect of college showed that senior females were less likely to feel that it had been socializing ($p = .054$). For the worst aspects of college, seniors more often mentioned financial problems ($p = .047$) and the opposite sex ($p = .013$). Four significant effects for the influence of college indicated that while seniors were less likely to mention self-development ($p = .022$), they were more likely to mention the development of coping and survival skills ($p = .009$), the ability to deal with people ($p = .043$), and cultural broadening ($p = .01$).

Similar results observed for both sexes in their ratings of various aspects of college suggest that senior men and women had more negative feelings about their experiences than freshmen men and women. From the analysis of environmental press, however, the findings for men and women were very different. Although the senior males were less concerned with failure than the freshmen males, they were more affected by institutional abandonment and at the same time more involved in extracurricular activities having the potential for cultural involvement or political protest. There is the suggestion here that their feelings of personal failure give way to dissatisfaction with the institution and that the tensions created become redirected into nonacademic pursuits having the opportunities for socializing. On the other hand, they seem to perceive more changes in themselves than do the men in terms of their ability to survive in their situation, to cope with their people in their environments, and to partake of the new cultural environment. In short, it seems that although men and women have similar feelings about the negative institutional aspects of the college environment, and although each sex experiences different strains, women get more out of the experience in terms of perceived positive changes in themselves.

On the six measures of academic performance, freshman and senior males show no difference on five; only on performance in the major subject is there a significant difference such that seniors actually score lower than freshmen ($p = .003$). In terms of their academic adjustment, senior males were less likely to feel that their teachers graded fairly ($p = .047$), gave lower ratings to the importance of grades ($p = .035$), were less likely to feel that grades in the major subject were essential to their careers ($p = .048$), and had lower estimations of their general ability relative to other students ($p = .051$). Seniors were also more likely than freshmen to be involved in extracurricular activities ($p = .0001$) and spent longer hours studying ($p = .054$). Differences observed in the future plans of males in white schools showed that while seniors were less likely to aspire to the B.A. as the terminal degree (p = .003), they were more likely to plan to go to graduate or professional school immediately after college (p = .006) and more often aspired to the master's degree as the terminal degree (p = .008). No differences were found for males on their vocational-interest profiles.

For females, there was also only one significant difference for academic performance, showing that seniors received higher overall grade-point averages for the most recent semester than freshmen (p = .046). On the indices of academic adjustment, senior females were less likely to express satisfaction with the decision to come to college (p = .0001), less satisfied with the teaching methods (p = .007), less likely to feel that teachers graded fairly (p = .001), gave less importance to the salience of grades (p = .001), and had lower estimates of their general ability (p = .015). Seniors were also more likely to be involved in extracurricular activities (p = .0001), to be satisfied with their majors (p = .035), to admire someone of the faculty or staff (p = .021), and to work well under pressure (p = .048). For future plans, senior women more often planned the M.A. as the terminal degree (p = .005) and exhibited a higher SES level of occupational aspirations (p = .033). Differences in their vocational-interest profiles showed that senior women displayed stronger conventional profiles reflecting clerical and numerical interests compatible with conforming personalities (p = .023).

These findings suggest that senior males show poorer intellectual adjustment than their female counterparts. Although senior males have higher future educational aspirations than freshmen males, the validity of these aspirations is not supported by the other sources of data. Whereas seniors might be expected to improve in their academic efficiency, black males do not do so in the major subject where the maximum motivation would be expected. Although senior males seem to put more time into studying, their grades seem less important, they have less faith in the fairness of the grading practices, and they actually come to think less of their own ability. The educational environment, furthermore, had no impact on their vocational interests. Although senior females only show a single significant difference from freshmen females in their academic performance, it is one toward increased academic efficiency and it is a difference that is complemented by other sources of data. Senior females, too, showed signs of academic dissatisfaction in terms of feelings about their decision to come to that college, the grading procedures, teaching methods, and so forth, but at the same time they exhibited evidence of attachment to positive role models, involvement in the major, and the ability to work under stress. These senior women have higher educational aspirations and occupational goals than freshmen women. It should, however, not be overlooked that they too demonstrate less faith in their perceived ability and that college may have altered their vocational interests in more conventional ways.

For both sexes, then, the nature of the academic experience seems to be characterized by an uphill fight that is frustrating and has consequences for their perceived ability. Women, however, seem to show better intellectual adjustment, perhaps because of their greater access to positive role models who may maintain interest in the major subject. It may also be that their demonstration of conventional profiles, which implies conforming personalities, is related to their seemingly better adjustment to the academic process.

In regard to psychosocial adjustment, senior males received lower scores than freshmen males on the social-adjustment scale ($p = .003$). On a series of sex-role items, the one difference among men was that seniors more often felt that marriage would help their careers ($p = .051$). For the stress indicators used, senior males reported a larger number of life changes ($p = .01$) and a larger number of illnesses ($p = .008$). On the factors of the life-changes questionnaire, senior males scored higher on personal-life changes ($p = .002$), academic-life changes ($p = .005$), and personal threat ($p = .003$) (see note 1). The only significant finding for thirty-six self-descriptions and five factors derived from them was that senior males described themselves as less energetic ($p = .04$). Seniors scored higher on the total Black Ideology Scale ($p = .002$) and lower on the acceptance of white authority factor of this scale ($p = .018$) (see note 2). Although there were no differences on the total social-assertiveness scale, seniors scored lower on the emotional-suppression ($p = .016$) and submissiveness factors ($p = .047$) (see note 3).

Senior females also received lower scores on the social-adjustment scale than freshmen females ($p = .005$). The sex-role items showed that senior females were less likely to think that marriage would interfere with a career ($p = .035$), less likely to think that it would be difficult to combine a family and career ($p = .032$), and less likely to think that marriage and family are more important than a career ($p = .021$). They were more likely, however, to feel that marriage would help a career ($p = .046$) and to indicate that later ages would be ideal for having children ($p = .028$). On the stress indicators, seniors scored higher on a number of psychosomatic complaints onset since college ($p = .0001$), medical assistance sought for psychosomatic complaints ($p = .001$), number of illnesses ($p = .0001$), number of life changes ($p = .033$), and the personal life-changes factor ($p = .026$) (see note 1). The self-concept results indicated that although senior females described themselves as less energetic than freshmen ($p = 0.54$), they also perceived themselves as less inarticulate ($p = .026$) and more outspoken ($p = .004$). Seniors scored higher on the Black Ideology Scale ($p = .046$) and the total social-assertiveness scale ($p = .05$), and scored lower on the emotional-suppression factor of the social-assertiveness scale ($p = .001$).

The data suggest then that the psycho-social adjustment of males and females in white schools is similar in some ways. Both sexes show evidence of significant differences in social adjustment. Both sexes show differences in a number of physical-stress indicators. Both show similar personality differences in regard to stronger black ideology and greater social assertiveness, especially in self-expression. There are, however, important differences in two areas. First, although there was minimal evidence of sex-role differences among the men, there was a consistent trend among women toward less sex-role traditionalism. The perceived obstacles to career posed by marriage seem less important to senior women than freshmen women either because the imminence of marriage is lessened in their constricted social surroundings or because they feel that marriage might help solve their problem of social adjustment. Second, although the seniors of both sexes report feeling less energetic, which suggests some emotional strain, females expressed more confidence than males in their ability to express themselves. Compared to males, then, females seem to exhibit a freedom from sex-role constraints on their behavior and future goals.

Taken together, the findings suggest that senior black women in white schools have derived somewhat greater benefits from the experience than have senior black males in terms of perceived changes in themselves, intellectual adjustment, and freedom from traditional sex-role constraints. Clearly, the experience is on the average a difficult one for both sexes that harbors serious sources of dissatisfaction, the strain of which saps many of their productive energies. The feelings of frustration and alienation on the part of males seem to divert their attention away from learning activities toward nonacademic pursuits. Although it seems clear that racism and isolation are difficult experiences for both black men and women, the educational process may be somewhat easier for women in that they can point to more sources of satisfaction that appear to offset some of the dissatisfactions.

Sex Differences in the Impact of Predominantly
Black Schools on Black Students

Among students in black colleges, the one difference in subjective assessments of the college experience observed in the rating scales was that senior males in black schools reported more informal contact with instructors outside the classroom than did freshmen males ($p = .005$). On the climate variables, seniors were less likely to feel that the best aspect of college was socializing ($p = .036$) but more likely to feel that the best aspect was extracurricular activities ($p = .024$). They more often reported the worst aspects of college as apathy and the lack of student involvement ($p =$

.013), race-related tensions and pressures from whites (p = .055), and un-fairness and favoritism in the classroom (p = .0001). Nonetheless, senior males more often reported that the influence of college was cognitive growth (p = .032).

Senior females in black schools also reported more informal contact with faculty outside the classroom than did freshmen females (p = .0001) and also expressed more positive feelings about the quality of instruction at their school (p = .042). Also, like the males, females were less likely to feel that the best aspect of college was socializing (p = .01) and more likely to think that the best aspect was extracurricular activities (p = .057). They were less likely to point to the worst aspect of college as the lack of institu-tional support (p = .048) but more likely to complain about race-related tensions from whites (p = .002) and about their instructors (p = .0001). Seniors more often felt that the influence of college was cognitive growth (p = .024) but were less likely to cite self-development (p = .014). They also were less likely to feel that college had not had much of an impact on them (p = .035).

The observed pattern of differences suggests more similarities than dif-ferences in the perception of male and female students in black colleges regarding their college experiences. Both sexes seem to feel that the best aspects of the experience are nonacademic and, in fact, complain most about classroom tensions with instructors and the perceived unfairness of classroom practices. But in spite of these complaints, students still indicate that the greatest impact of college has been in what they learned. It does seem that females are somewhat more positive about their academic ex-periences and the impact of college than are males. The increasing informal contact that students of both sexes report may well be linked to their cognitive development.

Senior males scored higher than freshmen males on two of the six measures of academic performance: overall grade-point average for the last semester (p = .018); and grades in the major subject for the last semester (p = .055). In terms of their academic adjustment, senior males scored lower than freshmen males on the salience (that is, importance) of grades (p = .001),[4] and they scored higher on their degree of extracurricular involve-ment (p = .0001).[5] Differences in the nature of their postgraduate plans showed that seniors were less likely to want to go to work right after gradua-tion (p = .009) but were less likely to want to work their way up in some business as an alternative to further education (p = .035), more often want-ing to pursue the master's as the terminal degree (p = .018). Two changes in their vocational-interest profiles showed that senior males were more likely to express enterprising, that is, entrepreneurial (p = .0001), and conven-tional (p = .001) occupational interests.

Senior females in black schools scored higher than their freshmen counterparts on five of the six measures of academic performance: overall grade-point average for the most recent semester (p = .0001), cumulative grade-point average (p = .0001), grades in the major for the last semester (p = .0001), cumulative grades in the major (p = .0001), and honors status (p = .0001). All these differences were highly significant. Other differences observed in academic adjustment showed that senior females scored lower on the salience (that is, importance) of grades (p = .005) but higher on extracurricular involvement (p = .0001), positive involvement with faculty members who provide assistance and whom they admire (p = .001),[6] involvement in their careers as indicated by having career-relevant jobs and seeking career-related advice (p = .0001),[7] satisfaction with their decision to come to that college (p = .016), satisfaction with their courses (p = .002), and satisfaction with their academic performance (p = .0001). Seniors were also, however, experiencing more academic problems than freshmen (p = .057). In terms of their future plans, senior women were less likely than freshmen women to be undecided about their future plans for graduate school (p = .042) and were more often planning either to rest after graduation (p = .03) or to work, with additional schooling planned for a later time (p = .042). More seniors were planning the B.A. (p = .005) and the M.A. (p = .004) as terminal degrees. Also, seniors more often planned careers in neutral (p = .037) and in male-dominated fields (p = .037). No freshman-senior differences were observed in the vocational-interest profiles of these women.

The data imply that males and females in black colleges are quite different in the nature of their intellectual adjustment. Although the differences observed for both sexes in academic performance were positive in nature, females showed far more consistent evidence of academic adjustment. Whereas declining importance of grades and an increasing importance of extracurricular activities characterized both senior men and women, women show far more positive involvement in their academic activities, in their careers, and with instructors. But the more positive academic involvement among women does not seem to have implications for postgraduate plans. The indications are that these differences in educational aspirations are similar for men and women in that seniors of both sexes plan more master's-level degrees and consider noneducational alternatives after graduation. Whereas senior women suggest in their career options that they are less bound by conventional sex-role boundaries, the vocational interests of men are more strongly influenced than those of women in enterprising directions. A fair summary would seem to be that females in black schools are more involved in the academic life of the institution than are males.

In regard to psychosocial adjustment, senior males in black schools received higher scores than freshmen (p = .047) on the social-adjustment scale. On the sex-role items, senior males were less likely to feel that it would be difficult to combine a home and career (p = .017) and less likely to feel that a career is more important than home and family (p = .041). They also were more likely to feel that a career and home/family were equally important (p = .019) and that marriage would have no effect on their careers (p = .048). The significant findings on the stress indicators showed that seniors experienced longer illnesses than freshmen (p = .027) and reported a larger number of recent life changes (p = .045). On the self-descriptions, seniors scored lower on feelings of fatigue (p = .0001)[8] and on feelings of intellectual incompetence (p = .002).[9] They also were more likely to describe themselves as enterprising (p = .026) and as gentlemen (p = .03). Seniors exhibited higher scores than freshmen on the Black Ideology Scale (p = .02) and scored lower on the black defensiveness factor of this same scale (p = .012).[10] Although there were no differences on the overall social-assertiveness scale, seniors scored lower than freshmen on the fear of confrontation factor of this scale (p = .042),[11] the shyness factor (p = .044)[12] and the submissiveness factor (p = .019) (see note 1)—all clearly pointing to greater social awareness in self-expression.

Females showed no freshman-senior differences in their degree of social adjustment. Scores on the sex-role items indicated that senior women were less likely to want to be single women (p = .007), less likely to think that a career was more important than home and family (p = .029), and less likely to think that marriage would interfere with a career (p = .004). They were also more likely to want to be working wives, that is, wives who worked for additional income but whose primary interest was home and family (p = .039), to feel that marriage and family were equally as important as a career (p = .044), and to think that marriage would help a career (p = .038). On the self-concept variables seniors were less likely to express feelings of intellectual incompetence (p = .004) and less likely to describe themselves as lazy (p = .052). They also described themselves as more independent (p = .045) and intelligent (p = .04). On the stress indicators, senior women scored lower on academic life changes (p = .054) but higher on the number of psychosomatic diseases since college (p = .0001) and the severity of their illnesses (p = .048). On the test-anxiety scale (fear of failure), seniors scored lower than freshmen (p = .004). On the factors of the social-assertiveness scale, seniors scored lower on emotional suppression (p = .002) but higher on fear of confrontation (p = .0001), shyness (p = .024), and submissiveness factor (p = .03).

The data thus suggest that in sex-role orientation similar differences were observed for both sexes in that both senior men and women felt that marriage and family goals were just as important as career goals. A similar incidence of physical symptoms were found for both sexes, although women did exhibit a difference in academic life changes. Also, very similar differences between freshmen and seniors in self-concept were found for both sexes, in that seniors thought of themselves as more intelligent and capable. The first notable sex difference is that senior males show a better social adjustment than do females. The major area of divergence, however, would appear to be in the personality differences between men and women. Whereas senior males seem more assertive than freshmen males, especially in their self-expression and dealings with others, senior women are more submissive and show more anxiety in their dealings with others than freshmen women. This pattern suggests a process of traditional sex-role conditioning in both sexes on social level. The implied ascendance among males and submission among females may also be linked to the differences in social adjustment for men, but not for women.

To the extent that sex differences were observed among black students at black colleges, they are in the direction of somewhat greater subjective satisfaction among women with academic experience and especially with their instructors, greater involvement among the women in the academic life of the college and in academic performance, and greater sex-role conditioning among the women, resulting in losses in social assertiveness. It may be that the major social difference on black versus white campuses for black students is that there are large numbers of black men and women in black schools and that the interactions between the sexes are at least one major source of social adjustment. Thus, although women may benefit as much or more from the academic life of the black institution as men do, they may also become more conforming to the traditional pattern of sex-role submission in their dealings with males. Such a pattern could well be related to evidence that the stronger academic involvement found among women does not seem to translate directly into enhanced educational or occupational aspirations.

Conclusions

Although the results presented in this chapter derive solely from cross-sectional data of freshmen and senior students in the seven colleges studied, they provide a strong data base from which to cull implications as to the differential impact of college environments. This data base can serve as a guide for future research. One of the most striking implications of these findings is that in general students in black schools show better intellectual adjustment than their counterparts in white schools. This pattern of results is important because it had never been predicted or suspected in any of the writings on the issue. If anything, the literature leads one to expect better social adjustment in black schools, but hardly more than that. What is so significant about this finding is that it seems to occur in spite of the fact that the black schools are at a considerable disadvantage, compared to their white counterparts, in terms of resources of every conceivable kind. By the same token, it appears that the interpersonal tensions encountered by black students in white schools, which seem to be of a racist nature, are sufficient to thwart their intellectual potential at schools with better objective attributes. The issue to be considered, then, in the debate over the continued existence of black colleges is not one of mere differences in institutional resources. More important for the educational experience of college is the nature of the latent psycho-sociological climate that apparently can have stronger consequences for intellectual adjustment. Thus, the contribution that black colleges make to black education is the greater academic and intellectual adjustment of their students despite impoverished resources.

It is not new to suggest that racism has less impact on black women. It does seem, however, that data from this investigation might place a different slant on why this seems to be the case. In addition to the subjective and intellectual experiences that black women receive in white schools was evidence of freedom from traditional sex-role constraints in their careers and in self-expression. At the same time, the data indicated that black women in black schools may experience more sex-role conditioning on a social level. This difference was linked to the presence in black schools of more males with whom they could interact on a social level. It may be that black women seem to show a blossoming of their coping capabilities in white settings because there are few black males who might subject them to the kinds of rewards and punishments known as sex-role conditioning, and because white males have less interest in dealing with black women socially. It does appear that the social arena is where this kind of conditioning takes place. Although the consequences of such a phenomenon for academic and career development are not clear at this point, the data clearly suggest consequences for self-expression—an important link in the chain of personal as well as intellectual adjustment. This kind of viewpoint also raises the question of whether the academic involvement observed among black women in black colleges is related to a kind of intellectual adjustment that will have consequences beyond college or whether it is specific to the values and expectations of the institution.

On the surface, these results might seem to support old notions about black matriarchy in that black women show better academic and intellectual adjustment than black men in both educational environments. The real question, however, is whether college experience has consequences for future educational and occupational goals. Although it has been said that black schools perpetuate the ascendance of black women (Jencks and Riesman 1968), the present data indicate that the biggest sex difference in future goals occurs in white schools. Furthermore, a previous analysis of this data showed that the goals of black women are actually lower than those of their male counterparts and are in a more traditional, sex-role-stereotyped direction (Fleming, forthcoming). It was also apparent in this data that the vocational interests of senior and freshman women in black schools were similar and that the startling differences in assertiveness do not bode well for highly competitive career choices. Among women in white schools, the more conventional-interest profiles among seniors are less than encouraging. Thus, the positive adjustment of black women found especially in black schools may not translate into higher aspirations for the kind of prestigious enterprising occupations associated with the crossing of sex-role boundaries.

The data presented in this chapter were extracted from the exploratory phase of a four-year undertaking. In the three succeeding phases of the study, the nature of the results continue to confirm the preliminary conclusions presented here. In addition, research plans are underway to provide longitudinal tests of the pattern of findings suggested here as students progress to new life stages, including the senior year of college and the assumption of postgraduate responsibilities after college.

Notes

1. Three factors are extracted from the twenty-one items of the Life Changes Questionnaire. The first was Academic Stress, composed of the following items: change in sleeping habits; change in alcohol or drug consumption; increase in unhappiness; change in study habits; failure in course; disagreement with an instructor; and a competitive event. The second was Personal Threat, composed of: violation of the law; legal troubles; change in political beliefs; and physical attack. The third was Personal Stress, composed of: a personal achievement; change in personal habits; change in social activities; and a major decision.

2. The Acceptance of White Authority factor is composed of the following items: Afro-Americans should not buy guns; police protect the black community; black schools do not need a black principal; and services need not be community-controlled.

3. The Emotional Suppression factor of the Social Assertiveness Scale consists of: "I am careful to avoid hurting other people's feelings, even when I feel that I have been injured"; and "If a close and respected relative were annoying to me, I would smother my feelings rather than express my annoyance."

The Submissiveness factor consists of: "If a salesman has gone to considerable trouble to show me merchandise which is not quite suitable, I have a difficult time in saying 'no!'"; and "To be honest, people often take advantage of me."; and "I have often had a hard time saying 'no!'."

4. The Salience of Grades factor is composed of: good grades are

essential to career goal; good grades in the major essential to career goal; and general importance of getting good grades.

5. Extracurricular Involvement factor refers to the number of extracurricular activities and offices held in extracurricular activities.

6. Involvement with Faculty factor is composed of: campus person has been helpful; and subject admires a person on the faculty or administration.

7. The Career Involvement factor consists of: subject sought career assistance; and job is related to career plans.

8. The Fatigue factor extracted from Self Descriptions is composed of the following items: lazy and tired.

9. The Incompetence factor is composed of the following items: scatter-brained; poor memory; slow-witted; irresponsible; and incompetent.

10. The Black defensiveness factor consists of: blacks more intelligent than whites; thick lips look better; and whites can't get down.

11. The Fear of Confrontation factor consists of: "I will hesitate to make phone calls to business establishments and institutions"; "I would rather apply for a job or for admission to a college by writing letters than by going through personal interviews"; "I find it embarrassing to return merchandise"; 'I have avoided asking questions for fear of sounding stupid"; and "During an argument I am sometimes afraid that I will get so upset that I will shake all over.'

12. The Shyness factor consists of: "Most people seem to be more aggressive and assertive than I"; "I have hesitated to make or accept dates because of shyness"; and "I often don't know what to say to attractive persons of the opposite sex."

Bibliography

Anastasi, A. *Differential Psychology.* New York: MacMillan, 1958.

Astin, A.W. *Preventing Students from Dropping Out.* San Francisco: Jossey-Bass, 1975.

Atkinson, J.W., and Litwin, G.H. "Achievement Motive and Test Anxiety Conceived as Motive to Approach Success and Motive to Avoid Failure." *Journal of Abnormal and Social Psychology* 60 (1960):52–63.

Baltes, P.B.; Reese, H.W.; and Lipsitt, L.P. "Life-Span Developmental Psychology." *Annual Review of Psychology* 31 (1980):65–110.

Baltes, P.B.; Reese, H.W.; and Nesselroade, J.R. *Life-Span Developmental Psychology: Introduction to Research Methods.* Monterey, Calif.: Brooks/Cole, 1977.

Boyd, W.M. *Desegregating America's Colleges.* New York: Praeger, 1974.

Clark, K., and Plotkin, L. *The Negro Student at Integrated Colleges*. New York: National Scholarship Service and Fund for Negro Students, 1963.

Feldman, K.A., and Newcomb, T.M. *The Impact of College on Students*. San Francisco: Jossey-Bass, 1969.

Fleming, J. "The Impact of College Environments on Black Students." Technical Report. New York: The United Negro College Fund, 1980.

————. "Sex Differences in the Educational and Occupational Goals of Black College Students: Continued Inquiry into the Black Matriarchy Theory." In M.S. Horner, M. Notman, and C. Nadelson, eds., *Perspectives on the Patterns of an Era*. New York: Plenum Press, forthcoming.

Gurin, P., and Epps, G. *Black Consciousness, Identity and Achievement*. New York: Wiley, 1975.

Hamburger, M. *A Revised Occupational Scale for Rating Socioeconomic Status*. Unpublished manuscript, New York University, 1971.

Hathaway, S.R., and McKinley, J.C. "A Multiphasic Personality Schedule (Minn.): Construction of the Schedule." *Journal of Psychology* 10 (1940):249–254.

Hedegard, J., and Brown, D. "Encounters of Some Negro and White Freshmen With a Public Multi-University." *Journal of Social Issues* 25 (1969):131–144.

Hinkle, L.E., Jr.; Christenson, W.N.; Kane, F.D.; Ostfeld, A.; Thetford, W.N.; and Wolff, H.G. "An Investigation of the Relation Between Experience, Personality Characteristics, and General Susceptibility to Illness." *Psychosomatic Medicine* 4 (1958):278–295.

Holland, S.L. *Making Vocational Choices: A Theory of Careers*. New Jersey: Prentice-Hall, 1973.

Jackson, J.J. "Black Women in a Racist Society." In C.V. Willie, B.M. Kramer, and B.S. Brown, eds., *Racism and Mental Health*. Pittsburgh, Pa.: University of Pittsburgh Press, 1973.

Jencks, C., and Riesman, D. *The Academic Revolution*. Garden City, N.Y.: Doubleday, 1968.

Lachman, S.J. *Psychosomatic Disorders: A Behavioristic Interpretation*. New York: Wiley, 1972.

McGrath, E.J. *The Predominantly Negro Colleges and Universities in Transition*. New York: Teachers College Press, 1965.

Maccoby, E., and Jacklin, C.N. *Psychology of Sex Differences*. Palo Alto, Calif.: Stanford University Press, 1974.

Mandler, G., and Sarason, S. "A Study of Anxiety and Learning." *Journal of Abnormal And Social Psychology* 47 (1952):166–173.

Mays, B.E. "The Black College in Higher Education." In C.V. Willie and R.R. Edmonds, eds., *Black Colleges in America*. New York: Teachers College Press, 1978.

Moynihan, D.P. *The Negro Family, A Case for National Action*. Washington, D.C.: U.S. Government Printing Office, 1965.

Pifer, A. *The Higher Education of Blacks in the United States*. New York: Carnegie Corporation of New York: 1973.

Rahe, R.H.,; McKean, J.D.; and Arthur, R.J. "A Longitudinal Study of Life-Change and Illness Patterns. *Journal of Psychosomatic Research* 10 (1976):355–366.

Ramseur, H. "Continuity and Change in Black Identity: A Study of Black Students at an Interracial College." Ph.D. diss., Harvard University, 1975.

Rathus, A.S. "A 30-Item Schedule for Assessing Assertive Behavior." *Behavior Therapy* 4 (1973):398–406.

Sowell, T. *Black Education: Myths and Tragedies*. New York: David McKay, 1972.

Staples, R. "The Myth of the Black Matriarchy." *Black Scholar* 1 (1970): 9–16.

Stewart, A.J. "Longitudinal Prediction from Personality to Life Outcomes Among College-Educated Women." Ph.D., Harvard University, 1975.

Willie, C.V., and Edmonds, R.R., eds., *Black Colleges in America*. New York: Teachers College Press, 1978.

Wylie, Ruth C. *The Self-Concept: A Review of Methodological Considerations and Measuring Instruments,* vol. I. Lincoln: University of Nebraska Press, 1974.

11

Undergraduates and Their Teachers: An Analysis of Student Evaluations of Male and Female Instructors

Sheila Kishler Bennett

Student perceptions and evaluations of their instructors are broadly consequential, not simply for instructors, but also for their students and institutions. Attribution and role-modeling theory suggests that students are more likely to identify with and hold in esteem individuals perceived as similar to themselves; the absence of attractive female role modes in academia is often cited as significantly inhibiting the movement of women into the professions and nontraditional areas of study and employment (Almquist and Angrist 1971, 1975; Carnegie Commission 1973, Tidball 1973, 1976; Tidball and Kistiakowsky 1976; Widom and Burke 1978). Instructors in turn become aware of student perceptions and reactions through informal communication and subtle reinforcement in the form of student performance, attitudes, and course enrollments, as well as through formal teaching evaluations. These last are often of particular concern since an increasing number of institutions incorporate some form of student evaluation into decisions on tenure and promotion. Therefore, to the extent that administrators and appointment committees use formal student evaluations in assessing male and female instructors, student bias in evaluation can lead to unintended institutionalization of gender preferences.

In broader context, the study of student perceptions and evaluations of instructors promises to extend our knowledge of institutional characteristics consequential to the educational experience of undergraduate women and the life-styles and career paths they chart in adult life. Research on the baccalaureate origins of female achievers has documented evidence that the undergraduate institutions from which women have gone on to doctorates, professional work, or public achievement differ from those that produce male achievers (Newcomer 1959; Tidball and Kistiakowsky 1976; Oates and Williamson 1978; Tidball 1980). Women's colleges stand out particularly in this respect, producing almost twice as many achievers per 1,000 women graduating in the decades 1910–1960 as did coeducational institutions (Tidball 1973). Tidball's (1973, 1980) analysis indicates that the productivity of

251

women's colleges correlates highly with the proportion of female faculty relative to female students, even when such factors as wealth, size, and the selectivity of the institution are taken into account. These findings, which suggest a link between contact with women in instructional roles and outcomes for students in later life, point to closer examination of students' orientations toward their instructors during the undergraduate years.

The studies described here examine student orientation toward their instructors, within the domain of the instructional role, in a variety of institutional settings. Background for these studies is provided by review of available research and methodological issues in the study of student evaluation of college instructors. An initial pilot study is then described and an analytic model developed that links visibility of female faculty to the perceptual and expectational orientation of students and to outcomes for instructors. Finally, there is an overview of a seires of subsequent studies that tested the generalizability of a number of these propositions within other institutional settings. As design and analysis of the pilot study and development of the research instrument are detailed elsewhere (Bennett forthcoming), summary statistical discussions only are provided here.

Background: Student Evaluation of College Instructors

Assessment of student bias and its institutional consequences is not a straightforward matter. The cognitive and attributive processes underlying gender-specific judgments are potentially complex. Further, although student perceptions, evaluations, and expectations have multiple implications, the few studies that have specifically assessed differences in teaching evaluation are often inconsistent in their findings. Contradiction and inconsistency in this literature is understandable. Available studies not only cover as much as a four-decade period, but also are set within strikingly different institutional contexts. Further, concern with development of student-evaluation instruments that conform to internal-consistency standards of reliability leads to instruments constructed on the premise that each student represents a replicate observation (Marsh and Overall 1979). This procedure can mask differences in the manner in which male and female students respond to instructors. Additional methodological and conceptual complications arise when studies based on direct student ratings of their instructors (Elmore and LaPointe 1974, 1975) are compared with studies using semi-projective and other procedures that confound sex-role stereotypes and evaluation of actual behavior (Kaschak 1978).

Available research offers little evidence that women, *as instructors,* are devalued by their students. When asked formally to evaluate the teaching effectiveness of a specific classroom instructor, using one of the number of widely adopted course-evaluation instruments, students are found generally to accord their male and female instructors equal marks—or to favor women slightly (Elmore and LaPointe 1974; Kulick and McKeachie 1975; McKeachie 1979). Students may, however, express a marked preference for same-gender instructors, in both course selection and satisfaction with course selection (Sternglanz and Lyberger-Ficek 1977; Kaschak 1978). Same-gender preferences may also extend to evaluation of qualitative aspects of teaching performance. Elmore and LaPointe report that "female students seem to perceive female teachers as more interested, and male students seem to perceive male teachers as more interested" (1975, p. 374).

Kaschak (1978), using a semiprojective protocol in which descriptions of differing teaching styles were attributed randomly to instructors with identifiably male or female names, found that male students rated male instructors as more effective, concerned, likable, excellent, and powerful than female instructors. Female students did not differentiate between male and female instructors in their evaluations (ratings of "powerful" excepted). However, quasi-projective protocols and the use of hypothetical descriptions of teaching styles may tell us more about the rater than about either actual differences among male and female instructors or the process of bias in ratings (Crittenden and Norr 1973). Further, the labeling of teaching styles as "masculine" (active, aggressive, directive) and "feminine" (passive, facilitating, listening) characteristic of such studies may have limited empirical validity (Sternglanz 1979). Studies such as Harris's (1975, 1976), reporting that hypothetical teachers with "masculine" styles are rated more highly than those with "feminine" teaching styles, may be observing in part the general social evaluation of men over women. In general, studies based either on direct student ratings of actual instructors' behaviors do not report either dramatic mean differences between ratings of male and female instructors or interactions between gender of student and gender of instructor.

Whether or not instructor gender—as a variable presumably extraneous to evaluations of performance—biases student ratings of instructors, specific gender-stereotypic attributes do identify instructors whom students evaluate more favorably and may account for any tendency for women to be rated above men. Primary among these attributes is warmth. Previous research has consistently documented positive correlation of student ratings of teacher performance and student perception of an instructor as a warm, supportive, interested individual (Baird 1973; Costin and Grush 1973; Elmore and LaPointe 1975; Elmore and Pohlmann 1978). Since warmth and a supportive, concerned interest in others are traits stereotypically attributed to women, students may assume or more readily recognize warmth in a female instructor. The question of whether or not such an assessment is consistent with an instructor's own self-image or actual interpersonal orientation may be secondary.

This chapter reports a series of studies assessing bias in student ratings of male and female instructors in two types of institutional settings. The initial pilot study was conducted in 1977 at a small coeducational college. Subsequent studies, designed to test the generalizability of specific propositions suggested by the initial study, were conducted in a variety of university settings during the period 1977–1980. Direct student ratings of specific instructors are the basis of analysis, following Kaschak's argument that typical rating items such as " 'made clear assignments' . . . may allow less room for the introduction of stereotypes and bias . . . than judgments involving such areas as competence, rationality, emotionality, etc. If attitudes are to be assessed, it would seem that rating scales must be constructed to reflect areas of cultural bias or stereotypical attitudes toward females" (1978, p. 237). In addition, our data include both formal ratings of teaching performance and more personal assessments of personal attributes, interpersonal style, and instructional approach.

In the following analyses, we will first assess whether students place male and female instructors within a common frame of reference—whether the elements of teaching style, personality, and interpersonal orientation that distinguish the male instructors for students are the same as those that distinguish the female. Second, using separate cognitive and evaluative measures, we will assess whether differences observed for male and female instructors in the *formal* evaluation of instructor effectiveness are related to differences in students' perception of the personal attributes of male and female instructors. Third, we will examine whether students are more demanding that female faculty conform to feminine stereotypes by being more available to their students, more supportive, and more personally concerned, and the consequences of such role pressure for female instructors.

The Initial Study: Teacher Evaluations in a
Liberal-Arts College

The initial investigation was conducted at a coeducational liberal-arts college and was based on a sample of all students enrolled in nonscience introductory courses. The research instrument was an anonymously returned questionnaire, which was also used with little modification in the subsequent studies.[1] Students were selected in such a way that gender of student and gender of instructor were balanced, a strategy that required substantial oversampling of students of female instructors. Women constituted a minority of full-time faculty at this institution, from one-third at the level of assistant professor to fewer than one-tenth in the higher, tenured ranks. As no full-time female faculty taught an introductory science course during the term of the study, no courses within that division were included. Eighty-two percent (253) of all questionnaires were returned; 56 percent of all respondents were female, and 43 percent were students of female instructors.

Summary of Analyses

Forty bipolar descriptive scales were developed that describe instructor attributes such as classroom mannerisms, teaching style, course organization, attitudes toward students, approachability, and personal characteristics and interpersonal style. These scales were constructed on the model of the semantic differential (Heise 1970); representative items may be examined in table 11-1. Factor analysis of these scales permits characterization of the structure of perceptual orientation underlying these student ratings, and scales constructed to index each dimension permit comparisons among instructors and students.

Factor analysis of these forty perceptual-orientation scales, derived from this first section of the questionnaire, indicates a common factor structure for male and female instructors (see table 11-1). The four facets of

Table 11-1
Student Perceptions of Classroom Instructor

F1	F2	F3	F4	
				Factor 1: Warmth (nonauthoritarian interpersonal style)[a]
.74				understanding/uncompromising
.51				approachable/unapproachable
.60	(.31)			nonauthoritarian/authoritarian
.53				fair/not always perfectly fair
.77				encouraging/critical
.62				modest/gives impression of being conceited
.58				permissive/strict
.62				tolerant of student with weak natural command of material/not sympathetic to student lacking natural talents in field
.70	(.36)			does not intimidate/intimidates
.58				permits interruption in classroom/discourages interruption
.61				patient/impatient
.71	(.40)			makes student feel important/makes student feel unimportant
				Factor 2: Charisma (potency)
	.52			hip/straight
	.59			engaging, involved/withdrawn, stolid
	.58			effective in eliciting discussion when desired/ineffective

Table 11–1 continued

F1	F2	F3	F4	
	.64			maintains eye contact with students/seldom makes eye contact
	.45			teaching reflects a critical social and political consciousness/teaching does not
				Factor 3: Self-assurance ("experienced")
		.73		confident/uncertain
		.73		relaxed in classroom/nervous
		.55		experienced/inexperienced
		.80		poised/ill at ease
				Factor 4: Instructional approach ("professionalism")
			.40	clearly outlines course requirements/lax in informing students
			.66	relatively structured lectures/relatively unstructured lectures
			.49	maintains tight control over discussion/tendency to let blabbermouths run on
			.73	presents material in organized manner/ presentations not organized
			.77	professional/unprofessional
7.34	2.94	2.11	1.89	eigenvalue[b]
29.3	11.7	8.4	7.5	percentage total variance accounted for
				N = 253

Note: Principal factors, varimax rotated, male-and female-instructed students pooled (initial study).

[a]Item descriptions edited for publication.

[b]Eigenvalues and percentage total variance accounted for by each factor reported for unrestricted forty-item principal-factors solution; item loadings (greater than .30 only) reported for restricted, four-factor solution, varimax rotated.

cognitive orientation identified by this procedure may be described as egalitarianism in interpersonal style ("warmth"); personal charisma ("ability to compel"); self-assurance (connoting to students that the instructor is "experienced"); and instructional approach (structured versus laissez-faire, connoting to students that the instructor is "professional," as opposed to "unprofessional"). The dominant warmth factor is consistent with other factor-analytic evaluation studies of instructor attributes (McKeachie and Lin 1971; Baird 1973; Costin and Grush 1973; Elmore and LaPointe 1975; Elmore and Pohlmann 1978). The first two factors are, however, also noteworthy in that they resemble the evaluative and potency dimensions characteristically found in factoring semantic differential response (Osgood, Tannenbaum, and Suci 1959).

This factor analysis supports the hypothesis that students do not have qualitatively different standards of reference for male and female instructors. Personal attributes and characteristics of teaching style that differentiated among male instructors were the same as those that differentiated among females. Nevertheless, when male and female instructors are compared on scales constructed to index each of these four facets of perceptual orientation, female instructors were found to be judged warmer and more supportive than male instructors. Additionally, female instructors were perceived as more personally charismatic (see table 11-2). Therefore, although students did not place instructors in gender-specific frames of reference, they did perceive systematic differences between male and female instructors on the common dimensions of comparison.

That women tended to be described as warmer and less authoritarian is consistent with conventional images of femininity. Charisma—implying power and authority—is not. However, the perception that female instructors are potent and able to compel is in accord with the perception that female *academicians* are exceptional. In an institutional environment in which women are a distinct and thereby visible minority, this perception may be constantly reinforced, quite apart from whether women who achieve such positions are in fact exceptionally competent individuals (Kanter 1977). This interpretation is strengthened by the finding that women in departments in which women held few appointments were found to be rated significantly more personally charismatic, although women in both token and simply skewed departments were nonetheless also rated higher on this dimension than male colleagues.[2]

In formal ratings of teaching performance, women were consistently rated higher on interpersonal aspects of teaching performance, such as willingness to assist, ability to encourage students to express opinions and viewpoints, and ability to arouse and sustain interest in a subject matter. Women also scored higher on the global rating of teaching effectiveness (see table 11-2). However, regardless of gender, an instructor's perceived warmth was highly predictive of each of these formal ratings of teaching performance; and women's higher ratings on interpersonal aspects of teaching performance were in fact accounted for by their higher perceived warmth (and, in the case of some ratings, higher perceived ability to compel).

The next step in the analysis was to ask whether the perceptual judgments that correlate with assessments of teaching performance are similar for male and female instructors. That is, do they "earn their marks" in a similar manner? To answer this question, bivariate relationships between perceptual and performance ratings were compared for male and female instructors separately. It was found that perceptual ratings that were consequential for the performance ratings of men were in many cases comparatively consequential for women, especially with respect to the perceptual attribute "warmth." However, two important gender differences were found when the correlate of the secondary factors (which reference more specific aspects of student perceptual orientation) are examined:

Table 11-2

Perceptual-Orientation Scales and Teaching-Performance Ratings: Differences of Means, by Gender of Instructor (Initial Study)

Scale or Rating	male N = 144 x	female N = 109 x	p
	Gender of Instructor		
Perceptual orientation scale			
Nonauthoritarian interpersonal style	− .34	1.00	.05
Charisma (potency)	− .29	.61	.001
Self-assurance	.08	− .19	n.s.
Instructional approach	.02	− .22	n.s.
Performance rating[a]			
Willing to assist students out of class	3.63	3.87	.05
Consistently encourages students to express opinions and viewpoints	3.49	4.08	.001
Able to arouse and sustain student interest in the subject matter	3.22	3.60	.009
Overall evaluation	3.57	3.75	.05

Note: $N = 253$.

[a]Instructor rated on five-position scale (high = "much better than average"; low = "much below average") relative to other faculty with whom student had worked. No statistically significant differences observed for command of material for classroom presentation; organization, clarity, and coherence of classroom presentation; organization and coherence of course as a whole; fairness of evaluation of students' work; balanced presentation of pertinent viewpoints.

1. When the question of acceptance of the content of instructional presentation was at issue (for example, whether the instructor presents a balanced interpretation of pertinent viewpoints), favorable perceptual impressions were far more consequential for women than for men. That is, if her students were to accept her intellectual authority in this respect, it was doubly important for the female instructor that she be judged compelling, self-assured, and "professional" in instructional approach.
2. Students were clearly more tolerant of what they perceived as a lack of formal professionalism in the conduct of teaching from their male professors, demanding of women a higher standard of formal preparation and organization.

Further, according to student reports, students do receive more time and personal attention from female instructors (see them more frequently, call them at home, discuss personal matters with them)—as would be consistent with the perception of greater warmth, as well as culturally conditioned expectations for women. However, female instructors were also described more frequently as "insufficiently available." In the case of female instructors, this judgment likely reflected the heavy student contact maintained by women. Students reporting a high level of contact and support were also likely to judge the instructor sufficiently available, and those reporting less contact and support were less satisfied with female instructors' availability. In contrast, male instructors were not judged by the time and attention the student had personally received, but rather by perceptual correlates of availability—how free, for instance, the student felt to stop by casually, regardless of the student's history of contact and supportive relationship. Similarly, judgments of an instructor's willingness to assist a student out of class correlated highly with history of contact for female instructors, but not for male. As was generally true for all analyses relating to the initial study, the student's gender did not make a difference.

Visibility: A Conceptual Model

Despite the limitations of the pilot study, important differences were documented between male and female instructors in their students' perceptual judgments of personal attributes frequently ascribed on the basis of gender ("warmth," "ability to compel") and in students' reports of contact and personal support. Further, the study suggested that women are held to different—but also more exacting—standards than men. These observations, as well as the thematic content of presurvey interviews with instructors, point to phenomena more complex than simple stereotyping, since students seemed to be subjecting female instructors to a particular scrutiny as well. The lack of independent data for instructors on warmth and role investment prevents us from determining whether students were simply reporting actual differences in instructor attributes and behaviors. However, if a *cultural* argument were a sufficient explanation, then we should find that ratings of women's willingness to assist and availability were largely independent of a student's actual experience of assistance and support. As described previously, this was not the case.

On the other hand, qualitative data obtained from instructors in the process of developing the student questionnaire suggests that a simple *behavioral* explanation would also not be particularly useful, at least in this specific institution. In presurvey interviews, female faculty repeatedly expressed concern over students' demands for time and personal attention (a theme absent from interviews with male instructors) and often spoke of conflict between the demands of teaching and the demands of other professional activities. The sentiment was expressed repeatedly that students expected "mothering" in a way not demanded of their male colleagues; other female faculty spoke of feeling "exposed" to such demands by virtue of being the only women in a department, of being a "lightning rod" or "riding point." Many spoke at length of strategies they employed to control student contact, distance themselves from personal involvement, and discourage personal demands. In contrast, male instructors spoke of the time required by course preparation and grading and described their students as either "dull" or "stimulating"—seldom as "demanding," except in an intellectual sense. Regardless of differences in individual feelings of personal responsibilities toward their students, female instructors clearly felt pressures on them as women not experienced by men as instructors.

On the basis of this evidence, an argument can be developed that as a numerical minority, female academicians are characteristically highly visible anomalies. As such, women are puzzles for their students—to be observed, categorized, figured out. They are likely to be thought of as different and therefore less predictable, both as individuals and in their role as classroom instructors. The visibility of female faculty then has the following consequences:

1. *Visibility increases attentiveness to personal characteristics of female instructors.* This is consistent with the research in person perception and attribution theory, which documents information gathering as an ambiguity-reducing response (Tagiuri 1969; Gruder 1977), as well as with research on stress and ambiguity in complex organizations (Kahn et al. 1964; Kanter 1977).[3]
2. *Visibility decreases students' tolerance for deviation from normative or stereotypic expectations for instructors within that narrowly defined role.* This proposition is consistent with research linking ambiguity and tolerance for ambiguity to students' evaluations of and orientations toward instructors (Baird 1973; Norr and Crittenden 1975).
3. *Visibility increases student pressures toward conformity to stereotypic gender-linked role expectations.* The female instructor may invest heavily in the teacher role, thereby reinforcing stereotypic expectations that a woman is supportive, warm, facilitative; or she may invest heavily in the external status role of researcher/professional, adopting deliberate strategies to limit student contact and to communicate her primary commitment to the "masculine" (instrumental rather than affective) aspects of career investment.[4]

A conceptual model suggested by the initial study and incorporating these and other propositions is depicted in figure 11-1. Visibility is a definitional construct by which institutions may be compared in terms of the degree to which women are proportionally represented and professionally and curricularly integrated. Proportional representation, institutional climate, and curricular segregation are observable indexes of visibility that may specify one or several referent levels (for example, school, division, department). Institutional variables enhancing the visibility of instructors are hypothesized to affect student perceptual and expectational orientations in the three ways just cited. Scrutiny and stereotyping mediate between

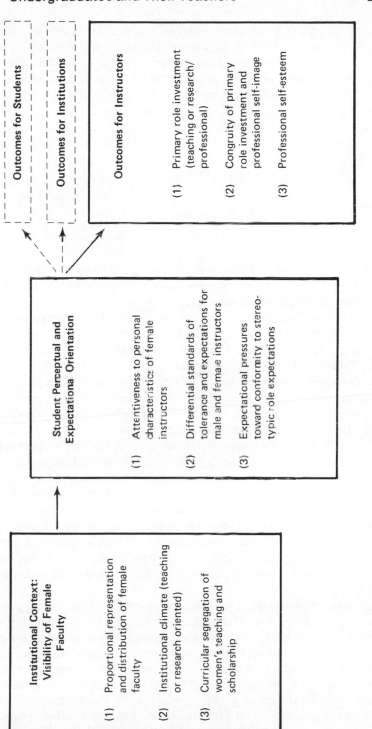

Figure 11–1. Relation of Women's Visibility in Institutional Context to Instructor's Role Definitions and Investment, as Mediated by Students' Perceptual and Expectational Orientations

institutional factors that heighten female instructors' visibility and consequences of heightened visibility for individual instructors. Primary among
the latter are the consequences of performance pressures implicit in pressures toward conformity—either to minimize or maximize investment in
teaching, the latter potentially at the expense of professionally rewarded
activities. The consequences of this behavior in teaching can include raised
expectations by students for interpersonal support and counseling, and
lowered prospects of women faculty for promotion and tenure.

The University Studies

Procedure

A subsequent set of studies was then conducted specifically to test the conceptual model with respect to the consequences of visibility for students'
increased attentiveness to personal attributes of female instructors, student
tolerance for deviation from normative or stereotypic expectations for
instructors, and pressures on instructors toward conformity to stereotypic
gender-linked role expectations. University questionnaires were distributed
in class by the researcher or an assistant and returned anonymously via campus mail. Response rates and summary of sample characteristics and administrative procedures for each institution are found in table 11-3. All classrooms sampled or included were taught directly, without the use of a teaching assistant or sectioning, by an instructor who held full faculty rank. In
three of the universities, all full-appointment women teaching an appropriate course in the specific departments or divisions in the study semester participated; in the remaining two universities, care was taken to ensure variation in rank of participating female instructors. As before, classroom selection was restricted to introductory or other courses offered without prerequisite, in order to minimize student preselection of instructor. "Visibility"
is indexed as the proportional representation of female faculty at three
referent levels: the undergraduate institution as a whole (usually, the College of Arts and Sciences or its equivalent), the disciplinary division, and the
department.[5]

In addition, participating instructors were provided with a log, constructed as a desk diary, in which each recorded the extent and nature of all
contact with members of the case class for one week late in the study semester. Telephone calls and social interactions were logged, as well as scheduled
office hours and individual student-instructor conferences. Instructors were
asked to describe each interaction as primarily "academic or class related
advising," "personal advising or counseling," "combination," or
"social." Use of student initial permits counting of the number, propor-

tion, and frequency of students seen. Thus it is possible to corroborate students' reports of the extent and nature of contact with specific instructors.

Summary of Analysis

Confirming initial analyses, separate factoring of the perceptual rating scales of female-instructed and male-instructed students produces nearly identical factor structures, indicating the absence of gender-differentiated cognitive frames of reference within the pooled university sample. This factor structure is comparable to that previously described, being composed of clusters of items referencing degrees of egalitarianism in interpersonal style ("warmth"), personal charisma, self-assurance ("experience"), and structured versus laissez-faire instructional approach ("professionalism"). Somewhat less separation than previously of the first two item clusters (warmth and charisma) is observed, but care was taken in subsequent scale construction to select only maximally valid (purely loading) items from each. The warmth index constructed for the university sample consequently contains somewhat fewer items than the initial study, although it is otherwise identical.

When aggregate ratings of female-instructed and male-instructed students are compared, women are again described as appreciably warmer and more supportive than their male colleagues ($X = 1.20$, .37, female- and male-instructed students respectively). This difference is greater than that observed in the initial study, perhaps reflecting the greater investment of male instructors in the instructional role and student support in the undergraduate liberal-arts institution. Further, as in the liberal-arts institution, female-instructed students generally described their instructors as more personally compelling and charismatic than did male-instructed students, but not different as a group in experience and professionalism. Adjusting mean warmth and charisma ratings for gender differences in years teaching (a control for classroom experience, roughly corresponding to instructors' academic rank) and each of the indexes of visibility indicates that high-visibility contexts do accentuate women's perceived personal charisma (see table 11–4).[6] Nevertheless, even in situations of *relatively* lower visibility, women are scored somewhat higher on this dimension. Of the three referent levels for visibility, institutional and departmental visibility are the best predictors both separately and together. Although all three visibility indexes are highly intercorrelated, in this sample divisional visibility appears to have the least predictive power.

Comparison for male and female instructors of the correlational correspondence between positive perceptual ratings (warmth, charisma, experience, professionalism) and positive evaluation of the degree to which the student judged his or her instructor as fair and balanced in presentation of course material clearly corroborate the earlier finding that positive percep-

Table 11-3
Institutional and Sample Characteristics

| | | | | | | Institutional and Sample Characteristics | | |
| | | | | | | Percent Female Faculty[a] | | |
Institution	N	Percentage Return	Female/Male Instructors	Field	Respondent Selection Procedure	Department (1)	Division (2)	School (3)
College A	Private coeducational liberal arts	253	82	11/28	All non-science entry courses	Stratified sample			18
University A	Private	256	73	5/8	Entry courses, two social-science departments	Total enrollment	19	14	9
University B	Public	251	65	5/7	Entry courses, two humanities departments	Total enrollment	29	31	17

University C	Public	183	61	7/11	Entry course, social-science department	50-percent sample, incorporated into department evaluation	37	35	21
University D	Public	385	89	5/9	Entry courses, two social-science departments	Total enrollment	24	19	14
University E	Private	165	80	3/4	Freshmen seminars, humanities department	Total enrollment	21	23	11
Total: University samples		1,240	73	25/39					

[a]Percentage calculated for full-time faculty holding rank at the level of assistant professor or above, or other tenure-track appointment. Data coded from appropriate catalog with aid of institutional informant. For universities, figure refers to Faculty of Arts and Sciences or equivalent.

Table 11–4
**Difference of Means in Personal Charisma, by Gender of Instructor,
Adjusted for Gender Differences in Years Teaching and Departmental and
Institutional Visibility of Female Faculty (Pooled University Sample)**

	Means, Personal Charisma			
Gender of Instructor	Unadjusted $\overline{x}$	Adjusted for Years Teaching $\overline{x}$	Adjusted for Departmental and Institutional Visibility $\overline{x}$	Adjusted for Years Teaching, Departmental, Institutional Visibility $\overline{x}$
Male	3.09	3.01	3.18	3.16
Female	3.92	3.87	3.46	3.43
	$p < .001$	$p < .001$	$p < .01$	$p < .01$
Multiple R		.04	.23	.24
$N = 1229$				

tual ratings are very important for women but not systematically so for men. Computing partial correlation coefficients that take into account institutional and departmental visibility attenuates these relationships for women with respect to personal charisma, but not to the point of statistical or substantive insignificance ($r = .57$, partial $r = .31$). That is, all women—and particularly those in higher-visibility contexts—must be perceived as particularly potent and compelling if their intellectual authority is to be accepted.

Results obtained with respect to professionalism in the conduct of teaching parallel those obtained for the salience of personal attributes for judgments about women's intellectual authority: for women only, the assumption of a great deal of responsibility for their students' performance is broadly consequential for the formal teaching evaluation of women. This anxiety-reducing strategy is, however, particularly consequential for women in high-visibility contexts. For example, professionalism in the formal conduct of teaching is highly predictive of women's global evaluating rating, but only moderately so for men ($r = .63, .24$); institutional and departmental visibility partly accounts for the relationship between these two judgments for women, but not totally so (partial $r = .32$).

It is clear from the instructor-contact logs that students' reports of greater contact with and personal support from female instructors is an accurate reflection of women's greater investment of time in advising and counseling activities. Female instructors see more students, see them more frequently, spend a greater amount of time in doing so, and are more likely to be sought for personal advice and called outside the office. The gender contrasts are more striking when observed from the contact logs than from student self-reports, because small differences in students' propensities to seek out male and female faculty translate into substantial differences for those faculty. For example, across the five university samples, male-instructed students report an average of 0.47 office visits, whereas female-instructed students report an average of 0.92. (University E freshmen seminars, with mandatory conferences, are excluded.) However, female instructors averaged 11 office visits with case-class members during the study week, whereas male instructors reported an average of 5. Differences in gender of instructor by gender of student interactions are not observed in overall contact, but rather in the nature of that contact. Male students were much more likely to engage in personal discussion with female instructors than with male instructors; no preference pattern is found for female students.

Unlike student respondents in the initial study, however, university students were more likely to report their female instructors sufficiently available than their male. However, as previously, a woman's ratings of her availability and of her willingness to assist her students reflected individual students' history of contact and assistance. Men not only were less likely to be judged available and helpful, but also were judged so independently of students' personal experience. The implications for male instructors are as striking as those for female. Women commit more time and energy to their students than their male colleagues do but are recognized for their effort, or lack of effort. On the other hand, although male instructors have greater latitude in meeting student expectations for time and assistance, the available, concerned instructor is not necessarily affirmed in his investment in the instructional role.

Conclusions

In summary, the university studies are consistent with the pilot study in providing no evidence of direct gender bias in students' formal evaluations of their male and female instructors. Rather, evidence of gender-specific standards of evaluation are observed in women's greater burden of student contact and informal counseling, and in examination of the relation of student contact to students' assessments in areas particularly open to gender stereotyping: expectations and judgments regarding willingness to assist and satisfaction with instructors' availability. Whether or not women are also more positively oriented toward teaching and interpersonal support than their male colleagues, their greater investment of time in the instructional role potentially reinforces students' expectations that they will be more available and supportive.

The university studies also support the conclusion that students are less tolerant of female instructors in a number of respects, subjecting women to a particular scrutiny in arriving at judgments of their teaching performance and holding women to a high standard of "professionalism" in the formal conduct of teaching. Institutional contexts of heightened visibility, in which women are an identifiable statistical anomaly, increase the likelihood that women will be perceived as exceptionally potent and personally efficacious individuals, but also seem to make women more subject than female instructors in other institutions to scrutiny, pressures toward conformity, and other anxiety-reducing strategies such as the demand for professionalism.

The university studies provide corroborative support for the fundamental proposition that the visibility of women in instructional roles does condition their students' cognitive and evaluative judgments—particularly the degree to which a female instructor is perceived as exceptional in her ability to command and compel. For the student, the apparently anomalous achievement of a woman in an observably masculine work setting may be explained by special personal attributes such as personal charisma and a high level of personal efficacy. The evidence of the studies described here indicates that such an explanation is less compelling in institutional settings in which women are not as anomalous. Therefore, we are led away from simple cultural explanations to the realization that institutions can differ appreciably in the degree to which they reinforce or delegitimate culturally based assumptions and stereotypes.

Assessed in relation to studies of institutional productivity of female achievers, this research lends additional support to the argument that institutions that provide an institutional environment supportive of equitable participation of women—students and faculty alike—are those characterized by a highly "*in*visible" female faculty, because a range of female instructors offers multiple examples and combinations of life-style choices and establishes a norm of achievement without reference to gender. Within this view, women's colleges may be more successful in providing a climate promoting interpersonal identification between female instructors and students precisely because gender is not a primary personal attribute.

The consequences of heightened visibility for the female instructor also bear examination. Incongruity of a woman's primary role investment and her professional self-image can be both stressful and damaging to her professional self-esteem. Female faculty repeatedly expressed the sentiment that "there is no middle ground for a woman," and resentment at the stark choice they felt they faced. As one put it, "If you open that door but the least crack, the flood rushes in. So you have to make it clear from the start that you're one of the boys in this respect—and that means that you're too busy to be every student's mother." Yet the same woman also spoke for many others when she continued, "but the feminist in me rebels at having to be [one of the boys]. I feel badly about that, that I'm cheating my students and myself, denying part of my nature and responsibility to care." Women were often painfully aware of the conflict between the time required to meet student obligations and the time required to achieve the research and publication needed for professional recognition, tenure, and promotion. The double binds in which women find themselves represent more than private personal dilemmas; rather, they are institutional problems requiring institutional responses.

The diverse implications of women's visibility for students and faculty places a special burden of responsibility on college and university administrators. Visibility as a construct may be conceptualized as not only the degree to which women are proportionately represented, but also, more generally, as the degree to which they are truly integrated within an institution. A variety of institutional factors may therefore be identified that can ameliorate the adverse effects of women's visibility: (1) the broader distribution of women across disciplinary divisions and academic ranks, as well as affirmative attention to the hiring and promotion of women; (2) the presence of women in diverse administrative and decision-making positions; (3) the participation of women in academic governance; (4) an affirmation of the contribution of teaching and student support, as well as of research and vocational and professional training, to fulfillment of institutional missions; (5) a care to avoid the curricular segregation of women and women's scholarships in special courses and isolated programs. Examination of an institution's policies and practices in each of these areas is demanded not simply by concern with issues of equity as they relate to female faculty, but also by the responsibilities educators face for providing educational programs and institutional environments supportive of both male and female students.

Notes

1. The student questionnaire was composed of three sections, corresponding to the three types of data required:

1. As described in the summary of analysis, forty bipolar descriptive scales were developed that describe classroom mannerisms, teaching style, course organization, attitude toward student, approachability, and instructor's personal characteristics and interpersonal style. Scales were constructed on the model of the semantic differential. Representative items may be examined in table 11-1.

2. Students were asked to rate the instructor directly on a variety of items used in the formal institutional evaluation of courses. A global rating of the instructor was also requested. These items emphasize "activity-process" aspects of instruction (for example, "organization, clarity, and coherence of classroom presentation") rather than "instructor's personality-trait dimensions" (Thorne 1980) and comprise the formal "teacher-evaluation" portion of the questionnaire.
3. Students were asked to report detail of their out-of-class contact with their instructor. Items included how many times the student had seen the instructor formally in the instructor's office, how free the student felt to stop by the office casually or to call the instructor at home; and whether the student had ever sought personal advice from the instructor.

2. Hesselbart reports a congruent finding that when females are rated differently from males, "they are rated as more competent or more favorable" (1977, p. 418), a finding she describes as surprising and as inviting further speculation. One explanation she proposes is that women in fields stereotyped as male oriented "are viewed as exceptional for achieving in prestigious professional fields" (1977, p. 419). The explanation proposed here is similar but is focused not on generalized stereotyping but on the actual gender representation within the specific organizational environment. In this sense the explanation is structural rather than cultural.

3. The proposition that visibility increases attentiveness to personal characteristics of female instructors does not necessarily stand in opposition to Kanter's proposition that token women in corporate organizations tend to be treated as symbols or as stereotypic representatives of a class (1977, pp. 211, 230). To the degree that visibility, in calling attention to the female instructor as a member of a class of objects different from the norm, arouses anxiety in a student with respect to those aspects of their relationship in which she or he feels vulnerable or dependent, a variety of strategies for dealing with that anxiety or removing its source might be employed. Both stereotyping and scrutiny (information gathering) increase the subjective sense of knowing and being able to anticipate another, although over time, presumably, scrutiny makes stereotypic assumptions less tenable. It is important to note that, from the student's point of view, the instructor-student relationship is one in which the instructor is thought to be able to exercise a significant degree of fate control over his or her students, in the sense that an instructor, by awarding higher or lower grades, can affect a student's outcomes (those contingent on grades) regardless of that student's efforts or reciprocal actions (Thibaut and Kelley 1959, p. 102). That is, the instructor can act arbitrarily, with significant consequences for the student, and the student has limited recourse. Although this perception on the part

of the student may ignore formal aspects of the instructor-student relationship, such as grievance procedures, as well as many informal aspects of the situation, this relationship is nonetheless intuitively more anxiety arousing than one in which fate control is converted to behavior control or in which the power relationships (fate and behavior control) between parties are more symmetrical. The latter are more characteristic of managerial roles and relationships in bureaucratic organizations, where complex norms govern formalistic procedures and social relationships limit individuals' usable power and create complex interdependencies.

4. The process described is similar to that which Kanter (1977) describes as "role encapsulation" resulting from assimilation of an individual's own characteristics to stereotypic characteristics of his or her social type. In this case, however, the encapsulating roles ("teacher," "academician") represent complementary roles within a single status set, rather than the clearly inappropriate and conflicting encapsulating roles female managers face ("secretary," "mother," "seductress").

5. As with the initial study, the analytic questions addressed deal primarily with *student* cognitive frame of reference, evaluative judgments, and contact histories, and therefore usually require comparisons among individual respondents. For this purpose, all university respondents were pooled into a single data file, and institutional, divisional, class, and instructor characteristics coded for each individual respondent. For example, proportion of women teaching in the department offering the course enrolled (a visibility indicator) and number of office visits logged by the instructor for all members of the case class are coded for each student. However, mean institutional differences have also been examined; and analyses have been performed on the basis of aggregated response levels for each instructor (class), when appropriate, in order to test the robustness of results obtained when the student respondent is treated as the primary unit of analysis.

6. Parallel analysis based on instructor (class) as the unit of observation ($N = 39$) produces consistent results.

Bibliography

Almquist, Elizabeth, and Angrist, Shirley. "Role Model Influences on College Women's Career Aspirations." *Merrill-Palmer Quarterly* 17 (1971):263–279.

————. *Careers and Contingencies.* New York: Kennikat Press, 1975.

Baird, L.L. "Teaching Styles: An Exploratory Study of Dimensions and Effects." *Journal of Educational Psychology* 64 (1973):15–21.

Bennett, S.K. "Student Perceptions of and Expectations for Male and Female Instructors: Evidence Relating to the Question of Gender Bias in Teaching Evaluation." *Journal of Educational Psychology* (in press).

Carnegie Commission on Higher Education. *Opportunities for Women in Higher Education.* New York: McGraw-Hill, 1973.

Costin, F., and Grush, J.E. "Personality Correlates of Teacher-Instructor Behavior in the College Classroom." *Journal of Educational Psychology* 65 (1973):35–44.

Crittenden, Kathleen, and Norr, James L. "Student Values and Teacher Evaluation: A Problem in Person Perception." *Sociometry* 36 (1973): 143–151.

Elmore, Patricia B., and LaPointe, Karen. "Effects of Teacher Sex and Student Sex in the Evaluation of College Instructors." *Journal of Educational Psychology* 66 (1974):386–389.

————. "Effect of Teacher Sex, Student Sex, and Teacher Warmth on the Evaluation of College Instructors." *Journal of Educational Psychology* 67 (1975):368–374.

Elmore, Patricia B., and Pohlmann, John T. "Effect of Teacher, Student, and Class Characteristics on the Evaluation of College Instructors." *Journal of Educational Psychology* 70 (1978):187–192.

Gruder, C. "Choice of Comparison Persons in Evaluating Oneself." In J. Suls and R. Miller, eds., *Social Comparison Processes.* Washington, D.C.: Halstead Press, 1977.

Harris, Mary B. "Sex Role Stereotypes and Teacher Evaluation." *Journal of Educational Psychology* 67 (1975):751–756.

————. "The Effects of Sex, Sex-Stereotyped Descriptions, and Institutions on Evaluations of Teachers." *Sex Roles* 2 (1976):15–21.

Heise, David R. "The Semantic Differential and Attitude Research." In Gene F. Summers, ed., *Attitude Measurement.* Chicago: Rand McNally, 1970.

Hesselbart, Susan. "Sex Role and Occupational Stereotypes: Three Studies of Impression Formation." *Sex Roles* 3 (1977):409–422.

Kahn, R.L.: Wolfe, D.M.; Quinn, R.P.; and Snoek, J.D. *Organizational Stress: Studies in Role Conflict and Ambiguity.* New York: Wiley, 1964.

Kanter, Rosabeth Moss. *Men and Women of the Corporation.* New York: Basic Books, 1977.

Kaschak, Ellyn. "Sex Bias in Student Evaluations of College Professors." *Psychology of Women Quarterly* 2 (1978):235–243.

Kulick, J.A., and McKeachie, W.J. "The Evaluation of Teachers in Higher Education." In Fred Kerlinger, ed., *Review of Research in Education,* vol. 3. Itasca, Ill.: Peacock, 1975.

Marsh, Herbert, and Overall, J.V. "Long-term Stability of Students' Evaluations: A Note on Feldman's 'Consistency and Variability Among

College Students in Rating Their Teachers and Courses'." *Research in Higher Education* 10 (1979):139–147.

McKeachie, Wilbert. "Student Ratings of Faculty: A Reprise." *Academe: Bulletin of the AAUP.* Washington, D.C.: American Association of University Professors, 1979.

McKeachie, W.J., and Lin, Y.C. "Sex Differences in Student Response to College Teachers: Teacher Warmth and Teacher Sex." *American Educational Research Journal* 8 (1971):221–226.

Newcomer, M. *A Century of Higher Education for American Women.* New York: Harper, 1959.

Norr, James L., and Crittenden, K. "Evaluating College Teaching as Leadership." *Higher Education* 4 (1975):335–350.

Oates, Mary L., and Williamson, Susan. "Women's Colleges and Women Achievers." *Signs* 3 (1978):795–806.

Osgood, Charles; Tannenbaum, P.H.; and Suci, G.J. *The Measurement of Meaning.* Urbana: University of Illinois Press, 1959.

Sternglanz, Sarah. "Sex Differences in Student-Teacher Classroom Interactions." Paper presented at the Research Conference on Educational Environments and the Undergraduate Woman, Wellesley College, September 1979.

Sternglanz, Sarah, and Lyberger-Ficek, Shirley. "Sex Differences in Student-Teacher Interactions in the College Classroom." *Sex Roles* 3 (1977):345–352.

Tagiuri, Renato. "Person Perception." In Gardner Lindzey and Elliot Aronson, eds., *The Handbook of Social Psychology,* vol. III. Reading, Mass.: Addison-Wesley, 1969.

Thibaut, John W., and Kelley, Harold H. *The Social Psychology of Groups.* New York: Wiley, 1959.

Thorne, G.L. "Student Ratings of Instructors: From Scores to Administrative Decisions." *Journal of Higher Education* 51 (1980):208–214.

Tidball, Elizabeth M. "Perspective on Academic Women and Affirmative Action." *Educational Record* 54 (1973):130–135.

———. "Of Men and Research." *Journal of Higher Education* 47 (1976): 373–389.

———. "Women's Colleges and Women Achievers Revisited." *Signs* 5 (1980):504–517.

Tidball, E.M., and Kistiakowsky, Vera. "Baccalaureate Origins of American Scientists and Scholars." *Science* 193 (1976):646–652.

Widom, C.S., and Burke, B.W. "Performance, Attitudes, and Professional Socialization of Women in Academia." *Sex Roles* 4 (1978): 549–562.

12

Sex Differences in the Implications of the Links between Major Departments and the Occupational Structure

James C. Hearn and
Susan Olzak

There is clear evidence that the department of a student's major is the college subenvironment most influential in undergraduates' career-related decision making and socialization (Feldman and Newcomb 1969). For example, Wilson et al. (1975) and Astin (1977) found that two major-related factors—the warmth and frequency of faculty-student interactions and the degree of involvement of students with their academic work—appear to be primary determinants of undergraduates' overall evaluation of their college experiences. In addition, Weidman (1974) found evidence that certain aspects of the normative and affective climate of major departments play significant roles in student attitude and value change in college (see also Beardslee and O'Dowd 1962; Wilson 1966; Gamson 1966; and Vreeland and Bidwell 1966).

Yet the research on the significance of departments has not fully addressed certain crucial theoretical and policy concerns. Although it provides us with evidence that departments differ significantly in the environments they present to undergraduates, and that those environmental differences are relevant to various undergraduate outcomes, we know too little about the factors explaining the nature of departmental climates, about the processes distributing individuals into different kinds of departmental climates, and about the role of individual background characteristics in short- and long-term major-department influences (Feldman and Newcomb 1969).

This manuscript is based on data from the first author's doctoral dissertation research at Stanford University. The research was supported in part by NIMH Grant MH6026 and NIAAA Grant AA02863. The authors wish to express their appreciation to Paula Antrum, Burton Clark, John Meyer, Rudolf Moos, JoAnn Stonebarger, Joan Talbert, and Jane Weiss for their valuable comments regarding the conceptualization, data analysis, and reporting, and to Larry Haffner for his assistance in the data analysis. In addition, the authors are grateful to the many members of the Social Ecology Laboratory, Stanford University, who participated in the necessary data collection over the years 1972 to 1976.

Of particular concern is the failure of the previous research to address the role in departmental influences of the socioeconomic structure of status and opportunity in the larger society. Departmental effects may not be independent of the societal expectations for, and ascribed status of, individuals undergoing college education in general and specific major programs in particular. Since sex-role differentiation and stereotyping in education and jobs are crucial societal concerns, the present research pays particular attention to the possibly distinctive influences of major departments on male and female students. The proposition that an individual's sex is crucial in these influence processes is based on a large body of research evidence that there are gender-based differences in the role of education, occupation, and vocation in one's affect, self-concept, and aspirations (see Maccoby and Jacklin 1974; Bielby 1978). Most important, there is evidence that (1) women and men are differentially distributed both into majors (Bielby 1978) and into occupations and income levels in the larger society (Treiman and Terrell 1975); and (2) in selecting and reacting to educational environments, women may tend more than men to base their responses on the personal supportiveness of those environments, whereas men may tend more than women to base their responses on externally validated environmental characteristics relating to achievement and status attainment (for example, see Coleman 1961; McDill and Rigsby 1973).

The present research addresses five central questions prompted by the previous research.

1. Can the different social and evaluative environments of major departments be explained by reference to differences in the status-based and occupation-based linkages of major areas to the larger socioeconomic structure? For example, do departments providing substantial future income and status payoffs to the undergraduate have distinctive environments?
2. Do the differential enrollment patterns of men and women by subject area imply that men and women encounter and experience different major-department educational environments? For example, are women more likely to major in departments characterized by supportive climates?
3. How do the differential enrollment patterns of men and women by subject area relate to status rewards after graduation? For example, do women tend to enroll in majors that are less empowering in the postgraduation job market?
4. Do men and women differ in their rates of enrollment in areas that are closely linked to specific occupations? For example, are women more likely to pursue "general education" at the expense of vocational training in college?

5. Are the determinants of satisfaction with major-department experiences different for men than for women? For example, do women in their evaluations rely more strongly than men on the social supportiveness of the major department?

Theoretical Perspective

Our perspective is in the tradition of the work of Meyer (1965, 1970, 1977, 1980), which calls on analysts to examine education as a social and economic institution, considering variables beyond the level of the classroom, the peer group, or the school as an organization. Meyer (1980) has proposed that educational organizations, such as schools or departments, tend to be arrayed along a continuum linking students to future adult roles. At one extreme of the continuum is the *externally validated* organization, which considers students to be in training for adult roles, objects of knowledge dispensation, and not currently in contact with the centers of meaning and value in adult life. At the opposite extreme is the *internally validated* organization, in which the curriculum and extracurriculum are organized to fit and validate the *present* interests and perspectives of students.

Meyer (1980) states that both extremes of emphasis can have negative influences on student satisfaction and commitment. In externally validated organizations the student role is defined by the presumed incompetence of its incumbents (see also Bernstein 1975). Because the instructional system organizes tasks in terms of the requirements of adult life, emphasizing selection, failure, and so on, it tends to generate and reinforce a sense of meaninglessness, dissatisfaction, and lack of commitment in students for whom the present is little more than an unpleasant prologue. The other extreme, however—that of the internally validated organization that expands and legitimates the student role—also has negative aspects. To some extent the student culture and social organization encouraged by such settings enhance learning, but links with the future are not strong; education is only tenuously related to the types of knowledge relevant to adult life. Students experience meaninglessness, dissatisfaction, uncertainty, and loss of commitment due to the absence of firm educational links to their occupational futures.

Arnove (1971) found support for the broad tenets of Meyer's argument in research in major departments in a Venezuelan university. He found that the institutionalized prestige of a field of study in the eyes of the larger society was significantly negatively related to the supportiveness of the departmental faculty toward students and to the liberality of departmental grading practices. Arnove also found, as Meyer would predict, that students in prestigious fields had high levels of satisfaction with their "professional efficacy" (vocational training and socialization), but low levels of satisfaction with the level and quality of their interactions with faculty members, whereas students in less prestigious fields exhibited the opposite pattern in their reported satisfaction. The Meyer and Arnove analyses suggest strongly that undergraduates' evaluation of their educational experiences will tend to be a direct function of two departmental dimensions: the quality of the departmental environment and the extent of the external rewards to the major B.A. degree.

The Meyer perspective suggests a hypothesis. In answer to our first central question regarding the structural determinants of the different social and evaluative environments of major departments, we propose that major departments with favorable status-based ties and/or close occupational links to the larger socioeconomic system will tend to be less supportive and more critically evaluative toward their undergraduate students, emphasizing training, discipline, and technical skills rather than humanistic attempts to aid the general intellectual or moral growth of students.

Several analyses uphold this argument. Students in such majors as engineering and business may value faculty-student interactions and other internal departmental features less than students in other majors (see Feldman and Newcomb 1969); thus they may not press faculty for supportiveness toward students. Also, because faculty in such areas may see their role as technical rather than moral training (see Vreeland and Bidwell 1966), they may orient their teaching, research, and consulting careers to audiences outside the university (such as business executives) and care less about broad, humanistic concern for undergraduates. To validate their external orientations, these professors may need to use strict academic standards to assure themselves and employers of their students' competence. Furthermore, faculty in these subject areas may be strict with students in order to justify the rigor of their discipline to others in more traditional disciplines on campus. In general, departments with close ties to, or high status in, the larger economic system are newer disciplines incorporated into the university setting relatively recently (that is, since 1875)[1]

Meyer and Arnove assume that external rewards of the major may be classified along a single dimension relating to prestige and professional certification. We extend their analyses by proposing that, for the departmental setting, there are not one but two continua along which major areas may be arranged according to their structural linkages to the external social and economic system. First, we may classify major areas by the status and power rewards of the major B.A. as generally perceived by employers, students, and faculty. Second, we may classify majors by the closeness of the focus of the major program to specific occupations in the larger society, as elaborated by the departmental faculty in course requirements and structure. Breaking down the external characteristics of major areas along these two dimensions addresses a fundamental qualitative distinction between the extent of the socioeconomic rewards of a major area and the extent of its closeness to specific external occupations.[2] We propose that these structurally based distinctions between majors relate systematically not only to the specific social and academic features majors present to undergraduates, but also to the selection patterns of undergraduates of different ascribed statuses into specific majors, and to the influences of specific majors on these undergraduates.

Support for a structural approach to investigation of major-department impacts has recently been provided from several sources. Wilson (1978) found clear links between major areas and employers' conceptions of potential individual power in their respective organizations and industries; and Griffin and Alexander (1978), as well as Wilson, present evidence that majors differ significantly in their postgraduation rewards. Wilson proposes that students are aware of employers' expectations and beliefs regarding graduates of different majors and may target their college educations with future competitions for power, income, and status in mind. This interpretation is strongly supported by the work of Ferber and McMahon (1979) on the earnings expectations of students in different major areas.

The role of institutionalized socioeconomic factors in college major choices, experiences, and rewards is not limited, however, to the rather clear-cut exchange notion explored by these researchers. There is evidence suggesting that ascribed status may play a significantly mediating or supplemental role in variations in attainment patterns by major areas. The income and status rewards to the college degree are generally worth more to individuals with higher ascribes status, particularly to males as opposed to females (Treiman and Terrell 1975; Featherman and Hauser 1978; Sorensen 1979). This pattern of differential returns may be due partly to discrimination in postgraduation labor markets. Two other explanations, however, are of more interest for the present research. The pattern may be due in part to the differential enrollment patterns into majors by members of various statuses; members of lower statuses may tend to enroll in majors that provide lower rewards after graduation. The pattern may also be due in part to different qualities of educational experiences encouraged by undergraduates; members of lower statuses may tend to encounter lower levels of facilitative concern for their educational well-being and socioeconomic advancement.

To explore the importance of ascribed status and derive hypothesized answers to our last four central questions, we work from the following theoretical conception of the major choice and influence process. We propose that a student chooses a major and evaluates his or her experiences in it on the basis of two kinds of criteria, intrinsic and extrinsic. *Intrinsic* criteria are founded on goals for personal growth and expression. That growth and expression may be related to general intellectual and moral concerns or to concerns in a specific content area of interest. Intrinsic purposes are satisfied by *internal* features of the major department as experienced by students. Positive internal features include generalized faculty concern for undergraduate education and liberal grading by faculty in an openly accepting educational climate. The internal features of departments would also include the specific experience of individual students relating to their major choice, such as the quality of their grades, job experience related to the major, and personalized interactions with faculty members.

Students also choose and evaluate majors on the basis of *extrinsic* criteria relating to postgraduation rewards in the larger occupational system. We propose that there are two dimensions of extrinsic purposes,[3] corresponding to the status and occupational linkages discussed previously: *allocation*—that is, the extent to which the major enables the student to obtain higher-status positions in the economic system—and *certification*—that is, the extent to which a department labels the student as competent in a particular content area. Unlike intrinsic purposes, extrinsic purposes are satisfied by the *external* features of the department—by its firm links to attractive elements of the larger occupational system. Students who value extrinsic rewards highly are likely to choose and stay in majors that provide significant extrinsic rewards, whereas students who especially value intrinsic rewards are likely to choose and stay in majors that provide significant intrinsic rewards.

We propose that status-differentiated early socialization and other factors may lead people of different ascribed statuses (for example, males as opposed to females) to place different weights on the respective criteria for major choice and evaluation. The second central question of our research is whether the differential enrollment patterns of men and women by subject area imply that men and women encounter and experience different major-department educational environments. Research in various areas suggests that males are more likely to be interested in extrinsic rewards than females, who may value supportive faculty-student interactions (intrinsic rewards) more (Coleman 1961; Lynn 1962; Spady 1971; Broverman et al. 1972; McDill and Rigsby 1973; Weidman 1974). Indeed, males may be more likely to be socialized to endure demanding and unsupportive social environments in order to attain higher economic or status rewards. Thus we could expect women to be more likely than men to choose majors with supportive social environments.

Our third question relates to how the differential enrollment patterns of men and women by subject area relate to status rewards after graduation. We propose that enrollment in majors along the structural dimensions of status postulated earlier will tend to reproduce the ascribed status distinctions in societal labor markets; that is, lower-status departments will enroll more people from lower ascribed statuses. In particular, women will be more likely than men to enroll in majors with lower-status payoffs, such as home economics. This proposition is based on an individual-level factor but has implications for the nature of social interactions, expectations, and evaluations at the contextual (departmental) level as well. The expected results are hypothesized to be due to one or a combination of the following factors:

1. Perceptions by lower-status individuals that discriminatory barriers exist to entry into higher-status occupations and positions may make pursuit of such occupations unrewarding, in a human capital sense, and possibly punishing as well (see Featherman and Hauser 1978; Polacheck 1978.

2. An association of lower-status majors and occupations with certain status-based goals may encourage lower-status individuals to pursue such majors. For example, a teaching career has been seen by many blacks as a valuable service to their status/cultural community (see Freeman 1976).

3. Status-differentiated early socialization into interests and occupations may produce status-differentiated choice patterns.

4. If women indeed place greater weight than men on intrinsic environmental features such as the level of social supportiveness, they will tend, in an institutional setting wherein lower-status departments are generally more supportive to their students, to choose the more supportive, lower-status environments over the less supportive, higher-status environments.

The fourth central question of our research was whether or not men and women differ in their rates of enrollment in areas that are closely linked to specific occupations. The hypothesis that men tend to rank extrinsic, externally oriented goals higher than do women leads to the expectation that men will be more likely than women to enroll in closely linked departments. Women may be more likely to favor general education and intellectual skills as goals of their college education, since (1) they are more likely than men to face intermittent participation in secondary labor markets where various potential jobs require a variety of necessary skills (see Treiman and Terrell 1975); and (2) males are more often than females socialized by their parents and others to occupational careers and achievement (see Maccoby and Jacklin 1974).

Nevertheless, although different people rank the various extrinsic and intrinsic goals differently depending on their life plans and interests, we propose that they maintain virtually the same ranking criteria for evaluating specific individual features of their chosen major departments. In other words, other things being equal, students will generally react positively to a highly supportive faculty, will generally prefer a status or occupational payoff to no extrinsic payoff whatsoever, and so forth. Thus, in answer to our fifth question as to whether the determinants of major-department satisfaction are different for men than for women, we hypothesize that there will be significant similarities in the way men and women evaluate their majors once they have chosen them. Men will not react negatively to supportive faculty, nor will women react negatively to significant extrinsic payoffs in a major.[4]

We expect that certain patterns in departmental effects will be more apparent among women than among men, however. Research by Weidman (1974) suggests that women may be more sensitive in their evaluations to personalized interactions in departments (as opposed to the general social climate); and research by several authors (for example, Maccoby and Jacklin 1974) suggests that women in cross-sex occupations and educational programs may be especially satisfied with their work. Women, as members of a disfavored status group in higher education—and particularly as members of a disfavored status group in male-dominated majors—may be more satisfied when individual faculty members show concern for their educational progress and may also be especially satisfied on completing the necessary work for a degree in a "male" area that provides higher-status rewards than those normally accorded women graduates.

Tying together the foregoing discussion produces the following specific hypotheses:

1. Structural factors are linked to departmental features in the following way: the closer the external ties to the larger socioeconomic structure, the less personally supportive the internal social climate and the less liberal the evaluative practices.

2. Student choice and evaluation of a major area is a direct function of the positiveness of two dimensions of departments:
   a. *internal factors,* such as (1) the department having a supportive social climate and liberal evaluative practices, and (2) the student receiving high grades relative to others, having job experience related to the major, and having supportive, personalized interaction with department faculty members;
   b. *external factors,* such as the department having rewarding status-based and occupationally based links to the larger socioeconomic system.

3. At the departmental level the status rewards of a major area tend to parallel the ascribed statuses of its enrolled students; and at the student level the status rewards of one's major choice tend to parallel one's ascribed status. Therefore, women, as a lower-status group, tend to choose majors with lower-status rewards.

4. Women tend to choose majors without direct occupational linkages, since labor-market factors, such as sex discrimination, and socialization factors produce less certainty about occupational career and work continuity among females.

5. Although men and women students, in choosing and evaluating majors, differentially weigh the relative importance of internal and external facets of majors, there is no ambiguity to the effects of these factors: other things being equal, faculty supportiveness, liberal grading, good grades, relevant job experience, close links to the occupational system, and higher status rewards of the major area are all positively evaluated by students. Women, however, may receive *added* satisfaction from certain major-department characteristics facilitating significant status gain (higher-status majors, personalized interactions with faculty members).

Research Design

This chapter describes the results of a modest test of the most basic implications of the foregoing argument. The students and departments of one campus are examined through the use of simple correlation and multiple-regression techniques.

Sample

The sample for this study consists of 346 seniors who responded to a questionnaire developed by Rudolf Moos and his colleagues (see Moos 1979 for details). The students represented twenty-one major departments at a large, state-supported university in a small rural community. The senior-year instrument, entitled the College Experience Questionnaire: 1976 Update (CEQ:76) was mailed to those who had completed a freshman questionnaire and remained at Campus A over the three-year period since the initial sampling. Over 85 percent of those receiving the senior questionnaire returned a completed CEQ:76. Students included in the present study were seniors who were majoring in departments with at least ten senior respondents and who had complete data on all relevant variables.

Indicators

The twenty-one major departments in the study were cross-classified according to the two kinds of linkages to the larger social structure specified earlier. This cross-classification leads to the breakdown presented in table 12-1. The breakdown of majors into high and low status and power rewards in the larger socioeconomic system is derived directly from the results of Kenneth Wilson's survey of employers in various fields regarding their perceptions of the capabilities of bachelor's degrees in various majors to empower graduates in the larger occupational arena and thus to promote the income and status attainment of those graduates (1978; also personal communication, 1979).

The *occupational-linkage* indicator was constructed by consulting course-catalog descriptions for the twenty-one departments. If practitioner or professional training were emphasized, the major was classified as closely linked. The construct validity of this categorization was assessed at the individual level by testing the proposition that students graduating in those majors classified as closely linked would exhibit significantly higher levels of instrumental attitudes regarding their college education. In other words, their responses to CEQ:76 items related to the purposes of college education would be marked by (1) a pronounced orientation to future vocation and (2) a lack of strong orientation to moral, social, or intellectual development in college. These two hypotheses were confirmed in the present sample, at the individual level. Students in majors categorized as closely linked scored significantly higher than students in majors not categorized as closely linked ($p \leq .05$) on an instrumentalism scale composed of the following two four-point importance-ranking items: "Provide vocational training; that is develop skills that are directly applicable to your job," and "Develop skills that will enable you to earn a high income." The students in closely linked majors also ranked significantly lower ($p \leq .05$) the importance of the following two items, making up a four-point "humanistic-education scale": "Help develop your knowledge and interest in community, national, and world problems," and "Develop your understanding of such subjects as philosophy, art, literature, and music."

Five indicators of internal, intrinsically rewarding features of majors were devised for the study. The *department student-orientation* scale assesses the perceived concerned for undergraduate education evidenced by professors in the departments. Such concern consists of the perceived encouragement, supportiveness, engagement, and innovativeness of the professors in their formal and informal interactions with undergraduate students. The indicator of department student orientation was derived from selected CEQ:76 items to tap the student's perception of the social climate of his or her major department. Students responded on four-point scales (hardly ever true, occasionally true, frequently true, almost always true) with respect to seven characteristics of their major-department professors. The seven perception items were combined into the department student-orientation scale: "Help and support students," "Provide opportunities

Table 12-1
Classification of Twenty-One Major Departments

	Links of Major B.A. to Specific Occupations	
	Closely Linked	*Not Closely Linked*
Status and power rewards of the major B.A.		
Higher status rewards	Economics, chemical engineering electrical engineering zoology	Biochemistry biology, genetics physiology,
Lower status rewards	Animal sciences, consumer sciences, environmental science and management food science, home economics, human development, physical education, plant science	Art, English, history political science, psychology

for social interactions with students majoring in the department," "Engage students in stimulating discussions," "Clearly explain departmental rules and requirements," "Encourage students to become involved in their work," "Respond to students' grievances over departmental issues," and "Emphasize variety and new approaches in student work." In analyses of variance of student responses, each of the items discriminates among departments ($p \leq .05$), as does the scale combination of all seven items ($p \leq .001$). Each student in an eligible senior-year major was assigned a mean scale score for his or her major department (as perceived by the student and fellow majors). Since a given student may perceive a departmental environment differently from peers in the same major or may encounter different courses and professors, an indicator of the student's *relative perception of departmental student orientation* was also devised. The term is equal to the given student's individually perceived department student-orientation scale score minus the consensus scale score for his or her major department.

The liberality of *department grading practices* is indicated by a measure of departmental-evaluation context consisting of the average of self-reported grade-point averages in courses in the department for all seniors majoring in the department.[5] A student's *relative evaluation in major courses* is indicated by the student's self-reported GPA in courses in the major minus the average GPA in courses in the department (for all seniors majoring in the department. *Job experience* related to the major area is indicated by a dichotomous question, so phrased, on the CEQ:76 (yes = 1, no = 0).

A final individual-level indicator necessary to the analysis is that for *individual satisfaction with experience in the major area*, as assessed by a generally phrased item seeking the respondents' overall evaluation of departmental experiences and professors on a four-point scale ranging from "very dissatisfied" to "very satisfied."

Results

Departmental-Level Results

Table 12-1 shows the relationships among the structural profile of the department, department social climate, department grading practices, and the percentage of the undergraduate majors who are female. The propositions regarding the links between structural factors, social climate, and evaluative practices are generally supported. The higher-status departments tended to have less supportive social climates, and the closely linked departments tended to give lower grades to their students. Also, the percentage who were female in the respective departments were significantly and negatively related to the status, but not the occupational-linkage dimension, of the major. In other words, many women and men choose vocationally linked majors, but those majors may be divided into two status levels, to which the sex-composition factor is closely linked.[6] Finally, there was a close positive relationship between percentage female in a department and the department student orientation.[7] Thus, supporting our argument, departments with large numbers of female students tended to be lower status but very supportive to their student clientele.

Individual-Level Results

This section examines the meaning of the foregoing results at the individual level, considering specifically the question of what the different department contexts and rewards, and the dispersal of people differentially by sex into major departments, imply for experiences in, and outcomes of, higher education.

In the numbers graduating in given majors and in the characteristics of those majors, students provide clues as to how they individually choose and evaluate major programs. Table 12-3 presents evidence on this question. The mean student orientation encountered by male students in their final major area was lower than that encountered by females, and the grading practices encountered by males were slightly less liberal than those encountered by females. Furthermore, women tended to perceive approxi-

Table 12-2
Relationships between Department Occupational Linkages, Status Rewards, Social Climate, Evaluative Practices, and Percentage, Female Enrollment

	Mean	Standard Deviation	1	2	3	4	5
1. Closely linked major	.52	.51	—	—	—	—	—
2. Major with high status rewards	.38	.50	-.23	—	—	—	—
3. Department student orientation	2.56	.30	.27	-.58**	—	—	—
4. Departmental grading practices (average GPA in major courses)	5.64[a]	.36	-.39*	-.33	.27	—	—
5. Percentage female of students majoring in the department[b]	50.81	25.38	.12	-.63***	.38*	.30	—

Note: $N = 21$. All departments have at least 10 respondents. Code for significance levels: ***$p \leq .001$, **$p \leq .01$, *$p \leq .05$.
[a]Converts to letter grades as follows: $7 = A$, $A+$; $6 = A-$, $B+$; $5 = B$; $4 = B-$, $C+$; $3 = C$; $2 = C-$, $D+$; $1 = D$ or less.
[b]Based on total enrollment in major for spring 1976, as provided by the registrar.

mately the same levels of student orientation in any given department environment as the men in that environment,[8] and the satisfaction levels among women were slightly higher than those among men. Finally, males were more likely than females to choose higher-status majors, whereas females were more likely than males to choose closely linked majors and were much more likely than males to have had job experiences closely related to their respective major choice area. We may conclude from these results that men and women in general do encounter significantly different kinds of departmental environment, as well as different kinds of departmental payoffs in the larger social and economic system. In general, men experience less supportive departments but receive greater immediate postgraduation status rewards.

Table 12-4 presents the relations found between reported evaluation of the major and the focal independent variables at the structural, organizational, and individual developmental levels. The multiple-regression results for the basic model are presented first. The basic model consists of all independent variables discussed in the hypotheses section of this chapter except that for relative individual perceptions of department student orientation. Because there is evidence that personalized interactions with faculty may play a crucial mediating role in departmental influence processes, particularly for women (see Weidman 1974), the basic model was tested before models containing the individual-level perception item; this stepwise approach provides some tentative clues to direct and indirect effects in the data. The results for the basic model support the propositions presented earlier for the intrinsic factors in student satisfaction. For both males and females, department student orientation and relative individual grades in the major played the most significant roles in determining individual satisfaction with major-department experiences. No support was found for the propositions relating extrinsic factors to student satisfaction.

The search for interaction effects revealed a significant extrinsic interaction term for the females, however. Specifically, a dummy product interaction term representing high status in conjunction with close linkage of the major department (see table 12-3) provided an important addition to the explanatory power of the basic model for women. The regression results for the basic model plus the interaction term (presented in table 12-4) plainly point to higher satisfaction levels among females in higher-status, closely linked departments. Those are the departments most closely associated with "male" occupational careers and, as evidenced in table 12-3, most clearly dominated in numerical terms by males (for example, economics, engineering).[9]

We hypothesized that the individual perceptions of major-department climate may not only mediate certain departmental influences on students but also may be more important in a given individual's major-area evalua-

Table 12–3
Correlations, Standard Deviations, and Means for the Focal Indicators, at the Individual Level for Males and Females

	1	2	3	4	5	6	7	8	9
Major with high status rewards	—	-.49	.33	-.58	.03	-.27	-.04	-.13	-.07
Closely linked major	-.22	—	.16	.52	.01	-.02	.08	.21	.17
Interaction of status in linkage (1 × 2)	.37	.65	—	-.14	.15	-.18	.03	-.11	.14
Department student orientation	-.59	.18	-.26	—	.00	.49	.07	.23	.25
Individual perception of department student orientation	-.01	.00	.03	-.02	—	-.01	.20	.10	.53
Department grading practices[a]	-.31	-.26	-.36	.26	.01	—	.00	.11	.09
Relative individual grades in major	.08	-.09	.01	-.07	.27	.01	—	.09	.29
Job experience related to major	-.12	.15	.00	.23	.04	-.02	.09	—	.17
Overall evaluation of the major	-.02	-.14	-.17	.24	.54	.15	.21	.16	—
Mean (male)	.68	.40	.22	2.44	-.04	5.58	-.05	.43	3.13
Standard deviation (male)	.47	.49	.42	.28	.51	.28	.93	.50	.59
Mean (female)	.24	.57	.03	2.58	.05	5.64	.03	.63	3.20
Standard deviation (female)	.43	.50	.18	.29	.55	.31	.88	.49	.64

Note: male data ($N = 167$) are below the diagonal, female data ($N = 179$) are above it.
[a]Converts to letter grades as follows: 7 = A, A+; 6 = A−, B+; 5 = B; 4 = B−, C+; 3 = C; 2 = C−, D+; 1 = D or less.

Table 12-4
Regression Analysis for Overall Evaluation of Major

	Males (N = 167)		Females (N = 179)			
	Basic Model	Basic Model, Plus Individual-Perception Term	Basic Model	Basic Model, Plus Interaction Term	Basic Model, Plus Individual-Perception Term	Basic Model, Plus Interaction and Individual-Perception Term
Major with High Status Rewards	.17	.20*	.12	.03	.10	.06
Closely linked major	-.14	-.15*	.05	-.04	.04	.00
Status X Link Interaction	—	—	—	.18*	—	.08
Department student orientation	.34***	.36***	.27*	.28**	.28**	.29**
Individual perception of department student orientation	—	.53***	—	—	.50***	.48***
Department grading practices	.08	.07	-.02	-.02	-.02	-.02
Relative individual grades in major	.20**	.06	.21**	.20**	.11	.11
Job experience in major area	.10	.09	.10	.12	.05	.08
R^2	.17	.43	.13	.15	.36	.37
F	5.40***	17.13**	4.29***	4.40***	13.94***	12.39***

Note: Standardized regression coefficients are reported. Code for significant levels: *$p \leq .05$, **$p \leq .01$, ***$p \leq .001$.

tion than the consensus perception of his or her peers in the major. Individuals may confront unique sets of courses and professors, and professors may interact with different students in different ways. As shown in table 12-4, the addition to the basic model of the term representing the individual's relative perception of major-department climate not only appreciably increased the explained variance of the basic model, but also provided some intriguing changes in the pattern of results. The consensus perception term for department student orientation remained significant, whereas the parallel individual-perception term, as expected, was also quite significant. However, the indicator for relative individual grades in the major, which previously was significant for both males and females, dropped from significance for both males and females.

This result strongly hints that the influence of relative grades on satisfaction levels is mediated through professors' interactions with individual students. Those students who are being rewarded most highly are also those who perceive an especially high and significant degree of concern for their education on the part of professors in the department. Several specific explanations may be proposed. High-achieving students may seek out interactions and support from their major professors. Also, professors may tend to favor such students with their interactions, since those students most clearly have potential for further accomplishment in the profession and potential for providing challenging discussions with the professors both in and out of class. Finally, achieving good grades may create a favorable feeling on the part of students regarding departmental experiences more neutrally or negatively interpreted by other students.

The addition of the individual-perception term had a further impact on the pattern of results. For males, higher-status majors appeared to have a uniquely positive effect, and closely linked majors appeared to have a uniquely negative effect, on males' satisfaction levels. For females, the addition of the individual-perception term did not change the nonsignificant results for the basic status and linkage indicators, and changed the status-link interaction term from significant to nonsignificant. These results suggest the overarching significance for women of individual-level interactions in the department setting. Women in high-status, closely linked majors, relative to the men in those majors, had rather favorable perceptions of departmental concern and support (see the respective correlations between relative perceptions of department student orientation and the status-link interaction term, reported in table 12-3); and when the individual perception data were entered, the relationship between these departments and satisfaction outcomes for women disappeared, suggesting the mediation interpretation. Apparently, in these high-payoff but male-dominated areas, the encouragement of mentors is crucial to women's persistence and satisfaction.

Summary and Discussion

This chapter provides supportive evidence from the higher-education setting for propositions that the socioeconomic structure of opportunity and status is related to the environments of various educational alternatives, to the selection patterns of students into various educational alternatives, and to the reactions of students to their educational experiences. These findings suggest strongly that the generation, testing, and refining of theoretical propositions relating to the status-based and occupation-based linkages of major departments to the larger society should be a focus of future research.

Several central research questions guided the present research effort. Tying the findings for the first four questions together suggests a significant conclusion: men and women can choose from an array of major departments in which the supportiveness of the social climate is negatively related to the significance of the status rewards. Confronting such choices, men tend to opt for the unsupportive departments with higher status rewards, whereas women tend to opt for the supportive departments with lower status rewards. This pattern suggests that the hypothesis of greater sensitivity of women to social factors in environments and the greater sensitivity of men to "external," achievement-related factors in environments (see Coleman 1961; McDill and Rigsby 1973) is supported in our research as it relates to the *choice* of educational environments. Interestingly, however, the results do not provide unqualified support for the hypothesis of greater tendencies toward instrumentalism in male students. Our data suggest that males, compared with females, are more strongly oriented to the eventual attainment of achieved status through their major choices, but are not more strongly oriented to vocational certification in those choices. Indeed, females may be more likely than males to choose vocationally oriented majors.[10]

Are the determinants of satisfaction with major-department experiences different for men and women? The answer provided here must be somewhat equivocal. Both men and women responded positively to supportive faculty attitudes and actions regarding undergraduate education, and individuals of both sexes responded positively to receiving higher grades than their peers. Nevertheless, women, but not men, apparently received special satisfaction from completing vocationally specific majors with higher status rewards, such as engineering and economics. Because these majors are those most closely identified with males, and numerically most clearly dominated by them, the finding strongly supports existing research findings that women choosing to participate in male-dominated fields are highly satisfied with their choices (Rossi and Calderwood 1973; Maccoby and Jacklin 1974).

When an indicator of the student's relative individual perception of departmental supportiveness was added to the regression model, the pattern of similarities and differences in results for men and women shifted significantly. Notably, the status-by-linkage interaction term became appreciably less important as a unique, influential factor for women. Since higher-status, closely linked major departments tend to have rather unsupportive climates overall, it can be tentatively inferred that supportive personalized interactions with certain departmental faculty members convey the special positive influence of these departments on women. In support of this interpretation, the data reveal that women in such departments, compared with their male peers, held significantly more favorable perceptions of the supportiveness and concern of their major-area professors.

These results hint strongly that our emphasis on socioeconomic structure and its links to major choices and experiences is fundamentally correct and fruitful with important implications for several areas of policy-relevant inquiry. The results most significantly connect the equity-based concerns regarding sex differentiation in educational and occupational choices, environments, and short- and long-term outcomes. Our findings suggest that women favorably evaluate male-dominated majors that are both closely linked to occupations and high in status rewards; and other research has shown that both sexes appear to receive certain affective benefits from pursuing cross-sex college major programs—that is, major programs providing sex-atypical academic rewards and socioeconomic linkages (see Hearn 1980). If we accept the policy goal of achieving parity in the distribution of the sexes into higher- and lower-status occupational positions, then the causes and the positive and negative consequences of cross-sex choices for both men and women should be researched and publicized.

Earlier, we posed two possible explanations for the pattern of differential returns to college education for men and women beyond the apparent factor of labor-market discrimination: sex-differentiated major choice patterns wherein men tend to choose majors with higher postgraduation payoffs, and sex-differentiated educational quality in the undergraduate years wherein men tend to be in departments providing better educational experience. The present research suggests that researchers and policymakers should devote more substantial attention to the former explanation—that is, to the structural as opposed to the educational-quality explanation. It appears from our results that undergraduate women tend to encounter *more* supportive major-area professors than do men, but receive appreciably lower status returns to the degree in the major area.[11] Indeed, we may infer from Wilson's (1978) results that not only the status returns but also the *income* returns to the degree for the women in our sample were destined to be lower. Future research in this area might investigate the relative role of various factors (for example, perceptions of occupational barriers versus sex-role socialization) in the major choice and influence patterns uncovered in the present study.

A final point merits discussion. The results generally point to positive effects on satisfaction for both men and women in areas with higher status rewards, but for women these effects occur only in those areas that are also closely linked to specific occupations. This intriguing pattern appears well worth further investigation. For now, we simply propose on possible explanation. It may be that, as part of a lower-status group, highly ambitious women strongly desire and need the security of *both* certification and status to overcome labor-market discrimination. Certification may be seen as a kind of passport, validating the individuals' right to cross certain heavily guarded occupational borders. Perhaps women are more often required to present the passport than men, who are granted entry by virtue of their favored ascribed status.

This explanation would imply that highly ambitious women may tend to view status and occupational linkage as integrally related in occupational plans, whereas highly ambitious men may tend to devalue undergraduate majors that provide occupational linkages but to value status rewards from majors. The classical conception of a college degree as a broad, vocationally unspecific endorsement of the educated man as a potential leader of society (Hofstadter 1963; Veysey 1965; Meyer 1970) seems relevant. Perhaps men are more willing and able to defer, or avoid altogether, vocationally linked college education. This interpretation, if valid, has important policy implications. If sex discrimination continues to be a serious problem in labor markets, women may be wise to require that their education certify them occupationally. Higher status rewards from the major, in themselves, may not provide as much mobility for women as for men, particularly in tight job markets for college graduates. Alternatively, in a more prosperous, less discriminatory occupational marketplace, efforts to encourage women's acceptance of the merits of less closely linked majors may be advisable. Such majors may provide pathways into a wider variety of graduate and professional programs and may also provide greater potential for job mobility and experimentation in the early occupational career.

Notes

1. Veysey (1965) points out that the latter part of the nineteenth century was marked by increasing conflict between the traditional, liberal-arts conception of U.S. higher education and an emerging utilitarian conception of the enterprise. Departments in such areas as business, education, engineering, and home economics were established for the first time at major institutions, but not without resistance from professors in the established liberal-arts disciplines (such as, philosophy, religion, and languages).

2. Departments that are high in status and power rewards *and* those that are closely linked to specific occupations may be considered to be *exter-

nally validated departments in that an audience beyond the confines of the college plays an important role in their actions, structure, and influence vis-á-vis undergraduates. Similarly, departments with only weak links to the occupational and status structure may be considered to be *internally validated,* oriented in their undergraduate program to general education and intellectual skills, and not especially responsive to audiences in positions of expertise and power in the larger socioeconomic system. Unlike Meyer, we propose that a major can be external along one dimension and internal along the other. For example, elementary education is a major that may be considered closely linked to a specific occupation and thus externally validated in one sense. Yet it also appears to have a rather low eventual payoff in terms of status and income, with few immediate rewards in either sense for the newly graduated holder of the degree (indeed, there are currently few available entry-level jobs at all in this area). From this viewpoint, the elementary-education major can offer very few external rewards and may be considered a major choice more oriented to present, on-campus rewards than to future benefits.

3. Criteria involving avoidance of postgraduation penalty undoubtedly play a role in the choice of major—for example, avoiding a major, however vocationally attractive, in which one's potential GPA is too low to ensure employment; avoiding a major, however, vocationally attractive, that is dominated by unattractive role occupants; or avoiding a major, however vocationally attractive, that is marked by declining job prospects. These avoidance criteria may be considered as parallel aspects of the positively phrased choice criteria described here.

4. Indeed, these positive features of majors may be a kind of unusual bonus to students. If students confront an array of majors in which positive extrinsic rewards are negatively related to positive intrinsic rewards, as hypothesized earlier, those students choosing majors with positive extrinsic rewards may have few positive expectations for intrinsic rewards, and vise versa.

5. The sample base for scores on this indicator and on the consensus student-orientation perception indicator described earlier was approximately twice the size of the present sample. Certain cases were dropped from the present analysis because of missing data considerations.

6. The question may be raised as to whether (1) a major or occupation has lower status in the eyes of the general public because women numerically dominate it or (2) women tend to choose lower-status majors. This distinction is substantively intriguing but must be largely ignored in the present study because of data limitations. Some evidence supporting position (1), however, may be found in the recent research of Heilman (1979) on the importance of projected sex ratios in determining high-school students' occupational-interest patterns.

7. The individual-level data were checked for evidence that this

department-level finding might be an artifact of sex differences in perceptions of any given departmental climate. The individual data show no significant relation between an individual's sex and his or her relative perception of department student-orientation, leading us to reject this alternative explanation of the results.

8. This finding provides no support for hypotheses that women are treated less positively than men in personal interactions with department faculty members in higher-education settings.

9. It could be argued that some or all of the assorted basic and interaction effects of the departments in the analysis represent little more than contextual effects attributable to the numerical dominance of one sex in certain departments. This possibility was tested by entering a term for sex composition into each of the equations reported in table 12-4. The results were essentially unaffected by inserting the new term into the equations. The findings in this new analysis thus uphold a more structural interpretation of the influence process.

10. This conclusion is tentative and bound by the sample institution. It should be tested more extensively in varying institutional settings such as private institutions or Southern institutions. Nevertheless, our exploratory analysis of national major choice data from the National Center for Education Statistics (1978) upheld the findings reported here: women were slightly more likely than men to receive bachelor's degrees in vocationally linked areas.

11. A potentially important caveat may be raised to the conclusion that women tend to encounter educational environments unequivocally superior to those of men. Highly supportive, liberally grading educational environments, such as those encountered by many of the women in our study, may tend to provide fewer academic challenges to their students. Research in secondary-school classrooms by Moos (1979) has suggested that student satisfaction tends to be greatest in supportive classroom environments but that academic gains tend to be greatest in intellectually challenging classroom environments wherein supportiveness levels are not especially high.

Bibliography

Arnove, R.F. *Student Alienation: A Venezuelan Study.* New York: Praeger, 1971.

Astin, A. *Four Critical Years.* San Francisco: Jossey-Bass, 1977.

Bardwick, J.M. *The Psychology of Women: A Study of Biocultural Conflicts.* New York: Harper and Row, 1971.

Beardslee, D.C. and O'Dowd, D.C. "Students and the Occupational World." In N. Sanford, ed., *The American College,* New York: Wiley, 1962.

Bernstein, B. *Class Codes and Control,* vol. 3. London: Routledge and Kegan Paul, 1975.

Bielby, D. "Career Sex-Atypicality and Career Involvement of College Educated Women: Baseline Evidence from the 1960s." *Sociology of Education* 51 (1978):7–28.

Broverman, I.K.; Broverman, D.M.; Clarkson, D.; and Rosenkrantz, F. "Sex-Role Stereotypes: A Current Appraisal." *Journal of Social Issues* 28 (1972):59–72.

Coleman, J.S. *The Adolescent Society.* New York: Free Press of Glencoe, 1961.

Featherman, D.L., and Hauser, R.M. *Opportunity and Change.* New York: Academic Press, 1978.

Feldman, K.A., and Newcomb, T.M. *The Impact of College on Students,* vol. 1. San Francisco: Jossey-Bass, 1969.

Ferber, M.A., and McMahon, W.W. "Women's Expected Earnings and Their Investment in Higher Education." *Journal of Human Resources* 14 (1979):405–420.

Freeman, R.B. *The Over-Educated American.* New York: Academic Press, 1976.

Gamson, Z.F. "Utilitarian and Normative Orientations Toward Education." *Sociology of Education* 39 (1966):36–37.

Griffin, L.J., and Alexander, K.L. "Schooling and Socioeconomic Attainments: High School and College Influences." *American Journal of Sociology* 84 (1978):319–347.

Hearn, J.C. "Major Choice and the Well-Being of College Men and Women: An Examination from Developmental, Organizational, and Structural Perspectives." *Sociology of Education* 53 (1980):164–178.

Heilman, M.E. "High School Students' Occupational Interest as a Function of Projected Sex Ratios in Male-Dominated Occupations." *Journal of Applied Psychology* 64 (1979):275–279.

Hofstadter, R. *Anti-Intellectualism in American Life.* New York: Knopf, 1963.

Lynn, D. "Sex-role and Parent Identification." *Child Development* 33 (1962):555–564.

Maccoby, E.E., and Jacklin, C.N. *The Psychology of Sex Differences.* Stanford, Calif.: Stanford University Press, 1974.

McDill, E., and Rigsby, L. *Structure and Process in Secondary Schools.* Baltimore, Md.: Johns Hopkins University Press, 1973.

Meyer, J.W. "Working Paper on Some Non-Value Effects of Colleges."

Unpublished manuscript, Bureau of Applied Social Research, Columbia University, New York, 1965.

————. "The Charter: Conditions of Diffuse Socialization in School." In W.R. Scott, ed., *Social Processes and Social Structures,* New York: Holt, Rinehart and Winston, 1970.

————. "The Effects of Education as an Institution." *American Journal of Sociology* 83 (1977):55–77.

————. "Levels of the Educational System and Schooling Effects." In C.E. Bidwell and D.M. Windham, eds., *The Analysis of Education Productivity: Issues in Macroanalysis,* vol. II. Cambridge, Mass.: Balinger, 1980.

Moos, R.H. *Evaluating Educational Environments.* San Francisco: Jossey-Bass, 1979.

National Center for Education Statistics. *Earned Degrees Conferred 1975–76: Summary Data.* Washington, D.C.: U.S. Government Printing Office, 1978.

Polachek, S.W. "Sex Differences in College Major." *Industrial and Labor Relations Review* 31 (1978):498–508.

Rossi, A.S., and Calderwood, A. *Academic Women on the Move.* New York: Russell Sage Foundation, 1973.

Sorensen, A.B. "A Model and a Metric for the Analysis of the Intragenerational Status Attainment Process." *American Journal of Sociology* 85 (1979):361–384.

Spady, W.C. "Dropouts from Higher Education: Toward an Empirical Model." *Interchange* 2 (1971):38–62.

Treiman, D.J., and Terrell, K. "Sex and the Process of Status Attainment: A Comparison of Working Women and Men." *American Sociological Review* 40 (1975):174–200.

Veysey, L.R. *The Emergence of the American University.* Chicago: University of Chicago, 1965.

Vreeland, R., and Bidwell, C.E. "Classifying University Departments: An Approach to the Analysis of Their Effects upon Undergraduate Values and Attitudes." *Sociology of Education* 39 (1966):237–254.

Weidman, J.C. *The Effects of Academic Departments on Change in Undergraduates' Occupational Values.* U.S. Department of Health, Education, and Welfare Project No. 1-E-111, Grant no. OEG-5-72-0010 (509). Minneapolis: University of Minnesota, 1974.

Wilson, E.K. "The Entering Student: Attributes and Agents of Change." In T.M. Newcomb and E.K. Wilson, eds., *College Peer Groups,* Chicago: Aldine, 1966.

Wilson, K.L. "Toward an Improved Explanation of Income Attainment: Recalibrating Education and Occupation." *American Journal of Sociology* 84 (1978):684–697.

Wilson, R.C.; Gaff, J.G.; with Dienst, E.R.; Wood, L.; and Bavry, J.L.
College Professors and Their Impact on Students. New York: Wiley,
1975.

**Part IV
College and Beyond: Issues of
Outcomes and Achievements**

13

Career Plans of College Women: Patterns and Influences

Marsha D. Brown

There is a large literature on the characteristics of college students and the changes in these characteristics across colleges and across time between college entrance and college graduation (Davis 1964, 1965; Feldman and Newcomb 1969; Folger, Astin, and Bayer 1970; El-Khawas and Bisconti 1973; Astin and Bisconti 1977; Astin 1977). Several major studies have been based on longitudinal data collected before, during, and after the students were exposed to the college experience (Alexander and Eckland 1973, 1974; Alwin 1976; Astin 1977). Many studies in the field have been limited to samples of men or samples of women on a single college campus.

Early studies based on longitudinal analyses of large samples of men and women (Sewell and Shah 1967; Flanagan et al. 1971) showed that college women had lower career aspirations than college men and that the gap in aspirations between women and men widened between college entrance and college graduation. Researchers who have limited their studies to the predictors of educational and career outcome for men (Jencks et al. 1972, 1979; Alwin 1976) have assumed that the effects of background and college environment on career outcomes are different for women than they are for men.

This study is a longitudinal analysis of the career plans of a national sample of college women who were in college between 1966 and 1971.[1] Women who entered U.S. colleges in 1966 were surveyed four times in five years. This paper describes the patterns in women's career plans across the college years and the influences of individual background and characteristics and college-environment characteristics on women's initial career plans and on the changes in these career plans over the college years.

Data for this study were obtained from the Cooperative Institutional Research Program (CIRP) at the University of California at Los Angeles (UCLA) on a national sample of women who first matriculated as college freshmen in 1966. Data collected at college entry in 1966 were merged with

Grant GI-34394 from the National Science Foundation to the American Council on Education, the University of California at Los Angeles Graduate School of Education, and the Graduate School of Public Affairs at the University of Washington supported this research.

303

follow-up data collected in 1967, 1970, and 1971—one, four, and five years after college entry. The sample for this study was restricted to women who were white, U.S.-born, and less than 22 years old when they first matriculated as freshmen in 1966. The sample was also restricted to students who stayed at the same institution from 1966 to 1970. These restrictions reduced the final sample to 2,430 women.

This is a very restricted sample that excludes important groups of college women, including minorities, older women, and transfer students. Women in small private four-year colleges are overrepresented in this sample, and women in selective women's colleges do not include women in any of the Seven Sister colleges.

These data are also ten years old. These students were in college between 1966 and 1971, during a unique historical period in the United States dominated by the women's movement and the Vietnam War. Therefore, generalizing from this study to college women today may be hazardous. National norms for college freshmen published by Astin and his associates (1967, 1970, 1976, 1980) show shifts in the career plans of college women between 1966 and 1980. The percentage of freshmen women in four-year colleges and universities who were planning a doctorate or professional degree beyond the master's level (PhD/Prof) increased from 9 to 13 percent in the five years from 1966 to 1971. In the five years from 1971 to 1976, the percentage increased from 13 to 22; in 1980 the percentage of freshmen women with PhD/Prof degree plans was also 22.

For most analyses, women in the sample were divided into two groups based on their freshman career plans. Women were coded as having PhD/Prof career plans if degree plans were LL.B. or J.D., Ph.D. or Ed.D., M.D., D.D.S, or D.V.M.; or if career plans were minister or priest, lawyer, researcher, college teacher, or doctor; there were 337 women with PhD/Prof career plans as freshmen in 1966 (14 percent of the sample). Women were coded as having BA/MA career plans if they did not meet the criteria for PhD/Prof career plans and planned a B.A. or M.A. degree; there were 2,093 women with BA/MA career plans as freshmen in 1966 (86 percent of the sample).

This study is based on the same data as Astin's (1977) major study of the impact of college on students' vocational, personal, social, and academic development. This study differs from Astin's in several important respects, however. First, the samples are different. This study focuses on two subgroups of women—women with initial plans at college entry for the Ph.D. or professional degrees, and women with initial plans for B.A. or M.A. degrees. These groups were further divided on the basis of achievement and self-esteem. Second, this study is based on one cohort of women who were surveyed at four points in time; Astin's study is based on different cohorts of students exposed to college for different lengths of time. Thus this study compares the effects of different college climates on the career outcomes of women with different backgrounds who entered college at the same time and were exposed to the college environment for the same length of time, whereas Astin compared institutional effects for different cohorts of men and women students who entered college at different times and were exposed to the environment for different lengths of time. Finally, this study focuses on career outcomes of women: career plans at three points in time— one, four, and five years after college entry; and whether women apply to graduate school and enroll in graduate school within one year after college graduation.

Astin (1977) studied many outcomes, including career development. Specifically, he analyzed persistence of career choice for the homogeneous groups defined on the basis of initial career choice at college entry, highest degree planned, and estimates of the likelihood of changing career plans. Men and women were combined except for the field of medicine, where separate analyses were performed. School teaching, nursing, and homemaking were the only fields with large numbers of women; business, college teaching, law, engineering, scientific research, and social work had fewer than 100 women each. Astin predicted implementation of original career plans. Therefore, his analyses assumed that freshmen know what career they want and that college environments either hinder or help them to implement their career goals. This assumption may be more realistic for men than for women since college women show less stability in career choice over the college years than college men (Astin 1968; Brown 1978). In this study PhD/ Prof career plans are predicted both for the women who enter college with PhD/Prof career plans and for those who enter college with BA/MA career plans. The backgrounds and college environments that facilitate or hinder women in choosing Ph.D. or professional careers between college entrance and five years later are examined.

This is a descriptive study, divided into two major sections. The first section describes the *patterns* of career outcomes during college for six groups of women defined by initial career plans at college entry, achievement measured by college-entrance exams and self-reported academic self-esteem. The second section describes the *influences* of individual background variables and college-environment variables on career outcomes for two groups of women with initial career plans of PhD/Prof and BA/MA.

Patterns

Tables 13-1 through 13-4 compare the six groups of women on many variables; the variables are defined in appendix 13A. The six freshman career groups are defined by initial career plans when the women entered college; achievement as measured by college-entrance examinations; and self-esteem as measured by self-rating scales on intellectual self-esteem, academic ability, and math ability. Achievement was coded high if it was above average (the National Merit Scholarship converted score was greater than or equal to 120); otherwise achievement was coded low. Self-esteem was coded high if the student indicated she rated herself "above average" on a composite of academic ability, mathematical ability, and intellectual self-esteem; otherwise self-esteem was coded low. The six groups are as follows:

1. BA/MA career plans, low achievement
2. BA/MA career plans, high achievement, low self-esteem
3. BA/MA career plans, high achievement, high self-esteem
4. PhD/Prof career plans, low achievement
5. PhD/Prof career plans, high achievement, low self-esteem
6. PhD/Prof career plans, high achievement, high self-esteem

Marriage plans are strongly related to career plans (Bayer 1969a, b; Brown 1978). Marriage plans were not included in the definition of career groups, however, since more than 80 percent of the freshman women said the likelihood they would marry within one year after college was "some" or "very good", even among those with PhD/Prof career plans. Many of the women with PhD/Prof career plans who were not planning to marry immediately after college were also Catholic women attending Catholic colleges, perhaps women planning vocations in the Catholic church.

Comparisons among these six groups show differences in backgrounds, in college experiences, in career outcomes, and in other attitudes and outcomes related to career plans. Comparisons among the six groups on career outcomes over time show whether career outcomes become more consistent with the women's measured achievement and their perceptions of their abilities as measured by academic self-esteem. Comparisons among the six groups on self-esteem over time show whether academic self-esteem becomes more related to objective measures of achievement.

Tables 13–1 through 13–4 present means and percentages for the six groups of women on background; types of colleges attended and characteristics of colleges attended; other attitudes and plans as freshmen in 1966 and in three follow-ups in 1967, 1970, and 1971; marriage plans, marriage, and children at all points in time; and career outcomes at all four points in time in 1966, 1967, 1970, and 1971. The data in these tables are unweighted; analyses based on weighting the data to approximate all college freshmen were comparable.

Backgrounds

Table 13–1 shows the means and percentages for the six groups of women on background characteristics. Group 6, freshmen women with PhD/Prof

Table 13-1
Means and Percentages of Background Characteristics, by Freshman Career Groups

Variables		Freshman Plans in 1966					
	BA/MA Low Ach N = 1,281	BA/MA High Ach Low S-E N = 488	BA/MA High Ach High S-E N = 324	PhD/Prof Low Ach N = 119	PhD/Prof High Ach Low S-E N = 72	PhD/Prof High Ach High S-E N = 146	Total N = 2,430
Father's occupation	56.62	64.14	62.27	60.51	61.44	64.97	59.72
Father's education	13.26	14.31	14.11	13.61	13.83	14.62	13.70
Mother's education	12.92	13.53	13.62	12.91	13.31	14.30	13.23
Parents' income	11,935	13,899	13,409	11,950	13,743	13,130	12,652
Reared Catholic (%)	36.5	36.3	35.8	35.3	38.9	43.8	36.8
Reared Jewish (%)	4.2	10.7	5.6	6.7	6.9	9.6	6.2
Home in South (%)	18.7	16.0	16.4	16.0	16.7	10.3	17.1
Home on farm (%)	10.8	5.1	7.1	5.9	1.4	6.2	8.4
Achievement (NMSC scale)	102.74	127.18	132.52	106.92	130.63	136.08	114.65
High-school grades	3.16	3.40	3.66	3.34	3.47	3.71	3.32
High-school honors (number)	0.46	0.89	1.22	0.56	1.03	1.42	0.73
High-school science awards (number)	0.04	0.03	0.06	0.07	0.03	0.17	0.05
Used library in high school	2.86	2.82	2.89	3.06	3.10	2.98	2.88

career plans and both high achievement and high self-esteem, differs from the other groups. These women were more likely to have been Jewish, more likely to have been Catholic, less likely to have been from the South, and more likely to have received high-school honors and high-school science awards.

College Characteristics

Table 13–2 shows the distribution of the six groups of women across twelve college types. Table 13–2 also shows the mean characteristics for the colleges attended by each of the six groups of women.

For the total sample of women, 24 percent were in unselective public institutions, 40 percent in small sectarian colleges, and 29 percent in women's colleges with 21 percent of those in sectarian women's colleges. Weighting these data show 19 percent of the women in sectarian colleges and 10 percent in women's colleges. Extrapolations from the national norms show 22 percent of freshmen women in sectarian colleges and 7 percent in women's colleges in 1966. Such differences between this sample and the norms could well be due to the characteristics of this sample—white, U.S.-born, under 22, attending the same college for four years, and responding to successive waves of questionnaires.

Women with low achievement were concentrated in the large, relatively unselective institutions, especially the public ones, and in the unselective sectarian colleges. Of those with BA/MA career plans and low achievement, 88 percent were in unselective colleges, compared with 64 percent of the other groups and with 54 percent of those with PhD/Prof career plans, high achievement, and high self-esteem.

Within colleges, women in group 6 with PhD/Prof career plans, high achievement, and high self-esteem were more likely to be in honors and research programs and less likely to be in sororities. They were also more likely to be Catholic women in Catholic colleges. Women with high achievement and high self-esteem also earned the highest grades in college.

Attitudes and Marriage Outcomes

Table 13–3 compares the six groups of women on attitudes correlated with career plans. Table 13–4 shows the percentage in each group who were married and had children. Group 6 women were more likely to say as freshmen that they had no religion and that they had liberal politics. The percentage of this group expressing no religion in 1970 at college graduation was still high. For all groups the percentage expressing no religious affiliation went up dramatically between college entrance and college graduation.

Table 13-2
Means and Percentages of College Characteristics, by Freshman Career Group

Variables	Freshman Plans in 1966						
	BA/MA Low Ach N = 1,281	BA/MA High Ach Low S-E N = 488	BA/MA High Ach High S-E N = 324	PhD/Prof Low Ach N = 119	PhD/Prof High Ach Low S-E N = 72	PhD/Prof High Ach High S-E N = 146	Total N = 2,430
College type							
Low SATs, public	29.9	17.0	18.2	27.7	11.1	9.6	23.9
Low SATs, university	5.5	3.7	3.7	7.5	1.4	5.5	4.9
Low SATs, coed nonsectarian	11.4	5.7	5.2	10.1	2.8	4.1	8.7
Low SATs, coed sectarian	19.0	12.1	17.9	17.6	6.9	11.6	16.6
Low SATs, women, nonsectarian	3.3	5.7	1.5	0.8	1.4	2.7	3.3
Low SATs, women, sectarian	18.6	21.5	16.4	16.0	19.4	20.5	18.9
High SATs, public	4.5	5.9	4.3	7.6	6.9	4.8	5.0
High SATs, university	1.3	8.4	13.6	2.5	20.8	15.1	5.8
High SATs, coed, nonsectarian	0.3	4.5	5.9	0.0	9.7	13.0	2.9
High SATs, coed, sectarian	2.6	2.3	3.7	1.7	2.8	5.5	5.1
High SATs, women, nonsectarian	2.4	9.2	6.8	5.9	15.3	5.5	5.1
High SATs, women, sectarian	0.6	3.9	2.8	2.5	1.4	2.1	1.8

Table 13-2 continued

Variables	BA/MA Low Ach N=1,281	BA/MA High Ach Low S-E N=488	BA/MA High Ach High S-E N=324	PhD/Prof Low Ach N=119	PhD/Prof High Ach Low S-E N=72	PhD/Prof High Ach High S-E N=146	Total N=2,430
			Freshman Plans in 1966				
College Characteristics							
Selectivity (SATV+M)	996.46	1,068.71	1,073.60	1,029.22	1,111.54	1,100.93	1,032.54
Affluence	1,072.74	1,210.64	1,238.71	1,076.63	1,341.08	1,357.78	1,147.83
Size	5,502	5,057	5,137	6,274	5,560	4,777	5,360
Percentage faculty—women	24.83	28.85	24.81	26.01	28.08	25.78	25.84
Percentage faculty—Ph.D.	36.97	42.79	42.91	38.57	46.01	45.31	39.78
Percentage B.A.'s awarded to women	44.33	36.78	43.14	45.35	40.15	37.98	42.20
Percentage B.A.'s in student's area	21.75	25.39	23.97	18.92	21.80	21.28	22.61
College Factors (ICA)							
Academic competitiveness	1.56	1.62	1.65	1.59	1.68	1.68	1.59
Used library	1.41	1.42	1.42	1.40	1.43	1.44	1.41
Familiarity with faculty	1.46	1.49	1.48	1.47	1.48	1.50	1.47
Concern for students	1.81	1.85	1.84	1.81	1.83	1.86	1.83
Students work	1.33	1.28	1.30	1.33	1.28	1.31	1.31
Career uncertainty	1.29	1.30	1.30	1.29	1.30	1.30	1.29
Liberal	1.56	1.61	1.61	1.58	1.67	1.68	1.59
Snobbish	1.74	1.77	1.78	1.75	1.79	1.78	1.76
Social	1.74	1.76	1.74	1.74	1.72	1.71	1.74

Interactions with environment							
Catholic students in							
Catholic colleges (%)	19.5	24.2	21.3	21.0	23.6	30.1	21.5
Protestant students in							
Protestant colleges (%)	23.0	16.6	22.5	21.8	8.3	14.4	20.6
College involvement (%)							
In honors program	11.20	12.00	12.90	11.71	12.24	13.42	11.78
In research program	12.32	12.60	12.64	13.03	13.43	14.01	12.59
In sorority	29.0	23.4	26.2	23.5	25.0	15.8	26.3
Lived on campus as							
freshman	77.0	84.6	86.4	71.4	87.5	84.2	80.2
College Grades							
Freshman GPA, 1967	2.56	2.80	3.07	2.60	2.83	3.11	2.72
Cumulative GPA, 1970	2.85	3.07	3.24	2.91	3.10	3.27	2.98

Table 13-3
Means and Percentages of Attitudes and Plans, by Freshman Career Group

| | Freshman Career Group | | | | | | |
Variables	BA/MA Low Ach N = 1,281	BA/MA High Ach Low S-E N = 488	BA/MA High Ach High S-E N = 324	PhD/Prof Low Ach N = 119	PhD/Prof High Ach Low S-E N = 72	PhD/Prof High Ach High S-E N = 146	Total N = 2,430
Attitudes and plans, 1966							
Intellectual self-esteem	54.22	56.83	76.99	59.69	57.89	79.16	59.66
Chances of marrying— good (%)	84.9	81.6	83.0	65.5	70.8	60.3	81.2
Religion—none (%)	2.0	5.1	4.0	0.8	6.9	11.0	3.5
Politics—liberal	3.05	3.09	3.08	3.13	3.17	3.23	3.08
Artistic interests	1.72	1.80	1.82	1.94	1.90	1.94	1.78
Business interests	1.89	1.66	1.68	1.87	1.75	1.68	1.80
Status interests	2.56	2.46	2.52	2.78	2.80	2.77	2.56
Altruistic interests	2.63	2.62	2.57	2.77	2.72	2.66	2.63
Stubbornness	3.15	3.24	3.28	3.24	3.29	3.31	3.21
Interpersonal self-esteem	3.10	3.01	3.19	3.17	3.05	3.18	3.10

Attitudes and plans, 1967, 1970

Intellectual self-esteem in 1967	53.98	50.70	72.66	57.08	63.28	74.72	59.29
High self-esteem in 1967 (%)	11.0	22.8	70.4	21.9	43.1	74.7	26.6
Intellectual self-esteem in 1970	55.99	61.34	72.18	59.47	63.07	73.75	60.67
High self-esteem in 1970 (%)	14.8	27.5	67.6	20.2	33.3	77.4	28.9
Religious preference—none (%)	11.2	20.9	21.0	17.6	22.2	28.8	16.1
Politics—liberal	3.18	3.42	3.40	3.29	3.62	3.64	3.30
Artistic interests	1.79	1.87	1.77	1.80	1.90	1.93	1.81
Business interests	1.59	1.43	1.45	1.54	1.45	1.43	1.52
Status interests	2.24	2.17	2.27	2.35	2.42	2.38	2.25
Altruistic interests	2.38	2.31	2.25	2.42	2.25	2.34	2.34
Stubbornness	3.27	3.41	3.41	3.31	3.35	3.37	3.33
Interpersonal self-esteem	3.27	3.20	3.26	3.27	3.26	3.28	3.26
Overall satisfaction with college	40.51	41.03	41.45	41.18	40.28	40.82	40.78

Table 13-4
Percentages of Marriage and Children Outcomes, by Freshman Career Group

Variables	Freshman Career Group						
	BA/MA Low Ach N=1,281	BA/MA High Ach Low S-E N=488	BA/MA High Ach High S-E N=324	PhD/Prof Low Ach N=119	PhD/Prof High Ach Low S-E N=72	PhD/Prof High Ach High S-E N=146	Total N=2,430
Married in 1967	0.5	0.0	0.0	0.0	0.0	0.7	0.3
Married in 1970	29.7	24.2	29.9	27.7	29.2	26.7	28.3
Married in 1971	49.0	41.2	44.8	38.7	41.7	41.8	45.7
Children in 1971	7.1	4.9	4.6	8.4	6.9	2.1	6.1

Women in group 6 were less likely as freshmen to say there was a good chance they would marry within the next five years; four and five years later they were almost as likely to marry as other women, although they were less likely to have children. Women with BA/MA career plans and relatively low achievement were most likely to be married and most likely to have children five years after college entry.

Career Outcomes

Table 13–5 compares the career outcomes for the six groups of women across time. Women with low achievement and BA/MA career plans were least likely to *expect* to have full-time employment (57 percent, compared with 68 percent for the other groups); these same women were also least likely to *prefer* full-time employment (54 percent, compared with 65 percent for the other groups). For the women in group 6 with PhD/Prof career plans, high achievement, and high self-esteem, 82 percent preferred full-time employment, and 80 percent expected it.

Career plans during and after college are highly related to freshman career plans and achievement. All these women were college graduates; yet few of them expressed PhD/Prof career plans when they were leaving college. Across groups, the percentage of all women with PhD/Prof career plans rose slightly, from 14 percent in 1966 to 18 percent in 1970; but by 1971, when most of the women had been out of college one year and 46 percent were married, the percentage with PhD/Prof career plans was back down to 15. Historically, these changes were occurring during the same time period when the national percentage of freshmen women planning Ph.D.'s or professional degrees rose from 9 in 1966 to 12.5 in 1971.

Patterns, by Freshmen Career Group

The patterns can be discussed for each group of women. When achievement was below average, very few women expressed PhD/Prof career plans at the end of college, regardless of their earlier career plans. For women with BA/MA career plans as freshmen and low achievement, fewer than 10 percent raised their career plans to the PhD/Prof level during college. Conversely, for women with PhD/Prof career plans as freshmen and relatively low achievement, 80 percent lowered their career plans to the BA/MA level by the time they graduated from college. These figures indicate a shift toward career plans more consistent with measured achievement.

Among the women who started college with high achievement, the percentage with PhD/Prof career plans at the end of college was only slightly higher. For women with BA/MA career plans as freshmen and high

Table 13-5
Means and Percentages of Career Outcomes, by Freshman Career Groups

Variables	Freshman Career Group						Total
	BA/MA Low Ach N=1,281	BA/MA High Ach Low S-E N=488	BA/MA High Ach High S-E N=324	PhD/Prof Low Ach N=119	PhD/Prof High Ach Low S-E N=72	PhD/Prof High Ach High S-E N=146	N=2,430
Career plans, 1966							
Degree plans	16.70	16.96	17.07	18.78	19.10	19.43	17.14
Career plans	62.51	60.33	62.66	77.80	76.08	77.24	64.13
BA/MA health (%)	14.6	11.5	8.6	0	0	0	11.2
BA/MA teaching (%)	45.5	36.1	34.9	0	0	0	35.9
BA/MA business (%)	6.3	1.2	2.8	0	0	0	4.0
BA/MA engineering (%)	0.2	0.2	0.0	0	0	0	0.1
BA/MA other (%)	33.4	51.0	53.7	0	0	0	34.9
PhD/Prof humanities (%)	0	0	0	52.1	48.6	36.3	6.2
PhD/Prof science (%)	0	0	0	23.5	22.2	38.4	4.1
PhD/Prof lawyer (%)	0	0	0	4.2	11.1	4.1	0.8
PhD/Prof doctor (%)	0	0	0	20.2	18.1	21.2	2.8

Career plans 1967, 1970, 1971 (%)

Prefer full-time employment	53.7	63.9	59.6	64.7	69.4	81.5	59.2
Expect full-time employment	57.4	64.3	67.0	69.7	70.8	79.5	62.4
PhD/Prof career plans, 1967	3.9	8.8	9.5	46.2	47.2	74.7	13.3
PhD/Prof career plans, 1970	8.4	17.0	21.9	38.7	56.9	60.3	17.9
PhD/Prof career plans, 1971	8.7	13.7	21.0	18.5	40.3	45.9	15.0
PhD/Prof in 1967 and 1970	1.4	3.3	4.9	27.7	36.1	50.0	7.5
PhD/Prof in 1970 and 1971	3.9	8.0	13.9	10.9	38.9	40.4	9.6
PhD/Prof in 1967, 1970, 1971	0.4	1.8	3.7	10.1	23.6	36.3	4.4
Same field in 1966 and 1970	57.5	48.4	39.2	26.1	40.3	38.4	50.0
Career outcomes (%)							
Applied to graduate school in 1970	25.4	36.1	40.7	41.2	56.9	63.7	33.6
Enrolled in graduate school in 1971	20.2	26.8	31.8	31.1	41.7	48.6	26.0

achievement, only 14 percent of those with low self-esteem and 21 percent of those with high self-esteem raised their career aspirations during college to the PhD/Prof level. Obviously, factors other than achievement and intellectual self-esteem were affecting the career plans of these women.

Patterns Across Time

By 1967, one year after first matriculation, fewer than 10 percent of the women who entered college with BA/MA career plans had changed their plans to PhD/Prof, even if they entered college with high achievement and high self-esteem. Among the women with PhD/Prof career plans as freshmen, over 40 percent changed their plans to BA/MA during the first year; over 50 percent of those with low achievement or low self-esteem lowered their career plans from PhD/Prof to BA/MA, and over 25 percent of those with high achievement and high self-esteem lowered their career plans to the BA/MA level.

By 1970, when most of the women were graduating, only 19 percent of those who entered with BA/MA career plans and high achivement had changed their career plans to PhD/Prof. Forty percent of those women who entered with PhD/Prof career plans and high achievement changed their plans to BA/MA.

Career plans as freshmen exerted a strong influence among the women with both high achievement and high self-esteem. By 1970, four years after college entrance, only 22 percent of those who entered college with BA/MA career plans planned a PhD/Prof career, compared with 60 percent of those who entered college with PhD/Prof career plans. By 1971, 21 percent of those women with high achievement and high self-esteem but initial plans for a B.A. planned a PhD/Prof career; and only 46 percent of the women who entered college with high achievement, high self-esteem, and PhD/Prof career plans were still planning a PhD/Prof career.

Career plans, achievement, and self-esteem also affect application to and enrollment in graduate school. Planning a PhD/Prof career initially in 1966 had the strongest effect for women with high achievement and high self-esteem. Of the women who entered college with BA/MA career plans, 30 percent applied to graduate school in 1970, and 24 percent enrolled in graduate school in 1971. Of those who entered college with PhD/Prof career plans, 54 percent applied to graduate school in 1970, and 41 percent enrolled in graduate school in 1971. For the women who entered college with high achievement and BA/MA career plans, 40 percent applied to graduate school in 1970 and 29 percent enrolled in graduate school in 1971; for those who entered college with high achievement and PhD/Prof career plans, 61 percent applied to graduate school in 1970, and 46 percent enrolled in graduate school in 1971.

Patterns across time vary for the six groups of women. For the women who entered college with high achievement but low self-esteem, the percentage expressing PhD/Prof career plans rose during the last three years of college, then dropped after college graduation. For the women with high achievement, high self-esteem, and PhD/Prof career plans at college entry, the largest shift to BA/MA career plans was during the first year of college (25 percent), and the smallest change was during the last three years of college (15 percent). For the women who entered college with high achievement, high self-esteem, and BA/MA career plans, the largest increase in shifts to PhD/Prof career plans was during the first year of college (10 percent).

For all groups of women, the changes in intellectual self-esteem were greatest during the first year of college (3-5 percent); over the next three years the changes were very small (no more than 2 percent).

These results indicate that women continue to change their career plans back and forth during the college years. Feldman and Newcomb (1969), and Astin (1977) have concluded that changes in attitudes occur gradually over the college years rather than on first impact. These data seem to show that patterns differ for different students. For women with high achievement and high self-esteem, the first year is most crucial in terms of their career plans and self-esteem; for women with high achievement but low self esteem, the greatest changes occur after the first year of college.

Influences

Tables 13 6 and 13-7 describe the influences of college type and freshman career group on five career outcomes independent of background characteristics. These tables show whether women's achievement and self-esteem and the type of college they attend increase or decrease the probability that the women will pursue a Ph.D. or a professional career.

Stepwise regression analyses were made of five career outcomes. Separate regression analyses were done for the two groups of women with PhD/Prof career plans and BA/MA career plans as freshmen. In the first step of the regression analyses, the background characteristics were entered; in the second step, college characteristics were entered. The results of these regression analyses were reported by Brown (1979b, 1980).

The regression analyses show that the effects for the college-environment variables are different for the two groups of women, indicating that colleges have different effects on different groups of students. These results conflict with Alwin's (1976) conclusions that for men there is no discernible interaction of the college categories with selection and recruitment variables.

A few background variables were significantly related to PhD/Prof

Table 13-6

Effects of College Type and Freshman Career Groups on Career Outcomes Adjusted for Background and Previous Outcomes for Women Who Entered College with BA/MA Career Plans in 1966

College Type	N	PhD/Prof Career Plans in 1967	PhD/Prof Career Plans in 1970	PhD/Prof Career Plans in 1971	Apply to Graduate School in 1970	Enroll in Graduate School in 1971
Low selectivity, public	525ᵃ	-2	-2	+1	-3	+1
Low selectivity, private university	100	+5	-2	-1	-1	-3
Low selectivity, coed nonsectarian	191	0	-3	+1	-3	-3
Low selectivity, coed sectarian	360	0	-1	-2	-4	-3
Low selectivity, women's nonsectarian	75	-1	-4	+1	+7	+2
Low selectivity, women's sectarian	396	0	+3	0	+4	+5
High selectivity, public	101	+3	+3	+1	0	-5
High selectivity, private university	102	-1	+1	-1	+4	-2
High selectivity, coed nonsectarian	45	+9	-1	-9	-3	-5
High selectivity, coed sectarian	56	-2	-4	-7	-9	+3
High selectivity, women's nonsectarian	98	+1	+10	+8	+10	-2
High selectivity, women's sectarian	36	+4	+14	+2	+16	+4
Grand mean	2,085ᵃ	6	13	12	30	24

Freshman Career Group						
BA/MA career plans, low achievement	1273[a]	0	-2	-1	-1	-1
BA/MA career plans, high achievement, low self-esteem	488	0	+2	-1	-1	0
BA/MA career plans, high achievement, high self-esteem	324	0	+7	+5	+3	+5
Grand mean	2,085[a]	6	13	12	30	24
F Probabilities						
Freshman career group		0.991	0.001	0.003	0.467	0.046
College type		0.058	0.006	0.054	0.018	0.249
Interaction		0.063	0.001	0.244	0.350	0.207
Multiple R square		0.039	0.092	0.238	0.116	0.111

Notes: Covariates for PhD/Prof career plans in 1967: ACHNMSC, HSHONORS, NONEP66, DEGPL66, ENGINR66. Covariates for PhD/Prof career plans in 1970: PINCOME, JEWISHR, DEGPL66, TEACHR66, PHDPL67. Covariates for PhD/Prof career plans in 1971: JEWISHR, HSLIBARY, DEGPL66, HEALTH66, PHDPL70. Covariates for Apply to graduate school in 1970: PINCOME, JEWISHR, HSGRADES, DEGPL66, CARPREF. Covariates for Enroll in graduate school in 1971: JEWISHR, DEGPL66, TEACHR66, PHDPL70, CARPREF.
[a]Eliminates eight students who met criteria for sample but whose institution was classified as two-year in 1966.

Table 13-7
Effects of College Type and Freshman Career Groups on Career Outcomes Adjusted for Background and Previous Outcomes for Women Who Entered College with PhD/Prof Career Plans in 1966

College Type	N	PhD/Prof Career Plans in 1967	PhD/Prof Career Plans in 1970	PhD/Prof Career Plans in 1971	Apply to Graduate School in 1970	Enroll in Graduate School in 1971
Low selectivity, public	55	+2	-6	+2	-4	0
Low selectivity, private university	18	+7	+17	-12	-27	-29
Low selectivity, coed nonsectarian	20	+12	-3	-14	-17	-9
Low selectivity, coed sectarian	43	-2	+10	-6	-1	-1
Low selectivity, women's nonsectarian	6	+13	-37	+25	+9	+5
Low selectivity, women's sectarian	63	-5	+2	+1	-4	+5
High selectivity, public	21	-6	-12	-10	-4	+1
High selectivity, private university	40	-4	-10	+9	+17	+14
High selectivity, coed nonsectarian	26	+4	+3	+4	+17	0
High selectivity, coed sectarian	12	+17	+10	-15	-18	+3
High selectivity, women's nonsectarian	26	-4	+6	+13	+9	-8
High selectivity, women's sectarian	7	-7	+12	+11	+32	+1
Grand mean	337	59	52	35	54	41

Freshman Career Group

PhD/Prof career plans, low achievement	119	−9	−8	−1	+1	0
PhD/Prof career plans, high achievement, low self-esteem	72	−9	+10	+1	+1	−2
PhD/Prof career plans, high achievement, high self-esteem	146	+12	+2	+1	−2	+1
Grand Mean	337	59	52	35	54	41
F Probabilities						
Freshman career group		0.001	0.037	0.941	0.878	0.921
College type		0.895	0.186	0.161	0.018	0.338
Interaction		0.297	0.772	0.487	0.290	0.627
Multiple R square		0.216	0.248	0.366	0.244	0.213

Notes: Covariates for PhD/Prof career plans in 1967: POPOC, CATHLICR, STUBRN66, DEGPL66, CARPL66. Covariates for PhD/Prof career plans in 1970: PINCOME, JEWISHR, NONEP66, LAWYER66, PHDPL70. Covariates for PhD/Prof career plans in 1971: JEWISHR, HSHONORS, DEGPL66, DOCTOR66, PHDPL70. Covariates for Apply to graduate school in 1970: JEWISHR, DEGPL66, DOCTOR66, GPA67, CARPREF. Covariates for Enroll in graduate school in 1971: ARTSTI66, DOCTOR66, CARXPECT, CUMGPA70, PHDPL70.

career plans for both groups of women with initial plans for PhD/Prof careers or BA/MA careers. The significant variables include achievement measured on college-entrance exams; being Jewish; preferring no religion as a college freshman; and higher initial degree plans (M.A. versus B.A. or M.D. versus Ph.D. versus LL.B.). These variables had stronger effects on women's career outcomes than did the usual measures of socioeconomic status, such as father's and mother's occupation and parents' income.

For women who entered college with BA/MA career plans, achievement had a strong impact on career plans during the first year of college but was no longer significant after college experiences such as grades and participation in honors programs were controlled. Attitudes and behaviors at the end of college were more strongly related to career plans at the end of college than were characteristics measured when the women entered college. Degree plans and self-esteem at college entrance continued to be significantly related to career plans, even after the women left college.

Grades in high school and college had significant effects on whether women applied to graduate school, although they did not affect women's career plans significantly. The traditional socioeconomic measures of mother's education and parents' income were also significant determinants of whether these women applied to graduate school, as was being Jewish.

During the first year of college, women who entered college with BA/MA career plans were less likely to raise their career plants in large, unselective public colleges and in relatively small departments within colleges. They were more likely to raise their plans if they were in colleges with more faculty with Ph.D.'s. By the end of college women were more likely to raise their career plans from BA/MA to PhD/Prof and apply to and enroll in graduate school if they attended selective women's colleges and unselective sectarian women's colleges.

For women who entered college with PhD/Prof career plans, being Jewish or Catholic was a significant factor in maintaining their high career plans. Also significant were being stubborn or self-critical and having high self-esteem. Planning not to marry was also significant. After the first year of college the significant effects on women's career outcomes were for experiences and attitudes developed during college: career plans and career expectations, participation in honors programs and grades, interests in status and recognition, and marriage.

Women who entered college with PhD/Prof career plans were more likely to apply to graduate school if they attended liberal colleges and were more likely to apply to and enroll in graduate school if they were in relatively large departments within colleges—that is, in major fields where a large percentage of the students were concentrated. Astin (1977) found positive effects for this variable on career outcomes; he interpreted this finding as the effect of other students' pursuit of the same career objectives.

The analyses in tables 13–6 and 13–7 are based on two-way analysis of covariance. The two factors studied were college type and freshman career group. Five career outcomes were analyzed—PhD/Prof career plans in 1967, 1970, and 1971 (one, four, and five years after college entrance); whether women applied to graduate school in the fall of 1970; and whether women were enrolled in graduate school in 1971. In each of the five analyses, five variables were covaried, including background characteristics and previous career plans. The choice of the covariates was determined from the regression analyses on the two groups of women with PhD/Prof or BA/MA career plans as freshmen. Previous career outcomes as well as background characteristics were covaried to measure changes in career plans over time. In these tables the effects of freshman career group and college type are measured as deviations from the total percentage for each outcome. The figures in tables 13–6 and 13–7 can be interpreted as the difference between the percentage of women in a particular group attaining that career outcome and the percentage of women in the total sample attaining the outcome. For example, an effect of − 2 in table 13–6 for low-selective, public institutions can be interpreted to mean that 2 percent *fewer* women in these institutions had PhD/Prof career plans in 1967 than the 6 percent (grand mean) for the total group of women who initially planned a BA/MA career when they entered college; this effect represents a difference in outcomes for women who have been statistically matched through regression analysis on achievement (ACHNMSC), number of high school honors (HSHONORS), preference for no religion as freshmen (NONEP66), degree plans as freshmen (DEGPL66), and career plans in engineering as freshmen (ENGINR66). The variables are operationally defined in appendix 13A. An effect of + 10 in table 13–6 for highly selective women's colleges, on the other hand, indicates that 10 percent *more* women in these colleges planned a PhD/Prof career after four years of college, compared with the percentage of women with similar backgrounds and freshman degree and career plans across all colleges.

Table 13–6 summarizes the effects of college type and freshman career group for women who entered college with BA/MA career plans. This table shows that women in selective women's colleges were more likely to raise their career plans from BA/MA to PhD/Prof during college; women in women's colleges were also more likely to apply to graduate school immediately after college graduation.

Women with both high achievement and high self-esteem were more likely to raise their career plans from BA/MA to PhD/Prof and more likely to apply to graduate school and enroll in graduate school.

Table 13–7 presents the effects of the twelve college types and the six freshman career groups for women who entered college with PhD/Prof career plans. Although the actual differences between the groups are quite large, these differences are not statistically significant. The lack of significance is due in part to the small size of the sample.

Women's colleges have positive effects on women's career plans and on applying to graduate school. Women in relatively unselective private universities were less likely to apply to graduate school and to enroll in graduate school immediately after college, but more likely to express PhD/Prof career plans in 1970.

Women with both high achievement and high self-esteem continued to maintain their PhD/Prof career plans. Women with high achievement and low self-esteem lowered their career plans during the first year, but then raised them to the PhD/Prof level after the freshmen year.

Influences, by College Type

In general, these analyses do not show consistent college-environment effects on women's career outcomes. Across groups, women in large, relatively *unselective public institutions*—the largest group of women—were slightly less likely to have high career plans and to apply to graduate school. Across groups, women in large, relatively *unselective private universities* were slightly more likely to express PhD/Prof career plans while they were in college but were less likely actually to apply to graduate school or to enroll in graduate school immediately after college graduation.

Women in relatively *unselective nonsectarian coed colleges* who entered with BA/MA career plans were slightly less likely than average to raise their career plans or attend graduate school. Women who entered these colleges with PhD/Prof career plans lowered them by five years out and were less likely to apply to or enroll in graduate school. Women who entered relatively *unselective sectarian coed colleges* with BA/MA career plans were less likely to apply to graduate school four years later. Otherwise, women in these colleges fared close to the average.

Women in relatively *unselective women's colleges* were no more likely or unlikely to change their career aspirations during college, but women in these colleges were more likely to apply to graduate school and enroll in graduate school four and five years later.

Women with BA/MA career plans who entered *selective large public institutions* were less likely to enroll in graduate school five years later; women who entered selective public institutions with PhD/Prof career plans were more likely to lower them by four and five years later. Women with PhD/Prof career plans in large *selective private universities* were more likely to apply to and attend graduate school and to express PhD/Prof career plans in 1971, five years after college entry.

Women who entered *selective nonsectarian coed colleges* with BA/MA career plans were more likely to raise them briefly on college entry, but by five years later they were less likely to have PhD/Prof career plans and less likely to be enrolled in graduate school. Women who entered selective non-sectarian coed colleges with PhD/Prof career plans were more likely to maintain them through college and to apply to graduate school, but no less likely to attend graduate school five years after college entry. Women in *selective sectarian coed colleges* who entered college with BA/MA career plans were slightly less likely to raise their career plans to the PhD/Prof level and to apply to graduate school, but they were no less likely to be enrolled in graduate school. Women who entered selective sectarian coed colleges were more likely to maintain their PhD/Prof career plans during college, but after college they were less likely to plan a PhD/Prof career and apply to graduate school, although they were no less likely to be enrolled in graduate school.

Selective women's colleges have generally positive effects on women's career outcomes. Women who entered selective women's colleges were more likely to have PhD/Prof career plans after four years of college and more likely to apply to graduate school. Their early plans and graduate-school enrollment were not much different from the average, once previous plans were controlled. These results are consistent for both groups of women who entered college with BA/MA career plans and PhD/Prof career plans.

Discussion

These analyses lead to some tentative conclusions about the college characteristics that influence women's career choice. The methodology used in this study affects our interpretation of the results. This is a descriptive study of differences in outcomes for women with different college experiences and different initial career plans. These data do not show a causal relationship between college environments and women's career plans; the data do not prove that college environments cause women to change their career plans or maintain their initially high career plans. These methodological problems are discussed by Spady (1976) and by Astin and Panos (1969). Withey (1971) has pointed to the inherent difficulty in analyzing the environmental impact of a natural process whereby people are selecting environments that in turn have effects on them.

When background and previous outcomes are controlled, the strongest college effects are for selective women's colleges. Women in selective women's colleges, regardless of their initial career plans, seem more likely to express PhD/Prof career plans at the end of college and more likely to apply to graduate school immediately after college graduation. These effects are strongest for women with high achievement. Women in selective sectarian coed colleges seem less likely to express PhD/Prof career plans at the end of college and less likely to apply to graduate school immediately after college graduation. In many ways these two types of colleges are alike: they are both small and selective; they are both perceived as academically competitive; they are both perceived as climates where the faculty are concerned about the students. They differ mainly in the percentage of women students and women faculty and in whether they are perceived as liberal, permissive climates. Astin (1971) also found that the climate in women's colleges was distinctively "cooperative."

The lack of stability in college effects on women's career outcomes is somewhat disconcerting. Some generalizations can be made, but results for one group at one time are not clearly replicated at other times or for other groups. The data do seem to indicate, however, that the effects of college type are different for different groups of college women. Future research should focus on identifying the characteristics of women's colleges that facilitate women's career plans. It is possible that climates similar to those in women's colleges can be provided in other types of institutions through subenvironments such as women's studies programs.

Note

1. This study is reported in greater detail in Brown (1979a, b, 1980).

Bibliography

Alexander, K., and Eckland, B.K. *Effects of Education on the Social Mobility of High School Sophomores Fifteen Years Later (1955–1970).* Chapel Hill: Institute for Research in Social Science, University of North Carolina, 1973.
———. "Sex Differences in the Educational Attainment Process." *American Sociological Review* 39 (1974):668–682.
Alwin, D.F. "Socioeconomic Background, Colleges, and Post-Collegiate Achievement." In W. Sewell, R. Hauser, and D. Featherman, eds., *Schooling and Achievement in American Society.* New York: Academic Press, 1976.
Astin, A.W. *The College Environment.* Washington, D.C.: American Council on Education, 1971.
———. *Four Critical Years.* San Francisco: Jossey-Bass, 1977.
Astin, A.W., et al. *National Norms for Entering College Freshmen: Fall 1966.* Washington, D.C.: American Council on Education, 1967.
———. *National Norms for Entering College Freshmen: Fall 1970.* Washington, D.C.: American Council on Education, 1970.

————. *The American Freshman: National Norms for Fall 1976*. Los Angeles: Laboratory for Research in Higher Education, Graduate School of Education, University of California, 1976.

————. *The American Freshman: National Norms for Fall 1980*. Los Angeles: Laboratory for Research in Higher Education, Graduate School of Education, University of California, 1980.

Astin, A.W., and Panos, R.J. *The Educational and Vocational Development of College Students*. Washington, D.C.: American Council on Education, 1969.

Astin, H.S. "Stability and Change in the Career Plans of Ninth Grade Girls." *Personnel and Guidance Journal* 46 (1968):961–969.

Astin, H.S., and Bisconti, A. *Career Plans of College Graduates of 1965 and 1970*. Bethlehem, Pa.: College Placement Council Foundation, 1974.

Bayer, A.E. "Life Plans and Marriage Age: An Application of Path Analysis." *Journal of Marriage and the Family* 31 (1969a):551–558.

————. "Marriage Plans and Educational Aspirations." *American Journal of Sociology* 75 (1969b):239–244.

Brown, M.D. "How Family Background and Institutional Environments Affect Career Aspirations of College Women." Paper presented at the Annual Meeting of the American Educational Research Association, March 1978.

————. "Independent and Interaction Effects of Significant Institutional Variables on the Career Aspirations of College Women." Paper presented at the Annual Meeting of the American Education Research Association, April 1979a.

————. "Career Plans of College Women: Patterns and Influences." Paper presented at the Research Conference on Educational Environments and the Undergraduate Woman, Wellesley College, September 1979b.

————. "The Effects of Background and College Environment on the Career Plans of College Women." Ed.D. diss., Harvard University, 1980.

Christian, C.E. "Patterns of College Experience: The Empirical Typology of Students and College Interaction." Ph.D. diss., University of California, Los Angeles, 1978.

Davis, J.A. *Great Aspirations: The Graduate School Plans of America's College Seniors*. Chicago: Aldine, 1964.

————. *Undergraduate Career Decisions: Correlates of Occupational Choice*. Chicago: Aldine, 1965.

El-Khawas, E., and Bisconti, A.S. *Educational and Career Progress: 1971 Followup of College Freshmen of 1961 and 1966*. Washington, D.C.: American Council on Education and Center for Human Services, 1973.

Feldman, K.A., and Newcomb, T.M. *The Impact of College on Students*, vol. 1. San Francisco: Jossey-Bass, 1969.

Flanagan, J.C.; Shaycoft, F.F.; Richards, J.M., Jr.; and Claudy, J.G. *Five Years After High School*. Palo Alto: American Institutes for Research, 1971.

Folger, J.K.; Astin, H.S.; and Bayer, A.E., eds. *Human Resources and Higher Education*. New York: Russell Sage Foundation, 1970.

Jencks, C.: Smith, M.; Acland, H.; Bane, M.J.; Cohen, D.; Gintis, H.; Heyns, B.; and Michelson, S. *Inequality: A Reassessment of the Effect of Family and School in America*. New York: Basic Books, 1972.

Jencks, C., et al. *Who Gets Ahead? The Determinants of Economic Success in America*. New York: Basic Books, 1979.

Sewell, W.H., and Shah, V.P. "Socioeconomic Status, Intelligence, and the Attainment of Higher Education." *Sociology of Education* 40 (1967):1–23.

Spady, W.G. "The Impact of School Resources on Students." In W. Sewell, R. Hauser, and D. Featherman, eds., *Schooling and Achievement in American Society*. New York: Academic Press, 1976.

Withey, S.B. *A Degree and What Else? Correlates and Consequences of a College Education*. Carnegie Commission on Higher Education. New York: McGraw-Hill, 1971.

Appendix 13A

A brief description of the 100 variables analyzed in this study follows. The background variables and outcome variables are described further by Astin et al. (1967); Christian (1978); and Astin (1971, 1977). The measures of attitudes and college involvent are described by Christian (1978). The college variables were obtained from the Higher Education General Information Survey (HEGIS) and by aggregating the UCLA data. The Inventory of College Activities (ICA) factors are described by Astin (1971).

Background

POPOC	Father's occupation coded on the Duncan scale
POPED	Father's education in years
MOMED	Mother's education in years
PINCOME	Parents' income in thousands of dollars
CATHLICR	Religion in which you were reared—Catholic = 1; else = 0
JEWISHR	Religion in which you were reared—Jewish = 1; else = 0
HOMSOUTH	Home—South = 1; else = 0
HOMFARM	Home—Farm = 1; else = 0
ACHNMSC	Achievement test scores converted to National Merit scale
HSGRADES	High-school grades converted to 4.0 scale
HSHONORS	Number of high-schools honors—National Merit, honor society
HSSCIENC	Number of high-school science awards—science award, National Science Foundation summer school
HSLIBRARY	Studied in library, checked out a book (sum: 0 = not at all . . . 4 = frequently)

Career Plans in 1966

DEGL66	Degree plans in 1966 in years
CARPL66	Career plans in 1966 coded on Duncan scale
PHDPL66	PhD/Prof in 1966—humanities or science Ph.D., doctor, lawyer = 1

331

HEALTH66	BA/MA career plans in health in 1966 = 1; else = 0
TEACHR66	BA/MA career plans in teaching in 1966 = 1; else = 0
BUSNES66	BA/MA career plans in business or farming = 1; else = 0
ENGENR66	BA/MA career plans in engineering = 1; else = 0
HUMPHD66	PhD/Prof career plans in humanities PhD = 1; else = 0
SCHIPD66	PhD/Prof career plans in science PhD = 1; else = 0
LAWYER66	PhD/Prof career plans as lawyer = 1; else = 0
DOCTOR66	PhD/Prof career plans as doctor = 1; else = 0

Attitudes and Plans

INTLSE__	Average percentile in intellectual, academic, and mathematical ability; 1966, 1970
MARRY66	Chances of marrying within one year after college—some or very good = 1
NONEP__	Present religious preference—none = 1; else = 0; 1966, 1970
LIBRAL__	Liberal, nonconservative—1 = lowest 10 percent . . . 5 = highest 10 percent; 1966, 1970

The following four variables were coded as follows: 1 = not important, 2 = somewhat important, 3 = very important, 4 = essential (1966 and 1970):

ARTSTI__	Artistic interests—writing original work, creating artistic work
BUSI__	Business interests—being well off financially, successful in own business
STATUS__	Status interests—becoming authority in field, obtaining recognition
ALTRSM__	Altruism—helping others, participating in Peace Corps

The following two variables were coded as follows: 1 = lowest 10 percent, 2 = below average, 3 = average, 4 = above average, 5 = highest 10 percent (1966, 1970):

STUBRN__	Stubborness, defensiveness, sensitivity to criticism
IPERSE__	Interpersonal self-esteem self-rating

College Types

PUBHI	Selectivity—SATV + M GE 1100, public
UHI	Selectivity—SATV + M GE 1100, university
NSECCOHI	Selectivity—SATV + M GE 1100, Nonsectarian, coed
SECCOHI	Selectivity—SATV + M GE 1100, sectarian, coed
NSECSSHI	Selectivity—SATV + M GE 1100, nonsectarian, women's
SECSSHI	Selectivity—SATV + M GE 1100, sectarian, women's
PUBLO	Selectivity—SATV + M LT 1100, public
ULO	Selectivity—SATV + M LT 1100, university
NSECCOLO	Selectivity—SATV + M LT 1100, nonsectarian, coed
SECCOLO	Selectivity—SATV + M LT 1100, sectarian, coed
NSECSSLO	Selectivity—SATV + M LT 1100, nonsectarian, women's
SECSSLO	Selectivity—SATV + M LT 1100, sectarian, women's

College Characteristics

SLECTVTY	Average SAT V + M
AFFLUENC	Education and general expenditures/enrollment
CSIZE	Size of college in thousands
PCTFACWM	Percentage faculty women
PCTFACPH	Percentage faculty Ph.D.
PCTBAWMN	Percentage B.A.'s awarded to women
PCTBAFLD	Percentage B.A.'s awarded in student's major field area

ICA College Factor Scores

ICAACAD	Pressure for grades, competition for grades, high-caliber students
ICALIB	Checked out books, studied in library
ICAFFAC	Knowing instructor's name, being in instructor's home, office
ICADNCRN	Warm, students not lost, not numbers in a book
ICASWORK	Students regularly employed during school
ICACARUN	Students change major field, change long-term career plans

ICALIBRL   Liberal, informal class manner, not Victorian
ICASNOB   Snobbish, not practical-minded, not realistic
ICASOCAL   Social, social life, personal contact with class-
                mates

Interactions of Student and College Characteristics

HIACHSSS   High-achievement students in selective women's
                colleges = 1; else = 0
HIACHSEL   high-achievement students in selective colleges =
                1; else = 0
HISESEL   High self-esteem students in selective colleges = 1;
                else = 0
CATHCATH   Catholic students in catholic colleges = 1; else =
                0
PROTPROT   Protestant students in Protestant colleges = 1;
                else = 0

College Involvement

INHONORS   Participated in a general or department honors
                program
INRESRCH   Assisted professor's research, independent re-
                search, lab assistant
INFRAT   Active member of a sorority = 1; else = 0.
LCAMPS66   Lived on campus freshman year = 1; else = 0

Satisfaction

OVALLSAT   Overall satisfaction with college in 1970 (1 = very
                satisfactory, 2 = unsatisfactory, 3 = satisfac-
                tory, 4 = good, 5 = excellent)

College Grades

GPA67   Freshman GPA in 1967 converted to 4.0 scale
CUMGPA70   Cumulative GOA in 1970 converted to 4.0 scale

Career Plans in 1967, 1970, 1971

CARPREF	Prefer employment to housewife = 1; housewife, occasional employment = 0
CARXPECT	Expect full-time employment = 1; expect housewife = 0
PHDPL67	PhD/Prof career plans in 1967 = 1; else = 0
PHDPL70	PhD/Prof career plans in 1970 = 1; else = 0
PHDPL71	PhD/Prof career plans in 1971 = 1; else = 0

Career Outcomes

APPLGS 70	Applied to graduate school in 1970 = 1; else = 0
ENRLGS 71	Enrolled in graduate school in 1971 = 1; else = 0

Marriage and Children in 1967, 1970, 1971

MARRYD	Married = 1; else = 0 1967, 1970, 1971
CHILDN71	One or more children in 1971 = 1; else = 0

14

Career Commitment of Female College Graduates: Conceptualization and Measurement Issues

Denise Del Vento Bielby

The dramatic changes in size and composition of the female labor force that began nearly four decades ago are now well documented. More women than ever before are either in the labor force or in preparation for entry into it. Nearly 90 percent of all women can expect to be employed at some point in their lives, and the proportion of women seeking post-high-school education is greater than ever (Davis and Bumpass 1976; Samuelson 1977). It is expected that these seemingly irreversible changes in women's labor-force participation will eventually have an equal impact on both sex-role behavior and attitudes (see Mason, Czajka, and Arber 1976).

Most social scientists now also agree that because of these changes, women have added a work cycle to their normative configuration of the life course (Perun and Bielby 1981), so that their historically central responsibility to the family is but one of several major activities in their life span (Van Dusen and Sheldon 1976). Consequently, social scientists have begun to raise questions about the actual degree of female involvement with the work cycle. The question is now being approached by members of several disciplines, with most of the inquiry devoted to an examination of social-structural influences on career commitment. Demographers and economists searching for more definitive answers have focused primarily on women's labor-market supply, including women's decisions to enter the labor force and to withdraw from it; their decisions about where to work and the number of hours they choose to work; and , more recently, women's decisions to make human-capital investments both before and after entry into the labor force (Sweet 1973; Mincer and Polachek 1974). Sociologists have directed

This chapter is a revised and expanded version of the paper presented at the National Institute of Education Research Conference on Educational Environments and the Undergraduate Woman, held at Wellesley College, Wellesley, Massachusetts, 13–15 September 1979. The author wishes to acknowledge the encouragement of Jane A. Piliavin and Diane Papalia-Finlay during the preliminary stages of this work. That work was supported by a Graduate School Grant from the University of Wisconsin–Madison. The helpful comments of William T. Bielby and James C. Hearn during its subsequent development are greatly appreciated.

their attention to the structural and technological aspects of work settings that shape opportunities for socioeconomic success (Kanter 1977). Others have focused on particular features of the occupational structure, including the impact of sex composition on training and entry into traditionally male-dominated, or sex-atypical, fields and work settings (Bielby 1978a; McIllwee 1980; Leuptow 1981). Male-dominated fields typically demand larger and more prolonged personal investments on the part of the individual and on the part of those who control access to these fields through testing, training, and other screening devices. Women who find themselves in career tracks are expected to be as committed to the job as their male counterparts. Thus one would expect more dedication to the job among women as their career choices and involvements change.

There is, however, only a small body of research on individual differences in the subjective dispositions that influence the work involvement of women. Laws has asserted that ". . . the topic of women's occupational aspiration and the related vicissitudes of work motivation during the working history has gotten short shrift from the scholarly community" (1976, p. 34). Five years later, it is still true that very little is known about this aspect of female career behavior. Existing evidence suggests that labor-force attachment is both temporary and goal directed to many, whereas for an increasing number of others the involvement is a distinct entree to the career cycle (see Laws 1979, p. 20). Beyond this point, most studies of individual dispositions are not very informative because they have been influenced by widely accepted myths about women and career commitment. The subjective career disposition of women has typically been evaluated by social scientists against a male criterion of career commitment, which according to Laws, is in itself "an undefined but honorific term usually associated with the myth of the heroic male professional" (1976, p. 36). In general, women evaluated against this criterion are seen as less career committed. Consequently, there has been little exploration beyond this of extrinsic sources of their commitment. As a result, research in this area is influenced by what Laws (1976) refers to as the myth of "female motivational deficit"—the assumption that women lack career commitment. The results of studies generated by this myth only reinforce it in turn.

Given the hypothesized importance of individual differences in career commitment for explaining changes in female labor-force behavior, it is surprising that we know so little about the relative importance and function of subjective investment in the job among women as they train for and enter the occupational career. Early in their employment history young women must reconcile their personal commitments with structural opportunities and constraints. Presumably, this is an extended process that involves balancing personal acceptance of the idea of a career with the limits of one's aspirations. Clearly, an important contribution to this area can be made by analyzing the continuity of intrinsic career commitment in young-adult women.

We must meet several objectives in order to make a valid contribution to this area of inquiry. First, the explanation we seek should capture the temporal as well as the situational determinants of women's career commitment. Thus a causal model based on longitudinal data should be specified in order to analyze women's subjective investment with a career. As an analytic approach, causal modeling identifies the relative relationships among time-organized independent variables, which, in turn, explain the dependent variable of interest. A causal model is therefore ideally suited for analysis of data collected over time. To explain career commitment adequately, such a model should include proximal and distal life experiences that are antecedents to it, subsequent determinants of it that occur during investments in education and on-the-job training, and factors affecting its status during the early career. For example, maternal employment is known to be an antecedent to the career salience of women; and since career sex atypicality is a problematic phenomenon in women's continuous career involvement, it should also affect their career commitment (Bielby 1978a, b).

Specifying such a model presumes the existence of a well-defined and clearly operationalized measure of career commitment. At present none exists, and until we have an acceptable measure of career commitment, completion of the first objective is beyond the scope of this chapter. However, resolution can be achieved in stages, the first being clarification of the conceptualization and measurement of subjective investment in the career. The purpose of this chapter, then, is to complete the initial task in specifying a causal model of women's subjective investment with a career by reviewing theoretical and methodological issues in intrinsic career commitment among women.

Issues in Conceptualization and Measurement

Most social scientists who study career commitment agree on its conceptual definition. Commitment to the career is a subjective investment in or overall attachment to an occupation. According to Kanter (1977, p. 256), commitment "seems clearly tied to the increasing rewards and chance for growth implied in high opportunity." Because commitment is closely tied to the existence of an opportunity structure, Kanter continues, the expectations for future rewards such as job mobility, growth, or increased status are essential for commitment to exist. Kanter also notes that career commitment is quite different from job satisfaction, which is the outcome of immediate material rewards or other job attributes. Thus, depending on the phase of the career cycle, it is possible for job satisfaction to be low at a time when career commitment is high, and vice versa. Furthermore, commitment can be expected to develop or increase as a function of accrued investments in a career. According to Becker (1960), once an individual realizes the impact on his or her life of previous involvement with and expectations from an opportunity structure, those previous involvements heighten a sense of attachment to the occupation. The outcome is a consistent line of activity over a period of time (Becker 1960).

Despite the clarity evident in the conceptual definition of career commitment, operational definitions are almost as numerous as are studies of it. Most research has operationalized career saliency relative to the saliency of other commitments and measured it in one of two ways: either as labor-force participation per se, or as a social-psychological indicator of intent to engage in paid employment instead of or in addition to homemaking.

When a career commitment is operationalized as labor-force participation, the pattern of behavior—that is, length and continuity of labor-force participation—is the focus of analysis. There are, however, three problems with this approach. First, this operationalization asumes that a psychological attachment to work exists by virtue of the presence of labor-force activity. For women in particular, this assumption is problematic. Women's work activity is typically marked by gaps for childbearing and child rearing or is interrupted by the geographic mobility of a socially mobile spouse. In short, whether or not a woman is in the labor force tells us little about her career commitment.

Second, measuring career commitment as presence in the labor force ignores assessment of career commitment during those gaps in participation. As Becker has noted: "A person remaining in the same occupation may engage in many kinds of activity in the course of his [sic] career. The diverse activities are seen by the actor as activities which, whatever their external diversity, serve him in pursuit of the same goal" (1960, p. 33). Thus, to an outside observer, an activity viewed in isolation at one point in time reveals nothing about the significance of that activity to the individual.

Third, analyzing labor-force behavior as commitment leaves women's motivations for working unanalyzed. Some married women work because of intermittent financial needs of the household; when those needs are satisfied, they are likely to withdraw from the labor force. It is presumptuous to assume that these women are career committed in the same way as are women who have long-term investments in their careers.

It is clear that career commitment has social-psychological components and that simple behavioral operationalizations such as labor-force participation are inadequate for analysis of it. However, mere use of a social-psychological measure does not guarantee solution of the problems associated with its operationalization. Several operationalizations exist, each with a different name. As a group they tend to be inappropriately linked to the concept and inconsistent with one another. Typical measures of career commitment range, for example, from women's intention to enter the labor force, to expressed desire to work independent of actual circumstances (Sobol 1963; Fogarty, Rapoport, and Rapoport 1971; Haller and Rosenmayer 1971; Richardson 1974). The problematic validity of many of the assessments in this group renders consideration of reliablity difficult. Consequently, it is hard to make any conclusive statements about women's career commitment from these studies.

An additional point must be made about social-psychological measures before our discussion of the limitations of current career-commitment operationalizations is complete. The underlying assumption in early definitions of career commitment is that the concept represents an enduring behavioral disposition that is stable over time. However, it is generally impossible to determine the stability of a concept completely without longitudinal empirical evidence. Nearly all existing research on career commitment is based on cross-sectional studies that simply *assume* the stability over time of individual differences in career commitment. Therefore, any stability that is presumed to exist is particularly problematic, given the extant weakness of individual operationalizations and their diversity. If our ultimate goal is specifying a causal model of career commitment—one that identifies and assesses the relative determinants of it at each stage in the life course—we must satisfy or at least acknowledge the problems noted here.

Thus the major problem with previous research on career commitment is the correspondence between the definition of the concept and the indicators used to measure it. In many instances the measures are of questionable validity, as, for example, in the case of measuring labor-force participation. However, there may be more than one reasonably valid operationalization of the concept, as, for example, with some of the social-psychological measures; but not all such operationalizations will be equally reliable. When no one indicator is both perfectly reliable and completely valid, multiple indicators are necessary to assess the properties of the underlying concept. This is particularly true in the secondary analysis of existing data sets, where the researcher has no control over either the operationalization or the methods of measurement.

The secondary analysis that follows is the outcome of just such a situation. Career commitment among college-educated women is examined empirically with a survey originally designed nearly two decades ago and with data collected from 1961 to 1968. The particular issue to be examined is the correspondence between the stability of career commitment, as implied by its definition as an investment and as measured in these data by multiple social-psychological indicators.

Data and Methodology

Data analyzed for this study were collected as part of a larger study conducted by the National Opinion Research Center (NORC) on a representative sample of the June 1961 college graduating class. Through self-administered questionnaires, the future plans of college seniors were assessed in 1961; then these individuals were followed up for each of the next three years, 1962, 1963, 1964. A fifth assessment was conducted in 1968, seven years after college graduation.

The universe for NORC's 1961 College Graduating Class Study was limited to all college students who completed requirements for a baccalaureate degree during the spring 1961 term and who received such degrees at the end of the term from an eligible institution of higher learning. The university excludes graduates of a five-year first professional degree. A two-stage probability sample was drawn from this universe. In the first stage, 135 schools were selected from the 1,039 eligible institutions. In the second stage, a sample of each institution's prospective graduates was drawn, yielding an N of 41,116. The sample for the final assessment in 1968 was based on the 20,254 respondents who had replied to all four previous assessments. A 30-percent subsample of these respondents was drawn, yielding a sample of 6,005 potential respondents. Of these respondents, 81 percent, or 4,868 men and women, returned usable questionnaires. All white females who responded to the 1968 questionnaire, who were under 30 years of age at graduation, and who were married by the fourth assessment made up the sample for the present analysis, yielding a sample of 1,070. These criteria eliminated nonwhites, single, and older women who are likely to have substantially different career patterns from the typical female college graduate who is educated, married, and embarks on a career in early adulthood. For example, we know on the basis of results reported elsewhere (Bielby 1975) that single female college graduates—a particularly "deviant" group in the early 1960s—are typically more continuously career committed because it is a less problematic involvement for them. Presumably they are more stable in their attitudes and will remain so.

Several measures of career commitment were used, one with apparent face validity and others with less (see table 14-1 for a detailed presentation of the variables and their codes). The more face-valid measure, assessed by the question, "Which of the following do you expect to give you the most satisfaction in life?" was assessed in 1962, one year after graduation from college (CC62); two years later, in 1964 (CC64); and again in 1968 (CC68). Two response categories were analyzed: career or occupation, or all other pursuits.

Other measures, presumed to be social-psychological indicators of career commitment, were also assessed in 1962 and 1964. In 1962 respon-

Table 14-1
Variables, Mnemonics, and Variable Codes

Variable	Mnemonic	Code
Career commitment (assessed in 1962, 1964, 1968)	CC62, CC64, CC68	Primary satisfaction from career or occupation = 1 From other pursuits = 0
Career preferences and expectations in 1962	CPR62, CEXP62	Housewife only = 1 Housewife now, employment later = 2 Housewife with occasional employment = 3 Combining housewife with employment = 4 Employment only = 5
Importance of a home in ten years (assessed in 1964)	TH64	Very important = 1 Somewhat important = 2 Not very important = 3 Not at all important = 4
Importance of a career in ten years (assessed in 1964)	TC64	Very important = 4 Somewhat important = 3 Not very important = 2 Not at all important = 1
Work expectations with young, grown children (assessed in 1964)	WK64, WG64	Full-time = 4 Part-time = 3 Do not expect to work = 2 Don't know = 1

dents were asked, "In the long run, which one of the following do you really prefer?" (CPR62), and "Which one do you realistically expect?" (CEXP62). Respondents chose one answer from the following possibilities: housewife only, several different patterns for combining housewife with employment, or employment alone. In 1964, respondents were asked to imagine how they would rate the importance in ten years of taking care of home (TH64) and of work or career (TC64). Respondents were also asked in 1964 the amount of time, if any, they expect to be working when their youngest child is between 6 and 12 years of age (WK64) and after their children are all working or married (WG64).

Results

Table 14-2 presents the zero-order correlation coefficients of the multiple indicators of career commitment that have been measured at three points in time. Should we look no further, the observed correlations, taken at face

Table 14–2
Zero-Order Correlation Coefficients, Means, and Standard Deviations of Multiple Indicators of Career Commitment among Female College Graduates

	CC62	CPR62	CEXP62	CC64	TH64	TC64	WK64	WG64	CC68
CC62	1.00								
CPR62	.174	1.00							
CEXP62	.121	.446	1.00						
CC64	.048	.277	.234	1.00					
TH64	.119	.114	.078	.055	1.00				
TC64	.206	.163	.097	.043	.150	1.00			
WK64	.039	.220	.107	.168	.206	.142	1.00		
WG64	.107	.349	.287	.385	.169	.135	.238	1.00	
CC68	.015	.304	.184	.439	.036	.046	.147	.371	1.00
X	0.038	2.602	2.673	0.048	1.233	2.765	2.647	2.814	0.056
S.D.	0.191	1.193	1.213	0.214	0.456	0.928	0.972	1.293	0.229

Note: N = 897. Analyses were conducted on only those cases in the sample of 1,070 with no missing data (listwise deletion).

value, seem to indicate that the stability of career commitment among these women is low. No time-lagged correlation is greater than .44, and most are much smaller. The most surprising result is that measures (CC62, CC64, CC68), which are closest in correspondence to the definition of career commitment, have low time-lagged coefficients. Were we to terminate our investigation here, we would have to conclude on the basis of this entire set of correlation coefficients that the career commitment is a transient phenomenon in the typical college-educated woman in early adulthood. That is, career commitment among typical female college graduates is virtually nonexistent. If present a year after college graduation, it does not persist over the next few years.

There is, however, an alternative interpretation of these results. The low correlations among multiple measures at a given point in time (1962 or 1964) also suggest that they are poor indicators of an underlying, unobserved concept. More specifically, even when what has been measured corresponds with the construct, measurement of that construct can be less than perfect. The analytic task becomes one of separating the unreliability due to poor measurement from the component shared by each measure; only then can the stability of the common component over time be assessed. Our analysis hypothesizes that there is an unobservable commitment that underlies the observable indicators but is imperfectly measured by any given indicator.

The results of this investigation using confirmatory factor analysis are presented in figure 14-1.[1] With just one indicator in 1968 (CC68), it was necessary to assume that its reliability equaled the reliability of the corresponding indicator in 1964 (CC64) in order to identify the model. As observed in figure 14-1, when the unreliability due to imperfect measurement is accounted for, the stability of individual differences in the underlying concept is quite high. Career commitment one year beyond college graduation (CC62) is correlated .60 with career commitment three years after graduation (CC64) and .81 with commitment seven years later (CC68). Commitment three years beyond graduation (CC64) is correlated .80 with commitment in 1968 (CC68). These findings are consistent with the definition of career commitment as a stable concept and support its measurement through a multiple-indicators approach. Furthermore, they seem to show that despite a period of less stability within three years of graduation, the original individual differences tend to be restored within seven years after graduation.

This model also tests the adequacy of the measures used here. It is surprising that the indicators that assess the primary source of satisfaction in life (CC62, CC64, CC68), and that are assumed to have the most face validity—that is, the closest correspondence with the definition of career commitment—had the lowest reliability relative to the other indicators. Reli-

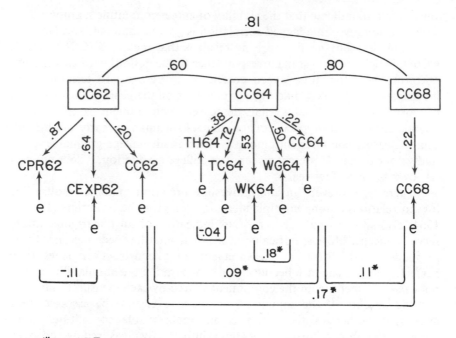

*p ≤ .05

Note: A complete description of variable mnemonics is presented in table 14–1.

Figure 14–1. Confirmatory Factor Analysis of Multiple Indicators of
Career Commitment among Female College Graduates

ability coefficients—that is, squared correlations between observed and true
components—hovered between .04 and .05 for these indicators, whereas the
others ranged from modest to quite large. This may be due in part to the
dichotomous measurement of CC62, CC64, and CC68. These dichotomous
measures classify women as either committed or not, whereas the other indicators differentiate among degrees of commitment.

The presence of statistically significant correlated errors among the
face-valid career-commitment measures indicates that they contain a common source of variation not shared with the other indicators. This could be
due to systematic response errors over time, but with such long intervals
between measurements it is more likely that the correlated errors reflect a
substantive source of variation unique to these indicators. It is, however,
encouraging to note that at the same time the most reliable indicators—career preferences in 1962 (CPR62) and importance of a career in ten years
(TC64)—are linked to the notion of career commitment as a long-term

investment. What the analysis indicates instead is that individual differences around the typical (low) level of career commitment are stable over time.

Finally, the analysis should be viewed as an attempt to validate the multiple-indicator approach to *measurement,* given the assumption of the stability of the underlying concept. The analysis presented here was not a direct attempt to validate the concept per se. Ideally, a discussion of the adequacy of measures of career commitment should proceed in conjunction with validation of the concept. For our purposes, validity of the concept is best assessed within the context of a substantive model of career commitment. That is, the unobservable variables posited here will be evaluated subsequently with respect to their determinants and consequences.

It is also important to add here that this investigation does not evaluate the overall *level* of commitment among these women at any one point in time or the pattern of mean commitment over time. The means in table 14–2 reveal a very low level of commitment among these women. Less than 4 percent expected primary satisfaction from a career in 1962 (CC62), and the proportion of women with such an expectation rose only slightly, to 5.6 percent, in 1968. These women were, however, members of the birth cohort born at the end of the Great Depression. They began high school in 1953, completed it in 1957, and graduated from college in 1961, coinciding with the ascendency of the "feminine mystique." Therefore, it was not until after these women had completed their formative years that broadly based attitudes supportive of women's careers began to be espoused. Thus we would expect these women to have a relatively low interest in commitment to an activity not fully endorsed by society. Given societal changes over the last few decades toward support of women's involvement in the labor force, we can expect that later cohorts of women have different expectations that predispose them to greater career commitment than their predecessors. This overall level of career commitment of contemporary women awaits assessment and explanation.

In closing, the analysis shows that when reasonable but imperfect multiple indicators are available, as is often the case in secondary analysis, it is possible to isolate the common sources of variation that are presumed to reflect the underlying concept of commitment. This analysis only addresses the patterns of common variation among the measures. As noted earlier, issues of validity must be assessed in a larger substantive context, a task that goes beyond the scope of this investigation.

Conclusion

Given the foregoing results, the next step is to specify and estimate a causal model of career commitment by building in exogenous and endogenous determinants. The present analysis revealed stable individual differences around an overall low level of commitment. Since it is known that higher education is a particularly crucial phase in establishing career commitment, the degree to which different aspects of higher-education environments are responsible for a level of commitment that will remain stable throughout early adulthood can now be examined. A causal model would determine what effect particular features of that environment have on interrupting or sustaining the stability of commitment (or lack of it), the relative impact of those features, and to what extent those features are responsible for apparent increases in career commitment among college-educated women.

The existing literature suggests a number of factors for examination. For example, previous research purports to show that academic ability, role models, and peers influence academic and career aspirations (for example, Epstein 1971; Tangri 1972). However, because only a few of these studies have assessed these determinants within a multivariate framework, their relative impact is unknown. In addition to these factors, features of the higher-education setting should be examined. These include whether the setting is a college or a university, the sex composition of the institution, the socially preferred sources of friends, and the ratio of males to females across majors (Astin 1977; Heilman 1979).

Furthermore, a valid model requires more broadly based causal factors. In particular, it is crucial that the relative importance of experiences in higher education be compared with features from other dimensions of women's lives. Thus the model should include independent variables that capture the direct and indirect career options, incentives, and deterrents women perceive throughout their lives; when they occur; how women act on them; and the duration of impact (Perun and Bielby 1981). Any subsequent efforts ought to assess longitudinally the extent to which those factors retain their relative importance in the low, albeit stable, career involvement we observed in the present analysis. For example, do education setting factors trade off in importance with or become mediated by other career or non-career factors, or do they retain importance over and above others as these women grow older? We can find those answers by concentrating more on how, when, and under what conditions young women act on their commitment and less on why they are committed (Laws 1976).

Finally, the present analysis, expanded to include determinants and consequences of career commitment, holds implications for educational policy. Once we determine the features of higher-education settings that are crucial to career commitment, the results can be used to advise programmatic opportunities for female undergraduates. Once the relative impact of educational settings and their features is more clearly understood, policy can be designed to attenuate the impact of structural barriers and to facilitate organizational and social support for women's careers.

Note

1. Confirmatory factor analysis is a procedure for specifying and estimating relationships between unobservable concepts and their empirical indicators. Whereas conventional factor-analysis procedures are typically used for exploratory data reduction, confirmatory factor analysis allows one to work from a specific measurement model that specifies the number of factors and, in effect, places constraints on permissible factor loadings (Joreskog and Sorbom 1978).

Bibliography

Astin, A. *Four Critical Years*. San Francisco: Jossey-Bass, 1977.

Becker, H.S. "Notes on the Concept of Commitment." *American Journal of Sociology* 66 (1960):32–40.

Bielby, D.D. "Factors Affecting Career Commitment of Female College Graduates: 1961–1968." Ph.D. diss., University of Wisconsin–Madison, 1975.

————. "Career Sex-Atypicality and Career Involvement of College-Educated Women: Baseline Evidence from the 1960's." *Sociology of Education* 51 (1978a):7–28.

————. "Maternal Employment and Socioeconomic Status as Factors in Daughters' Career Salience: Some Substantive Refinements." *Sex Roles* 4 (1978b):249–264.

Davis, N., and Bumpass, L. "The Continuation of Education After Marriage Among Women in the United States: 1970." *Demography* 13 (1976):161–174.

Epstein, C.F. *Women's Place*. Berkeley: University of California Press, 1971.

Fogarty, M.; Rapoport, R.; and Rapoport, R.N. *Sex, Career, and Family*. Beverly Hills, Calif.: Sage Publications, 1971.

Haller, M., and Rosenmayer, L. "The Pluridimensionality of Work Commitment." *Human Relations* 24 (1971):501–518.

Heilman, M.E. "High School Students' Occupational Interest as a Function of Projected Sex Ratios in Male-Dominated Occupations." *Journal of Applied Psychology* 64 (1979):275–279.

Joreskog, K.G., and Sorbom, D. *LISREL IV: Analysis of Linear Structural Relationships by the Method of Maximum Likelihood*. Chicago: International Educational Services, 1978.

Kanter, R.M. *Men and Women of the Corporation*. New York: Basic Books, 1977.

Laws, J.L. "Work Aspiration of Women: False Leads and New Starts."
     Signs 1 (1976):33–49.
———. *The Second X.* New York: Elsevier, 1979.
Lueptow, L.B. "Sex-Typing and Change in the Occupational Choice of
     High School Seniors: 1964–1975." *Sociology of Education* 54 (1981):
     16–24.
Mason, K.O.; Czajka, J.; and Arber, S. "Change in U.S. Women's Sex-
     Role Attitudes, 1964–1974." *American Sociological Review* 41 (1976):
     573–596.
McIllwee, J.S. "Organization Theory and the Entry of Women into Non-
     Traditional Occupations." Paper presented at the Annual Meetings of
     the American Sociological Association, New York, 1980.
Mincer, J., and Polachek, S. "Family Investments in Human Capital:
     Earnings of Women." *Journal of Political Economy* 82 (1974):76–111.
Perun, P.J., and Bielby, D. "Towards a Model of Female Occupational
     Behavior: A Human Development Approach." *Psychology of Women
     Quarterly* in press (1981).
Richardson, M. "The Dimension of Career and Work Orientation in Col-
     lege Women." *Journal of Vocational Behavior* 5 (1974):161–172.
Samuelson, P. "Shameful Sex Economics." *Newsweek,* 12 December 1977.
Sobol, M.G. "Commitment to Work." In I.F. Nye and L.W. Hoffman,
     eds., *The Employed Mother in America.* Chicago: Rand McNally,
     1963.
Sweet, J. *Women in the Labor Force.* New York: Seminar Press, 1973.
Tangri, S. "Determinants of Occupational Role Innovation Among College
     Women." *Journal of Social Issues* 28 (1972):177–200.
Van Dusen, R., and Sheldon, E. "The Changing Status of American
     Women." *American Psychologist* 31 (1976):106–116.

15

Family Formation and Educational Attainment

Karl L. Alexander,
Thomas W. Reilly, and
Bruce K. Eckland

Although the historic tendency for women, on the average, to terminate their schooling earlier than men is well documented (Duncan 1968; Ferriss 1971), explanation of this deficit has remained elusive. It appears clear, however, that the personal resources and school experiences otherwise so important to educational attainment do *not* account for this liability. That is, the higher attainments of men do not derive to any significant degree from sex differences in social supports for college, educational goals, high-school track placement or academic performance. How, then, are such inequalities to be understood if not in terms of the "traditional" determinants of educational outcomes? Perhaps tradition is misguided.

Research on educational attainment typically neglects many extra-schooling aspects of life-course development that might be quite relevant to this question. As youth mature beyond the age of mandatory school attendance and assume increasing independence from parents, they enter into new commitments and confront increasingly complex, often immediate, career decisions. Among the most consequential of these are commitments and decisions regarding marriage and parenthood. Certainly, one's educational progress is not insulated from such family events; and it may well be that, beyond midadolescence, the family of procreation—in both its anticipation and its actuality—comes to rival, if not exceed, the family of orientation in its importance for schooling.[1]

There is a widely scattered literature that suggests that such family factors are indeed important for educational attainment, especially for women. Of course, a substantial association between marriage timing and levels of education is well documented (Tietze and Lauriat 1955; Glick and Carter 1958; Rele 1965). Both theory (Elder 1975) and research (Burchinal 1959; Elder 1972; Bacon 1974; Elder and Rockwell 1976) indicate that early

Paper prepared for the Research Conference on Educational Environments and the Undergraduate Woman, Wellesley, Mass., 1979. This research was supported in part by Contract No. 1–HD52836, National Institute of Child Health and Human Development. Portions of this chapter are reprinted from Karl L. Alexander and Thomas W. Reilly, "Estimating the Effects of Marriage Timing on Educational Attainment," *The American Journal of Sociology* (July 1981), by permission of the University of Chicago Press.

entry into marriage and motherhood often incurs numerous disadvantages: "Early marriage identifies a life course of relative deprivation—low socioeconomic origins, restricted formal education, marriage into the lower strata, heavy childcare burdens and inadequate material resources" (Elder and Rockwell 1976, p. 51).

Even under circumstances less extreme than these, early assumption of the role responsibilities of spouse and parent (referred to by Bacon 1974, as "accelerated role transitions") would certainly limit extrafamilial pursuits, and perhaps especially would limit continuing investments in education in view of the past ambivalence of many domestically oriented women toward labor-force careers (Empey 1958; Matthews and Tiedeman 1964; Turner 1964; Gysbers, Johnston, and Gust 1968; Astin and Myint 1971; Watly and Kaplan 1971; Dowdall 1974).

The strain between marriage and schooling is also apparent in much of the literature on school attrition. Marriage and parenthood are among the strongest predictors of dropping out of college (Bayer 1968; Folger, Astin, and Bayer 1970) and are often offered as reasons for either not beginning or not completing college by both men and women, although much more so by the latter (Iffert 1957; Trent and Medsker 1968; Astin and Panos 1969). Additionally, there is reason to suspect that these constraints are not entirely situational but, rather, reflect in part the successful negotiation of life plans formulated much earlier. Bayer, for example, has demonstrated a strong association between *intended* age at marriage and educational *plans* among adolescents (Bayer 1969b) and that such intentions are reasonably good forecasters of actual marriage timing (Bayer 1969a).[2]

Thus, ideally, analysis would entertain the possibility that family events *and* schooling patterns impinge on one another over the individual's life course. There is, however, little research overall that touches on these issues; and most of that which is available has assumed priority of family commitments over school attainments (Call and Otto 1977; Waite and Moore 1977).[3] Now, however, there are available at least three exceptions to this generalization (Voss 1975; Marini 1978; Moore and Hofferth 1978); and these are most germane to our interest in the educational consequences of early marriage.

Although these studies differ from one another in their procedural details, the assumptions that govern their treatment of the crucial educational attainment–age at first marriage relationship are virtually identical. At the most general level all three studies recognize that occurrences in one institutional setting may have implications for what transpires in the other— in particular, that school progression and continuation will likely be affected somewhat by family events and, in turn, that family events may be influenced by schooling considerations. The three studies then straightforwardly apply this general imagery to the specific measures of family and educational experience at issue. They assume that age at marriage and educational attainment are mutually influential. Hence, all three studies develop models in which age at marriage and educational attainment are reciprocally related, and employ structural-equations estimation procedures for which the assumption of recursivity is not required.[4]

As a general characterization of the research process, this scenario is not at all exceptional; however, as increasingly powerful statistical tools have become generally available, their application often has become excessively stylized and routinized. As a result, questions of their detailed appropriateness to the substantive issues under study are sometimes neglected. This appears to be the case with the existing literature on the educational attainment–age at marriage relationship. There is, of course, a tremendous gap between the general sense that family and school factors may have relevance for one another and the formal assumption that two specific measures originating in the family and school are reciprocally related. To move from the general to the specific, substantive arguments must be offered to justify the use of these research variables and the assumption that they stand in reciprocal relationship to one another. In this instance, however, no such justifying rationale is advanced. Moreover, consideration of the nature of the variables themselves seems to make a prima facie case against their being reciprocally related.

To begin with, the timing of marriage and the age at which schooling is concluded differ widely in relation to one another across cases. Among the men and women of the present sample, for example, 27 percent of the men and 16 percent of the women report two or more years of additional academic enrollment after marriage. Similarly, many men and women do not marry for several years after completing their educations. Overall, only 13 percent of the men and 29 percent of the women who obtained no additional schooling after marrying concluded their educations in the first year of their marriages.[5] Although it is not necessary for events to be in close temporal proximity to one another in order to be reciprocally related, it is unlikely that any simple model of mutual influence could account for this diverse pattern of timing and sequencing.

More generally, variables that index the occurrence of life-course events are of such a nature that they probably cannot conform to the assumptions that underlie statistical-estimation models of the sort employed in this research. Simultaneous-equations procedures for estimating reciprocal influence, such as two- or three-stage least squares, assume a system in equilibrium. Inferences about how variables have adjusted to changes in one another's values within cases are drawn from comparisons across cases in the currently stable situation (this is referred to as *comparative statics*). Age at first marriage and level of educational attainment are not, however, the sort of variables that *can* adjust to one another successively within cases. That is, they both happen only once over the life course and are invariant thereafter. The imagery of variables mutually adjusting to shifts in one another's values until an equilibrium point is reached does not seem especially applicable to events that are unique and invariant over the life course.

It may be, then, that such statistical models are not appropriate to variables of this sort and, conversely, that such variables cannot stand in relation to one another in the way assumed by these models. Therefore, it is difficult to know what interpretation should be lent to the coefficients of reciprocal influence presented in these studies. It is conceivable, of course, that they do not in fact quantify what they are intended to quantify, but this is hardly self-evident. Until it is demonstrated explicitly, caution and skepticism are warranted.

Fortunately, there is an alternative research strategy that avoids these uncertainties and still allows us to address the issues most central to the studies we have just critiqued: whether early marriage is a deterrent to high educational attainment and, if it is, whether it is more so for women than for men. We can do so by distinguishing education accumulated prior to marriage from that obtained afterwards and by focusing on this second component. This enables us to ask how the likelihood of continuing in school after marrying differs as a function of the age at which the marriage occurs. If early marriage is in fact a liability, as both theory and conventional wisdom suggest, then this should be revealed in differences in the postmarriage school experiences of early and late marriers.

This approach is parallel to that employed in several recent studies of earnings attainments (Griliches and Mason 1973; Mason 1974; Griffin 1978), in which valuable resources such as work experience and schooling are segmented into the quantities obtained before and after some other salient life experience (such as military service). Expressed in this way, the separate consequences of each component can be estimated. Theory often suggests that these effects should differ. In the present instance, distinguishing schooling obtained after marrying from that obtained before allows us to isolate more clearly the educational consequences of marriage timing. In fact, Bielby, Hawley, and Bills (1977, p. 59) recently have made a similar observation about the advantage of distinguishing postbirth schooling from total schooling.

There remains, however, one further complication in making substantive sense out of the relationship between age at marriage and educational attainment, another age-graded variable. Age at marriage subsumes two major components: age, and the fact that some socially significant role transition has occurred. It is important, therefore, that these two components be distinguished. In failing to do so, we run the very real risk of mistaking age effects for those of marriage timing. Since school enrollments themselves tend to be age patterned, there is a negative association built into the relationship between age at marriage and years of postmarriage schooling. That is, we would expect older marriers to have fewer years of later enrollment simply because older persons generally will already have completed more of their education.

What we want to do, then, is isolate how enrollment patterns following on marriage at a particular age depart from the cohort's educational experience overall beyond that age. Thus marriage effects would show up as deviations from the cohort baseline, with beneficial consequences of marriage appearing as enrollment beyond that which is typical, and liabilities of marriage being revealed as shortfalls from the average.

To take account of the typical age grading or patterning of school enrollments, we have constructed two control variables, one for premarital schooling and one for postmarital schooling. Each is based on the *entire sample's* enrollment history. The first indexes, for every age at marriage represented in the data, the average number of years of enrollment, *across all respondents,* prior to a particular age. The second does the same for years of enrollment subsequent to particular ages. To partial out the age component from age at marriage, we then simply express *each individual's* pre- and postmarital schooling as deviations from the control values for the age at which that respondent married. For example, if a woman in our sample who married at age 20 received thirteen years of premarital schooling and half a year of postmarital schooling, and the sample as a whole (regardless of marriage timing) received on the average 12.7 years of schooling prior to age 20 and 1.2 years of schooling after age 20, then the respondent's age-adjusted scores would be $+0.3$ for premarital enrollment and -0.7 for postmarital enrollment. The figures in this example are, incidentally, the actual sample averages for our female sample and are the age-adjustment values for age 20. These deviations from the sample's age-normed averages are the variables actually employed in the analysis.[6] With this backdrop of procedure and rationale, we now are in a position to discuss the particulars of the model that will guide our analysis.

The framework that guides our analysis is portrayed in figure 15-1. In it, status origins and academic ability are considered as exogenous influences. These have been found previously to affect both marriage timing and educational attainment, although only modestly so for the first. Higher-ability and higher-status youth tend, on the average, to marry somewhat later, perhaps in part because they continue further in school. Educational plans and a dummy variable indicating whether or not the respondent met his or her spouse while in high school appear next in the model. These serve as instrumental variables in identifying the nonrecursive age at marriage and educational-attainment equations.

The remaining variables and relationships are of most immediate substantive interest. Age at first marriage and years of enrollment up to mar-

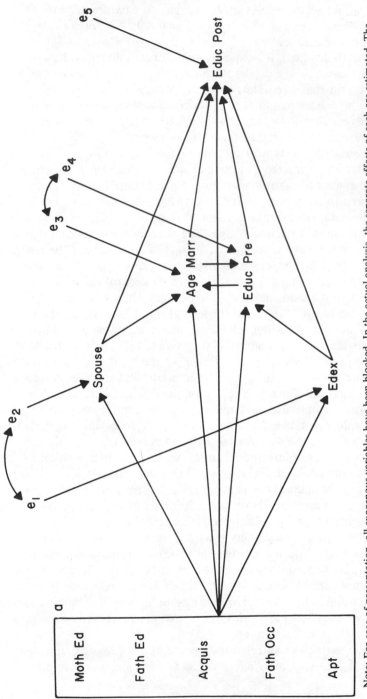

Figure 15-1. Nonrecursive Structural Model of Educational Attainment, with Age at Marriage and Education Prior to Marriage Reciprocally Related.

Note: For ease of presentation, all exogenous variables have been blocked. In the actual analysis, the separate effects of each are estimated. The following variable abbreviations are used here and throughout the remaining figures and tables: *Moth Ed*, mother's education; *Fath Ed*, father's education; *Acquis*, the household-acquisitions index; *Fath Occ*, father's occupation; *Apt*, aptitude; *Spouse*, whether the respondent met his/her spouse in high school; *Edex*, educational expectations; *Age Marr*, age at marriage; *Educ Pre*, age-adjusted years of school enrollment prior to marriage; *Educ Post*, age-adjusted years of school enrollment after marriage.

riage are reciprocally related. Although the first is a discrete event and the second cumulative over time, we assume that the timing of marriage is dictated partly by the circumstances of one's other career and career-preparatory commitments, and that schooling patterns similarly are organized partly around intentions regarding family formation (recall Bayer's finding that intended age at marriage predicts rather well actual age at marriage). Since these intentions are unmeasured in our data, we specify the outcomes of that planning as jointly dependent.

It should be recognized that this particular aspect of our model is not much more defensible than were the models we criticized earlier, which evaluated age at first marriage and level of educational attainment within a similar framework of reciprocal influence. There are, however, three minor differences that distinguish the present application from these others. First, the school-enrollment data here are bounded by the marital event itself and hence are not subject to the diversity of sequencing and patterning that complicates the earlier studies. Second, we recognize that the relationships evaluated are proxies of unknown adequacy for the planning process that actually is of substantive interest, and hence that we should not be too taken with the seeming precision and concreteness of our estimations. Finally, these uncertainties are less troublesome here because we are interested mainly in postmarital schooling, and our assumptions regarding the premarital enrollment age at marriage relationship have no bearing on the analysis's implications regarding this outcome. Both age at marriage and premarital enrollment are predetermined relative to postmarital enrollment. In this respect the model is block recursive.

School enrollment after marriage, then, is the final variable considered; we are especially interested in how this is affected by prior schooling and age at first marriage. Recall here that the enrollment measures analyzed are adjusted for the characteristic age grading of school enrollments so as to distinguish the effects of marriage timing from those of age. Note also that we do not give explicit consideration to level of educational certification in this analysis. This is because certification follows definitionally from enrollment patterns, and it would be redundant to consider both. To the extent that this is not the case in our data, this results from the crudeness of our enrollment data rather than from substantively interesting considerations.[7]

This last stage of the model, then, addresses the major issues of the analysis. We are especially interested in whether differences in the consequences of marriage timing account for women's lesser average educational attainment. Parallel analyses will be conducted for men and women and their results compared. At issue is whether family constraints weigh more heavily on the educational progress of women, thereby contributing to their educational shortfall relative to men.

Methodology

Sample and Measurement

The data for this analysis are from a national sample of youth, first studied in 1955 as high-school sophomores and followed up in 1970. The original 1955 survey, conducted by the Educational Testing Service, includes all sophomores in ninety-seven schools. The analyses that follow are based on the subsamples of once-married men and women for whom data are available for all variables included in the models, numbering 657 and 794, respectively. The survey consisted of two instruments: a twenty-item test of academic aptitude (constructed for the project) that measured both verbal and mathematical ability, and a questionnaire.

The 1970 follow-up survey was conducted under the auspices of the Institute for Research in Social Science at the University of North Carolina. Schools constituted the basic sampling units and were stratified by region and size and to some extent by parental education, group test scores, and school dropout and college-going rates. The final sample (targeted) consisted of forty-two schools with 4,151 sophomores. Detailed descriptions of the schools are available elsewhere (Eckland and MacGillivary 1972). Usable follow-up data were obtained for 2,077 of these students, 1,130 females and 947 males. The 50-percent overall nonresponse consists of 32 percent refusals, 16 percent lost cases (for whom current addresses could not be located), and 2 percent known deceased. The major sample and response biases involved an underrepresentation of urban and large schools and, not surprisingly, an underrepresentation of low-aptitude students (the questionnaire required about three hours to complete). These sample biases, of course, temper the generalizability of our results, especially since the project design excludes those likely to marry extremely early. Nevertheless, careful assessment of the biases arising from various sources of sample attrition has found them in general to be surprisingly modest (see Alexander and Eckland 1973, pp. 57–69).

Table 15–1 presents descriptions of the variables to be used in the analysis and their measurement.

Analysis

Joreskog's program for the evaluation of complex covariance structures, LISREL IV, is used to provide parameter estimates for these nonrecursive models. Since we employ only one indicator per construct, the measurement portion of the program is completely fixed, and only the structural relations are estimated. Although the LISREL IV program provides maximum-likelihood estimates, in this application these correspond quite closely to

Table 15-1
Variable Description

Variable	Label	Measure
Mother's education	Moth Ed	Level of educational certification rescaled to years of schooling completed
Father's education	Fath Ed	Level of educational certification rescaled to years of schooling completed
Father's occupation, while respondent in high school	Fath Occ	Duncan SEI
Acquisition index	Acquis	13-item factor-weighted index of possessions in respondent's high-school household
Academic aptitude	Apt	20-item test from 1955 survey that gives equal weight to vocabulary and arithmetic reasoning
Educational expectations	Edex	Measured in 1955 survey: 1 = not expecting to go to college 2 = possibly expecting to go to college 3 = expecting to go to college
Early acquaintance with spouse	Spouse	0 = did not attend same high school as present spouse 1 = attended same high school as present spouse
Age at first marriage	Age Marr	Age in years
Premarital enrollment, not age adjusted	—	Number of calendar years in which some academic schooling had been obtained through the first year of respondent's first marriage[a]
Postmarital enrollment, not age adjusted	—	Number of calendar years in which some academic schooling had been obtained following the first year of marriage through 1970
Premarital enrollment, age adjusted	Educ Pre	Respondent's number of years of enrollment prior to marriage (defined above in premarital enrollment, not age adjusted) minus the mean number of years of enrollment realized by the sample overall up to and including the age that corresponded to the respondent's age at marriage

Table 15-1 continued

Variable	Label	Measure
Post-marital enrollment, age adjusted	Educ Post	Respondent's number of years of enrollment after marriage (defined above in postmarital enrollment, not age adjusted) minus the mean number of years of enrollment realized by the sample overall beyond the age which corresponded to respondent's age at marriage

Note: Unless otherwise indicated, items are from the 1970 schedule.

[a]This operationalization was used for all respondents except those who were enrolled both in the year of marriage and the following year. For these cases, schooling during the marriage year was credited to post-marital enrollment.

what would be obtained from least-squares procedures for the estimation of systems of nonrecursive structural equations, such as two-stage least squares. The model is just identified. Only respondents with usable data for all variables are used in the analysis.

Results

As mentioned earlier, all analyses in this section pertain to subsamples of once-married men and women. It turns out that, overall, school attendance after marrying is a rather rare occurrence, and more so for women than for men. The second panel of table 15-2, which presents selected bivariate cross-tabulations as a backdrop to the regression analyses that follow, indicates that 70 percent of men and 81 percent of women receive no formal schooling after the year in which they marry. Overall, men average 1.2 years of postmarital enrollment, as compared with an average of only 0.6 year for women. This difference of about 0.6 year in school enrollment after marriage amounts to about 40 percent of the mean difference between men and women in total years of enrollment (which is about 14.9 years for men and 13.4 years for women, with the difference thus being 1.5 years). This strikes us as a notable contribution to the female educational deficit relative to men, especially in view of the fact that men marry, on the average, about 2.3 years later than women and therefore have even more opportunity to pursue their schooling *prior* to marrying.

The first panel of table 15-2 presents the relationship of total years of enrollment to age at marriage, separately for men and women. It reproduces the moderate, positive association between the two that has been

Table 15-2
The Relationship between Age at Marriage and Total Educational Enrollment and Postmarital Enrollment, for Men and Women

| | Age at Marriage | | | | | | | |
| | Men % | | | | Women % | | | |
	19	20/21/22	23+	Total	19	20/21/22	23+	Total
Total enrollment								
≤ 12	64	50	38	48	84	47	36	64
13–16	15	26	21	22	15	35	30	24
17+	20	24	41	30	2	18	34	12
N	(143)	(305)	(324)	(772)	(481)	(315)	(140)	(936)
Enrollment after marriage (not age adjusted)								
0	66	68	73	70	81	78	85	81
1–2	6	10	13	10	10	11	7	10
3+	28	23	14	20	9	11	8	9
N	(143)	(305)	(324)	(772)	(481)	(315)	(140)	(936)
Enrollment after marriage (age adjusted)								
≤ −1	66	25	0	22	86	31	0	55
−1 < × ≤ 0	4	44	73	49	5	48	85	32
> 0	30	32	27	29	9	21	15	14
N	(143)	(305)	(324)	(772)	(481)	(315)	(140)	(936)

observed in numerous other studies. The tau c coefficient (a measure of association for ordinal-level data that can range from $+1$ to -1) for this relationship is .183 for males; for females it is .344. Thus we find that older marriers tend to obtain more total schooling and that this relationship is notably stronger among women.

The last two panels of table 15-2 focus on schooling after marriage and how it varies with the age at which marriage occurs. The middle panel presents these relationships for actual years of postmarital enrollment, whereas the last panel employs our difference measures. These, it will be recalled, adjust for the general age patterning of school enrollments. This comparison demonstrates the importance of such adjustments. In the first instance, postmarital schooling (unadjusted) has a small negative relationship with age at marriage among men (tau $c = -.066$) and is unrelated to age at marriage among women (tau = − .001). This seems to suggest that, if anything, early marriage enhances one's prospects somewhat for continuing in school, in that young marriers tend to receive somewhat *more* schooling after marrying than do older marriers.

This enrollment measure, however, is not adjusted for age differences in school progressions. Hence the suspicion remains that what we are seeing here are simply age effects rather than the consequences of marriage timing. The bottom panel of table 15–2 confirms this suspicion and underscores the importance of taking aging patterns into account in making such assessments.

Enrollment after marriage here is expressed as deviations from the total sample's enrollment experience referenced to the particular age at issue.[8] Hence, a score of − 1 indicates that the respondent received one year less education beyond his or her age at marriage than did the sample overall beyond that age. Positive deviations indicate that the respondent's experience exceeded the sample average for that age. With this scaling of post-marital enrollments, we obtain substantial *positive* relationships with age at marriage, with tau c being .238 for men and .485 for women.

Thus it appears that marrying young depresses prospects for later educational enrollments relative to what would be expected otherwise beyond that age and that it does so markedly for women. For example, whereas 86 percent of the women who marry before age 19 fall short of the schooling generally received beyond age 19 by at least one year, this severe a liability is observed for only about two-thirds of the men. In fact, about 30 percent of the men who marry this young receive *more* schooling subsequently than is typical, compared with only 9 percent of the women. Sex differences in enrollment relative to the norm are less marked among older marriers, but still favor men.

Overall, the sample averages on these age-adjusted enrollment measures differ in sign for men and women, being .406 and − .824 respectively. This suggests that across the entire sample the average male receives more schooling beyond his marriage age than is typical for that age generally, and the average woman receives less. In all likelihood this results from both the average earlier age at marriage for women and from the greater effects of family experiences for women overall. This last possibility is pursued more formally in our regression analyses, to which we turn next.

Table 15–3 presents the correlation matrixes, means, and standard deviations from which the regression results in table 15–4 are calculated. We already have referred to some of the differences in means between men and women reported in table 15–3. The zero-order correlations between age at marriage (Age Marr) and age-adjusted postmarital schooling (Educ Post) also deserve note). These are .064 for men and .401 for women, suggesting that the educational benefits from deferring marriage are far greater among

Table 15-3
Means, Standard Deviations, and Interitem Correlations for Variables included in the Nonrecursive Model of Family Influences on Educational Attainment (Age Adjusted)

Males N = 657

	Edex	Spouse	Educ Pre	Age Marr	Educ Post	Moth Ed	Fath Ed	Acquis	Fath Occ	Apt	X̄	SD
Edex		.0302	.4496	.1205	.3029	.2793	.3089	.3456	.2739	.3421	1.9496	.8416
Spouse	-.0394		-.1407	-.3601	-.0216	.0325	.0218	-.0125	-.0346	-.0062	.2983	.4579
Educ Pre	.4511	-.0869		.5421	.2521	.2216	.3117	.3850	.3350	.4604	.6009	2.2778
Age Marr	.1870	-.2024	.3689		.0540	.0414	.1001	.1687	.0868	.1491	22.2268	2.9901
Educ Post	.2708	-.0741	.2937	-.013		.1197	.1744	.1726	.1453	.2280	.4062	2.2601
Moth Ed	.3763	.0274	.3715	.1467	.2112		.5679	.3814	.2895	.1922	10.8828	2.8627
Fath Ed	.4076	-.0237	.4027	.1973	.2429	.5699		.4295	.4305	.2834	10.2359	3.6364
Acquis	.4167	-.0318	.3948	.2633	.2397	.5034	.5409		.4207	.2922	.0247	.8727
Fath Occ	.3530	-.0391	.3354	.1690	.2792	.3840	.5737	.4887		.2098	39.8767	21.6439
Apt	.2440	.0047	.3556	.1218	.2360	.2690	.2860	.1910	.2176		7.6347	3.9587
X	1.9156	.2620	.3108	19.5471	-.8240	10.6977	10.0504	.0381	39.4987	7.6121		
S.D.	.9049	.4400	1.6864	2.7762	1.5618	3.1249	4.0529	.9557	22.3938	4.1065		

Females (N = 794)

Note: Data for males above the diagonal, data for females below the diagonal.

women. It remains to be determined, though, whether this holds up when assessed within the framework of the school-attainment model reviewed earlier in figure 15-1.

These results are reported in table 15-1, separately for men and women. The patterns of influence on the first two dependent variables—educational plans and a dummy variable indexing whether or not the respondent met his or her spouse while in high school—are entirely unexceptional. These variables are included mainly for technical reasons, to serve as instrumental variables in identifying the equations involving patterns of reciprocal influence (the Educ Pre and Age Marr equations), although plans for college are, of course, also of substantive interest in their own right. It turns out that the spouse variable is virtually unrelated to any of the predictors. This is of little concern substantively, and it is actually something of a virtue technically, for it implies that the measure is unconfounded with any of the other measured determinants of Educ Pre. Plans for college, on the other hand, are moderately responsive to both status origins and measured ability, although the latter is a good bit less important for women. These results are consistent with other research dealing with background influences on educational plans.

The next stage of the model considers age at marriage and schooling prior to marriage as they are affected by background influences, by the two instrumental variables, and by one another. The coefficients for the various predetermined variables in these equations are largely as expected. The only substantial influence on marriage timing is the variable pertaining to early acquaintance with one's spouse. Those who marry a high-school boyfriend or girlfriend marry considerably earlier than those who do not (about one year and two years so, respectively, for women and men—see metric coefficients). Status origins as indexed by the acquisitions measure also have a modest influence, but only for women. Since modest associations between marriage timing and both status origins and academic ability have been observed in much of the relevant literature (see Voss 1975 for a review of this material), it is likely that the selectivity of our sample (which includes few high-school dropouts and overrepresents high-ability youth) has attenuated these relationships somewhat. This qualification applies throughout the analysis and suggests that our parameter estimates may actually be somewhat conservative. Nevertheless, background correlations with age at marriage have never been found to be large, and our zero-order correlations are appropriately patterned. Again, we think the distortion owing to sample biases is likely quite small.

Next we find that high-status origins, high academic ability, and plans for a college education while in high school are all associated with greater premarital enrollment, and more strongly so for men than for women. Moreover, as has been found in numerous other studies, including a number

Table 15-4
Nonrecursive Model of Family Influences on Educational Attainment (Age Adjusted), by Sex

Predetermined Variables	Men (N = 657)					Women (N = 794)				
	Edex	Spouse	Educ Pre	Age Marr	Educ Post	Edex	Spouse	Educ Pre	Age Marr	Educ Post
Moth Ed	.1022* (.3000)	.0369 (.0059)	-.0013 (-.0050)	-.0446 (-.0466)	-.0166 (-.0131)	.1264* (.0366)	.0735 (.0104)	.0922* (.0498)	-.0413 (-.0367)	.0247 (.0124)
Fath Ed	.0723 (.0167)	.0317 (.0040)	.0307 (.0192)	.0348 (.0286)	.0514 (.0320)	.1314* (.0293)	-.0269 (-.0029)	.0716 (.0298)	.0242 (.0165)	-.0181 (-.0070)
Acquis	.1681* (.1621)	-.0171 (-.0090)	.0945* (.2467)	.0890 (.3050)	.0161 (.0418)	.2112* (.1999)	-.0388 (-.0179)	.0562 (.0992)	.1633* (.4744)	.0252 (.0413)
Fath Occ	.0935* (.0036)	-.0503 (-.0011)	.1294* (.0135)	-.0485 (-.0067)	.0097 (.0010)	.1020* (.0041)	-.0346 (-.0007)	.0454 (.0034)	-.0044 (-.0005)	.1400* (.0098)
Apt	.2332* (.0496)	-.0068 (-.0008)	.2577* (.1453)	.0194 (.0147)	.0920* (.0525)	.0199* (.0242)	.0075 (.0008)	.1874* (.0770)	.0030 (.0020)	.1256* (.0478)
Edex			.2370* (.6414)		.2056* (.5521)			.2318* (.4321)		.1076* (.1857)
Spouse				-.3261* (-2.1297)	-.0218 (-.1076)				-.1728* (-1.0901)	.0030 (.0105)
Educ Pre				.2399 (.3149)	.1123* (.1114)				.2630 (.4330)	.0207 (.0192)
Age Marr			.3921* (.2987)		-.0287 (-.0217)			.3752* (.2279)		.3285* (.1848)

Disturbances	Edex	Spouse	Educ Pre	Age Marr	Educ Post	Edex	Spouse	Educ Pre	Age Marr	Educ Post
Edex	.7856 .0321					.7431 -.0236				
Spouse		.9921					.9947			
Educ Pre			.6054 -.2755					.6358 -.2777		
Age Marr				.7784					.8182	
Educ Post					.8775					.7571

Note: Asterisks signify coefficients at least twice their standard errors. Figures in parentheses are metric coefficients.

using these same data (Alexander and Eckland 1974a,b), much of the relevance of background characteristics for educational outcomes is mediated through goal-orientations. Since these relationships are very much like those obtained for educational attainment generally and are thoroughly documented and discussed in many other sources, we do not dwell on them here.

The reciprocal effects of age at marriage and premarital enrollment are of particular interest. Although the extent of enrollment prior to marriage appears to be of little consequence for marriage timing, there is the suggestion of modest influence in the other direction. That is, each year of deferred marriage is estimated to accrue about one-fourth of a year of age-adjusted schooling. These estimations suggest, then, that the coordination of schooling and family formation entails mainly limitations on enrollment that follow from marriage-timing decisions. There is no indication that the age at which one marries is at all dictated by school commitments. This pattern is very much the same for men and women.

Finally, we come to schooling after marriage. Here we are particularly interested in how marriage timing affects continuation in school after marriage, but other results also deserve comment. Postmarital education is affected directly by earlier educational goals and measured ability. The enduring importance of educational plans, though modest, indicates that even despite the complications surrounding family formation, earlier goals continue to structure educational progress. That this is especially so for men (compare metric coefficients) suggests that women either are more likely to have their extrafamilial plans deflected by family obligations or that they are more obliged to take steps toward the actualization of such plans prior to marriage. This last possibility is consistent with the considerably stronger effect of plans on premarital schooling than on postmarital schooling obtained for women, whereas for men the two effects are much more similar. Moreover, the sex disparity in the importance of educational plans for attendance is somewhat less for premarital enrollment, although in both instances the male coefficient is the larger of the two.

The consequences of schooling prior to marriage for attendance after marriage are perhaps somewhat surprising. For men but not for women, greater investments in schooling prior to marriage modestly increase the likelihood of continuing in school after marrying. Although these effects would hardly be considered substantial, something of a trade-off between pre- and postmarital enrollment might well have been expected, but this certainly is not at all evidenced in our results. Rather, a cumulative advantage is suggested, with additional schooling accruing most often to those with greater premarital enrollment. Although it might be interesting to learn whether this derives from differences in achievement orientation, from circumstances that might facilitate or retard continuing investments in education, or from the costs and benefits persons expect they would realize from such investments, the size of this effect suggests that the matter itself is not of great practical importance.

Finally, we consider how age at marriage affects schooling subsequent to marriage. Here our results have clear implications. For men, the timing of marriage has no effect on later academic progression. For women, on the other hand, the liability that follows from marrying early is quite substantial. For each year that marriage is deferred, it is estimated the women realize about one-fifth of a year of age-adjusted schooling. In other words, age at marriage is irrelevant for men's subsequent school enrollment, but quite important for women's. For women, early marriage is an educational liability; and it no doubt is an important factor in women's depressed educational attainment relative to men. In fact, these estimations suggest that if women married at the same age as men (raising their average age at marriage by about 2.3 years), they would obtain about one-half year more age-adjusted schooling, again on the average, then is now the case. This is approximately one-third of the observed sex difference in age-adjusted postmarital enrollment.[9]

Summary and Discussion

It seems clear from the foregoing analysis that family obligations have important consequences for school-attendance patterns. It also appears that the extent and nature of family intrusions on educational progress differ somewhat for men and women, with the educational liabilities that follow from early marriage being much more severe for women. These conclusions suggest the need for a much broader framework than is customary in school research. The traditional perspective, in concentrating on experiences within educational settings neglects important facets of career development that, though situated outside the school, might have profound academic applications.

The model of the socioeconomic life-cycle implicitly ascribed to in most research on educational and socioeconomic attainment is actually a rather crude characterization of the life course, uninformed by an explicit theory of either careers or career development. The timing, sequencing, and patterning of significant life events and of various institutional involvements have, through their neglect, been assumed either unproblematic or unimportant; but emerging perspectives on life-course development (see, for example, Clausen 1972; Jordaan 1974; Atchley 1975) and the results of the research reported herein with regard to educational attainment both suggest quite the contrary. It is hoped that this project will encourage serious consideration of the various dimensions of career patterning and how these might be incorporated into models of the attainment process. See Spilerman (1977) for a related recommendation and a preliminary, though still incomplete, formulation of such an expanded framework.

In terms of the immediate questions posed in this analysis, we conclude that family contingencies are important constraints on educational attainment. We focused on the implications of age at marriage and accumulated enrollment up to marriage for the likelihood of continuing in school after marriage. As anticipated, age at marriage was considerably more important for women than for men, with early marriage being found to depress women's later enrollments once the characteristic age grading of school-enrollment patterns was taken into account. For men, the age-at-marriage patterns hardly departed at all from the normal age patterns. Our evaluation of the relationship between age at marriage and enrollment prior to marriage also suggested that marriage timing is more of a factor in limiting school enrollments than the reverse. This last conclusion applies similarly to men and women.

It is hoped that future research will shed further light on the ways in which men's and women's school attendance differ, how these differences might be constrained by family obligations, and the relevance of family circumstances to other aspects of career development. It would be especially interesting to explore whether, and how, changing patterns of family formation and changes in family-oriented sex roles and sex-role attitudes might account for recent increases in female college attendance. These inquiries should inform our understanding not only of individuals' academic progress, but also of the conditions of the contemporary family, and in so doing should provide much useful information for career planning and counseling.

Along more purely procedural lines, we would encourage greater caution in mechanical applications of powerful statistical tools. It first needs to be determined—and this can be can be done only on a case-by-case basis—whether the nature of the variables and of the relations among them conform at least reasonably well to what is assumed by the statistical model one wishes to employ. Too often, it appears that insufficient attention is given to the compatibility of substantive and statistical models. Finally, our exercises also underscore the importance of taking into account the age grading of life-course events in research of this sort when age differences per se are not of immediate interest. Had we neglected to do so in the present instance, our empirical results and their seeming substantive implications would have been very different; in fact, they would have been almost the reverse of those that were obtained. Clearly, then, such procedural decisions should not be sloughed off as simply methodological fine tuning, since how they are resolved may fundamentally alter our understanding of the issues under study.

Notes

1. For youth who succeed in gaining access to college, for example, socioeconomic origins bear little relation to subsequent educational attainment (Wolfle 1954; Spaeth 1970). See Eckland (1964), however, for the suggestion that the continuing importance of status background may be underestimated in much of this literature.

2. Unfortunately, Bayer was unable to consider how one's plans for marriage and education affect one's educational attainments.

3. Waite and Moore (1977) acknowledge sidestepping the matter of causal priorities in these relationships, whereas Call and Otto (1977) disavow responsibility for their model specification, evaluating uncritically the framework developed by Nye and Berardo (1973).

4. The paper by Moore and Hofferth (1978) considers both age at marriage and age at the birth of one's first child as factors affecting educational attainment. The other two focus exclusively on marriage timing, as does the present study. Our comments about the modeling of life-course events would be applicable to research on both aspects of family formation, marriage and fertility.

5. Pertinent tables are available on request. *Years of enrollment* in this context refers to the number of calendar years during which the respondents received some formal academic preparation, rather than completed academic years. See the discussion of Educ Pre and Educ Post in the methodology section for a complete description of the data used in this analysis.

6. We explored the possibility of working with the unadjusted enrollment measures in the analysis and using the adjustment variables as statistical controls, but this resulted in excessive collinearity in elements of the data matrix. We therefore decided to remove age effects first and to use the residualized enrollment measures in the analysis.

7. Our pre- and postmarriage enrollment measures together account for about 75 percent of the variance in men's levels of educational certification and 66 percent of women's.

8. We now think it is better to adjust the enrollment measures on the basis of sex-specific subsamples of those not yet married at each age. The same general pattern of regression results is produced by this procedure, but the sex difference in the estimate of the effect of age at marriage on postmarital enrollment is somewhat attenuated. For a detailed description of results produced by sex-specific norming, see Alexander and Reilly (1981).

9. We should note, incidentally, that the results obtained when the unadjusted enrollment measures are used in this analysis are quite different in apparent implication. Using these measures, the effects of age at marriage on postmarital enrollment are *negative* for both men and women, and more than twice as large for men (metric coefficients are, respectively,

− .203 and − .076). Thus, these results are completely the reverse of those reported in the text. Clearly, the age adjustments have considerable consequence; and these striking contrasts should make us quite wary of studies that neglect this concern in dealing with other age-graded phenomena.

Bibliography

Alexander, K.L., and Eckland, B.K. "Effects of Education on the Social Mobility of High School Sophomores Fifteen Years Later (1955–1970)." Final Report, U.S. Office of Education, Project no. 10202 (00E-4-71-0037), 1973.

―――. "School Experience and Status Attainment." In S.D. Dragastin and G.H. Elder, Jr., eds., *Adolescence in the Life Cycle: Psychological Change and Social Context*. Washington, D.C.: Hemisphere, 1974a.

―――. "Sex Differences in the Educational Attainment Process." *American Sociological Review* 39 (1974b):668–681.

Alexander, K.L.; Eckland, B.K.; and Griffin, L.J. "The Wisconsin Model of Socioeconomic Achievement: A Replication." *American Journal of Sociology* 81 (1975):324–342.

Alexander, K.L., and Reilly, T.W. "Estimating the Effects of Marriage Timing on Educational Attainment: Some Procedural Issues and Substantive Clarifications." *American Journal of Sociology* 87 (1981): 143–156.

Astin, A.A., and Panos, R.J. *The Educational and Vocational Development of College Students*. Washington, D.C.: American Council on Education, 1969.

Astin, H.S., and Myint, T. "Career Development of Young Women During the Post-High School Years." *Journal of Counseling Psychology Monograph* 18 (1971):369–393.

Atchley, R.C. "The Life Course, Age Grading, and Age-Linked Demands for Decision Making." In N. Datan and L.H. Ginzberg, eds., *Life-Span Developmental Psychology: Normative Life Crises*. New York: Academic Press, 1975.

Bacon, L. "Early Motherhood, Accelerated Role Transition and Social Pathology." *Social Forces* 52 (1974):533–541.

Bayer, A.E. "The College Drop-Out: Factors Affecting Senior College Completion." *Sociology of Education* 41 (1968):305–315.

―――. "Life Plans and Marriage Age: An Application of Path Analysis." *Journal of Marriage and the Family* 31 (1969a):551–558.

―――. "Marriage Plans and Educational Aspirations." *American Journal of Sociology* 75 (1969b):239–244.

Bielby, W.T.; Hawley, C.B.; and Bills, D. "Research Uses of the National Longitudinal Surveys." SR18, Institute for Research on Poverty, Ann Arbon, Mich., 1977.

Burchinal, L.G. "Adolescent Role Deprivation and High School Age Marriage." *Marriage and Family Living* 21 (1959):378-384.

Call, V.R.A., and Otto, L.B. "Age at Marriage as a Mobility Contingency: Estimates for the Nye-Berardo Model." *Journal of Marriage and the Family* 39 (1977):67-79.

Clausen, J.A. "The Life Course of Individuals." In M.W. Riley, M. Johnson, and A. Foner, eds., *Aging and Society,* vol. 3. New York: Russell Sage, 1972.

Dowdall, J.A. "Women's Attitudes Toward Employment and Family Roles." *Sociological Analysis* 35 (1974):251-262.

Duncan, B. "Trends in the Output and Distribution of Schooling." In E.B. Sheldon and W.E. Moore, eds., *Indicators of Social Change.* New York: Russell Sage, 1968.

Eckland, B.K. "Social Class and College Graduation: Some Misconceptions Corrected." *American Journal of Sociology* 70 (1964):36-50.

Eckland, B.K., and MacGillivary, L. "School Profiles: Working Paper No. 1." Chapel Hill, N.C.: Institute for Research in Social Science, 1972.

Elder, G.H. "Role Orientations, Marital Age, and Life Patterns in Adulthood." *Merrill-Palmer Quarterly* 18 (1972):3-24.

———. "Age Differentiation and the Life Course." In A. Inkeles, J. Coleman, and N. Smelser, eds., *Annual Review of Sociology,* vol. 1. Palo Alto: Annual Reviews, 1975.

Elder, G.H., and Rockwell, R.C. "Marital Timing in Women's Life Patterns." *Journal of Family History* 1 (1976):34-53.

Empey, L.T. "Role Expectations of Young Women Regarding Marriage and a Career." *Marriage and Family Living* 20 (1958):152-155.

Featherman, D.L., and Carter, T.M. "Discontinuities in Schooling and the Socioeconomic Life Cycle." In W.H. Sewell, R.M. Hauser, and D.L. Featherman, eds., *Schooling and Achievement in American Society.* New York: Academic Press, 1976.

Ferriss, A.L. *Indicators of Trends in the Status of American Women.* New York: Russell Sage, 1971.

Folger, J.K.; Astin, H.S.; and Bayer, A.E. *Human Resources and Higher Education.* New York: Russell Sage, 1970.

Glick, P.C., and Carter, H. "Marriage Patterns and Educational Level." *American Sociological Review* 23 (1958):294-300.

Griffin, L.J. "On Estimating the Economic Value of Schooling and Experience: Some Issues in Conceptualization and Measurement." *Sociological Methods and Research* 6 (1978):309-335.

Griliches, Z., and Mason, W. "Education, Ability, and Income." In A. Goldberger and O.D. Duncan, eds., *Structural Equation Models in the Social Sciences.* New York: Academic Press, 1973.

Gysbers, N.C.; Johnston, J.A.; and Gust, T. "Characteristics of Homemaker and Career-Oriented Women." *Journal of Counseling Psychology* 15 (1968):541–546.

Iffert, R.E. *Retention and Withdrawal of College Students.* Washington, D.C.: U.S. Government Printing Office, 1957.

Jordaan, J.P. "Life Stages as Organizing Modes of Career Development." In E.L. Herr, ed., *Vocational Guidance and Human Development.* Boston: Houghton Mifflin, 1974.

Marini, M.M. "The Transition to Adulthood: Sex Differences in Educational Attainment and Age at Marriage." *American Sociological Review* 43 (1978):483–507.

Mason, K.O. *Women's Labor Force Participation and Fertility.* Research Triangle Park, N.C. National Institutes of Health, 1974.

Matthews, E., and Tiedeman, D.V. "Attitudes Toward Career and Marriage and the Development of Life Style in Young Women." *Journal of Counseling Psychology* 11 (1964):375–383.

Moore, K.A., and Hofferth, S.L. "Factors Affecting Early Family Formation: A Path Model." Unpublished manuscript, Urban Institute, Washington, D.C., 1978.

Nye, F.I., and Berardo, F.M. *The Family.* New York: Macmillan, 1973.

Rele, J.R. "Some Correlates of the Age at Marriage in the United States." *Eugenics Quarterly* 13 (1965):1–6.

Sewell, W.H.; Haller, A.O.; and Ohlendorf, G.W. "The Educational and Early Occupational Attainment Process: Replications and Revisions." *American Sociological Review* 35 (1970):1014–1027.

Sewell, W.H.; Haller, A.O.; and Portes, A. "The Educational and Early Occupational Attainment Process." *American Sociological Review* 34 (1969):82–91.

Spaeth, J.L. "Occupational Attainment Among Male College Graduates." *American Journal of Sociology* 75 (1970):632–644.

Spilerman, S. "Careers, Labor Market Structure, and Socioeconomic Achievement." *American Journal of Sociology* 83 (1977):551–593.

Tietze, C., and Lauriat, P. "Age at Marriage and Educational Attainment in the United States." *Population Studies* 9 (1955):159–166.

Trent, J.W., and Medsker, L.L. *Beyond High School.* San Francisco: Jossey-Bass, 1968.

Turner, R.H. "Some Aspects of Women's Ambition." *American Journal of Sociology* 70 (1964):271–285.

Voss, P.R. "Social Determinants of Age at First Marriage in the United States." Ph.D. diss., University of Michigan, 1975.

————. "Social Determinants of Age at First Marriage in the United States." Paper presented at the Annual Meetings of the Population Association of America, St. Louis, Mo., 1977.

Waite, L.J., and Moore, K.A. "The Impact of an Early First Birth on Young Women's Educational Attainment." *Social Forces* 56 (1977): 845–865.

Watley, D.J., and Kaplan, R. "Career or Marriage? Aspirations and Achievements of Able Young Women." *Journal of Vocational Behavior* 1 (1971):29–43.

Wolfle, D. *America's Resources of Specialized Talent.* New York: Harper and Brothers, 1954.

16 Life after College: Historical Links between Women's Education and Women's Work

Pamela J. Perun and
Janet Z. Giele

Life after college has never been a simple matter for female graduates. Unlike their male counterparts, who know from childhood that their adult lives will be devoted to work and whose undergraduate education is a means toward that end, college-educated women have been faced with contradictory and ambivalent societal assumptions about their adult lifework. The decisions to be made by women after college from among a set of competing alternatives—to marry; to work for pay; to continue in school; or to do all, some, or none of the above—have always been complex and difficult. The research reported in this chapter examines the life patterns of the graduates of a single-sex women's college since the turn of the century in order to explore the different ways in which women made their decisions and the different means by which they linked their educations to their adult lifework.

If the question for individual women has been, "How do I use my education after college?" the question for educators has been, "Toward what end is a woman's education a means? Opposing positions on that question are clearly evident in the remarks of two male educators at the turn of the century. According to Charles W. Eliot, a former president of Harvard University, women's work is in the home and women's education should reflect their ultimate destinies as wives and mothers. He asserted:

> It has been perfectly natural that the higher education of women should have been directed toward bringing women into new occupations. . . . But

This research has been supported by Wellesley College through a faculty research grant to Janet Z. Giele in 1969–1970 and a grant from the President's Discretionary Fund in 1973. In 1979 Pamela J. Perun received a Biomedical Research Support Grant from Wellesley College, which funded the research reported at the Research Conference on Educational Environments and the Undergraduate Woman. Our current work with these data has been funded by a grant from the Lilly Endowment, Inc., to Brandeis University (Janet Giele, principal investigator; Pamela Perun, co-principal investigator) in support of our project entitled "College Women's Changing Life Patterns, 1900–1980." We thank Arlene Rozzelle, Margaret May, and Mary Modoono for their assistance in the preparation of this chapter. We also thank Ann Stueve for her comments on its earlier versions.

wiser ways and methods will come into play, because it is not the chief happiness or the chief end of women, as a whole, to enter these occupations; to pursue them through life. They enter many which they soon abandon; and that is good—particularly the abandonment . . . the prime motive of the higher education of women should be recognized as the development in women of the capacities and powers which fit them to make family life more intelligent, more enjoyable, happier, more productive—more productive in every sense, physically, mentally and spiritually. [Eliot 1908, p. 105]

Professor D. Collin Wells of Dartmouth College, in contrast, cautiously gave women's education and work a broader definition:

The training of women in high school, college and professional schools is a late nineteenth-century notion and some of the new questions raised by it are our present concern. Permit me to say at the start that, in my opinion, the whole movement is natural and inevitable. . . . It is the demand of native powers to be given a chance to develop freely. In it the insistence of the human personality upon the right to express itself has come to full consciousness. In it women protest that they are no longer to be regarded merely as mothers of men or as housekeepers to minister to the comforts of men as autonomous persons with all the privileges appertaining to such. If motherhood and the activities of the home satisfy a woman of today she will be content with these, if they do not sufficiently express her personality enlightened justice will afford her appropriate educational opportunities equal to those of any man. To continue to exclude half of humanity from the cultivation and exercise of native talent would appear to involve economic wastes as well as an a priori assumption of the inferiority of women. [Wells 1909, pp. 731–732]

The link between education and work was never articulated as clearly for women as for men. Continually in dispute were whether or not a woman could choose her lifework or have it chosen for her, whether or not a woman should fit her lifework to her own personal needs and interests or to her biological capabilities, and whether or not a woman would spend her adult life inside or outside the home. The challenge to both college educators and college women has been to find ways to integrate higher education with individual women's adult life choices and goals in accordance with prevailing norms of women's work. (See chapter 2 by Antler for a historical analysis of educators' responses to this challenge.)

Historical changes in the roles deemed appropriate for women also have compounded the choices facing college-educated women. American women in 1900, for example, were presented with a much more complicated range of alternatives than women of fifty to seventy-five years earlier. Before the Civil War women had few role choices outside of marriage and motherhood. In some instances, they had a brief period of paid employment in a factory, elementary school, or cottage industry before attachment to some family either as a wife and mother or in the more precarious role of maiden aunt or spinster daughter (Cott 1977; Norton 1980). Educational opportunities for women beyond the secondary school were extremely limited. But after 1870 new possibilities for paid employment outside the home began to multiply. Women became laborers in shoe, garment, and textile factories and joined the trade-union movement. Middle-class women had more chance of completing a high-school education; by 1895 more women than men were graduated from high school (Women's Bureau 1969, p. 13) Women also had improved opportunities for a college education as the institution of higher education grew and matured in the late nineteenth century with the founding of new colleges, the expansion of the curriculum, and the development of the modern research university. They could attend female institutions such as Vassar or Smith or coeducational institutions like Cornell or the University of Michigan. But the question of how women were to *use* their educations after college remained unresolved.

As historians have noted, young female college graduates at the turn of the century faced a very real dilemma—"after college, what?" Antler (1977, 1980) documents the frequent incidence of postcollege depression in the members of the Wellesley College class of 1897 who, after four years of rigorous training in the liberal arts, found only extremely limited occupational opportunities and families eager to reimpose filial responsibilities. A college education, then, led women to no independent future and fulfilled no special purpose. The role it was intended to play in their adult lives was still undefined. Were women to use their education for professional and occupational advancement? Or were they to be women of culture while their male counterparts were to be men of learning and industry? The link between women's education and women's work remained ambiguous, drifting somewhere between the traditional homebound female pattern of the past and the more autonomous and adventurous pattern of college-educated men.

In this chapter we explore how some college-educated women of these early generations structured their adult lives from among the set of competing options open to them. We also examine the extent to which succeeding generations of these women made different choices to correspond with changing norms of education and work and the means by which they forged links between their educations and their chosen life work. Because a college education usually has a different meaning and purpose for individual women, addressing these issues is a complicated task. Explaining how women fashioned their life patterns requires taking into account both social and historical changes in definitions of women's work. Therefore, in order to examine how such changes are related to women's individual life histories in this research, we have utilized a life-course perspective in analyzing and interpreting our data. This perspective has emerged during the last decade as a new, multidisciplinary approach to the study of lives in time (see Har-even 1978; Riley 1979; Back 1980; Brim and Kagan 1980). Increasingly adopted by life-span developmental psychologists, sociologists of age and aging, social historians and anthropologists, and developmental biologists, the life-course perspective incorporates the following assumptions:

1. The human life span is viewed as an integrated whole from birth to death rather than as the sum of age-defined stages.
2. Individual development is seen as possible throughout the life course.
3. Behavioral change does not occur through a specific series of psycho-social crises, but from the interaction of biological, psychological, and social processes that are systematically linked in individual lives.
4. The life course of individuals and the life patterns of groups are affected by social and historical change. Hence, the life-course perspective is concerned with both social and historical change and individual developmental change processes and with their interactions (Neugarten and Datan 1973; Elder 1974; Baltes and Willis 1976; Riegel 1979; Perun and Bielby 1979, 1980).

Empirically, life-course researchers characteristically focus at the individual level of analysis on the antecedents and consequences of transitions in social roles and developmental processes and on their cumulative impact over the life span. At the societal and historical levels of analysis, the focus shifts to the ways in which cultural, economic, and sociodemographic changes alter existing normative systems of behavior and the allocation of individuals to major social roles. Life-course researchers view the social structure as dynamic rather than static in nature. Hence, normative systems with respect to age and sex roles are viewed as highly responsive to social change (Neugarten 1969; Riley, Johnson, and Foner 1972), and life-course research seeks to document the mechanisms through which such change transforms individual lives. In brief, then, the life-course perspective represents an innovative, multidisciplinary approach to the study of changing lives embedded in changing social systems (Elder and Rockwell 1979).

The changing life patterns of college-educated women, then, represent an empirical problem appropriate to the life-course perspective. Through an analysis of the life histories of the graduates of Wellesley College, this chapter traces the diverse ways in which these women linked education and work in their adult lives in the fifty years between 1911 and 1960. Given the nature of our data, our focus will not be on the psychological or developmental processes relevant to a woman's choice of a particular life pattern, but on the historical context and its relationship to women's changing choices of life patterns as a function of social, economic, and demographic change. This chapter therefore contributes to life-course theory and research through its examination of the role of education as a mediating influence between social change and individual change, a role largely unexamined to date for women. By analyzing the life patterns of many generations of college-educated women, this chapter seeks to illuminate the relationships between history, social change, and the individual life course with respect to women's education and women's work.

The College, the Data, and the Sample

Wellesley College, the source of our data, has long been a leader in the higher education of women. Founded in 1870 specifically for "women of modest means" (Glasscock 1975, p. 47), the college has remained remarkably unchanged as an educational institution and has maintained its tradition of liberal-arts education for women by providing a rigorous intellectual training in the physical sciences, social sciences, and humanities. Although the curriculum did undergo major revisions as new fields of inquiry and science were added and outmoded courses were dropped, no departments or curricula defined for women only, such as domestic science or home economics, were ever adopted (Onderdonk 1975). Although the college motto—"to serve, not to be served"—emphasizes a commitment to social reform and social service (Hawk 1975) as an important aim of higher education for women, the curriculum has always been integrally tied to the traditional liberal-arts education. Given the continuity of its curriculum and the high caliber of its faculty and resources, Wellesley College has always offered its students an educational experience equal if not superior to that available to men at comparable institutions. As a result, Wellesley graduates provide an important highly selected population in which to study the changing life patterns of college-educated women because they have shared in a stable, continuing educational heritage largely identical to that provided for their male counterparts.

The data on which this research is based come from the Alumnae Census conducted by Wellesley College in 1962. Its purpose was to collect information on the lives of its alumnae in preparation for a major review of the curriculum. Through a questionnaire designed to gather life-history data from the graduates, the college obtained information on their demographic characteristics; educational, marital and occupational histories; and community and cultural activities. Some 17,000 alumnae returned usable questionnaires, for an average 74-percent response rate by class. The data available to us from the census are quite extensive in terms of the numbers of people surveyed, the many historical eras covered, and the magnitude of the life-history material collected. We do not have complete life-history data from this survey; for example, some information important for life-course research on the precollege years of these women is incomplete by the social-science standards of 1980. Nevertheless, the breadth and depth of the life-history data found in the Alumnae Census of 1962 enables us not only to determine the current life patterns of these women, but also to examine how those patterns changed as a function of historical time and individual characteristics and experience after college.

The analyses reported in this chapter are based on a subsample of the total census population. Although the college had defined *alumnae* to include women who had attended without receiving a degree, we have limited our sample to those alumnae who earned baccalaureate degrees and to those who graduated after 1910 (the class of 1907 being the earliest in which 50 percent of its members were living in 1962). From this restricted population of some 13,000 cases, we selected a random 20-percent subsample for study. The findings reported here are based on our analysis of the life history of some 2,200 graduates in the fifty years between 1911 and 1960. We have also made rather arbitrary groupings of the classes studied into five-year intervals for reasons of economy and efficiency, recognizing that these divisions only roughly approximate the pre- and postwar and pre- and post-Depression eras of this century.[1]

It is important to note that we do not have available to us comparative data on other college-educated women during this period. As a result, we can not estimate how representative Wellesley College graduates were, at any one point in time, of the general female college population in the United States. We do know, for example, that Wellesley College students came from better-educated families and married better-educated husbands over time (Perun and Giele 1979), but we cannot determine whether these and other trends present in the Wellesley data reflect the experience of other college graduates as well. Our purpose in this research, however, is not to determine how the graduates of Wellesley College can be compared with the graduates of other institutions since the turn of the century. Rather, it is to demonstrate how the life patterns within this specific group of women who experienced a similar college education, and therefore had similar life chances and choices available to them after college, changed over time. The changes we detect in their life patterns should reflect crucial turning points in social definitions of women's education, women's work, and the links between the two.

Analysis of Women's Major Life Patterns, 1911–1960

To observe the life patterns of some women in the transitional decades around the turn of the century is to detect the gradual formation of a new normative system of age and sex roles that stretched the boundaries of appropriate behavior to fit the opportunities newly opened to women. The emerging life patterns of women took into account three important realities: (1) that the single state could be a viable and positive alternative to marriage; (2) that women needed independent means of support—that is, jobs—in an urban economy; and (3) that higher education was a necessary prerequisite to an occupation and hence to independence. At the same time, however, these new patterns developed within a social context that still largely prescribed limited education, marriage, and motherhood rather than a career for women. For the college graduate of these generations of change, the challenge was somehow to steer a course that allowed her to design an individual combination of new and traditional alternatives in adulthood. The following analyses describe the logical structure of major life patterns and their changing frequencies for these women and their successors.

It is important to note that there is no single obvious way to classify life patterns. As with any typology, the distinguishing characteristics between types selected by researchers according to their interests, and the variables utilized are related to the theories and questions that guide the research. Thus there are any number of ways to describe the predominant life patterns that emerged among college graduates after the turn of the century, depending on the factors used to distinguish the decisions or choices confronting women. By and large, researchers have built their typologies of women's life patterns to reflect one or more of the following major dimensions: (1) the choice of role from among such categories as never-married, housewife, or dual-career couple; (2) the demographic prevalence of important life events such as marriage and childbearing; and (3) the sequence and timing of variations in life transitions with respect to education, employment, marriage, and motherhood. Both the measures used in other studies and the findings themselves are instructive in suggesting how the shape of women's lives has changed in this century.

Previous Findings

One of the most familiar ways to chart women's life patterns is by type of role choice. The common distinction in earlier research was between women who chose a "traditional" pattern of marriage and motherhood with no paid employment outside the home, and those who chose a "pioneer" pattern, usually defined as including all possible deviations from the dominant pattern. More sophisticated terminologies and analyses of women's lives have just begun to appear in the social-science literature (Marini 1978; Perun and Bielby 1981), reflecting a belated concern with female role choice by scientists as a result of long-term changes in the status of American women. Chafe (1972), for example, in his history on American women, has documented the intense concern with women's roles that followed World War II; whereas feminists argued that educated women should be able to choose careers and achievement outside the home, antifeminists developed rationales for restricting women's destinies to the roles of wife and mother. In this climate, psychologists studied role conflict and the psychodynamic motives behind the choice of one pattern over another; not until the late 1960s, however, did an attractive image of the career woman as a role choice appear (Helson 1972). Sociologists like Young and Willmott (1975) focused on the correlation between the traditional pattern for women and the patriarchal family of preindustrial society and demonstrated that it was much less prevalent in the modern "symmetrical family" of the urban, industrial era. Level of education as a crucial determinant of role choice in women has rarely been studied. In the midst of the postwar ideological and scientific debate over women's roles, Newcomer (1959) surveyed female college graduates to determine whether they had used their educations primarily as scholars, artists, homemakers, or civic workers; but she gave no clear figures on the distribution of her sample among these categories. Only such studies as Ginzberg's (1966) study of highly educated Columbia women documented that most in fact were employed and earning good salaries.

Social historians and demographers have focused on the changing prevalence of particular events in women's lives. Uhlenberg (1969) demonstrated the shift in predominant life patterns among women after 1890 by counting the proportion of women who experienced crucial life events. He defined the typical or preferred life course as the chance to marry, have children, and survive to age 55 with marriage intact. Five major deviations from this pattern were the abbreviated (death before age 20), the spinster, the barren wife, the mother who dies young, and the widow (husband dies before age 57) patterns. Uhlenberg found that until 1980 the predominant pattern among women was the abbreviated life course but that subsequently the preferred life course far outstripped the others, representing nearly two-thirds of all women from 1920 on. Labor-force participation of women represents another measure of the prevalence of a particular role choice. For example, among women born in the decade before 1895, labor-force participation at age 20 was relatively high, about 30 percent, but at age 30 the level of participation was about 10 percent lower. By contrast, women born between 1895 and 1935 showed a very different profile. Although their percentage in the labor force also dropped slightly between the ages of 20 and 30, they reentered the labor force in large numbers in their middle years. Women born since 1935 exemplify yet another profile, one of continuously rising labor-force participation after age 20 (Kreps and Leaper 1976; see also Perun and Bielby 1981). Again, level of education has rarely been investigated in the prevalence of role choice and life pattern among

women. A very early study by Van Kleeck (1918) of the 17,000 female graduates of nine colleges demonstrated that over a third had some further graduate training beyond college and that 70 percent were gainfully employed at
some time. Only 39 percent had married (at a mean age of 27.3 years); and,
of those married, 70 percent (only 20 percent of the sample) had children,
with an average number of children per married woman of 2.1; Data on succeeding generations of college-educated women are sparse, however.

A third focus for typologies of life patterns, one of particular concern
to life-course researchers, is the timing and sequence of major life events.
The normative timing schedule of life events has been shown to vary significantly from generation to generation. For example, as succeeding generations live longer, the life event of widowhood is occurring later in people's
lives on the average. The early years of the life course have also had their
normative schedules of events altered over time. Modell, Furstenberg, and
Hershberg (1976) have demonstrated that the period of transition to adulthood, during which men and women finish their educations, marry, enter
the work force, and establish households, is concentrated into fewer years
for twentieth-century youths than it was for nineteenth-century youths. As
a result, historical and social change appear to have a major impact on the
timing of life events. There appears to be no fixed or perfect age at which a
life event should occur; the "ideal" age to marry, to have children, or to be
educated is merely a reflection of contemporary age and sex norms, not an
absolute or universal standard.

The scheduling of life events has also been examined with respect to
their consequences for individual lives both within and across generations.
People who deviate significantly from peers in their experience of life events
have been hypothesized to suffer the sanctions attached to violations of
social norms. Whether the deviant timing schedule is early or late, behavior
that is "off time" in comparison with contemporary norms is presumed to
affect the individual's life course adversely (Neugarten and Datan 1973).
Evidence exists, moreover, that contemporary norms in relation to the timing of life events are differentiated by such important social categories as
socioeconomic status, gender, and level of education; and the consequences
of being off time vary accordingly. Elder and Rockwell (1976) showed, for
example, that educated women who marry late are more likely to have husbands with equal or higher educational and occupational status, compared
with the husbands of women who marry early. Moore et al. (1979) documented the impact of early childbearing on white women's subsequent
chances for education and employment. Alexander and Reilly (1981) reported that age at marriage significantly affects the quality and type of
women's subsequent education (see also chapter 15 by Alexander, Reilly,
and Eckland). The sequence of life events is also an important empirical
issue; Boocock (1978) has articulated six different sequential patterns of

transitions in life events, such as entering the labor force, establishing a household, or marrying. Perun and Bielby (1980) distinguished three major categories in an early generation of academic women who were married: marriage before, after, or simultaneously with the attainment of the doctorate. The mean age of both marriage and the attainment of the doctorate was strongly related to the type of career established by women in each of the three categories.

The development of life-pattern typologies has by now reached the point where the most complete classifications include all three major dimensions: the *type* of role chosen, the *prevalence* of those choices, and the *timing* of life events and transitions. For example, Elder (1974) studied the life histories of sixty-five women born in the early 1920s on the west coast. Although unable to provide comparative data over time for women of different generations, he did identify the following major life patterns by 1964, distributed in his sample in this order to importance: (1) *Double track,* 34 percent who worked, married and had children, and then returned to work; (2) *conventional,* 25 percent who worked and then married; (3) *unstable,* 20 percent who were intermittently employed after marriage; (4) *stable homemaking,* 8 percent who had no work history either before or after marriage; and (5) *delayed employment,* 6 percent who worked only after marriage (Elder 1974, p. 234). In a recent study of Australian women, Young (1978) found that women's work sequences in relation to marriage and childbearing are related to the historical and economic circumstances of their youth. Women who married in the 1930s were unlikely to work at all after marriage until their children were at school. Those who married in the 1940s were likely to work after marriage but before childbearing and to return to work after the children had started school; among the most recently married groups, a sizable proportion worked continuously throughout marriage, even when the children were of preschool age. Overall, of women who had one of more children in primary school, Young found that 35 percent were not employed since marriage; 24 percent were employed before having children, but not since; 22 percent were employed only if all children were at least in primary school, and 10 percent had been continuously employed (Young 1978, p. 403). Her comparative figures for Britain and Europe showed somewhat higher proportions of women who became employed when their children reached primary school and over 20 percent who had been continuously employed. Finally, using data from the Five Thousand Families Study, Corcoran (1978) classified women's work patterns by number of interruptions since school completion. Generally speaking, black women have experienced more continuous employment and fewer interruptions than white women. Corcoran's results show that 36 percent of white women have experienced pattern A (continuous work since school); 30 percent, pattern B (nonemployment, then work); 15 percent, pattern C (work, nonemployment, work); 8 percent, pattern D (nonemployment, work, non-employment, work); and 12 percent, pattern E (at least five periods of alter-nating employment and nonemployment)(Corcoran 1978), pp. 61–62).

These earlier studies demonstrate that numerous classification schemes are possible—indeed, necessary—in order to represent accurately the vari-ability in life patterns of women of different eras, countries, and socioeco-nomic and educational backgrounds. Almost all address issues common to the life patterns of women: the various alternative ways of combining education, marriage, childbearing, and employment. In a few instances, researchers have been able to chart changes in these patterns over time and to investigate the timing and sequence of life events differentiating each pat-tern when longitudinal data are available. However, the role of education, and particularly of a college education, in determining the life patterns of women remains an empirical question.

Life Patterns in the Alumnae Census Data

In the case of the Wellesley College alumnae, for whom we have cross-sec-tional data collected from women of many different age groups at only one point in time, we cannot reconstruct the complete life history of each grad-uate. We do, however, have substantial information on the lives of these women from their graduations from college through 1962; and we can use this retrospective data effectively to examine their histories in detail. In order to distinguish between the married and the unmarried, those with and without children, those who did or did not receive further education, and those who were or were not employed after college, our analyses focus on four major components of role choice in their lives: their marital histories, their fertility histories, their educational histories, and their employment histories. The sample is grouped into five-year intervals by year of gradua-tion so that long-term trends can be seen more clearly.

The data presented in table 16–1 indicate several important long-term trends. Women who graduated near the early part of the century were more likely never to have married than those who graduated from the period of World War I onward. Beginning with women who graduated in the classes of 1916–1920, the proportion remaining single was cut in half, to an average 15–20 percent during the 1920s and 1930s. Among women who graduated in the 1940s, the proportion remaining single declined further, to under 10 per-cent. Although our data do not represent the completed marital histories of the classes of the 1950s, it is expected that never-married women constituted a similar, if not smaller, fraction of their members during those years of the baby boom. As more women married, more women became mothers. There is almost a linear increase in the percentage of married women who became

Table 16-1

Components of Role Choice, Wellesley College Alumnae, 1911–1960

	Percentage Experiencing Each Component of Role Choice			
Class Groupings, by Year of Graduation	*Marriage*	*Childbearing*	*Graduate Education*	*Employment*
1911–1915	69	57	56	87
1916–1920	81	69	58	88
1921–1925	78	69	61	92
1926–1930	86	75	62	89
1931–1935	88	83	71	90
1936–1940	88	80	71	89
1941–1945	94	92	56	95
1946–1950	92	87	55	92
1951–1955[a]	89	84	56	89
1956–1960[a]	78	51	61	94

[a]These figures probably do not represent the completed histories of women in these class groupings.

mothers from the earlier to the later class groupings. For example, in the classes of 1911–1915, 12 percent of the married women never had children, in contrast to only 2 percent of such women in the classes of 1941–1945. This trend occurred, moreover, in the face of relatively little change in the average number of children born to a married woman. Our data show the following mean number of children (per married woman with at least one child) for each class grouping: 1911–1915, 2.4; 1916–1920, 2.3; 1921–1924, 2.1; 1926–1930, 2.4; 1931–1935, 2.5; 1936–1940, 2.9; 1941–1945, 3.2; 1946–1950, 3.1; 1951–1955, 2.4; and 1956–1960, 1.6. More mothers evidently did not mean significantly more children.

With respect to the educational and employment data in table 16-1, however, the indications of an increased prevalence among these women in their experience of each of these components of role choice are more ambiguous. It is the women who graduated in the 1930s who completed some graduate training in the highest proportions. This finding is difficult to explain, given that these women graduated in the worst years of the Great Depression; perhaps further education was a necessity because jobs held by college graduates were reserved for men in those troubled economic times; or perhaps the percentages of women in subsequent classes attaining graduate education were depressed by their relatively higher fertility. Further analyses will be necessary to account for this trend. The surprising finding with respect to employment is, in contrast, the absence of any trend. About

Table 16-2
Timing of Events in Role Choices, Wellesley College Alumnae, 1911-1960

Class Groupings, by Year of Graduation	Mean Age at Marriage (Ever-Married Women)	Mean Age at Completion of Graduate Education
1911-1915	30	37
1916-1920	29	35
1921-1925	27	37
1926-1930	27	34
1931-1935	27	32
1936-1940	26	29
1941-1945	25	29
1946-1950	24	28
1951-1955[a]	23	26
1956-1960[a]	22	24

[a]These figures probably do not represent the completed histories of women in these class groupings.

90 percent of each class grouping reported having been employed after graduation. Because the data on employment are somewhat ambiguous, interpreting this finding must await the more detailed work-history data that will be collected in our follow-up study.[2] However, this preliminary evidence suggests substantially more labor-force participation by these women than would have been predicted on the basis of earlier research.

The timing information present in the data set reveals interesting trends, particularly with respect to marital and educational histories.[3] As table 16-2 indicates, the mean age at marriage fell from 30 in the classes of 1911-1915 to 22 in the classes of 1956-1960. As more women in each subsequent class grouping married, they did so at earlier ages on the average. At the same time, the mean age at completion of graduate education was similarly dropping; the classes of 1911-1915 experienced this event, on the average, at age 37, whereas the classes of 1956-1960 did so at age 24. In the later class groupings, graduate education appears to have become an event of the early rather than the middle years of adulthood. These findings confirm those of Modell, Furstenberg, and Hershberg (1976): the tempo of events in early adulthood has accelerated for women in the course of this century. The women of the earlier class groupings seem to have had more time to make their major life choices about marriage or further education. The women in the later class groupings concentrated those events in their twenties—increasingly, in their early twenties. It is interesting to note that although the mean age at marriage was dropping and the number of women marrying and having children was increasing, the average number of children held relatively steady. This suggests that childbearing, in addition to marriage and graduate education, was also becoming an event of the twenties. As a result, the adult life course assumed a very different structure and format for succeeding generations of alumnae. Members of the earliest class groupings experienced adulthood at a more leisurely pace, with several of their most important role choices occurring some ten to twenty years after college. Members of the later class groupings, in contrast, made important decisions (some, like childbearing, being irreversible in nature) immediately after college. The consequences of this dramatic shift in the timing of life events among college-educated women for their later lives will not be apparent, however, until the analyses of our follow-up data are completed.

Although these data on the major components of role choice, their prevalence over time, and the timing of life events have illuminated some important facets of the changes in educated women's lives during the course of this century, they fail to capture entirely the complexity of life histories. To establish the life patterns of these women requires more than an analysis of disaggregated roles and discrete events; women fill multiple roles and experience multiple events simultaneously throughout their lives. A life pattern is an expression of the ways in which women have woven the different strands of their lives into a colorful fabric; and analytical representations of life patterns should be able to show not just a swatch of material, but the whole cloth. In the next stage of our analysis of the life histories of these Wellesley College graduates, we bring together the dimensions of roles and life events that we discussed in isolation in order to illustrate the diverse life patterns found in our sample over time.

Figure 16–1 illustrates twelve possible combination of our four components of role choice: marriage, childbearing, graduate education, and employment. It is important to note that the diagrams represented in figure 16–1 depict only whether or not an individual woman participated in a specific component of role choice, not the temporal sequence of components in her life. As is immediately evident from the percentages, some of these patterns are rare in real life; only eight patterns are actually represented in our data. The woman with graduate education who never worked, the single woman who never worked, and the childless woman who never worked are not found in large numbers, if at all, among Wellesley College alumnae during this period. The most common pattern (pattern 1) is one in which all four components of role choices are represented. The second most common pattern (pattern 3) is composed of women who married, had children, and worked without additional education. Among single women, pattern 7, with a combination of graduate education and work, predominates and is the third-most-common pattern as well. The remaining five patterns each represent less than 10 percent of the sample, although they do illustrate important permutations of the three major patterns.

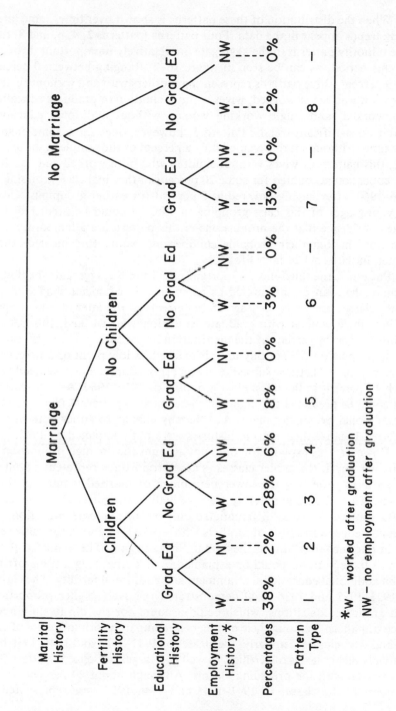

Figure 16-1. Typology and Distribution of Life Patterns among Wellesley College Alumnae, 1911–1960

When the distribution of these patterns is shown over time, some interesting trends appear in the data. Four patterns (patterns 2, 4, 6, and 8) that were minority patterns in the aggregate are relatively unimportant throughout this period, as can be seen in figure 16-2. Ranging between 0 percent and 9 percent, these patterns representing mothers with and without further education who never worked, wives without children or graduate education who worked, and single working women without additional education exhibit no significant trends. Pattern 5, however, does show some change over time. Although it represented only 8 percent of the sample in the aggregate, this pattern of wives without children who both worked and had further education accounted for some 20 percent of the final class grouping of 1956-1960, after having hovered at 5 percent for earlier groupings. Given the young ages of this class grouping in 1962, it could be predicted with some confidence that the proportions in this pattern are a temporary phenomenon, in that their probable childbearing would find most of these women in pattern 1 in later life.

Pattern 7, the third-most-important pattern in the aggregate, exhibits a U curve that can be interpreted as an indication of social change in the earlier classes and as an artifact of age effects in the later classes. Representing single women with graduate education who worked, this pattern accounted for 26 percent of the distribution in the earliest class groupings, but its proportion fell steadily until it reached its low point of 5 percent in the classes of 1941-1945; subsequently its proportions again rose steadily to reach 18 percent in the latest class grouping of 1956-1960. As with pattern 5, it could be predicted that many of the women in pattern 7 from the later classes would eventually marry and thereby change to either pattern 5 or pattern 1 because their marital histories were not completed by 1962.

However, this explanation does not account for the high proportion of single women in the earlier classes. These proportions represent stabilized life patterns reflecting the lower percentage of married women in those classes, a trend that apparently was gradually extinguished by the early 1940s. Patterns 1 and 3, differentiated only by the graduate-education/no-graduate-education status of mothers who worked, maintain the same relative importance over time as they did in the aggregate. The trends exhibited in both these patterns could be explained by hypothesizing a trade-off between additional educational attainment and additional fertility. The classes of 1931-1935 and 1936-1940 demonstrated relatively higher proportions with graduate educations, which could account for the dip in the importance of pattern 3 among their members as compared with members of earlier and later classes. Similarly, the classes of 1941-1945 and 1946-1950 had relatively higher levels of fertility, as well as a larger presence in pattern 3 in comparison with the preceding classes. Although about 40 percent of the members of the classes of 1941-1945·and 1946-1950 were represented in

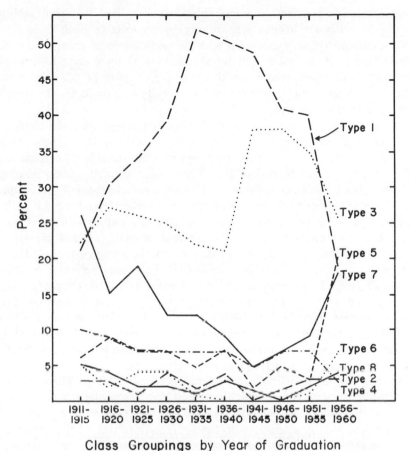

Class Groupings by Year of Graduation

Figure 16-2. Distribution of Eight Major Life Patterns, by Class
Groupings, Wellesley College Alumnae, 1911–1960

pattern 1, indicating that this trade-off was not absolute, the evidence does
suggest an important relationship between childbearing and educational
attainment in particular class groupings that should be examined in subsequent analyses of these data.

The distribution of life patterns over time found in figure 16–2 has
documented some long-term trends related to social and historical changes
in the proportions of Wellesley College alumnae marrying, having children,
and obtaining additional education. At the same time, some short-term

trends related to age effects in our sample have illustrated the lack of stability to be found in the life patterns of very young women. Both these phenomena demonstrate the strengths and the weaknesses of cross-sectional, historical data. As a result, our interpretations of these data have been made with caution; we expect that the follow-up data to be collected from Wellesley College alumnae will enable us to verify and to clarify the trends established in this research.

In summary, the life patterns of Wellesley College alumnae changed considerably during the course of this century. Among the earliest graduates, nearly 30 percent never married, but by 1930 roughly 90 percent did marry. Similarly, by the end of the 1930s, more women were attending graduate school; but by the end of the 1950s the percentages with such education were identical to those recorded by the earliest classes. Such shifts seem to signal the emergence of multiple-role life patterns. Rather than having to make an either-or choice between marriage and a career, it became increasingly possible for women to maintain two or more roles at once, or at least to structure their lives in such a way that both employment and families were feasible. As figure 16–2 demonstrated, the proportions of never-married women (patterns 7 and 8) show significant decreases in the fifty-year period from 1911 to 1960 when age effects are controlled. Concomitant with these declines are the relative increases in patterns 1 and 3, the mothers with some record of employment. More or less stable throughout this period are the less frequent alternatives, such as patterns 2 and 4, the married women with children who were never employed. These emerging multiple-role patterns were facilitated not just by long-term social trends of increased employment and education opportunities open to college-educated women, but by alterations in the normative timing of life events as well. The increased concentration of crucial events related to marriage, childbearing, and graduate education in the very early twenties in the lives of the later alumnae resulted in a significant alteration in the structure and format of their lives, the consequences of which remain an empirical question.[4]

Conclusions

Understanding the links between women's education and women's work in the lives of our Wellesley College alumnae requires us to take a step backward into history in order to place them within a relevant context. In an analysis of the biographies of the nineteenth-century graduates of Emma Willard's Troy Seminary, Scott (1979) discovered the proportion of ever-married women fell from 87 percent in the classes of 1821–1832 to 75 percent in the post–Civil War classes. Although the proportion of married alumnae with no children held steady at 30 percent, the mean number of children per married woman also fell from 4.5 for graduates of the 1820s to only 2.6 for graduates of the 1860s and 1870s. The percentage of married women employed outside the home remained around 7 percent throughout this period (Scott 1979, p. 16). Marriage data for early Mount Holyoke College graduates, a college that was also started as a seminary, exhibited a similar trend; some 78 percent of graduates before the Civil War were married, but only about 50 percent married in the classes of 1885–1910. Among Vassar graduates from the Civil War to the turn of the century, only 55–60 percent married. The average number of children per married woman was 2.1 in both groups (Newcomer 1959, p. 212). These low marriage and birth rates of college-educated women raised intense fears of "race" suicide among leaders influenced by the ideas of Social Darwinism and eugenics then popular (Wells 1909).

Against this historical backdrop, the post-1900 Wellesley College alumnae showed a restabilization of life pattern with respect to marriage and childbearing. Although the nineteenth-century data from Troy, Mt. Holyoke, and Vassar are quite limited in terms of their quantity, quality, and comparability with the twentieth-century Wellesley data, these findings taken together indicate a long sweep of change in college-educated women's life patterns during these years. Although any conclusions drawn from these data should be regarded as tentative, a preliminary comparison suggests that between 1880 and 1910 a substantial transformation took place in the normative systems of age and sex roles that governed women's life patterns. During that period the proportions of college graduates remaining single reached its peak, stabilized, and then eventually fell to its contemporary level of about 10 percent. Although the average number of children remained between two and three per family, there was a dramatic change in the numbers of married women who worked outside the home. In the nineteenth century, only 5–8 percent of the married Troy graduates were employed after marriage. In contrast, among twentieth-century Wellesley alumnae, only about 9 percent were *not* employed at some time after college. The most prevalent life patterns in the Wellesley data were those representing married women, with and without children, who had some record of postcollege employment. These statistics clearly indicate the workings of a long-term process of change that resulted in the emergence of an intricate multiple-role ideal in which marriage, childbearing, graduate education, and employment were combined in various ways in the adult lives of college-educated women by the mid-twentieth century.

Beyond the scope of the present analysis lie questions related to short-term alterations in marriage, childbearing, employment, and graduate-education attainment rates. Clearly, graduates of different eras had dissimilar life chances with respect to their opportunities to assume such roles.

Were these long- or short-term shifts due to changes in ideology, technology, or economic conditions? Why did certain life patterns become more prominent in one era than another? Easterlin (1968, 1980), for example, hypothesizes that women increase their educational attainment when chances for marriage are poor because of economic slumps and high rates of unemployment for men. Our preliminary analysis suggests that college women's chances to be both employed and married are associated to some extent with the social and economic conditions prevailing during their early years of adulthood (Giele 1973). Our further investigation of cyclical shifts in life patterns will appear in an examination of the relationships between social and historical change and women's roles (Giele and Perun, 1982). Our subsequent analyses will also focus on the factors associated with particular life patterns, both as antecedents and as consequences. We will be exploring such variables as husband's educational and occupational status, alumna's type and level of graduate education, alumna's participation in social or cultural volunteer activities, estimates of the extent of an alumna's labor-force participation, and so on, which may be crucial determinants of an individual woman's choice of life pattern. From these analyses will emerge a clearer picture of the trade-offs inherent in specific life patterns and of the characteristics of women who selected one over all others.

Our major conclusions from this stage of our research are threefold. First, the either-marriage-or-employment dichotomy assumed at the turn of the century to structure women's adult lives was largely an illusion even then. Our analysis of the life histories of Wellesley College alumnae has revealed intricate combinations of family *and* employment *and* graduate education constituting their most common life patterns throughout this period. Consequently, our second conclusion is that women's work is a concept complex in both definition and practice. As college-educated women became a common phenomenon in the twentieth century, their adult lives deviated less from contemporary norms of age and sex roles. At the same time, as their numbers grew, their lives after college gradually reflected a multiple-role ideal as contemporary expressions of women's work incorporated additional dimensions. Finally, we conclude that women's adult life patterns are not solely determined by women's individual abilities, attitudes, goals, or educational preparation. Although women's attributes and experiences contribute to their choices of particular life patterns, this research suggests that the range of life patterns available at any point in time is determined by the social structure and hence is beyond the control of individual women. A college education remains an important element in preparing individuals for their adult lifework; but women's outcomes and achievements after college must always be evaluated in relation to the social, economic, and historical conditions surrounding their lives.

Notes

1. Through a generous grant from the Lilly Endowment, Inc., we have just begun two-year study of historical changes in the life-course pattern of college-educated women from 1900 to 1980. During the first year, our primary task will be to complete our analysis of the existing data set and to describe and document the major trends in life patterns found among this specific population of educated women. In the second year of this project, having identified in that analysis particular classes that seem to represent crucial turning points in terms of historical eras of social change, we will collect follow-up data on the graduates of Wellesley College exactly twenty years after the initial survey. In addition, we will survey comparable graduates of a black women's college and a small, coeducational institution. Our tasks in the final year of the study are therefore to verify the existence of our identified patterns and to determine the relative importance of socio-economic origins, type of college attended and degree received, historical time, and social change in explaining changes in the life-course patterns of college-educated American women during this century.

2. The questionnaire item asked merely whether or not the individual had ever been employed. Although some survey questions did relate to the type of job the individual had and the length of time she was employed, much of those data were lost in the coding process. Therefore, we are unable to construct employment histories for each woman, although we do have several additional variables on employment that we will be analyzing at a later stage in our research.

3. We have relatively incomplete timing data on the lives of these women. For example, we know only the number of children they had by 1962, not their ages at each birth, so accurate timetables of their fertility histories cannot be constructed.

4. The follow-up data for alumnae of the classes of the 1950s should be particularly interesting. Perun (1981) has suggested that these women belong to a generation whose lives have been dramatically altered by changes in the social norms and roles about women's work in the years after they graduated from college.

Bibliography

Alexander, K.L., and Reilly, T.W. "Estimating the Effects of Marriage Timing on Educational Attainment: Some Procedural Issues and Substantive Clarifications." *American Journal of Sociology* 87 (1981): 143–156.

Antler, J. "The Educated Woman and Professionalization: The Struggle for a New Feminine Identity, 1890–1920." Ph.D. diss., State University of New York at Stony Brook, 1977.

————. "'After College, What?': New Graduates and the Family Claim." *American Quarterly* 32 (1980):409–434.

Back, K., ed. *Life Course: Integrative Theories and Exemplary Populations.* Boulder, Colo.: Westview Press, 1980.

Baltes, P.B., and Willis, S. "Toward Psychological Theories of Aging and Development.' In J.E. Birren and K.W. Schaie, eds., *Handbook of the Psychology of Aging.* New York: Van Nostrand Reinhold, 1976.

Boocock, S.S. "Historical and Sociological Research on the Family and the Life Cycle: Methodological Alternatives." *American Journal of Sociology* 84 (1978):S366–S394.

Brim, O.G., Jr., and Kagan, J., eds. *Constancy and Change in Human Development.* Cambridge, Mass.: Harvard University Press, 1980.

Chafe, W.H. *The American Woman: Her Changing Social, Economic, and Political Roles, 1920–1970.* New York: Oxford University Press, 1972.

Corcoran, M. "Work Experience, Work Interruption, and Wages." In G.J. Duncan and J.N. Morgan, eds., *Five Thousand American Families: Patterns of Economic Progress,* vol. VI. Ann Arbor: Institute for Social Research, University of Michigan, 1978.

Cott, N.F. *The Bonds of Womanhood: "Woman's Sphere in New England, 1780–1835.* New Haven, Conn.: Yale University Press, 1977.

Easterlin, R.A. *Population, Labor Force, and Long Swings in Economic Growth: The American Experience.* New York: National Bureau of Economic Research, 1968.

————. *Birth and Fortune.* New York: Basic Books, 1980.

Elder, G.H., Jr. *Children of the Great Depression.* Chicago: University of Chicago Press, 1974.

Elder, G.H., Jr., and Rockwell, R.C. "Marital Timing in Women's Life Patterns." *Journal of Family History* 1 (1976):34–53.

————. "The Life Course and Human Development: An Ecological Perspective." *International Journal of Behavioral Development* 2 (1979): 1–21.

Eliot, C.W. "Woman's Education—A Forecast." *Association of Collegiate Alumnae* 3 (1908):101–105.

Giele, J.Z. "Age Cohorts and Changes in Women's Roles." Paper presented at the Annual Meeting of the American Sociological Association, New York, 1973.

Giele, J.Z., and Perun, P.J. "Historical Swings in Women's Life Patterns." Paper submitted for presentation at the Annual Meeting of the American Sociological Association, 1982.

Ginzberg, E. *Life Styles of Educated Women.* New York: Columbia University Press, 1966.

Glasscock, J., ed. *Wellesley College 1875–1975: A Century of Women.* Wellesley, Mass.: Wellesley College, 1975.

Hareven, T.K. *Transitions: The Family and the Life Course in Historical Perspective.* New York: Academic Press, 1978.

Hawk, G.E. "A Motto in Transit." In J. Glasscock, ed. *Wellesley College 1875–1975: A Century of Women.* Wellesley, Mass.: Wellesley College, 1975.

Helson, R. "The Changing Image of the Career Woman." *Journal of Social Issues* 28 (1972):33–46.

Kreps, J.M., and Leaper, R.J. "Home Work, Market Work, and the Allocation of Time." In J.M. Kreps, ed., *Women and the American Economy: A Look to the 1980s.* Englewood Cliffs, N.J.: Prentice-Hall, 1976.

Marini, M.M. "Transition to Adulthood." *American Sociological Review* 43 (1978):483–507.

Modell, J., Furstenberg, F.F., Jr., and Hershberg, T. "Social Change and Transitions to Adulthood in Historical Perspective." *Journal of Family History* 1 (1976):7–32.

Moore, K.A.; Hofferth, S.L.; Caldwell, S.B.; and Waite, L.J. "Teenage Motherhood: Social and Economic Consequences." Washington, D.C.: Urban Institute.

Neugarten, B.L. "Continuities and Discontinuities of Psychological Issues into Adult Life." *Human Development* 12 (1969):121–130.

Neugarten, B.L., and Datan, N. "Sociological Perspectives on the Life Cycle." In P.B. Baltes and K.W. Schaie, eds. *Life-Span Developmental Psychology: Personality and Socialization.* New York: Academic Press, 1973.

Newcomer, M. *A Century of Higher Education for American Women.* New York: Harper, 1959.

Norton, M.B. *Liberty's Daughters: The Revolutionary Experience of American Women, 1750–1800.* Boston, Little, Brown, 1980.

Onderdonk, V. "The Curriculum." In J. Glasscock, ed., *Wellesley College 1875–1975: A Century of Women.* Wellesley, Mass.: Wellesley College, 1975.

Perun, P.J. "Age and the Woman: A Comment of Rossi's 'Life-Span Theories and Women's Lives.'" *Signs* (forthcoming).

Perun, P.J., and Bielby, D.D.V. "Midlife: A Discussion of Competing Models." *Research on Aging* 1 (1979):275–300.

———. "Structure and Dynamics of the Individual Life Course." In K. Back, ed., *Life Course: Integrative Theories and Exemplary Populations.* Boulder, Colo.: Westview Press, 1980.

———. "Towards a Model of Female Occupational Behavior: A Human Development Approach." *Psychology of Women Quarterly* (forthcoming).

Perun, P.J., and Giele, J.Z. "The Changing Function of Education in Women's Lives." Paper presented at the Research Conference on Educational Environments and the Undergraduate Woman, Wellesley College, 1979.

Riegel, K. *Foundations of Dialectical Psychology*. New York: Academic Press, 1979.

Riley, M.W., ed. *Aging from Birth to Death: Interdisciplinary Perspectives*. Boulder, Colo.: Westview Press, 1979.

Riley, M.W.; Johnson, M.; and Foner, A. *Aging and Society: A Sociology of Age Stratification*, vol. 3. New York: Russell Sage, 1972.

Scott, A.F. "The Ever Widening Circle: The Diffusion of Feminist Values from the Troy Female Seminary, 1822–1872." *History of Education Quarterly* 19 (1979):3–25.

Uhlenberg, P.R. "A Study of Cohort Life Cycles: Cohorts of Native-Born Massachusetts Women, 1830–1920." *Population Studies* 23 (1969): 407–420.

Van Kleeck, M. "A Census of College Women." *Journal of the Association of Collegiate Alumnae* 11 (1918):557–591.

Wells, D.C. "Some Questions Concerning the Higher Education of Women." *American Journal of Sociology* 14 (1909):731–739.

Women's Bureau. *Trends in Educational Attainment of Women*. Washington, D.C.: U.S. Department of Labor, 1969.

Young, C.M. "Work Sequences of Women During the Family Life Cycle." *Journal of Marriage and the Family* 40 (1978):401–411.

Young, M., and Willmott, P. *The Symmetrical Family*. New York: Pantheon, 1975.

17 Issues of Educational Equity in the 1980s: Multiple Perspectives

Pamela J. Perun,
Jeanne J. Speizer,
Mary Ann Gawelek,
Lourdes Rodríguez-Nogués,
Oliva M. Espín,
Carmen R. Besterman,
Florence C. Ladd,
Sumru Erkut, and
Lilli S. Hornig

We have every reason to be proud of the progress of women in higher education in the 1970s. By the end of that decade, more women than ever before were in college and receiving degrees; more women than ever before were going on to graduate and professional training; more women than ever before were using their educations in the labor force; and with respect to higher education itself, more women than ever before were making their way into faculty and administrative positions. It is therefore abundantly clear that Title IX, the federal law eliminating discrimination on the basis of sex in education, has begun to fulfill its promise, and that its policies of equal access and equal opportunity have been fully justified. Throughout the 1970s women successfully pursued their educational goals and, through their own perseverance, have conclusively demonstrated the irrationality and inefficiency of barriers to their full participation in higher education.

In the 1980s, however, different challenges for women in higher education will arise. Because we now represent the statistical majority in undergraduate education, it is clear that women have achieved some measure of equality in higher education. Nevertheless, we are all aware that, although mere numerical superiority provides some impetus toward change, it assures no lasting or fundamental institutional accommodation to the needs and concerns of women. Consequently, our efforts in the 1980s are less likely to be focused on issues of blatant discrimination or incidents of outright hostility toward women; the momentum and presence that women have achieved in higher education have largely eliminated the most obvious instances of sexism. As our critical examination of the processes and setting

We thank Mary Modoono and Maria Collins for their contributions to the preparation of this chapter.

399

of undergraduate education for women proceeds, the issues to be highlighted in the 1980s will undoubtedly be more subtle and therefore more difficult to identify and resolve. Our efforts to change institutions created of, for, and by men will require multiple agendas for action as well as research. The purpose of this chapter is to begin the drafting of such agendas using the following essays written by women from a variety of constituencies and perspectives in higher education as a basis for thought, discussion, and action.

One way of thinking about our future goals, as distinct from those already achieved, is to consider the differences between the concept of *equality* and that of *equity*. Throughout the 1970s women were largely concerned with issues of equality in higher education: equal access, equal opportunity, equal representation in the faculty ranks, and so on. In large measure, equality was defined as parity, on the reasoning that women were entitled to benefits and rewards of higher education equivalent to those that men received. Recognizing that women often obtained an education inferior in scope, quality, and utility to that provided for men, our efforts were directed toward placing women in the mainstream of higher education. In this, as the record shows, we have been very successful. At least at the undergraduate level, we have reached the goal of parity with men, with the result that simple issues of equality now seem anachronistic and secondary in importance.

We have come to realize, however, that the goal of mere equality was rather shortsighted and unrealistic. We have discovered that simply assuring women the right to sit in the same classrooms and attend the same colleges and universities as men was accompanied by little identifiable change within the institution of higher education itself. We also learned that the education men were receiving and that we wanted was in many cases no bargain. We already knew that higher education had significantly shortchanged female students in the past, but is now became increasingly clear to us that it was failing male students in important ways as well. As we reflected on this observation, we came to see that aspiring to a "man's" education was irrelevant, if not counterproductive, to our aims. We therefore found ourselves presented with a dilemma because our aspirations, as usual, had been too low. We had been prepared to don a man's education like a new suit of clothing taken at face value, but our closer examination had revealed how frayed was the material, how clumsy the construction, and how inadequate the styling that its purchase price alone should have guaranteed. Our solution to this dilemma was to refuse to accept this ready-made garment is and to request substantial alterations in order to improve its fit to our own needs and purposes.

Consequently, by the end of the 1970s, we had concluded that accepting the status quo in higher education would be a retreat rather than an advance toward our ultimate goal of placing women in the mainstream of U.S. society. It became clear that we would be better served in the long run by concentrating instead on making the institution of higher education more responsive to both male and female students. In our survey of the processes and settings of undergraduate education during the 1980s, for which this book is intended as a stimulus, our attention will therefore be focused on crucial issues of equity. By this we mean that our task is now to examine both the structural and the social-psychological aspects of higher education for practices, processes, and policies that are unfair and unjust to women. Once problems are identified, we expect to devise and implement creative solutions that serve both male and female students and, in the final analysis, measurably improve the practice and science of education. Issues of equity are therefore our primary concern in the coming decade. We have reached a crucial turning point in the history of women in higher education, and our own concerted efforts in the pursuit of justice and equality will determine our success or failure. Mindful of the legal maxim that "equity aids the vigilant, not those who slumber on their rights," we have no choice but to press forward.

The rest of this chapter is devoted to sections written by women presenting issues of equity from many perspectives in higher education. Jeanne J. Speizer, an educator, discusses an issue of equity in the classroom; and Mary Ann Gawelek, Lourdes Rodrígues-Nogués, and Oliva M. Espín, all counseling psychologists, illustrate issues of equity in the counseling center. Carmen R. Besterman, a community-relations analyst, then presents some equity issues in higher education for Hispanic women. Pamela J. Perun, a human developmentalist, and Florence C. Ladd, a psychologist, discuss the issues of equity that affect the faculty and administrative ranks in higher education for women and minorities. Finally, Sumru Erkut, a social psychologist, and Lilli S. Hornig, a chemist and human-resources analyst, raise equity issues that link the institution of higher education to the family and to the world of work.

Students Should be Seen *and* Heard
Jeanne J. Speizer

Imagine for a moment an undergraduate college where half the students, faculty, and administrators are women; where each discipline has an equal number of female and male students; and where every classroom has an equal representation of women and men. Utopia? The answer to all equity issues in education? No—even in this apparently utopian educational environment, the female and male students may still not be getting an equal education. Look closely at the classroom interaction. Who does most of the talking? Who tests their ideas and thoughts? The female students? Unlikely. Women are socialized early in their school careers to remain silent so as not to appear "brainy." Boys do not like smart girls, according to the myth, so girls should hide their intelligence; a girl who keeps her mouth shut and lets the boys do most of the talking might succeed in being popular and smart at the same time. With each passing year of school, more and more of the girls put their energy and talent into written assignments that allow them to outline their ideas clearly and logically for their teachers' eyes only. These same girls are often unwilling or unable to express their thoughts in classroom discussions; if they talk in class, they might find themselves labeled as aggressive and thus as too smart and independent for boys to want to date.

This profound silence of female students may start in elementary school, where many teachers equate students' neatness, silence, and orderliness with a good education. Boys receive the same message; but somehow the boys conform minimally, if at all. Thus in elementary school many more boys than girls are sent for special help or to special classes. Silent, withdrawn girls are usually not identified by the teacher as needing help because they do not cause any disturbance in the classroom. It is the exceptional teacher, indeed, who identifies silent students as needing special attention.

Educational expectations change after elementary school. Students are encouraged to test their ideas and to defend their approaches and solutions to problems. Bright boys, who never really conformed or believed the rules in elementary school, often respond to the new expectations with gusto. Bright girls often do not respond as readily, for they are confronted with a dilemma: to speak up and perhaps be labeled smart, hence unfeminine, or to remain silent and maintain the secret of their intellectual ability. Remaining silent and putting one's thoughts in writing is often the chosen solution. These written ideas, however, often are untested because the female student has not learned to defend her thoughts in public. She does not know how others will react to those ideas or how to use interactions with others to expand initial ideas and shape new thoughts.

Of course, some female students do not conform to the stereotypic expectation of silence. They speak up in high school and enjoy the interchange of ideas with their teachers and peers. By college, however, the pressure to remain silent in a classroom situation appears to increase, along with the pressure to find a mate. By the junior year of college, faculty members report, that a majority of their female students do not speak in class unless the teacher takes special steps to require and support verbal participation. Even in all-female classrooms, many faculty members report that only a handful of the students participate in classroom discussion. Instead, at the end of a spirited classroom discussion, a faculty member may be approached by female students who wish to share their ideas and thoughts. A positive response by the faculty member to those ideas and encouragement to speak in class next time does not necessarily guaranteee that the student will do so.

Thus we find female college graduates with comparable or even better grades than their male peers, yet somehow unable to fulfill the potential that those grades promise. Female professionals rarely advance as rapidly as their male cohorts, even in those fields comprising an equal number of women and men. Perhaps some of the lack of equal success may be explained by the female students' lack of preparation in testing their ideas verbally. The perceived risk of expressing their thoughts out loud may be so high that it is easier to follow other people's ideas than to expose their own. Advancement comes slowly to those who do not take verbal risks. Of course, everyone cannot be an idea person, a leader in his or her field—leaders need followers. Given equal selection criteria, however, one must seek explanations other than native ability alone for the phenomenon that most leaders are men and most followers women. One possible explanation is the relative silence in discussions that female students learned and practiced in school and carried into the work world.

In general, women do not talk less than their male peers. In fact, the opposite is more often true; in many situations women talk *more* than men. Women's verbal domination is most often in social situations, however. Early socialization has trained women to be aware of social nuances and the underlying feelings and subtleties in a conversation or an event. In these instances women work to handle or control the conversation and to intervene as negotiators. Skill in social interactions is certainly important in promoting harmony in communication, but it is not the only verbal skill needed for success. It is also important to be able to speak effectively, express opinions, and take the risk of saying something unpopular or against the general drift of the conversation. In other words, women must learn not only to be soothers and negotiators, but also, on occasion, to be sources of discomfort or conflict in exchanges of controversial or contradictory ideas.

The school years are an important training period for learning how to take verbal risks. If those years are used effectively, then speaking up or arguing for another, perhaps unpopular, approach to a problem would not be too difficult. But if women remain silent in school, the fear of speaking grows larger with each passing year. In fact, by the time women leave school, the risk of verbal confrontation in a group situation may be too threatening even to contemplate. One example of the power of such a self-censor was described by a middle-aged woman who recalled the first time she spoke in a meeting against the prevailing opinion. She said, "I broke out into a sweat and began to shake all over. The shaking continued throughout the meeting and reoccurred each time I risked expressing my ideas or opinions at meetings over the next few years. It took all my powers of concentration to overcome my dread of the shaking and to continue to speak up and state my views." How much easier it would have been for that woman had she overcome her dread of speaking and her self-censorship while still in school.

Faculty members who allow students to remain silent in class discussion are thereby doing them a disservice. An education that permits or promotes silence is preparation for the world of work only if followers are being trained. We certainly need educated followers, but they should not be the primary end product of an undergraduate education. For a classroom to approach utopia, it must be filled with women and men who speak out and test their ideas equally. Promoting classroom interaction is not a simple task, however. Faculty members may have to learn how to create an educational environment in which discussion flourishes. Silent students may need special help to break the hold of their self-censors. Whatever is needed must be done if we are to ensure that an undergraduate education, particularly a liberal-arts education, is useful to individuals when they enter the world of work and when they interact with each other as equals. Men will then hear their heretofore silent partners, and women will express and test their heretofore silent thoughts and ideas.

Counseling Issues of College-Age Women
Mary Ann Gawelek, Lourdes Rodríguez-Nogués,
and *Oliva M. Espín*

The counseling psychologist working in a college setting is concerned with the developmental issues of both men and women. However, in order to serve college-age women best, the counseling psychologist must be aware of the specific sociocultural factors that frame the developmental issues of women. Thus the purpose of this section is to discuss the unique needs of college-age women with respect to counseling. The fundamental issues encountered by this population will be presented and discussed briefly. Traditional and more creative intervention strategies will be presented. The use of primary prevention techniques will also be suggested.

In order to understand the needs of college women better, one must examine the conflicts of late adolescence. The primary concern of this developmental period is the struggle to gain healthy autonomy (Erikson 1968). This struggle is compounded for the adolescent woman by the increased intensity of mother-daughter bonding (Chodorow 1978) and by societal role expectations (Frieze et al. 1978). Attempts to resolve a peaceful separation from family and healthy individuation are often wrought with tension resulting from increased feelings of aggression. Because society neither sanctions the expression of aggression in women nor promotes female independence, these young women attempts to suppress their aggressive feelings or longings for separation may result in inappropriate behaviors or intrapsychic conflicts.

Although these developmental issues are experienced by women in late adolescence, their manifestations are dependent on variables such as early-childhood relations, socioeconomic class, ethnic background, and religion. The age at which these conflicts emerge varies, and the conflicts may re-emerge throughout the adult life cycle if resolution is not completed during adolescence. The manifestations of these conflicts range from severe distress to manageable discomfort. The coping behaviors of college-age women are unique and individually developed. However, there are several thematic issues that are most often presented by this population.

The brevity of this section allows us only to mention the most frequently presented themes in counseling college-age women. These issues are separation from family and issues of autonomy, career and role expectations, and body-image concerns and sexuality.

Separation from Family and Issues of Autonomy

For most women, entrance into college represents their first formal and major separation from their family. This period is a crucial time in the formation of peer relationships and is also a time in which there is an emphasis on the development of intimate dyadic coupling. Additionally, the young woman's decision-making skills are tested as she confronts her first significant independent adult choices. These conflicts may be expressed as homesickness, difficulties with peers and dilemmas with roommates, inability to relate to authority figures, (such as professors or residence-hall directors), withdrawal from social activities, and academic difficulties. These women may report feelings of general discomfort, unhappiness and depression, and anxiety; also, somatic complaints are frequently noted. It is common for these women to seek out counseling services on their own volition.

Career and Role Expectations

Developmentally, the college years are a time in which the individual must make decisions about the path her life will take. For women these choices are compounded by societal role expectations that may be in conflict with their inner strivings and career desires. Despite the apparent broadening of opportunity, stereotypic attitudes about appropriate careers for women still remain (for example, nurse, clerical worker, teacher, wife and mother). A college-age woman is faced with a conflict between her self-perception as a woman, which may still include being a wife and mother, and the wish to become a successful professional. Seldom can the young woman imagine becoming a successful woman and a successful professional at the same time.

Career conflicts are often expressed in the following manner: inability to entertain nontraditional careers; changing of majors and other career crises; failure in major courses in one's concentration; generalized low achievement; overall sense of indecisiveness; and conflicts with parents over career choices, which are compounded by the separation issues previously presented. These college women are often referred to counseling by concerned professors or may be self-referred to career counseling.

Body-Image Concerns

In general, women are more concerned about their bodies than men (Secord and Jourard 1953). This is particularly true in college-age women. The "ideal woman" as presented by the media constitutes an unobtainable goal. Therefore, women are caught in an unending struggle to reshape their bodies, change their faces, and clothe themselves in expensive and often uncomfortable clothing. This consistent societal emphasis on a woman's body leads women to use their bodies as a primary source of validation. This physical objectification creates a climate in which women compete against one another for male attention. Body-related concerns are often demonstrated in an increased emphasis on physical activity, an obsessional concern with clothing, a constant dieting pattern, and acute disturbances in eating behaviors. Women often enter counseling with an awareness that their concerns and behaviors are exaggerated and consuming too much time and energy.

Sexuality

Adolescence is a time of sexual awareness. During this period the development of sexual identity becomes obvious and crucial. The college-age woman, faced with new independence, confronts important decisions about how to exercise her sexuality. Crucial questions concern when and with whom to become sexually active; choices of sexual preference; and conflicts with parental, religious, societal, and cultural values. For women, there is a constant confusion between sexual desires and affectionate needs. Sparse or inaccurate information about sexuality compounds the difficulty in decision making. For those who are heterosexually active, pregnancy concerns and appropriate decisions about birth control are of paramount importance.

These sexual concerns are often illustrated by the following behaviors: (1) avoidance of the topic of sexuality or constant discussion of sexual issues; (2) rigid sexual abstinence or promiscuous behavior; (3) repeated pregnancy; (4) contraction of venereal disease; (5) social withdrawal; and

(6) depression or anxiety. Although these women may seek out counseling, sexual concerns are seldom the presenting problem and usually do not surface until later in treatment.

Counseling Interventions

Having presented issues most commonly faced by college-age women, we can now address the various means of counseling interventions. Traditional approaches to counseling emphasize the importance of early developmental history and intrapsychic difficulties. Often treatment consists of long-term verbal counseling. Although for some women this approach may be beneficial, there is the inherent danger of perpetuating stereotypic role expectations for women. The classic Broverman et al. (1970) study illustrates this point dramatically.

Currently we have recognized the need to develop theoretical concepts and intervention strategies that focus on the unique developmental and behavioral concerns of women. The sociocultural expectations that women face must be considered in developing a treatment strategy for the female client. Therefore, counselors of women must be aware of the specific internal psychological process the individual woman confronts, as well as her broader phenomenological world. In other words, feminist understandings of women should constitute an integral component of the counseling process.

The interaction between the counseling psychologist and the college-age woman must be a dynamic process. Emphasis should be placed on problem-solving, assertiveness training, education, and helping the clients understand their personal conflicts in a broader cultural context. It is particularly important to emphasize the counseling alliance because of the need to promote healthy autonomy, increased self-esteem, and the ability to experience support within appropriate boundaries. Often the counseling psychologist's most crucial task is that of a role model. In addition to individual counseling, group work and support groups have proved beneficial.

Realization of the aforementioned needs and conflicts of college-age women makes it possible for the counseling psychologist to intervene before problems emerge. Primary prevention illustrates an emphasis on mental health for women. Suggested interventions for this population are the following: (1) *consciousness-raising groups* for women focusing on women's role in society, women and social class, women and ethnicity, and women and sexuality; (2) *educational workshops* focusing on the biological concerns of women, birth control, career development, and sexual discrimination; and (3) *support groups* related to issues of intimacy, sexuality, career choice, and role conflicts. The counseling psychologist should be involved

in consultation with residence staff and academic advisors. It is often helpful to create a network of female professionals to serve as resourses and role
models to this population.

Active attempts to educate and support college-age women during this
crucial period may result in a less frequent need for secondary and tertiary
counseling interventions.

Hispanic Women's Issues for the 1980s in Undergraduate Education
Carmen R. Besterman

One of the greatest problems of Hispanics in the United States is their inability to find ways to integrate themselves into the American community.
Conversely, it is also a problem for Americans to comprehend the difficulties people from other cultures have in appreciating American values and
points of view.

The word *Hispanic* relates to the people, speech, or culture of Spain,
Portugal, and Latin America. Even though the origins are Hispanic, each
country—indeed, each region within these countries— has developed its
own national identity, customs, and cultures. In the United States these
differences are ignored primarily because of lack of knowledge. This general national cultural problem pervades academia as well as other areas of
our society.

Traditionally, Hispanics, and particularly Hispanic women, have been
poorly represented in U.S. universities and colleges. This is true not only of
students at the undergraduate level, but also of graduate students. Faculty
members with Hispanic backgrounds are few in number, as are Hispanic
administrators. Cultural, language, and socioeconomic differences have
contributed greatly to this situation. If this is to change, there must be a
firm commitment on the part of the educational institution to make every
effort to ensure that qualified Hispanic female students are given access to
an undergraduate education, and that qualified Hispanic female faculty and
administrators are recruited. All of them should be provided with an opportunity for upward mobility and for integration into the American mainstream.

In common with other minorities, Hispanic students, especially
women, have not had the opportunity to get a sound foundation in mathematics, science, and English at the junior-high-school level. Therefore, they
do not have much basis for considering careers in the science-based professions in which, to date, they have been virtually unrepresented. Unfortunately, they also lack the home environment in which these skills and
ambitions are nurtured. It would appear that specially targeted programs

are needed at both the high-school and undergraduate levels to cater to the special cultural needs of Hispanics.

Furthermore, colleges and universities should strive to provide professional counselors who are aware of the needs of the Hispanic student population and who are able to deal with their problems in their own language. Support systems through peer groups, advisers, and social and cultural organizations should be encouraged.

With the government's reduction of student-loan funds and other support to higher education in general, along with the escalating costs of tuition and decrease in financial aid, the problems of the Hispanic female student of the 1980s are extremely serious. Handicapped by a dual minority status— being Hispanic and being female—and burdened by linguistic problems, the challenge for her is great. Education is clearly the road to opportunity for Hispanic women. A sound undergraduate education will enable the student of the 1980s not only to bridge the cultural gap, but also to understand how the social and political system operates in the United States and what she can do to benefit and to contribute to the strengthening of that system. The Hispanic community in the United States itself requires a large number of leaders to work at different community levels to build the harmonious society of the future.

The Mythic Search for the Qualified Woman
Pamela J. Perun

To date, women have been more welcome on college and university campuses as tuition payers than as salary earners. Although female students have surpassed men in numbers at the undergraduate level and are approaching parity at the graduate- and professional-school level, no such equality has been achieved in the faculty or administrative ranks of higher education. When asked to account for this discrepancy, most faculty and administrators responsible for hiring decisions point to a profound and prolonged dearth of women qualified to occupy their available positions.

To some observers, this rationale is suspect. The contemporary "qualified-woman gap" seems analogous to the highly publicized "missile gap" of the 1950s in that it appears to exist more in rhetoric than in fact. Particularly in the 1970s, those same colleges and universities that are so far unable to locate qualified women to employ and promote are themselves busily cranking out vast numbers of women with appropriate, earned degrees. As students, women pay the same fees, pass the same courses, fulfill the same requirements, and receive the same degrees as men. What, then, are those magical qualifications that they lack? What distinguishes an unqualified woman from a qualified woman or man? How are such qualities to be developed and demonstrated in order for women to obtain employment in a discipline or position for which they have already spent long, expensive years in preparation? As yet, no one has advanced a satisfactory definition of a "qualified" (a term applied exclusively to women) woman or an explanation of the process required to produce one. To some observers, this suggests that the answers to the foregoing questions will not be found by examining the records of individual women for examples of their training and competence. A more likely place to find some answers is in the economics of the situation, with particular attention to be paid to the demand-side variables because the supply side of the equation is well in order.

Prominent among issues of educational equity in the 1980s, then, should be those of employment, promotion, and pay for women in higher education. It is natural and inevitable that many women, as a result of the educations for which they have paid in time, energy, and money, will aspire to full academic participation as scholars, teachers, and administrators. Any individual or institution that denies women the opportunity to do so largely because of gender is behaving unjustly and unethically. Even given the difficult financial position in which many colleges and universities find themselves, there is no justification in equity for their refusal to employ on equal terms with men the women whom they themselves have produced. It is further to be hoped that there will soon be no justification in law either. The protection of Title IX *must* be extended to questions of fair employment practices in higher education. Not to do so is to send a clear message to colleges and universities that sex discrimination in employment and promotion will be both permissible and legal. By any standards, that would be a hypocritical travesty of justice for all concerned. It would be a personal tragedy for all women in higher education, as well as for higher education itself

Women and Minorities in Higher Education
Florence C. Ladd

The future of education in the United States will be determined by the actions of independent institutions and individuals, who must have the courage to promote the movement of women and minorities into the mainstream of education. The thrust must come from independent colleges and universities that should demonstrate their belief in equity in education in the following ways: (1) reaffirmation of policies related to educational equity; (2) successful searches for women and minorities; and (3) effective promotion of the careers of women and minorities.

In a pluralistic society that has designated its educational system as the nation's laboratory for social change, schools, colleges, and universities now are primarily responsible for providing experiments that demonstrate the possibility of blending pluralism with equity successfully. In primary and secondary schools the experiment has relied on busing students; encouraging parental participation in policymaking; and, in urban systems, giving minorities and women more visible and responsible positions. Increases in the representation of female students, faculty, and administrators in colleges and universities have been accomplished through changes in policies and patterns of admission and in hiring practices. The redistribution of financial aid, the creation of third-world studies, and the introduction of minority personnel in student services have contributed to an increase in minority representation. In the 1960s and 1970s there were heartening examples of progress toward social reorganization in colleges and universities. There was movement toward the restructuring of educational opportunity.

The shift in the economic and political character of the nation in the 1980 national election brought a diminution in public concern about educational opportunity and the withdrawal of federal support for progressive social and educational programs that had benefited minorities and women. When federal support falls away, we must look to the private sector for financial resources and moral reinforcement. Independent institutions once more are needed to provide the moral leadership that will serve to reaffirm the commitment to educational equity and to ensure compliance with the policies and laws that favor educational equity. Independent colleges and universities now must take the lead in demonstrating that integration and academic proficiency not only are compatible, but also serve to enhance the quality of higher education. The most prestigious institutions must lead the way. They should begin by reexamining the composition of their administrative offices and faculties. At every level and in every department, key individuals should feel responsible for creating employment and advancement opportunities for those of their colleagues who are minority-group members and women.

In higher education, public institutions often look to independent institutions, particularly the older independent institutions, for leadership and direction in academic matters. The recruitment of students, staff, and faculty members matters greatly to academic institutions. The social composition of colleges and universities contributes significantly to the intellectual wealth of institutions. In recent years, most historically male and white institutions of higher education have been enriched and broadened by the inclusion of women and minorities. The value of their (our) contributions should be assessed and acknowledged. With this acknowledgment should come statements that reaffirm the value of equity and diversity in the classrooms, conference rooms, and boardrooms of those institutions.

Beyond reaffirmation of the value of educational equity, we need further evidence of credibility through successful searches for women and minorities, particularly at the senior level. When predominantly white male institutions conduct searches for senior-level faculty members and administrators, minority-group candidates often emerge, are interviewed, and then, with few exceptions, are quietly ignored or cordially rejected. Such searches usually focus on the candidate's attributes, accomplishments, and potential. When one is not selected, it is assumed that personal or professional inadequacies are the reason. But what about the attributes, accomplishments, and potential of the institution? Is it prepared to place minorities and women in senior faculty and management positions? Is the institution prepared to have a woman or a minority-group member in a senior post? If search committees were to analyze the readiness of the students, faculty members, and adminstrative staff of their respective institutions to accept people from "nontraditional" backgrounds in positions of authority, it is conceivable that we would find an increase in the numbers of blacks, Asians, Hispanics, native Americans, and women of all groups in the upper levels of college and university administration and instruction.

Ventures that focus on women with adminstrative talent (some of them members of minority groups), such as the American Council on Education's National Identification Programs for the Advancement of Women in Higher Education, should shift their focus occasionally from individuals to institutions. Among the goals of such programs should be the development of strategies to prepare institutions for a changing image of leadership figures and the identification of colleges and universities where those strategies could be used. It is frustrating and futile to prepare people for opportunities that do not exist for them. The expansion of opportunities and options for women and minority-group members in academic institutions could be accomplished through the affirmative preparation of the people who determine those institutions' destinies. In addition to working with identification and recruitment programs, institutions that intend to hire women and minorities at the senior level should make a special effort to involve female and minority-group administrators and faculty members in the planning. Such collaboration could lead to more searches in which minority-group candidates emerge, are interviewed, and are then cordially selected.

At every level it is important for women and minorities to work in institutional environments that promote their professional growth and development. Success in searching for and finding women and minorities is not sufficient. Keeping them on in a climate that elicits their best performance and enhances the institution is essential. This can be accomplished in institutions that trust their selection procedures and determine that the persons selected meet the institution's requirements ideally. Confidence in positive institutional decisions regarding women and minorities should be fostered in colleges and universities. The belief that women and minorities can continue to serve successfully must be expanded.

Men Have Families, Too
Sumru Erkut

Issues of educational equity for women are at once a part and a reflection of the total social order. Any social change toward achieving educational equity for women will necessitate changes in the other parts of the system. Moreover, having been the underprivileged party, women cannot be expected to shoulder the responsibility for social change alone. To assume that educational equity for women—or, for that matter, any underprivileged group—will come about solely through the efforts of the underprivileged is at best overly optimistic and, at worst, tantamount to blaming the victim. In my plea for concerted effort by all parties to bring about educational equity for women, I will focus on the necessity to share the responsibilities for the family. That women will be the ones to shoulder the responsibility for maintaining home and family has long been held against women who wished to pursue a serious education. For women to achieve educational equity, men must assume their part of the household and child care responsibilities. Educational institutions must be willing to prepare men to assume a more encompassing family role. Moreover, there must be social recognition and support for men and women sharing the responsibility for maintaining a family life.

A review of the literature on women's postsecondary education suggests that many women, educators, and researchers have not been able to separate concern for women's education, and its intended outcome, from women's assumed responsibility for forming and maintaining a family. Until the early 1970s this issue was identified as the career-versus-family dilemma. Several solutions were offered. One was to regard college education as a "finishing" process: during college the young woman would meet the future husband who would provide for her financial security in life. Many women majored in liberal arts with no corresponding career path to the labor force. Another solution was to look on college as a way of preparing for life's uncertainties. Although meeting a future husband who can provide for their needs would be the best of all outcomes, many women realized that they might spend at least part of their adult life alone. Hence they prepared for the contingency of having to earn a living if no husband existed or was willing or able to support them. Such contingency planning often resulted in preparation for careers in teaching, nursing, or secretarial work that could be done intermittently as the need arose. The occupational segregation created by the concentration of women into these low-paying jobs has been a major contributor to women's lower earnings relative to men. A third solution was to recognize the family-versus-career dilemma as an insurmountable barrier and to opt for a career. It is no coincidence that many of the achieving women of this century have been single women (unmarried, divorced, or widowed) or women who married later in life. Finally, a few courageous women fought to combine a career with family. The stories of their struggle can be found in any feminist journal or anthology.

Since the 1970s the family-versus-career dilemma facing women has been recast as the problems facing working couples or dual-career families. This shift in the focus of the problem from the woman to the couple or family is clearly a step in the right direction. However, even a cursory perusal of the two-worker- or dual-career-family literature points out that all parties involved (wife, husband, and the researcher who conducts the studies) expect the woman to be the person responsible for making the two-worker or dual-career family work. This issue is most vividly illustrated in a recent study of coeducation that surveyed student attitudes in six selective liberal-arts colleges in 1978. Female students were asked if they thought they would stop working to stay home to care for their young children. Male students were asked if they wanted their *wives* to stay home from work to care for their young children. No one seems to have entertained the possibility that a man, too, might stay home to care for his children. Since it takes a woman and a man, both of whom are presumably employed, to make a baby, it is not too farfetched to suggest that it need not always be the woman who cares for the children. Indeed, contrary to popular opinion, men can make excellent care givers to children of all ages. They also can be good housekeepers.

The idea that women need not be the sole or primary family care givers has tremendous implications for educational equity. This idea would make it realistic for women to choose rigorous educational paths leading to a variety of challenging and fulfilling careers. Educators and educational institutions would be more likely to encourage women to pursue a first-rate educational experience knowing that women can successfully combine a career and family if they so choose.

However, sharing the responsibility for the family will not come about simply because career-oriented women wish it to happen. Men must be psychologically prepared to assume household and child-rearing responsibilities. Employers, and also society at large, must be able to reward men for sharing these responsibilities. At present, both men and women who carry their part of the load of making a two-career family work are placed in a disadvantageous position relative to their fellow workers who marshall not only their full energy but those of their stay-at-home wives to promote their career development.

Colleges and universities have never explicitly taken on the responsibility of preparing students for family roles. The reluctance—one can go so far as to say failure—of educational institutions to prepare men and women for all aspects of adult life has been a serious handicap to all parties concerned. However, they have certainly been cognizant of women's family-versus-career dilemma and, lately, of problems women face in making two-career families work. This recognition has taken a variety of forms; on the positive side, it has led to the provision of special career counseling for women. The challenge for the 1980s is for colleges and universities to recognize that men, too, have a family life. There are at least two ways institutions of higher education can demonstrate that recognition. One obvious way is to incorporate into career counseling for men the idea that men will have family roles in addition to the traditional breadwinner role (which they are likely to share with their wives). Just as counselors discuss family-life implications of different careers with female students (at least in some college counseling centers), the same issues can be discussed with male students.

The second way is more indirect but likely to be more effective: to have male faculty, administrators, and staff serve as role models for successfully combining career with family life. Colleges and universities can encourage their male employees to combine these two aspects of their lives more visibly in a variety of ways. Some examples include providing paternity leave when there is a newborn, making it socially acceptable for fathers to stay home with sick children, not scheduling so many meetings after hours and on weekends (or providing child care when such meetings are unavoidable), and making flex-time and part-time careers available to men (and of course to women). We know that female students already look to female employees to see how a professional life can be combined with a family life. Male students will surely benefit from male role models who can successfully combine work with family responsibilities. Sharing of family responsibilities by men and women is but one of the many changes that must occur if women are to achieve educational equity. But it is an important change. Only when women can use college to prepare for a working life in which they will not be disproportionally burdened with family responsibilities can strides begin to be taken to assure equity in education for women and for men.

Issues and Answers
Lilli S. Hornig

The 1980s will be a crucial period for women in higher education; for the first time in history women will be a clear majority of undergraduate students and will approach parity in graduate and professional enrollments, barring renewed institutional action to limit their access. In the face of the financial and demographic pressures facing higher education, the possibility of such limitation may seem farfetched, but we need to remind ourselves that it has happened before. The threat of "feminization" of any field or institution that wields power and influence has always been regarded as grave; instances of imposing quotas on women in one form or another when their enrollments rose to near parity abound in educational history, from the early days of coeducation to the late 1960s, when strict, low limits on women's admissions were maintained in nearly all graduate and professional programs. The overriding equity issue for women in higher education will be to maintain the momentum of the last twenty years toward achieving full equality not only in numbers of students, but also in increasing the proportions of women faculty and administrators to the end that academic institutions may become more equitable in fulfilling the total educational needs—curricular, social, and developmental—of all their students.

Whatever the current (or even the traditional) arguments about liberal versus career-related education, there is little doubt that higher education in the United States has always been conceived of as vocational training—for men. Brown University's charter was granted in 1764 for the purpose of educating "men of usefulness and reputation"; few men since then have had the luxury of going to college without the firm knowledge that the threads of their education must somehow weave the fabric of a career. Women, on the other hand, have often become truly educated by virtue of being forcibly excluded from most professional or career aspirartions and therefore being relatively free to follow wherever their intellectual interests led. Note, however, "relatively." Women's colleges and those divisions of coeducational institutions to which women were admitted (subject, almost always to availability of properly supervised housing, provision for bathrooms, and so on) imposed their own assumptions about the kind of education that is suitable for women. Engineering, for instance, the single largest professional field for male students, was not accessible to women; the hard sciences and mathematics, deemed overly taxing to the female intellect, formed a minor and neglected part of the curricula open to them.

Many such limitations are now history, useful for understanding why so many differences have traditionally existed between the education of men and women. But have they not been obliterated in the changes of the last two decades, so that they need not be a concern for the future? The changes have indeed been remarkable; the great influx of women into higher education, the sheer impact of numbers, masks other trends that also have long-range importance. Perhaps the most influential of these is the growing convergence between male and female educational patterns. That convergence is evident with respect to all aspects of higher education—timing, completion rates, types of institutions attended, curricular choices, and progress to graduate and professional programs—and carries profound implications for higher-education policy in the 1980s.

Not only have women stepped up the pace of their education while men have relaxed theirs somewhat, but women also are preparing in ever growing numbers for what used to be almost exclusively male careers—in the sciences; in law, medicine, and business; and, most notably, in the most stereotypically male fields such as engineering and agricultural sciences.

Simultaneously, women's propensity to major in the arts and humanities is declining to levels more nearly comparable to those of men. The resulting overall shift of enrollment away from the traditional core fields of the curriculum accounts for many of the management problems in higher education, creating surpluses of faculty (and new Ph.D.'s) in the humanities and some of the sciences at the same time as shortages develop in engineering and business-related fields.

What accounts for these fundamental changes in women's view of themselves and their own future? The single most important change in women's aspirations comes from their *expectations* of equal access to careers; that for the most part those expectations remain exaggerated or unrealistic is beside the point. People, female and male, act on their perceptions—and the perception of equality has been fostered by legal mandates, by the media's insistence that "women can do anything now," and certainly also by hopeful feminists. For the first time in history, then, large numbers of young women about to embark on advanced education are making the first serious choice about the shape of their lives—whether to pursue a career or not.

This choice is a new one, since most serious professional careers previously were not open to women except in unusual cases; but it raises further problems of balancing personal and professional needs and obligations. Society still leaves the burden of solving these very largely to the individual woman.

The first step—the decision whether or not to pursue a career seriously—is an enormous added burden for women compared with men, who have known since early childhood that they must do so. Relieved of this fundamental inner debate, by the time they enter college they have already had several years in which to explore interests and options aided by a whole array of social supports, and are prepared to make at least interim choices. Women, on the other hand, having had to settle the prior question of whether to pursue a career at all, are only beginning to think seriously about which field to pursue, and few social supports exist to help them clarify the issue. Potential role models, mentors, and sponsors of their own sex are scarce in the learned professions, in business, or in public life; college faculty of a status and influence that might inspire emulation are men; women who could say to them, "I've done it, and the rewards outweigh the problems," are hard to find. All these problems certainly contribute to the often-noted lack of career commitment of women students, the contingent nature of their educational and career decisions. They are gambling not only with a few years possibly spent in the wrong pursuits, but with the central structure of their lives.

The women now reaching young adulthood are the first generation to have to face these choices on a large scale, the first to have spent all its conscious years in a social and educational climate that assumes a measure of equality for them but as yet does little to support it. They have none but male precedents by which to solve those urgent equations that will measure trade-offs among opportunity costs, human-capital formation, and returns to educational investment. Little information from the past serves to guide them: the working lives of women are not yet an integral part of the historical, religious, philosophical, or social traditions offered for their study. The counselors who should help them make these decisions are characteristically ill informed about career issues for women and tend to favor traditional choices. The competitive sports that colleges and universities support to foster both individual achievement and collaborative effort among men are only grudgingly being opened to women. When Judge J. John Fitzgerald of Connecticut, in ruling against the plaintiff in a Title IX case, stated that "athletic competition builds character in our boys. We do not need that kind of character in our girls, the women of tomorrow" (Duffy 1981, p. 1), he surely spoke for a host of academic administrators.

The assumption that young women will continue to flock into higher education in the 1980s, supporting an institutional structure that does so little to support them, is a leap of faith that colleges and universities cannot afford in a period when they will have to take pains to ensure that all their customers are satisfied. Among all the adjustments that academe faces in the coming decade, a new orientation toward female students is high on the list of priorities; without it, the possibility of losing female enrollment, in addition to the demographic decline, is real.

Throughout the coming decade the labor market for college-educated personnel is expected to continue softening. Since educated women are still in effect a marginal labor supply despite equal opportunity legislation, such a situation presents a classic social temptation to ameliorate the effects on men by shifting the burden to women. In the past, public policy, with the cooperation of academic institutions, has responded by limiting women's access (and that of other minority groups) to education, either directly through imposition of quotas or indirectly through subsidies to male students. Women's enrollment rates in such formerly exclusionary programs as engineering, medicine, dentistry, veterinary medicine, law, and business therefore must be closely monitored throughout the 1980s; any signs of leveling off below parity should be regarded with profound skepticism.

What should a new orientation toward women students encompass? Real equality of access is high on the list; our most selective universities still maintain predominantly male student bodies, whereas the least selective ones remain predominantly female. Once on campus, women must be helped to attain full academic citizenship, for they come to it from a long tradition of being second class. Ideally, of course, half of all faculty should be women, to guide, challenge, and inspire them; but that is not a realistic prospect in the next decade, although one may hope that it remains a goal. Still, equitable promotion rates for women junior faculty would demonstrate to female students an institution's commitment to women's future, and hence to their own aspirations. Curriculum revisions must include the incorporation of women's studies; the current trend toward reinstituting a core or general curriculum provides an opportunity for this that should not be neglected. The purpose of these revisions is an attempt to pull together, out of the educational diversity we take such pride in, a common tradition that informs and enlightens our individual experience. Women are inexorably part of that tradition even though their contributions to it have been ignored. The new scholarship on women of the last two decades has begun to tap a previously neglected body of information that expands the scope and greatly enriches the content of all the humanistic fields and the social sciences. The established professional fields have not welcomed this new area of inquiry, although one might have hoped that the pursuit of truth would outweigh the pettier concerns of traditional hierarchy. Still, this new scholarship illuminates the human experience in new ways, and it is essential that it become part of the core of learning.

All these changes need to be made not just for the benefit of women students, but for men as well. The areas in which higher education short-changes women the most are just the ones that give men extra value—a sense of themselves as lords of the universe. Men and women are destined to live together in partnership, not as master and slave; in the most fundamental sense, higher education must learn to reflect that partnership.

Bibliography

Broverman, I.K.; Broverman, D.M.; Clarkson, F.E.; Rosenkrantz, P.S.; and Vogel, S.R. "Sex-Role Stereotypes and Clinical Judgments of Mental Health." *Journal of Consulting and Clinical Psychology* 34 (1970):1–7.

Chodorow, N. *The Reproduction of Mothering*. Berkeley: University of California Press, 1978.

Duffy, D. "Public or Private? Athlete Associations Charged with Sex Bias, Secret Meetings." *In the Running* 3 (1981):1, 3.

Erikson, E.H. *Identity, Youth and Crisis*. New York: Norton, 1968.

Frieze, I.H.; Parson, J.E.; Johnson, P.B.; Ruble, D.N.; and Zellman, G.L. *Women and Sex Roles: A Social-Psychological Perspective*. New York: Norton, 1978.

Secord, P.F., and Jourard, S.M. "The Appraisal of Body Cathexia: Body Cathexia and the Self." *Journal of Consulting Psychology* 17 (1953): 343–347.

Index

Abramson, J., 128
Adjective Checklist, 235
Admissions processes, institutional, 87–90
Admissions Testing Program (ATP) Physics Achievement Test, 116, 121
Age, nontraditional students and data on, 60–64
Agency, 163, 174, 176, 179
Alexander, Karl L., 11, 86, 135, 136, 151, 279; on age at marriage and subsequent education, 383; and National Longitudinal Survey, 47–48
Almquist, E., 186, 190, 208
Alwin, D.F., 319
American Association for University Women, 24–25
American College Testing Program Assessment (ACT), 130, 132, 232
American Home Economics Association, 26
American Indian college women. *See* Native-American college women
Angrist, S.S., 186, 190
Antioch College, 16
Antler, Joyce, 9, 15, 376, 377
APA Standards for Educational and Psychological Tests, 114
Arnove, R.F., 277–278
Association (Associates) of Collegiate Alumnae (ACA), 17, 24, 25
Astin, Alexander W., 51–52, 130, 131, 132, 135, 275; and career plans of college women, 304–305, 319, 324, 327, 328; his longitudinal surveys of college women and men, 186–187, 193, 194
Astin, Helen S., 10, 85, 89, 91; and National Longitudinal Study, 76, 77, 82; and Project TALENT, 81, 82

Attendance. *See* College-attendance and -selection processes

Baca Zinn, M., 207
Bacon, L., 352
Baltes, P.B., 189
Barnard College, 26
Bayer, A.E., 352, 357
Beck, Michael D., 112
Becker, H.S., 340
Bengelsdorf, Winnie, 76
Bennett, Sheila, 10–11
Bennington College, 30, 184–186
Bernard, Jessie, 30, 190
Besterman, Carmen R., 12, 401, 408
Bias. *See* Sex bias in aptitude and achievement tests
Bielby, Denise, 11, 384
Bielby, W.T., 354
Bills, D., 354
Bird, Joyce, 9, 127, 131, 151, 152, 189; and sex differences in college choice, 132, 135
Bishop, John, 129
Black Ideology personality scale, 236, 240, 244
Black students: sex differences in impact of college environments on, 229–231, 245–247; analysis of, 236–237; black schools, 241–245; design of study on, 231–232; instruments used in study on, 232–236; white schools, 237–241
Blodgett, Minnie, 30
Bob, Sharon, 84
Boocock, S.S., 383–384
Breckinridge, Sophonisba, 28
Brigham, Carl C., *A Study of Error,* 115
Broverman, I.K., 407
Brown, Marsha D., 11, 47, 49, 319
Brown Project, 191

About the Contributors

Karl Alexander is associate professor in the Department of Social Relations at The Johns Hopkins University. His primary research interests involve school organizational effects on educational achievements and attainments.

Joyce Antler is assistant professor of American studies and director of the Women's Studies Program at Brandeis University. She is currently working on a biography of Lucy Sprague Mitchell, the founder of the Bank Street College of Education.

Helen Astin is professor of higher education at the Graduate School of Education at the University of California at Los Angeles and vice-president of the Higher Education Research Institute in Los Angeles. Her research interests are in the fields of educational progress and career development, with special emphasis on women, adults, and ethnic minorities. She has been chairperson of the American Psychological Association's Task Force on the Status of Women in Psychology and president of its Division of the Psychology of Women.

Sheila Bennett is assistant professor of sociology at Bryn Mawr College. Dr. Bennett's principal areas of interest include life-course and cohort-historical analysis and the study of institutional environments. She is also involved in a study of the patterns of entry and advancement among successive cohorts of women entering higher-education administration, which includes an analysis of institutional barriers and strategies of empowerment for women.

Carmen Besterman is special assistant, Office of the Chairman of the Massachusetts Institute of Technology (MIT) Corporation. Her primary responsibilities in this position are managing internal and external community relations.

Denise Bielby is lecturer in the Department of Sociology and the School of Education at the University of California, Santa Barbara. She has been a postdoctoral Fellow of the Institute of Human Development, University of California at Berkeley, and of the Department of Psychiatry and Sociology at the Duke University Medical Center. She has published on the topics of women's careers, the life course, midlife, and cognitive functioning in the elderly. Her areas of specialization are life-span human development and adult development and aging.

Joyce Bird is a graduate student in the Department of Sociology at the University of California at Berkeley. Her dissertation is on the topic of programs in higher education for women and other nontraditional students. She has taught at the University of California at Berkeley and at San Francisco State University.

Marsha Brown is assistant professor in the Graduate School of Public Affairs at the University of Washington. She also teaches in the Women's Studies Program as adjunct professor. She received the Ed.D. from the Graduate School of Education of Harvard University in 1980.

Blythe Clinchy is associate professor and chair of the Department of Psychology at Wellesley College. Her major research interest is in cognitive development, especially in adult women, but also in young children. She is currently codirector of the project "Education for Women's Development" supported by the Fund for the Improvement of Post-Secondary Education of the Department of Education. She and Claire Zimmerman have also been chosen Shaughnessy Scholars by the Fund for the Improvement of Post-Secondary Education for their work on a model of cognitive development.

Bruce Eckland is professor of sociology at the University of North Carolina at Chapel Hill. His present research deals with patterns of educational and socioeconomic inequality, and he has written extensively in the field of sociobiology.

Sumru Erkut is currently research associate at the Wellesley College Center for Research on Women, where she is associate director of the national review process of educational materials developed by grantees of Women's Educational Equity Act Program. Her research focuses on women's educational and occupational attainment, sex differences in the expectancy and attribution of academic achievement, and models and mentors for college students. Dr. Erkut has held full-time teaching appointments at the Middle East Technical University and Boston University, and has also taught part-time at the University of Washington, Boston College, and Wellesley College.

Oliva M. Espín is assistant professor in the Counseling Psychology Program at Boston University, a practicing psychotherapist, and a National Institute for Mental Health research Fellow at Harvard University. Dr. Espín is particularly interested in research and mental-health issues of women from a variety of cultural backgrounds.

Jacqueline Fleming is consulting psychologist at the United Negro College Fund and lecturer in the Department of Psychology at Barnard College. She is principal investigator of a grant from the Carnegie Corporation to study "The Impact of Predominantly White and Predominantly Black Environments on the Functioning of Black Students" under the auspices of the United Negro College Fund. Her research interests are in the areas of human motivation, achievement orientation in black women, and the psychology of sex differences.

Mary Ann Gawelek is assistant clinical professor in the Counseling Psychology Program at Boston University, where she is engaged in training and supervising counselors of women. She is also a practicing psychotherapist in the Boston area. Dr. Gawelek is particularly interested in the developmental issues of women and the clinical concerns presented by eating-disorder clients.

Janet Giele has been senior research associate and lecturer in family policy at the Heller Graduate School of Social Welfare at Brandeis University since 1976. She previously taught at Wellesley College and has been a Fellow and senior Fellow of the Radcliffe Institute. While at the Radcliffe Institute, she also served as principal consultant to the Ford Foundation's Task Force on Women. Her publications focus on changing sex roles, family policy, and aging. Her current research project, "College Women's Changing Life Patterns, 1900–1980," with Pamela Perun, was funded by the Lilly Endowment, Inc.

Katherine Hanson was formerly the vice-president and associate director in the Office of the Budget at the University of Massachusetts System, and assistant director of analytical studies and planning, Boston University. She is currently executive director of the Consortium on Financing Higher Education in Cambridge, Massachusetts.

James Hearn is principal analyst in the Social Science Operations Center of Advanced Technology, Inc., of McLean, Virginia. At the time of his contributions to this book, however, he was director of social and economic research for the Washington, D.C., office of the American College Testing Program. His current research interests include educational policy and program evaluation, analysis of educational organizations and their effects on students, and assessment of alternative conceptions of postsecondary educational equity.

Barbara Heyns is professor of sociology and director of the Center for Applied Social Science Research at New York University. She has taught at the Graduate School of Education at Harvard University and in the Department of Sociology at the University of California at Berkeley. She has published numerous articles on education and schooling, and her recent book on summer learning examines such activities as reading and sports that further children's achievement outside school.

Lilli Hornig is executive director of Higher Education Resource Services (HERS) at Wellesley College. Founded in 1972, HERS conducts research on women in higher education and programs designed to improve the status of academic professional women. Dr. Hornig has been a faculty member at Brown University and at Trinity College (Washington, D.C.) where she chaired the Department of Chemistry. She is a member of the National Academy of Sciences' Commission on Human Resources, chairing its Committee on the Education and Employment of Women in Science and Engineering, and of the Committee on Equal Opportunities in Science and Technology of the National Science Foundation. Dr. Hornig is currently conducting a comprehensive study of women in the humanities, a project funded by the National Endowment for the Humanities.

Florence Ladd is dean of students at Wellesley College. She was previously associate dean in the School of Architecture and Planning at MIT, and she has taught at Harvard University's Graduate School of Education and Graduate School of Design.

Larry Litten was formerly the director of institutional research at Carleton College and associate study director at the National Opinion Research Center in Chicago. He is currently associate director of the Consortium on Financing Higher Education, Cambridge, Massachusetts.

Marlaine Lockheed was previously research associate and coinvestigator of a study of interracial interaction in junior-high-school classrooms at Stanford University. She then joined the Educational Testing Service's Research Division, where she is currently a senior research sociologist in the Division of Educational Research and Evaluation and directs a program of research on sex equity in education.

Patricia McNamara is research analyst at the Higher Education Research Institute. She has been a member of the HERI research staff working with the National Commission on the Higher Education of Minorities for the past several years. She is the author of publications related to sex discrimination in access to postsecondary education, minority access to graduate and professional school, the status of native Americans in higher education, and women's business ownership. Her current project is a study of women scientists and engineers.

Susan Olzak is assistant professor in the Department of Sociology at Yale University. Her major teaching and research interests include ethnic mobilization, family conflict and instability, and determinants of ethnic and sexual stratification in the occupational structure.

Thomas Reilly is a doctoral candidate in the Department of Social Relations at The Johns Hopkins University. His current work centers around the examination of family transition points.

Lourdes Rodríguez-Nogués is staff clinician at the Counseling Center at Simmons College and a doctoral candidate at Boston University's Counseling Psychology Program. Her primary clinical interest is the interface between socioethnic and religious factors and ego development for women.

Rachel Rosenfeld taught at McGill University and the University of Chicago before going to the University of North Carolina at Chapel Hill. While in Chicago, she was also a senior study director at the National Opinion Research Center. Her research interests are in the area of women's careers and higher education.

Jeanne Speizer is associate director of Higher Education Resource Services at Wellesley College. In that capacity, she directs the Administrative Skills Program for Women in Higher Education. Her research interests include career paths and outcomes for educational administrators and evaluation of educational processes.

Claire Zimmerman is professor of psychology at Wellesley College. She is interested in the psychology of higher education, including the study of college environments, experimental curricula and teaching methods, and faculty-development programs, as well as the relationship between intellectual and personality development during the college years. She currently holds a Shaughnessy Scholarship, with Blythe Clinchy, from the Department of Education's Fund for the Improvement of Post-Secondary Education, for a project entitled "Using a Cognitive-Developmental Model to Improve Liberal Arts Education."

About the Editor

Pamela Perun is currently research associate at Higher Education Resource Services at Wellesley College. She was previously a postdoctoral Fellow in the Department of Sociology at Duke University. Her primary research interests are in life-span development, and her publications have focused on such topics as the structure of the individual life course, theories of midlife, and the adult development of women. With Janet Giele, she has received a grant from the Lilly Endowment, Inc., to study historical changes in life patterns among college-educated women.

About the Editor

...
...
...
...
...
...